English Baptist History and Heritage

English Baptist History and Heritage

Second Edition

Roger Hayden

2005

Published on behalf of The Baptist Union of Great Britain
by Nigel Lynn Publishing & Marketing Ltd
106 High Street, Milton under Wychwood, Chipping Norton
Oxfordshire, OX7 6ET, United Kingdom

The Baptist Union of Great Britain
Baptist House, 129 Broadway, Didcot
Oxfordshire, OX11 8RT, United Kingdom

First published 1990
Second edition published 2005

British Library Cataloguing in Publication Data
Data available

ISBN 0 901472 79 4

1 3 5 7 9 10 8 6 4 2

Cover design by Wheeler & Porter Ltd, Banbury

Printed in the United Kingdom
on acid-free paper by
The Alden Group, Oxford

Contents

Preface

THE Church of Jesus Christ preaches a Gospel that is rooted in history. The moment when 'the Word became flesh and dwelt among us' within a nation that had spent thousands of years looking for God's anointed one, his Messiah, is crucial for those who are concerned with the historic facts of Christ's life, death and resurrection as foundational for their faith.

A Baptist Old Testament scholar of the last century, J. N. Schofield, who taught at Cambridge University, enlivened his chosen area of Old Testament study with conundrums. He once posed the question to his class: 'Why is an Old Testament prophet like the winner of the Diamond Sculls at Henley?' Schofield's succinct answer was: 'They both move forwards by looking backwards.' There is real wisdom in taking Isaiah's words to heart, 'Look to the rock from which you were hewn, to the quarry from which you were dug, look to your father Abraham, and to Sarah who gave you birth.' (Isaiah 51.1–2) Denominational history is part of this concern, as well as history written on a much broader canvas. It is properly viewed from this perspective, and it is always worth remembering, as George Santayana put it, that 'the fate of those who forget their past is to have to relive it'.

It is also important to recognise that the interpretation of history begins with the person who writes it down. Baptists who have written about their heritage prior to the twentieth century have usually been motivated by a measure of distinctly polemical concerns. A helpful review of historians of English Baptists from Crosby to McBeth, is found in Appendix II of B. R. White, *The English Baptists of the Seventeenth Century*, revised edition, (1996), pp.164–170. Working through the Baptist Historical Society, contemporary Baptist historians have produced a new history of English Baptists, first under the general editorship of its former President, Dr B. R. White, and latterly by its current President, Dr Roger Hayden. The first volume covering the seventeenth century, was written by Dr B. R. White and published in 1983. A thoroughly revised and expanded second edition, prepared by John Nicholson was issued in 1996. The eighteenth-century volume by Dr Raymond Brown was published in 1986. Professor John Briggs' nineteenth-century volume was published in 1994. In 1982 Dr Keith Clements had edited a series of papers from the Baptist Historical Society's Summer School on *Baptists in the Twentieth Century*. Dr Ian Randall has prepared a more detailed history of the twentieth century for publication in 2005.

Dr Kenneth Dix's *Strict and Particular* (BHS, 2001) tells the story of independent Baptists who, outside the Baptist Union, remained High Calvinist in doctrine, with closed membership and communion as the heart of their church order. Geoffrey Breed has honoured the Strict communion position, who worked both within and beyond the Baptist Union, in *Particular Baptists in Victorian England*, (BHS, 2003).

The definitive history of BMS World Mission was written by Dr Brian Stanley for the bi-centenary of the Baptist Missionary Society in 1992, and this was published by T & T Clark. Dr Michael Walker's *Baptists at the Table* (BHS, 1992) provided a major discussion of Baptist eucharistic theology from 1800 to the present. Dr Anthony Cross dealt with baptism in the last hundred years in *Baptism and the Baptists,* (Paternoster, 2000). Baptists in Europe have been researched in two volumes by Bernard Green. *Crossing the Boundaries,* (BHS, 1999) is the story of Baptists in Europe from 1905 onwards, majoring on the history of the European Baptist Federation which came into being in 1948. *To-morrow's Man* (1997), is a biography of the Revd Dr James H. Rushbrooke, a significant English European Secretary of the Baptist World Alliance. In *The Welsh Baptists* (1977), published by the Welsh Baptist Union, Swansea, T. M. Bassett provided a comprehensive study of Baptists in Wales. An edited volume on *The Baptists in Scotland: A History* (1988), by Professor David Bebbington, was published by the Scottish Baptist Union. Dr Joshua Thompson wrote *A Century of Grace* (1995), a short history of the Baptist Union of Ireland. An important and vital contemporary discussion of 'Baptist Identity in Church and Theology', will be found in Paul S. Fiddes' *Tracks and Traces* (2003).

A wealth of historical material has been published in the Baptist Historical Society's *Transactions* and *Baptist Quarterly* since 1908. This present volume is a major revision and extension of *English Baptist History and Heritage* (1990) first published as a Christian Training Programme Manual by the Baptist Union of Great Britain. It describes the life of the two major Baptist communities in England since the seventeenth century, chronicling their story and setting out their primary beliefs, down to their merger in the ongoing life of the Baptist Union of Great Britain in 1891. Dr E. A. Payne's *The Baptist Union: A Short History* (1958) gives a detailed study of the Union from 1812. The rest of this book recognises the unity of Particular and General Baptists in the Baptist Union since that date and carries the story to 1990. This has difficulties, since the author has lived through much of that period as a minister within the Baptist Union and for fourteen years was one of its Superintendents in the west of England. I therefore acknowledge that my own perceptions have undoubtedly shaped the final part of this book. Further, this present volume would not have been possible without the work of my former secretary, Mrs Pat Miles, and my thanks are here offered. No one person can have all the detailed knowledge necessary to write the history of the English Baptists and I gladly recognise I am forever in the debt of many who have written relevant doctoral dissertations, and published research in the *Baptist Quarterly* and similar publications. If I have misrepresented any, I apologise, and if I have used work that has not been acknowledged, I ask forgiveness.

To all who encouraged me to revise this volume I give special thanks, for there was more than one occasion when I despaired of finishing it.

ROGER HAYDEN

July 2004

Acknowledgements

Several people have granted permission for material to be reproduced in this book. The co-operation of the following is acknowledged with gratitude:

The British Library; the Baptist Missionary Society; the East Midlands Baptist Association; Bristol Baptist College; Regent's Park College, Oxford; Broadmead Baptist Church, Bristol; Arnesby Baptist Church; Haven Green Baptist Church; Horsham Unitarian Church.

Thanks are due to John Houseago for preparing the illustrations for this edition.

Whilst all due care has been taken in the preparation of this book, the publisher and author apologise if any copyrights have been inadvertently infringed. They will be pleased to include the appropriate acknowledgement in the next available reprint.

Abbreviations

BQ Baptist Quarterly
BHS Baptist Historical Society

Introduction

Who were the Baptists?

WHEN and where was the first English Baptist church formed and by whom? What factors most properly account for Baptist origins? The questions are easily posed but the answers by no means simple, brief or straightforward. Baptists were the children of the Reformation and their origins are best determined from within that context. It will help to paint some broad strokes with the brush on the canvas of Baptist history before considering the details.

Baptist Christians first emerged in early seventeenth-century England and the Netherlands. They were part of the radical movement produced by the Reformation in Europe, initially influenced by the life and work of Martin Luther, Ulrich Zwingli and John Calvin. Each sought a personal spiritual reformation in their life as well as the renewal of the Church. The Bible in English was probably the most significant factor as it brought Christians in the British Isles towards a radical faith. Thomas Linacre, a young student in Cambridge, was typical of this awakening: when confronted with Scripture as he read Erasmus's newly published Greek New Testament, he reputedly said: 'Either this is not the Gospel, or we are not Christians.'

Congregations were created that were 'separate' from the church established by the law of the land, comprising believers only, who sought a 'purer' form of worship, and whose work and witness was to replicate the life-style of New Testament Christians. These separatist groups did not conform to the Church of England as by law established and were described by a variety of terms. Among these were those who practised the baptism of believers by total immersion in water, in the name of the Trinity. They were nicknamed 'Anabaptists' because they baptised for a second time those who had already been baptised as infants.

The name linked them to a very extreme group that had emerged in Münster in 1533–34, under the leadership of a Dutchman, Jan Matthys, and his successor as leader, John of Leyden. Catholic mercenaries surrounded Münster to put an end to the apocalyptic community that had been established. After a long siege, in which all kind of atrocities were perpetrated, the city was put to the sword by the mercenaries. 'Münster' and 'Anabaptist' became by-words of religious abuse, to Catholics and Protestants alike.

Baptists in England

Two main groups of Baptists emerged in England in the seventeenth century: the General Baptists and the Particular Baptists.

General Baptist churches came first, and were so named because their theological beliefs led them to understand the work of Christ on the cross at Calvary, to have a 'general' application. They believed that whoever voluntarily puts faith in Christ would be saved. In this belief they were influenced by the Dutch theologian, Jacob Arminius, a successor of John Calvin, who made a place for the freedom of the will in matters of salvation. The General Baptists also taught, as did Arminius, that it was possible for a Christian to 'fall from grace', in contrast to Calvin who had claimed that once people become Christian they continue as such, a doctrine known as 'the perseverance of the saints'. A .J. Baines writes:

> The General Baptists held 'that the way of salvation is not confined to particular persons, but is open to all, because Christ died for all and the Holy Spirit strives with all, so that if any perish their destruction is of themselves. This was their distinguishing doctrine of general or universal redemption. They held it to be the duty of and right of all followers of Christ, on profession of faith and repentance, to enter His visible church by baptism, followed by laying on of hands by a Bishop or Elder to receive the promised Holy Spirit. They held that the holy sacrament of the Lord's Supper ought often to be celebrated to show forth the sacrifice of Christ and to confirm the faithful in all the benefits of His death and resurrection. They did not admit infants to communion … but they held that all children dying in infancy became members of the invisible church and enjoy life everlasting. They regarded liberty of conscience not merely as a civil right but as part of the faith …'[1]

The church structure of the General Baptists allowed significant autonomy to congregations but gave some church power to regional Associations and their usually annual General Assembly.

John Smyth, (1570–1612) an Anglican clergyman, who first became a separatist, then led a group of English exiles to Amsterdam, in the Netherlands, where they adopted believer's baptism, is recognised as the founder of the English General Baptist Churches. A wealthy layman in the group, a lawyer Thomas Helwys, assisted Smyth. Together they formed the first English Baptist church on Dutch soil in 1609.

Particular Baptist churches emerged in the late 1630s from a London Independent church led by Henry Jacob where eventually some members decided to adopt believers' baptism as the only right and proper form of the sacrament. The church was Calvinist in theology and separatist in outlook. The Jacob-Lathrop-Jessey church, as it is usually called after the succession of ministers who led it, was then led by a Baptist pastor, Henry Jessey. From this congregation developed a number of other Baptist churches, among them those led by Hanserd Knollys and William Kiffin. All of these taught a Calvinist view of the work of Christ on the cross which believed that Christ's death was not effective for all people but only for 'particular' individuals, elected by God in his grace from all eternity. It was this that gave them their name—Particular Baptists. They understood that God had elected only some to salvation and those 'elect people' would persevere and enter upon eternal life. Particular Baptists gave each local congregation all necessary church power, while Associations and Assemblies had only an advisory capacity. Starting a generation later than General Baptist churches, the Particular Baptists were destined to become the larger of the two groups.

By 1650 both General and Particular Baptists were flourishing in Britain, with emerging congregations established in Wales and Ireland. The General Baptists were very strong in London, the Midlands and Kent, with at least 47 churches

[1] A. J. Baines in Roger Hayden, ed., *English Baptist Records*, Vol. i, *Chesham, Bucks*, BHS, 1985, p.vii

sharing in local Associations and a General Assembly. The Particular Baptist churches had developed a London base for their national organisation and were engaged in vigorous evangelistic work in the Midlands, North, and West of England, as well as in Wales and Ireland.

1

Renaissance and Reformation in Europe

FOR more than a century before the first English Baptist congregation was formed, a revolution in Christian understanding, literature and art, and in perceptions of the relationship of church and state, resulted in the emergence of a pluralist view of church and world that broke for ever the mould of European unity enshrined in the Holy Roman Empire.

The corruption of the Roman Church in head and members, together with its failure to effect meaningful reform from within, brought Luther to add his voice to others calling for reformation in 1517. He identified administrative and financial abuses in the Church. Worldliness and laxity in religious communities were prevalent. Theologians were failing to meet the challenge of so-called 'Renaissance' scholars who emphasised the difference between Christ's words and example, and current practice in the Church.

The Renaissance and Erasmus

The Renaissance and the Reformation were both 'movements of reform. Unlike many of the revolutionary movements of the twentieth century they looked with no disdain upon the past, but sought to correct the immediate past by a return to a past more remote. For the Renaissance this meant classical antiquity, for the Reformation the gospel. The glory of Greece, the grandeur of Rome, the grace of Galilee, should restore society and revivify the Church.'[1] Erasmus spent his time holding all this together, while at the same time seeking 'to purge the church and refashion the world'.

Erasmus was a leading scholar of the Renaissance in northern Europe, who challenged the use of Latin as the universal language of the church's Scripture and liturgy, and made himself responsible for printing and publishing in 1516 the first modern Greek New Testament in England. In subsequent writings he did not hesitate to contrast the existing Catholic Church with the picture of the Apostolic Church in the New Testament, to the detriment of the former. To this he added the Old Testament paradigm of the King in control of the state, priests and people. This scriptural warrant was welcomed not only by Henry VIII in England, but also by German Princes seeking authority to put down a peasants' revolt in 1525. It is impossible to overestimate the influence of the Old Testament

[1] R. H. Bainton, *Erasmus of Christendom*, 1970, p.14/15

precedents for the 'godly prince' in the Reformers' cause. The new power of the press which the development of printing had brought to Europe made the results of Biblical and historical studies, pursued with scholarly detachment in universities, the common talk of the market place, where moderation and restraint were less highly prized.

At the heart of medieval Catholicism was the celebration of Holy Communion, commonly called the Mass. It was believed to be effective, independent of the faith of either the celebrant or the congregation. This encouraged the saying of masses for their own sake, particularly to help those in purgatory gain heaven. Many clergy spent a lifetime only saying the Latin Mass, in the various chantry chapels across the land. This mechanistic view of religion led to a remarkable growth of mysticism, as people sought an immediate sense of the presence of God through a personal daily discipline of following Christ. A fine expression of this was Thomas à Kempis's *Imitatio Christi* (1418). Other Christian groups sought 'immediacy' in Christian living, and of these 'The Brethren of the Common Life' in southern Germany were a typical example. They contrasted their contact with God, which resulted in an experience of forgiveness and peace, with the empty, repetitive sacramental life of the Church, an experience which would, in time, give strength to the Reformation insistence on justification by faith alone.

Continental Reformation Leaders

The Reformation was carried through by number of leading theologians in various European countries, but Luther, Zwingli, and Calvin were fundamental for all reform groups of the time.

Martin Luther (1483–1546)

Martin Luther was a German Roman Catholic priest—an Austin Friar—who spent his teaching life at Wittenberg, a small town 'perched on the edge of beyond'. More than most he let history come to him. He went to the heart of things only three times, when he went to Rome, Augsburg and Worms. However, with his pen he filled the Christian world with a desire for reformation.

By 1512 the one-time lawyer had become a doctor of theology succeeding his friend, John Staupitz, as Professor at Wittenberg. He lectured on *The Psalms* between 1513 and 1515; on *Romans* between 1516 and 1517; *Galatians* and *Hebrews* between 1517 and 1518. By 1520 Luther had made Wittenberg a centre for the new theology of 'justification by faith alone'. Personally he 'hated this just God who punishes sinners' but through his Biblical studies realised the justice of God was to be interpreted passively. By this 'the merciful God justifies us by faith'. Luther felt himself to be born anew, and to enter through open gates into paradise itself.

In Luther's day the selling of indulgences to raise Papal finances was part of the Catholic way of life. Penance was a long established practice in the Roman Church. The idea behind penances was that Christ had acquired a treasury of merit for the Church on earth which the Pope could dispense as he pleased. In the Middle Ages the church authorities introduced a secular notion whereby it was agreed that moral offences could be forgiven by a monetary payment. The money raised was used initially to finance crusades to the Holy Land. Luther was deeply offended by Tetzel, who came offering an indulgence that, if

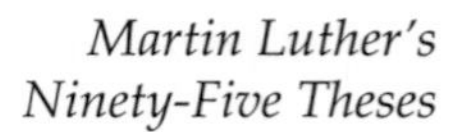
Martin Luther's Ninety-Five Theses

purchased, would secure personal forgiveness for the purchaser or a loved one, and the funds raised finance the building of St Peter's in Rome.

Luther published his objections to indulgences in the usual academic manner, nailing his ninety-five points (called theses) to the Cathedral door. What he did not foresee was a local printer translating his theses into German, then printing and selling them locally. The Reformation had begun. Luther's action led to his excommunication by the Pope. Frederick, Elector of Saxony, saved Luther by having him ambushed while on a journey and took him into protective custody. Once there Luther worked furiously and soon his tracts were selling all over Europe, including England.

Ulrich Zwingli (1484–1531)

Ulrich Zwingli, after studying classics at Berne, Basel and Vienna, was appointed priest at Glarus, where he joined Erasmus and other Renaissance scholars. In 1518 he was appointed 'people's priest' in Zurich. Zwingli resolved to preach through Matthew's Gospel, exegetically, with his congregation, which led Professor Gordon Rupp to claim that Zwingli's reformation was begun, continued, and ended by the agency of prophetic preaching. In a unique experiment each day Zwingli related the Bible to the needs of a small community who knew each other well, and among whom were the city fathers of Zurich. A near-death experience for Zwingli in 1519 brought him close to Scripture. Prophesyings—which were Biblical exposition followed by congregational comment—became a regular part of worship. 'I came to the conclusion that you must leave all the rest and learn God's meaning out of his simple word. Then I asked God for light and light came.'

Zwingli introduced various reforms. He banned images, pictures and music from public worship. In 1525 he introduced a new form of the Lord's Supper. He presided at a table, with wooden beakers and plates, while the congregation remained seated. The congregation took the bread and wine first, the minister last, and it was understood to be a commemorative rite of great simplicity.

John Calvin

John Calvin (1509–1564)

John Calvin, a lawyer trained at the Sorbonne in Paris, was also a great classical scholar who studied the writings of Luther and other contemporary theologians, before undergoing a spiritual experience in 1532. Of this he wrote, 'God subdued my heart to docility by a sudden conversion.' His conversion forced him into hiding and it was while he was passing through Geneva that he was persuaded to become the city's 'reader in Holy Scripture'. Calvin published the first edition of *The Institutes of the Christian Religion* in Basel in 1536, a book that became a classic statement of his reformed theology after going through several revisions and extensions over the years.

Calvin refused to be controlled by the Geneva city authorities, and was expelled in 1538 to Strasbourg, where he met Martin Bucer (d.1551). Here Calvin learnt to apply Scripture to the doctrine of the Church, including within it a ministry that involved pastors, elders and deacons. When Calvin eventually returned to Geneva he developed these insights in further editions of his *Institutes,* where he advocated a weekly Eucharist. He reluctantly accepted a quarterly observance, and dropped the laying on of hands from ordination. He proposed a church court that had the right to discipline and excommunicate unrepentant members. In Geneva people could see a theocratic state in action and many in England thought it the best model of a reformed church.

> Protestantism had been slowing down, its initial impetus spent, divided, tired, disheartened. After Calvin it is once more on the move, singing on the march, ready to strike new blows for liberty. He restored the

exhilaration of Christian comradeship. He renewed the brave vision of the Word going forth conquering and to conquer.[2]

Anabaptist Beginnings

The re-baptising movement began in Southern Germany and Switzerland. In 1521 three 'prophets' visited Wittenberg from Zwickau. Thomas Müntzer, a Zwickau preacher, proposed a radical reformation of church and society that went far beyond anything suggested by other reformers. The purification of the church must be accompanied, claimed Müntzer, by radical social change. He supported the peasants in the revolt against the established regime and eventually lost his life in the tragic aftermath. Luther was away from Wittenberg when the 'prophets' came. His colleague Carlstadt was greatly influenced by them, but Luther was not convinced and adopted a strongly argued defence of infant baptism.

In Zurich two friends of Zwingli, Conrad Grebel and Felix Manz, both keen for reformation, believed that Zwingli was too cautious in respect of new forms of church life. From 1523 they met in a private home of an evening for bible study, and in order to re-create the true environment of Lord's Supper, using ordinary bread. By June 1524 they were pressing for a 'confessing' church in which all members would personally testify to faith in Christ and receive baptism on account of that faith. Grebel rejected the idea of a church for 'everybody' and advocated that baptism, signifying cleansing from sin, should be administered only to believing adults. The Lord's Supper he described as a simple meal in the home of the believer, when only the words of institution would be read. Here, in fact, was one of the earliest expositions of what came to be called 'the gathered fellowship of believers'.

In December 1524 Manz wrote to Zwingli arguing that infant baptism was invalid. A disputation was arranged for 17 January, 1525, but this was pre-empted by the Zurich town council. Zwingli convinced the city council the Bible supported the baptism of infants. Consequently, the council passed an order that all parents who had been influenced against baptising their children should do so within eight days or face expulsion from the city. A few days later, on 30 January, a group of friends met with George Blaurock and Conrad Grebel at Zollikon, three miles from Zurich. Blaurock invited Grebel to baptise him by affusion, which he did, and then Blaurock baptised the others. Over the next seven days there were 39 more baptisms, as the candidates regarded their Catholic infant baptism as null and void. The idea of a confessing, separated church, linked with believer's baptism, was first established in Zurich in 1525. On 5 January 1527 Felix Manz was arrested by the authorities that decreed he be tied to a bedstead and drowned in the River Limmat in Zurich. Blaurock escaped to the South Tyrol as a wandering evangelist who planted many new congregations. He was eventually caught by the Innsbruck authorities, sentenced and burned to death at Kalusen in September 1529.

H. S. Bender, a Mennonite historian, claimed first and fundamental in the Anabaptist vision was the conception of the essence of Christianity as

[2] E. G. Rupp, *The Cambridge New Modern History*, Vol. VI, p. 117

Burning at the Stake

discipleship.[3] The church is to be understood as a brotherhood that offers a new ethic of love and non-resistance. The movement spread to Strasbourg, the Tyrol and into Moravia.

Balthazar Hubmaier, termed 'the theologian of Anabaptism',[4] in 1524 wrote a fine defence of toleration in matters of religion, *Concerning Heretics and Those Who Burn Them.* His argument turned on the point that to put a heretic to death did not honour Christ but denied him, since the Lord's purpose in coming was to give life. In fact, persecution was an invention of the devil. Hans Denck, (1495–1527), who was a considerable Biblical scholar, propounded a doctrine of the 'inner light' in his pamphlet *To Those Who Really Love the Truth*,[5] an idea which played a substantial part in English Baptist seventeenth-century life and was eventually embodied in the beliefs of the Society of Friends. In the Low Countries and Germany the Anabaptist leader was Melchior Hoffman. He held a docetic view of Christ, teaching that Jesus was born out of Mary, but not of Mary. He was a millenarian who believed the end of the world would be in Strasbourg in 1537 and that he was Elijah, one of the witnesses who would appear before Christ's coming again. His views of the person of Christ affected English General Baptist thought a century later when Matthew Caffyn promulgated them.[6]

Michael Sattler was the probable author of the earliest Anabaptist Confession of Faith, known as the Schleitheim Articles, written 24 February 1527. Sattler was Swabian, and had been a Benedictine Prior before coming to Reformation views. Expelled from Zurich, he gathered the first Anabaptist congregation in

[3] G. F. Hershberger, ed., *The Recovery of the Anabaptist Vision*, 1957, p.42
[4] H. W. Pipkin and John Yoder, *Balthazar Hubmaier, Theologian of Anabaptism, Classics of the Radical Reformation*, 5, 1989
[5] A. Coutts, *Hans Denck, 1495–1527, Humanist and Heretic*, 1927, pp.96–115
[6] For a modern biography, K. Deppermann, *Melchior Hoffman: Social Unrest and Apocalyptic Visions In the Age of Reformation*, Edinburgh, 1987

Strasbourg. The Articles[7] made seven points:

i Baptism ought to be administered only to those 'who have been taught repentance and a change of life and in truth believe their sins to have been blotted out through Christ, and wholly wish to be buried with him into death that they may be able to rise again'.

ii Church discipline is an important aspect of the 'gathered church' concept with its emphasis on holy living.

iii Only baptised believers are able to share fellowship at the Lord's Table.

iv The necessity of separating the 'true' from the 'false' church is established.

v This notes the qualifications and functions of a pastor.

vi The sword is an ordinance of God outside the perfection of Christ, by which the evil man is punished ... but the good man defended. A Christian should not accept the office of magistrate since it would involve using the power of the sword.

vii It is forbidden to swear oaths, on the basis of Matthew 5.34. This stand made a deep impression on a society which had for centuries rested on the oath as a basis for establishing truth and justice in the courts of the land.

Types of Anabaptists

Anabaptism uniquely united both Protestant and Catholic in their opposition to any manifestation of it. A major reason for this antagonism was the Anabaptist denial of a fundamental medieval conviction, inherited by the Reformers, that church and state are indissoluble. Baptism not only admitted to the church, it also admitted the person to the secular community. To remove this rite from children was not only a spiritual disaster but also a revolutionary political statement.

Anabaptist was a term 'covering a motley collection of beliefs and behaviour which range from mad millenarianism to pietism, from the reckless use of force to pacifism, from the extremes of personal egoism to humble piety and devotion. All these men and women have one thing in common: they do not fit in with any of the established religions and thus offend the principle of uniformity wherever they go ... The fact that Anabaptism drew its following from the underprivileged is significant enough'.[8]

Who the Anabaptists were is difficult to answer; but the distinctions of Ernest Troeltsch are useful, where he writes of Evangelical, Spiritualist and Anti-Trinitarian Anabaptists.[9]

The **Evangelical** Anabaptists took the Bible very literally, believing it to be God's Word, authoritative for mankind and capable of interpretation by the Holy Spirit's work. This led to a belief in the visible church as a fellowship of

[7] *Classics of the Radical Reformation*, 1, 1989, pp.27–43

[8] *The Cambridge New Modern History*, Vol. VI, p.6. See also 2nd edn, 1990, for new chapter by J. M. Stayer, on 'Anabaptists', pp.118–143

[9] E. Troelstch, *The Social Teaching of the Christian Churches*, Tübingen, 1912

believers, who alone would be allowed to share the benefits of the Lord's Table. Conrad Grebel (1489–1526), Felix Manz (d.1527), George Blaurock (d.1529) and Balthazar Hubmaier (1481–1528) were among their gifted leaders.

The **Spiritualists** set the direct, personal, inspiration of the Holy Spirit above the Word of God, although they were not averse to checking any revelation against the revealed Word of Scripture. They owed much to medieval mystics, played down the 'visible church' concept, and had no interest in the sacraments. Thomas Müntzer (1490–1561), Andreas Carlstadt (1481–1541) and Caspar Schwenkfeld (1489–1561) belonged to this group.

Anti-Trinitarian Anabaptists, as their name suggests, were those who denied the Trinitarian understanding of God's person. Their two most famous leaders were Michael Servetus (1511–1553) and Faustus Socinus (1534–1604) whose ideas persisted in Europe throughout the next two centuries.

The Anabaptist movement was large numerically, drawing many thousands to follow them because they were, as Henry Bullinger wrote, 'living saints'. The reason for their small influence in the Reformation period is their complete lack of organisation and state support; the violent persecution of their leaders by various state authorities in the 1530s; the total rejection of their ideas by reformers such as Luther, Zwingli and Calvin; and their own 'lunatic fringe' which carried some Anabaptists into political extremes thought to herald the return of Christ. Anabaptism was a child of the Reformation, and of Zurich in particular. Its thought forms were entirely religious but its challenge to church-state relationships had political implications which no state authority could tolerate at that period.

Anabaptist Principles

It would be misleading to suggest that Anabaptists produced clear ecclesiological structures for the churches to adopt, but some clear principles emerge from a wealth of written materials, which were well summarised by Morris West.[10]

The Bible is the Word of God, and absolutely authoritative. Only practices specifically mentioned in the New Testament should be followed. The New Testament was the final court of appeal, the new covenant having abrogated the old. They were Bible Christians of a precise kind. When opponents claimed they had Zwingli's word on a situation, their reply was that they had God's Word on it!

They had two weaknesses. They jumped from Scripture to their own time as if the Holy Spirit had not been active in the intervening period. They failed to distinguish between Biblical practices that were essential because they arose out of the Gospel and those that were only a response to a first-century custom.

They advocated a church model that was free from any state control and known as a fellowship of believers. They claimed that the Roman model of the church, when measured against Scripture, was entirely false. They were convinced that the reformers' models also fell far short of the New Testament. They taught that the church required restitution, not reformation. They put

[10] W. M. S. West, 'The Anabaptists and the Rise of the Baptist movement', in A. Gilmore, ed., *Christian Baptism*, 1959, pp.223–272

considerable blame for all this on the Emperor Constantine, and thought the reformers only 'half-way' men. They understood themselves to be a covenanted people, with believer's baptism a covenant sign of a good conscience with God.

For Anabaptists the New Testament taught only the baptism of believers upon a confession of personal repentance for sin, and faith in and allegiance to Christ: a concept which opposed the medieval church-state relationship and brought the charge of anarchy on the Anabaptists.

They were convinced that Christianity was a way of life rather than a series of beliefs. They applied Christian principles to themselves as individuals and administered a strict moral discipline within the church. They were aggressively evangelistic, working as missionaries to win people to Christian faith out of a sinful world. The Christian way meant embodying the principles of Christ's life and teaching. It was not that they believed that after baptism a person could do no sin but that he or she *should* not sin. Knowing they were on a collision course with the world at large, they developed a 'theology of martyrdom' which encouraged most of them towards pacifism, a refusal to swear oaths, and an unwillingness to hold the office of magistrate.

Anabaptists were deeply committed to religious toleration on four grounds.

1 The example of Christ and the Apostles showed no compulsion in bringing people to faith.

2 Christians have an obligation to love all people, even their enemies, which led them into pacifism as well as toleration.

3 Church members should be on a voluntary principle, free from state control, a church people joined only by a personal, conscious step of faith.

4 Faith is a gift from God: so burning a heretic might prematurely uproot a soul that God planned to harvest tomorrow.

The Münster Tragedy and aftermath

The Continental Anabaptists were not a homogeneous group. Their unity was expressed in three primary disagreements with mainstream churches. They insisted that faith was the key to the Gospel, and this faith was a conscious choice. Therefore baptism could not be administered to infants, who are unable to make such a conscious decision. Most were also convinced that a pacifist life-style was a major part of Christian living. Christians must 'turn the other cheek' and have no part to play in society as enforcers of law or in the army. On a different issue they were convinced that the Bible is the Christian's sole guide to life, and there was no need for the language of the early church or theologians to explain its meaning. Among the few educated leaders of Anabaptist thought, phrases like the 'Holy Trinity', or 'of one substance' were doubted or even denied, and a creed was dismissed as irrelevant. These Anabaptists saw the Church as an elite group on the edge of the world. They effectively repudiated the widespread understanding of the Church as the religious aspect of all society.

In the Netherlands the movement's apocalyptic element was at its strongest and introduced a contrary view that the Kingdom of God must be established by force of arms.

The issue came to a head in Münster, Germany. In February 1533 after a period of political and religious unrest, a treaty was achieved which granted legal rights to the Protestants within it. A Münster citizen, formerly a teacher, who became a minister, and was a very charismatic preacher in the city, led the group. In 1531 this minister, Bernhard Rothmann was banned by the Bishop of Münster, who thought his views too radical. The Bishop who had surrounded the city with a mercenary force, died. His successor made a treaty, which legitimised the Protestant stance of the city, and Rothmann became the Lutheran pastor.

In the nearby Netherlands, the Anabaptists were severely persecuted and some fled for refuge to Münster. Once settled, they persuaded Rothmann of the wrongness of baptising infants, a view that he accepted and fiercely advocated. In 1534 the Anabaptists won a constitutional election and came to power in Münster. Many more Anabaptist refugees streamed into the city, and when Jan Matthys, the leader, was killed, the responsibility passed to Jan Bockelson, known as John of Leyden. He proclaimed himself king, officially advocated polygamy on the basis of Old Testament precedent and waited for the return of Christ.

The end came when a deserter betrayed the city's defences allowing the besieging army to enter. The slaughter was total. The notoriety of Münster swept across Europe, putting an end to Anabaptists as an effective force. After the Münster episode the word Anabaptist was a general 'smear' term without precise meaning, and its use in documents does not imply Baptistic beliefs without further evidence. Some of those who escaped persecution gathered around a former Roman Catholic priest, Menno Simons, whose brother had been killed in the Münster affair, and his name is the origin of the later Mennonite communities. Some Anabaptists fled to England and there is evidence of their presence in Kent and Essex. Benjamin Evans records that thirty Dutch Anabaptists were taken into custody and examined in a house in Aldgate, London, on Easter Day 1575, and again examined at Pentecost.[11] From their evidence it is clear that they denied infant baptism, accepted a Hoffmanite theology, and held a Zwinglian view of the Lord's Supper. Five went to prison, five recanted, two were burnt as heretics at Smithfield, and others were banished and imprisoned.

English Baptist origins

It has been a constant matter for discussion between Baptist historians as to just how far Baptist roots are in the Anabaptist movement. W. T. Whitley, followed by A. C. Underwood, sharply separated the Anabaptists from Baptists in England. John Smyth inherited some Mennonite ideas, among them that Christians ought not to take oaths, should not be magistrates, should marry within the church family, and should be pacifist. However, Thomas Helwys, not Smyth, founded the first English Baptist church in England. Helwys disagreed with Smyth on a number of matters. He rejected the Hoffmanite theology of the Dutch group, but supported Christians taking oaths and accepted the magistracy. In this he was at one with other early English Baptist congregations in Coventry, Tiverton, and Salisbury, who corresponded with the Mennonite Waterlander community in 1626.

[11] B. Evans, *Early English Baptists*, i, pp.151–165

Winthrop Hudson, an American Baptist historian, has argued that early English Baptists specifically repudiated the 'Anabaptist' tag and condemned several Anabaptist ideas. He was convinced that the English Baptist tradition is much more properly allied with those who emerged from Puritanism and Congregational dissent and who theologically aligned themselves with Calvinism.[12]

E. A. Payne claimed this ignored the complex nature of Anabaptist belief, arguing that although some Baptists repudiated some Anabaptist views, they did not reject all the distinctive doctrines.[13] He noted that separatism was treading a similar path to that trodden earlier by many in Switzerland and Germany. Payne also argued that 'ideas have wings as well as legs' and the 'early English Baptists provided only one of many bridges by which the ideas of the continental radicals passed over into Britain and the new lands across the Atlantic' in the sixteenth and seventeenth centuries. The name was rejected, but not ideas like the 'gathered church', believer's baptism, Scriptural authority and religious toleration. Payne noted that Hudson virtually ignored the General Baptist tradition, but the fact is, not all English Baptists were Calvinist.

Gunnar Westin pointed out that the Dutch Mennonite refugees in England also denied the Anabaptist title. The relationship was not one of identity or succession. The pilgrimage of the Puritans into the Baptist camp did not take place till the Separatists had settled in Holland, where Anabaptists had been active for 70 years.

Dr Barrie White claimed there is little connection between European Anabaptists and the first English Baptist groups.

> It is rather difficult to demonstrate any direct debt to the continental Anabaptists, except in the case of John Smyth, and even in his case it may seem, upon closer examination, somewhat insubstantial. Rather do the Separatists appear to have been the most impatient embodiment of Elizabethan and Jacobean Puritanism; similarities between the forms of English Puritanism and continental Anabaptism seem to derive more from a similar type of appeal to the norm of the Church in apostolic times than to any observable sixteenth-century cross-fertilisation. At most it may be claimed that somewhat parallel developments did take place, but that, given the original New Testament source material and the nature of the contemporary Protestant appeal to it, such developments need not imply, and without clear evidence ought not to be taken to imply, any direct borrowing.[14]

Dr White put the onus of proof on those who would assert that European Anabaptists had any measurable influence on English Separatism. He is convinced there is no explicit testimony for such a view, and therefore rejects it.

Those churches that came to be known as Baptist evolved slowly and began with individual congregations, not a coherent group of churches called Baptist.

[12] W. S. Hudson, 'Who were the Baptists?', BQ 16, pp.303–12

[13] E. A. Payne, *The Anabaptists of the Sixteenth Century*, 1949, p.19; BQ, 16, pp.339–42

[14] B. R. White, *The English Separatist Tradition* 1971, pp.xii–xiii

> The essence of English nonconformity was the creation of non-parochial protestant congregations, or 'separate churches' as contemporaries described them. This term, denominationally neutral, permits us to see the underlying unity of nonconformity. It also suggests the fundamental truth that the later nonconformist denominations were organized from pre-existing congregations.[15]

The early English separatists were Puritan idealists who totally repudiated the Church of England, which they perceived to be a completely false church, and put in its place a new model of the Church, born out of a careful study of Scripture. However, the Puritan separatists fell out with each other over the details of the paradigm for the new church in England. Most Puritans had no intention of leaving Britain, being prepared to work for reformation within the existing parish system, but others tried to establish their new congregations in an atmosphere that was free from government interference either by Queen Elizabeth or King James, by moving first to Europe and then the New World.

The Reformation in England

The English Reformation smouldered into life with the refusal of the Pope to annul the marriage between Henry VIII and Katharine of Aragon. This eventually led to the separation of both the English church and state from the Roman Church, the diversion of taxes into the royal coffers, along with the revenue from the dissolution of the monasteries led by Thomas Cromwell. The 1534 Act of Supremacy declared: 'The King's majesty justly and rightly is, and ought to be and shall be, reputed the only supreme head in earth of the Church of England called Anglicana Ecclesia.'

The *Ten Articles* (1536) were drawn up to include references to the authority of the Scriptures, justification attained by contrition and faith joined with charity. The Bible in English, built on Tyndale's translation work, was provided in every parish church and a lectionary of readings established. But the marks of the old religion were still evident. Henry himself approved the use of images, the invocation of departed saints, of purgatory, transubstantiation with communion in one kind only, and the celibacy of the clergy.

What Henry began was developed by Renaissance studies of the Bible, the influence from continental universities, and the far-reaching measures of the advisors of Edward VI, Henry's son and successor. Thomas Cranmer helped secure the Reformation position of the Church of England by two editions of the *Book of Common Prayer*, 1549 and 1552, which in turn were greatly influenced by refugee theologians. These editions largely removed the ceremony and liturgical practice of the Roman Church from England. Rome was declared to be in the wrong, transubstantiation was decisively rejected, celibacy abolished, and communion offered in both kinds.

Protestants under Mary and Elizabeth

This revolutionary programme was completely reversed when Mary succeeded Edward VI. Her attempt to re-establish Roman Catholicism eventually failed,

[15] M. Tolmie, *The Triumph of the Saints: the Separate churches of London, 1616–1649*, 1977, p.1

but not before Cranmer and others were burnt at the stake. Many other English exiles imbibed deeply at the wells of Geneva and Strasbourg, and this is a primary root of Calvinistic Puritanism and the Protestant principles of later Dissent.

When Elizabeth came to the throne in 1558 she was determined to have peace in the land. She closely guarded her personal religious convictions, but at the opening of her reign she was declared 'Supreme Governor of the Church' and a revised Prayer Book of Cranmer's was reinstated. All clergy were required to subscribe to the *Thirty-Nine Articles*. The Romanizing bishops of Mary were deposed and the Pope replied by excommunicating Elizabeth, which effectively put the new Queen's life in danger from various Popish plots. R. C. Walton commented:

> Religion as established by law under the Elizabethan settlement was Calvinistic in theology, Erastian in church order and government, and largely mediaeval in liturgy. It was a typical English compromise, acceptable to those who had no desire to live under the rigour of the Genevan discipline, but little to the taste of Puritans.[16]

The Puritans and Separatism

The Puritans, many of them in the first instance returned exiles who had fled England during Queen Mary's reign, came to prominence in Queen Elizabeth's reign. They felt it was imperative to establish a pattern of church life that was in accordance with the Scriptures. Initially they campaigned for the removal of bishops, but were unsuccessful. They sought to establish a covenanted church on the pattern of the Calvinistic Presbyterians.

A 'shadow' church was attempted, organised on Presbyterian lines, to take over the state church when the opportunity came. Puritans were well represented in Elizabeth's Parliaments and among her bishops and clergy. Taking full advantage of the anti-Roman feeling, many of the Puritans campaigned for their objectives through a variety of pamphlets. In 1572 Elizabeth made a determined but ineffective attempt to silence such pressure.

Thomas Cartwright, of Cambridge University, proposed a purified Church that would mirror New Testament patterns. He advocated the abolition of archbishops; wanted bishops to have only spiritual power; and believed bishops should be elected by ministers and presbyters. He still favoured giving a considerable place to temporal power in church affairs, arguing that the state should enforce church attendance, test congregations on what they had learnt in worship, and if people were found wanting provide appropriate punishments! Cartwright was prepared to give the Church of England time to put its own house in order, but many of his contemporaries were not so minded. Another Cambridge man, Robert Browne, published *A Treatise of Reformation without Tarrying for Anie* (1582), a title which aptly described the urgency of the situation for many. Browne and his friend Harrison gathered a church of forty members in Norwich. They were soon in trouble with the authorities and fled to Middleburg on the continent. There the congregation developed a doctrine of the Church

[16] R. C. Walton, *The Gathered Community*, 1946, p.59

as a covenanted community, members being bound to God and each other in obedience to Christ, whose will was known through Scripture.

During the 1590s another Separatist church was formed in London under the leadership of John Penry. He advocated a covenanted church membership and the scriptural text of crucial importance was Matthew 18.17: 'Tell it to the church.' But the question was: Who comprised 'the church'? Henry Ainsworth stated the church meant all its covenanted members. Another leader, Francis Johnson, claimed it meant only the eldership. This congregation emigrated to Holland, where the issues were further discussed with other exiled groups, one of them led by John Robinson who eventually settled in Leyden. It was from his group that some members departed for America, first on the 'Speedwell' and then on the 'Mayflower' to become America's 'Pilgrim Fathers' in June 1620.

One group that stayed in Amsterdam came from Gainsborough, Lincolnshire, led by an Anglican clergyman, John Smyth. In his own person he epitomises the emergence of Baptists from Elizabethan Separatism. He describes his journey from 'the profession of Puritanism to Brownism, and from Brownism to true Christian baptism'. It is here that the origins of the General Baptists are to be found.

Part One:
The General Baptists

2

Early English Baptist Separatists

John Smyth

JOHN Smyth, who was probably born in 1570, was studying at Christ's College, Cambridge, by 1586. Among his tutors was Francis Johnson from whom he first received Puritan teaching. Smyth, ordained by the Bishop of Lincoln, was elected a Fellow at Christ's College in 1594.

Smyth was first in trouble with the church authorities when at Cambridge. He objected to the burial service, the churching of women and the wearing of the surplice. Smyth vacated his fellowship in 1600 and was appointed a City Lecturer at Lincoln where he preached four sermons on Psalm 22, later published as *The Bright Morning Star* (1603). This volume reveals him as a loyal Puritan member of the Church of England, who is well aware of Separatist criticisms, particularly those related to the use of set prayers in worship. Smyth's stance upset some people at Lincoln and in October 1602 he was described as a 'factious man', and his appointment terminated.

There was a legal dispute over his dismissal and what was called his 'personal preaching'. In *A Paterne of True Prayer* (1605), he offered an exposition of the Lord's Prayer. The Archdeacon's court convicted him of preaching in Lincoln without proper authority and 'factious doctrine' was added as a further irregularity after his dismissal. While this dispute was in progress Smyth received from Whitgift, the Archbishop of Canterbury, permission to preach in any part of his province, which included Lincoln. When the Bishop of Lincoln protested, Whitgift withdrew his authority. Smyth moved to Gainsborough but was soon in trouble with the Archdeacon's court when, at the diocesan visitation of 23 August 1605, he was preaching in that parish. Smyth appeared before the Archdeacon's court held at Huntingdon on 26 March 1606 charged with preaching on 2 March without a licence at Gainsborough. Apparently he had taken a service when the minister appointed did not arrive, and judgement was given against him. In November 1606 he faced a new charge of 'practising physic without licence'.

Gainsborough, on the borders of Nottinghamshire, was a gathering place for a number of ministers who had been in trouble with the authorities for their Puritanism. In an exchange of letters with Richard Bernard, Vicar of Worksop, between 1607–9, Smyth styled himself pastor of the Gainsborough church.

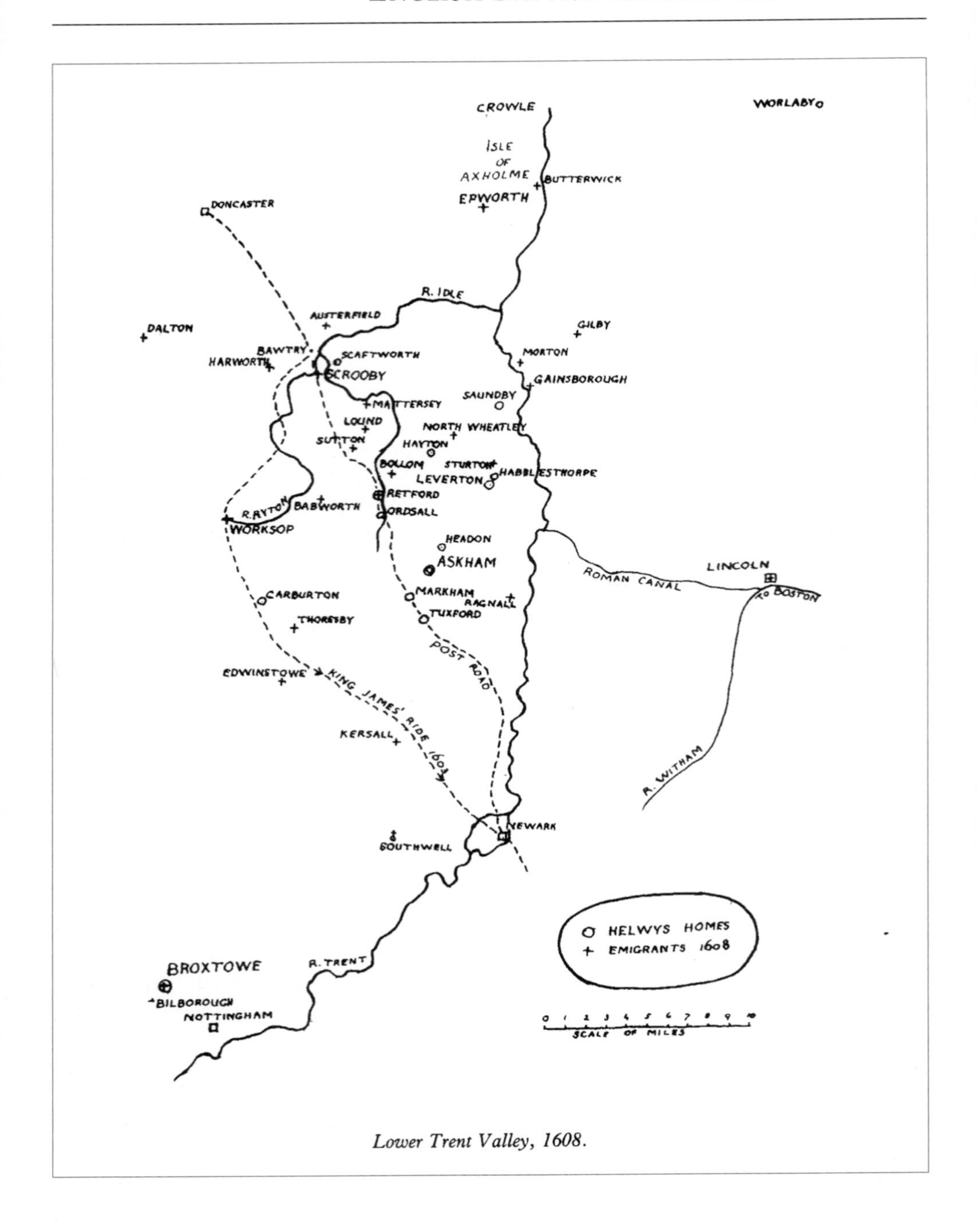

Lower Trent Valley, 1608.

Among those involved with Smyth at this time were Richard Clifton, rector of Babworth, who went to Amsterdam in 1608; William Brewster who went to Leyden; together with Thomas Helwys and his cousin Gervase.

Thomas Helwys

Edmund Helwys, father of Thomas was a lawyer, a staunch Protestant, who lived at Broxtowe Hall, in the parish of Bilborough, near Nottingham. Edmund died in 1590. Thomas had three years in London securing a legal training at Grays' Inn before he returned to Nottinghamshire in 1595, when he married Joan Ashmore at the Bilborough parish church. They settled at Broxtowe Hall. Though little is known of Helwys in the next few years, Broxtowe Hall was associated with known Puritan sympathisers. Among those who came were Richard Bernard of Worksop, John Robinson of nearby Scrooby, and John Smyth.

A group of Christians had formed a covenanted church at Gainsborough and one of them, William Bradford, said that they 'as the Lord's free people, joined themselves (by a covenant of the Lord) into a church estate, in the fellowship of the Gospel, to walk in all his ways, made known, or to be made known unto them, (according to their best endeavours) whatsoever it should cost them, the Lord assisting them'.[1] They believed 'the visible Church of the New Testament with all the ordinances thereof, is the chief and principal part of the Gospel'. Smyth's writings reveal his indebtedness to Francis Johnson, particularly in his understanding of the use of set prayers in worship. At a conference in the Coventry home of Sir William Bowes, in 1606, Francis Johnson's views were the centre of discussion. Smyth's own *Principles and Inferences Concerning the Visible Church,* (1607) is the documentary evidence that he was a willing heir to the Separatist tradition. His outline of the visible church's structure and practice owed almost everything to Johnson and Barrow.[2]

In January 1604 Puritan hopes were dashed when a new set of canons and discipline for the government of the Church of England were approved. It provided Archbishop Whitgift with the means of enforcing obedience to his policies regarding the Puritans. The effects were felt in Gainsborough, and the leadership decided that they should leave for Holland, a land of religious toleration, as quickly as possible. The emigration took place in small parties, with Thomas Helwys playing a leading part in the arrangements for Smyth's congregation.

Helwys and Smyth developed a very deep relationship. Reflecting on having left his wife and children in Broxtowe Hall, Helwys wrote in 1611,

> have we not neglected ourselves, our wives, our children and all we had and respected him? And we confess we had good cause to do so in respect of those most excellent gifts and graces of God that did abound in him.

Even when Helwys and Smyth parted, Helwys wrote: 'All our love was too little for him and not worthy him.'[3] When the party arrived in Amsterdam, a

[1] E. A. Payne, *Thomas Helwys and the First Baptist Church in England*, 1959, p.6
[2] B. R. White, *The English Separatist Tradition*, 1971, p.123
[3] E. A. Payne, *Thomas Helwys and the First Baptist Church in England*, 1959, p.7

haven for seventeenth-century objectors to the impure state of the Church of England, they were housed in the great bakehouse of the Mennonite Jan Munter. Here they were free to worship according to the dictates of their consciences as guided by the Holy Spirit, and free to experience 'all the evils of overcrowding, from exacerbated tempers to the plague'.[4]

Smyth's thought

The fundamental question was the nature of the Church, its officers, and its mission. Smyth recognised three specific issues for which he was indebted to earlier Separatists like Francis Johnson:

> Herein therefore especially are those ancient brethren (of the separation) to be honoured, that they have reduced the Church to the true primitive apostolic constitution which consisteth in these three things.
>
> 1 The true matter which are saints only.
> 2 The true form which is the uniting of them together in the covenant.
> 3 The true property which is communion in all holy things, and the power of the Lord Jesus Christ, for the maintaining of that communion.[5]

In Amsterdam the crucial issue to be faced was the nature of the Church and its relationship to covenant theology. In 1607 Smyth had defined the visible church as 'two, three, or more saints joined together by covenant with God and themselves ... for their mutual edification and God's glory'. On the one side God covenanted to be their God, 'to give Christ' and 'with Christ all things else'. On the other, the faithful covenanted 'to obey all the commandments of God'.[6] Within the covenant there was also a 'horizontal' responsibility, as Barrie White terms it, accepted by the faithful for each other, which 'mutually containeth all the duties of love whatsoever'. Such ideas went beyond Johnson and Robinson.

Smyth argued for all books of prayer, even the Scriptures themselves, to be removed not just during the time of prayer, but during the 'time of prophesying and singing'. He insisted that within the congregation the 'brethren jointly have all power both of the kingdom and priesthood immediately from Christ'. Such a church had power to administer the 'seals of the covenant', baptism and the Lord's Supper, and also the right to remove the elders' power 'upon just cause'. Whereas Johnson's congregation would receive help from outside for needy members, Smyth insisted that the church should take full responsibility for all its own members. 'In the covenant promise of the local congregation the eternal covenant of grace became contemporary and man's acceptance of it was actualised in history'.[7]

The Church

The concept of an independent gathering of adult believers, who pledged personal loyalty first to Christ and then to each other as members of the body

[4] A. C. Underwood, *The History of the English Baptists*, 1947, p.35
[5] B. R. White, *The English Separatist Tradition*, 1971, p.123
[6] W. T. Whitley, ed., *The Works of John Smyth*, Cambridge, 1915, i, p.252
[7] B. R. White, *The English Separatist Tradition*, Oxford, 1971, p.128

of Christ, was completely foreign to the Church of England as established by Queen Elizabeth and her successors. The Anglican understanding of itself was essentially an inclusive idea. The baptism of infants signified not only their acceptance within the church community of divine grace, but also their initiation into the temporal community of the nation. The Reformation in England had resulted in the severance of all links with the ecclesiastical and temporal powers of the see of Rome. Control in the Church of England, as in the nation, was now directly under the Sovereign, who worked through bishops in the House of Lords, to appoint ministers in the Church of England, and through both Lords and Commons in controlling the laws and liturgical practice of the established church.

However, for the Separatists and Puritans who eventually emerged as General Baptists, the independency of the local congregation, where Christ was King, was paramount. The members themselves provided from their own physical and spiritual resources for their own ministers. Christian commitment was worked out in the holy living of members of the congregation, and in a Christian life-style in the local community. They also shared in a wider association of churches with a similar outlook, an interdependence worked out with Christians of a like mind on the basis of common doctrinal beliefs, ecclesiastical polity and in mission to an unbelieving world. Each congregation understood itself accountable to God and each other, as it shared in God's covenanted love made known through Christ.

A covenanted people and a priestly people

Long before John Smyth adopted a General Baptist position, the concept of the divine covenant dominated his thought about the Church. He defined a 'visible community of saints' as 'two or more joined together by covenant with God and themselves.' Christians also had a duty to each other as believers, which he termed 'the duties of love'. This was put in a meaningful context as people accepted it within a local congregation.

The final seat of church authority was in the covenant community. 'Unto whom the covenant is given, unto them the power of binding and loosing is given. The covenant is given to the body of the Church … therefore the power of binding and loosing is given to them.' For Smyth, believers' baptism 'doth visibly declare' a promise that had been inwardly received, a covenant already entered, involving the 'mutual consent of both persons contracting together'.

Separatism provided an understanding of the independence of each gathered fellowship of believers, which was fundamental to the interdependence these churches also shared. The clearest statement of this is in *The Differences of the Churches of the Separation* where Smyth developed the idea of the visible church as a 'kingly priesthood … and the Saints are Kings and Priests unto God'.[8]

Smyth argued that the congregation could be defined by the phrase, 'saints as kings', and it is they who rule the visible church. As children of the Kingdom they accept the government of Christ the King in each congregation. The parallel of this was in congregational kingship, where the 'saints as priests' have the responsibility of offering up spiritual sacrifices acceptable to God. Smyth

[8] W. T. Whitley, ed., *The Works of John Smyth, Cambridge*, 1915, i, pp.274ff

deals at length with how such worship is to be conducted and elaborates on the responsibilities of presbyters or elders. The eldership 'is to lead and moderate the Church actions and speeches' where the ultimate authority rests with the 'saints' who are 'kings and priests unto God'. The saints are 'all interested in all parts of administration though the elders lead and moderate them'. It is the saints 'jointly who have all power both of the kingdom and the priesthood immediately from Christ'. Therefore, if there is no elder in a congregation, it does not lack power 'to preach, pray, sing psalms and ... administer the seals of the covenant' and can properly 'admonish, convince, excommunicate, absolve, and all other actions either of the kingdom or the priesthood'.

Even when the church has chosen elders it 'loses none of her former power, but still retains it entire unto herself to use' when occasion demands. 'The presbytery has no power but what the Church has and gives to it, which the church upon just cause can take away.' In fact the church has some power that the eldership on its own does not possess, that is the power to elect elders to office and also to excommunicate.

This ultimate congregational control of the life of the church has been distinctive for Baptists from the beginning. Indeed, Smyth went so far as to say that though the deacons 'are the hands of the church' and servants of the congregation, nonetheless, 'the church is the owner and primary possessor of the treasury, and the chief lord of it under Christ: and unto the church must account be made finally.'

Parting of the ways

The final breaking point with other Separatists came when Smyth advocated believer's baptism, in *The Character of the Beast* (1609). As a result, the group disbanded themselves from their former church state because they came to believe they had not been validly baptised. Smyth first baptised himself by affusion, then the rest of the group, beginning with Helwys. A shock of horror swept round the English refugees in Amsterdam. Why had not Smyth approached the Mennonites for baptism? Apparently it was their heretical Christology that repelled him.

Later he decided that perhaps he had been wrong to baptise himself. Regarding baptism he argued:

> Baptism is not washing with water: but it is the baptism of the Spirit, the confession of the mouth and the washing with water: how then can any man without great folly wash with water which is the least and last of baptism, one that is not baptised with the Spirit, and cannot confess with the mouth.[9]

If the church is built on a covenant, Smyth's opponents asked, why are children excluded? Were not Abraham's seed all sealed? Smyth replied that two covenants were made with Abraham. One related to his children who were his physical heirs, of which the covenant seal was circumcision. The other was a covenant with his spiritual children of which the Holy Spirit, not baptism, was the seal. Concerning infants, who obviously could not exercise faith for

[9] *Ibid.*, i, p.567

themselves, Smith claimed either, that they are all saved, 'or that they are one of the Lord's secrets, not to be searched into'.[10]

The status of baptism, in Smyth's view, changed from being a seal of God's grace, to being the means which 'doth visibly declare' a promise which has been inwardly received, the existence of a covenant which had already been entered.[11]

Baptism was for Smyth his entry into a covenant with God when 'Christ was visibly put on'. His own self-baptism was possible because all present believed they were re-constituting the church as in apostolic times. It meant a total repudiation of any idea of 'apostolic succession'. It led Smyth to claim that 'all power ecclesiastical or ministerial is derived from Christ to the Church, and then through the Church to elders'. For Smyth, the ministry was firmly subordinated to the church and the church was led by the Spirit of Christ. No Separatist had as yet placed the final seat of authority in the church so clearly.

One other factor determinative for the congregation before it divided was the Arminianism that was gaining a foothold in Dutch churches, who believed that Christ's redemption 'stretcheth to all men' and that all people are capable of faith. Baptists who held this view of a general redemption were called General Baptists and in England this theological perception significantly distinguished them from the Particular (Calvinistic) Baptists who emerged in England in the late 1630s.

Baptists and Mennonites

In February 1610 John Smyth, with thirty-one others, sought membership among the Mennonites, convinced that they had been wrong to baptise themselves, but they were not immediately accepted. Within a year Thomas Helwys and those who had not sought union with the Mennonites became a distinct church.

In 1611 Helwys shared in the production of three pamphlets. *A Declaration of the faith of English People Remaining at Amsterdam in Holland* was the earliest English Baptist Confession of Faith, in twenty-seven articles. The next pamphlet was a forthright attack on Calvinism, *A Short and Plain Proof by the Word and Work of God, that God's decree is not the cause of man's sin or Condemnation*. The third was an *Admonition* in which Helwys dealt with the main points of difference between himself and the Mennonites and stated he had separated from Smyth because he believed 'there is no succession or privilege in holy things'. His congregation maintained that church officers should hold office only in the church where they have been ordained to that office.

Helwys differed from Smyth and the Mennonites in a number of ways. He strongly repudiated belief in human freedom, and would have nothing to do with any idea of 'succession or privilege in holy things'. He defended the taking of oaths because for him the magistracy was a holy ordinance of God, not an office that debarred a person from membership in the Church of Christ. Against the Hoffmanite views of some Mennonites he contended that 'Christ took his flesh of Mary, having a truly earthly, natural body'.[12]

[10] *Ibid.*, ii, p.634
[11] *Ibid.*, i, p.567
[12] Underwood, *op. cit.*, p.47

Heare o King, and dispise not ye counsell of ye poore, and let their complaints come before thee.
The king is a mortall man, & not God therefore hath no power over ye immortall soules of his subiects, to make lawes & ordinances for them, and to set spirituall Lords over them.
If the king have authority to make spirituall Lords & lawes, then he is an immortall God, and not a mortall man.
O king, be not seduced by deceivers to sinne so against God whome thou oughtest to obey, nor against thy poore subiects who ought and will obey thee in all thinges with body life and goods, or els let their lives be taken from ye earth.

God Save ye Kinge

Spittlefeild neare London.

Tho: Helwys.

Helwys to the King

Plea for freedom of conscience

Helwys published in Amsterdam in 1612 *A Short Declaration of the Mistery of Iniquity*. It was the first claim for religious toleration and freedom for worship according to conscience to be published in English, declaring that the Church must bear witness to the truth whatever the cost. On the copy that Helwys sent to King James 1, now in the Bodleian Library, Oxford, he wrote on the fly-leaf:

> Hear, O King, and despise not the counsel of the poor … The King is a mortal man and not God: therefore hath no power over the immortal souls of his subjects, to make laws and ordinances for them, and to set spiritual Lords over them.

General Baptists persistently argued this point of religious freedom. They did not believe that anyone was destined by a divine decree to damnation, but that all people had the possibility of repentance and believing the Gospel. They argued vigorously that nobody should be killed for mistaken beliefs since this might defeat God's purposes in salvation. People must be free to hear spiritual truth and receive it without coercion of any kind.

Return to England

Helwys was now convinced that he had been wrong to leave England. Parting with Smyth caused Helwys personal pain, but he was convinced that 'the days of great tribulation spoken of by Christ' had now arrived and he must get back to England and appeal to James I to stop persecuting the faithful.

Helwys' own family position entitled him to think he might gain access to the King. His uncle, Geoffrey, was a City of London alderman, living in Walbrook. His cousin, Gervase, had been knighted and was soon to be Lieutenant of the Tower of London. Helwys and the small group with him established themselves at Spitalfields. Thomas Helwys' signed copy of *The Mistery of Iniquity* was presented to James I, though we do not know if Helwys did this personally. The King's reaction was swift. Helwys was lodged in the Newgate Prison where he died sometime before 1616.

John Murton, a Gainsborough furrier who had gone to Amsterdam with Smyth's group in 1608, and in that year married another group member from Worksop, Jane Hodgkin, followed Helwys as pastor. They returned with Helwys in 1612, but Murton was also soon in prison. He led the small church for twelve years, writing a number of tracts. *Objections Answered* (1615) was a bold plea that no person should be persecuted just for religious belief. *Truth's Champion* (1617) defended the Arminian view of redemption against Calvin's teaching. In 1620 he addressed an appeal to King James I on behalf of those who were being persecuted for the sake of their religion.

Leonard Busher, another member of the church, in 1614 published *Religious Peace*, suggesting it was

> lawful for every person or persons, yea, Jews or Papists, to write, dispute, confer and reason, print and publish any matter touching religion, either for or against whomsoever; always provided they allege no further proofs for any point of religion, but only the Holy Scriptures.[13]

Helwys, Murton and Busher made plain both their Arminian theology and their concern for religious liberty and were founders of the General Baptist tradition in England.

Other General Baptist churches were known to exist by about 1620 in Lincoln, Coventry, Salisbury and Tiverton. A few years later there was correspondence between these congregations and the Dutch Mennonites. By 1618 the Spitalfields church had moved to Crosby House, and in 1625 Elias Tookey led a splinter group that established a new church, meeting in Southwark. By 1639 the church met in London in two sections, one led by Thomas Lambe, a soap-boiler, in North Folgate and the other by Edward Barber, an upholsterer, in Bell Alley.

[13] E. B. Underhill, *Tracts on Liberty of conscience*, 1846, p.51. See also John Coffey, 'From Helwys to Leland: Baptists and Religious Toleration in England and America, 1612–1791', pp.13–37, in D. W. Bebbington, ed., *The Gospel in the World*, 2002

3

English General Baptists

AS the seventeenth century opened, James VI of Scotland became James I of England and thus the Scottish Stuarts and the Welsh Tudor dynasties united without bloodshed. Catholic conspirators, led by Robert Catesby, failed to assassinate James in 1605. The Puritans had many supporters in Parliament, but disliked James' claim to uphold the 'divine right of kings'. The new colonies in North America were slowly emerging. Some Puritans from the Midlands sought freedom of worship first in Holland, then in 1620 a group set sail in the *Mayflower*, for Virginia, but were blown off course and landed at Cape Cod. These Pilgrim Fathers founded what became the New England colonies, but the religious liberty they sought was not always present.

Charles I came to the throne in 1625, and facing considerable opposition and frustration from Parliament, he dissolved it in 1630 and for eleven years ruled without it. Archbishop Laud was entrusted with the affairs of the Church, suppressing, and imprisoning the Puritans, driving many overseas to Europe or North America. Thomas Wentworth, earl of Strafford, dealt with matters of state in a similar high-handed fashion. Eventually Charles sacrificed both Laud and Strafford to the demands of Parliament. Charles and the 'Long Parliament' fell out, the King moved to York and the first battle of the Civil War was at Edgehill in October 1642. Lancashire, Yorkshire, the Midlands and Wales, together with the far South-west largely supported the King. Parliament controlled the customs and key ports, which was financially vital, together with London, the south and southeast. It was Oliver Cromwell, MP turned soldier, who emerged in charge of the New Model Army, who eventually defeated the King's army. In 1648 Cromwell sided with the Army in calling for the execution of the King, and this happened in January 1649, at which point a republic was formally established in England. In 1653 Cromwell was installed as 'Lord Protector' and in April 1654 moved with his family into the Palace of Whitehall. He refused the crown when offered it in 1657, and was then installed as Lord Protector for a second time, dying soon afterwards in 1658. His son Richard took over from his father briefly, but once Charles II had agreed terms at Breda in 1660 and the monarchy resumed in 1661, and the 'restoration of the monarchy' began, with dire consequences for all nonconformists.

When the first English General Baptist churches were later caught up in the wider religious and political discussions of Cromwellian England, the vital connection between church and state was deeply challenged. Infant baptism tied Church and Society closely together. But General Baptists challenged this fundamental connection by witnessing to the truth of believer's baptism and the church as a gathered fellowship of believers only, bringing a radical political challenge to contemporary society which could not be ignored by either church or state. A challenge sharpened as some significant Anglican clergy were influenced in a variety of ways towards a Baptist position.

By the mid-1640s General Baptist congregations in London were achieving a clear identity based upon their Arminian theology and their understanding of the Church as a 'gathered community'. As they came together in a serious missionary endeavour to evangelise both London and the provinces, in accordance with the 'Royal commission of King Jesus', An advanced and sophisticated network developed by 1653, perhaps earlier, of church meetings, quarterly associations and annual national General Assemblies. Once new churches were planted it was the responsibility of the Assembly Messengers, appointed to serve the whole General Baptist constituency, carefully to consolidate the new congregations within the network.

Missionary concern

Ruth Butterfield has pointed out it was not only in London that the missionary impulse developed.[1] John Sims, a Southampton shoemaker, for example, who had been baptised by James Sicklemore was acknowledged as 'an emissary all the West over', when he was arrested in Bridgwater, Somerset, in May 1646. John Chandler, of Chichester, was bound over to appear at the Winchester assizes for his evangelistic activities on the Isle of Wight in August 1645. He returned to missionary endeavour on the island where, in May 1647, he was arrested with Bartholomew Buckley, a mercer of Lymington, and Markes Dewey, a Wimborne butcher, for evangelistic preaching in Newport, Isle of Wight.

There was a General Baptist publishing offensive to persuade people of the Baptist position. Henry Denne, for example, followed up his preaching tour in Kent with *Grace, Mercy and Peace* (1646) in which he set out the gospel message for the inhabitants of Rochester. Benjamin Cox, the vicar of Tiverton, Devon, records how he was introduced to General Baptist ideas by reading Thomas Lambe's book on the work of Christ, *A Treatise of Particular Predestination* (1642). It was a similar experience for Samuel Fisher, vicar of Ashford, Kent, who having read a book by General Baptist, Richard Jackson of Biddenden, was brought into the General Baptist community.

An individual's successful evangelistic thrust was most marked when the person concerned decided to become resident in an area, as when Samuel Oates decided to settle in Oakham, Rutland; James Browne in Bridgenorth, Shropshire; and Henry Haggar in Stafford. In each location a General Baptist church took root and grew significantly.

The organisation of missionary campaigns by the General Baptists in Kent, London and the Midland counties, the development of hierarchical quarterly and general meetings during the 1650s, and networking between individuals and churches, suggests a high degree of co-ordination among General Baptists.

[1] R. Butterfield, 'The Royal Commission of King Jesus', BQ 35, pp.56–81

Preaching

Civil War and Commonwealth

After ruling without Parliament for eleven years, Charles I finally called the Long Parliament, which met from November 1640 until 1653. By 1641 some MPs believed enough had been done to limit the monarchy's powers. Others, led by John Pym, wanted to be sure that Charles I could not go back on his reluctant agreement to Parliament's wishes. Among those who supported Pym was Oliver Cromwell, (1599–1658), then MP for Cambridge. Cromwell had gone through a conversion experience prior to 1638, and now was prepared to fight for a 'godly' church that would reform people's spirituality and morals, supporting those in Parliament who legislated for 'liberty to tender consciences'.

By January 1642 Parliament believed it was in a position to effect a thoroughgoing reform of religion. Its first move, to abolish episcopacy, had failed because parliamentarians could not agree which form of church government should be adopted in its place. In June 1643 an 'Assembly of Godly Divines', comprising 31 lay people and 121 ministers, was called to advise Parliament on the best solution of the matter. The discussion of the *Thirty-Nine Articles* in the Westminster Assembly was slow. There was considerable dissension and eventually a Presbyterian form was constructed on an entirely new basis, culminating in the Westminster Confession that provided a common statement of faith for the three kingdoms of England, Wales and Scotland. A *Directory of Worship* was produced to replace *The Book of Common Prayer.*

Influence through preaching

The following brief cameo typifies what was happening all over the country as Baptist churches were founded in the Commonwealth period. Francis Cornwell was a vicar of Marden, Kent, whose Puritan views had led to his imprisonment by Archbishop Laud. His own study of the situation, particularly as it related to baptism, led him to accept baptism as a believer at the hands of the General Baptist Messenger, William Jeffery, and thereafter he gathered his own baptised congregation in Marden. On one occasion Francis Cornwell was invited to address nearby clergy and he took the opportunity to commend a General Baptist position. Among those who heard Cornwell and considered his claims was Christopher Blackwood, a Cambridge graduate, who was vicar of Staplehurst. Eventually he too accepted General Baptist ideas and founded the Spillshill church in Kent. When in 1653 Blackwood moved to Ireland, he adopted Particular Baptist views, was a preacher for six years at Dublin Cathedral having taken over from Thomas Patient when he returned to London.

Public disputations

Within the university tradition there was an academic discipline that encouraged scholars to argue for a particular theory or idea. The 'theses' would be published, as when Luther nailed his 95 theses to the door of the Cathedral, then a time was set for an academic discussion, or 'disputation' as to the truth or otherwise of the proposition. In the Commonwealth period this method was taken out of the rarefied atmosphere of scholastic theology, to be debated in churches or other public places, with two disputants or more joining in.

Baptists developed the public disputation as means of church growth. Between 1641 and 1700 there were at least 109 public disputations, most occurring in the Commonwealth period. A quarter of them were held in London, the rest took place throughout the British Isles. By this means Baptists preached the Gospel, refuting slanders about so-called 'Anabaptists', and recruiting new members, often Anglican clergy, like Francis Cornwell and Christopher Blackwood.

One of their opponents claimed they arranged the place and subject for disputation, and then divided the local Baptists into two groups, initially for and against the resolution. As the disputation progressed all the Baptists would then come out in favour of their own position, thus hoping to persuade all present to accept the Baptist position.

Each side wanted to put their case before a wider public through the printed word. For example, the vicar of Leominster, John Tombes, debated baptism publicly no less than nine times in these years. B. R. White calls Tombes a Baptist who had held a paid appointment within the English Church establishment of the 1650s, who 'led a gathered congregation where believers' baptism was taught', then lost his post during the 1660–62 period.[2] Yet through these debates, and the accounts of them that were later published, he made a major contribution to the growth of both types of Baptist churches.[3]

New Model Army

Unlike most continental Anabaptists, English General Baptists had no objection in principle to Christian involvement with the magistracy and, when necessary, the armed services. As the civil wars progressed, both streams of Baptists found a significant place in the New Model Army in which they enlisted and were prepared to fight and plan for civil and ecclesiastical liberty. A few General Baptists achieved high rank but most served in the lower ranks.

Henry Denne joined Colonel Scroope's regiment as a 'cornet', a commissioned

[2] B. R. White, *The English Baptists of the Seventeenth Century*, 2nd edition, BHS, 1996, p.104
[3] A. C. Underwood, *A History of the English Baptists*, 1947, p.69

cavalry officer who carried the regimental colours. Among the captains of Colonel Thomas Pride were John Mason, a former apprentice to a coach harness maker in London, and John Pym, who both later joined Fairfax's regiment. In Colonel Whalley's regiment William Russell was a trooper elected as an 'agitator' in 1647. When in 1647 Parliament tried to disband the New Model Army without paying it, the-rank-and-file elected officers and two soldiers from each regiment to form a General Council of the Army to run their affairs. Among General Baptist Chaplains to the Parliamentary forces were James Brown (1616–85) from Bridgnorth, who was Chaplain to Col Fairfax's regiment in 1652–3, and Christopher Blackwood, in Chester with Col Robert Duckenfield at the same time before going to Ireland. In the second civil war Jeremiah Ives succeeded Hanserd Knollys as chaplain of Whalley's New Model Regiment of Horse. The Army was purged of Baptists more than once by senior staff, but General Baptists continued to support the political radicals after the Particular Baptists had broken with them, probably because 'they had more to loose from an intolerant government'.[4]

Restoration England

When Charles II returned to the English throne he was prepared to offer a compromise on the religious issue, but he came under great pressure from the restored Church of England to enforce a religious conformity centred on the *Thirty-Nine Articles* and the *Book of Common Prayer*. He wished also to provide a measure of toleration for Roman Catholics, under the guise of similar relief for Dissenters. Edward Hyde, Charles' Lord Chancellor (created Earl of Clarendon in 1661), skilfully presented legislation that would have allowed for comprehension and toleration. The rising of Fifth Monarchy men, led by Thomas Venner, in January 1661, encouraged the spread of growing alarm about the political intentions of religious dissenters prior to the May 1661 Parliament. The Savoy Conference, which ran from April to July 1661, brought Anglicans and Presbyterians together to discuss the future state church. Presbyterians wanted to be part of this. Richard Baxter proposed an alternative service book, and that ministers who had not episcopal ordination would not be required to seek re-ordination. In the end most Presbyterians were unable to accept the proposed *Prayer Book*, which came into force in August 1662 when two thousand clergy were ejected from the Church of England.

However, political and church leaders in England and Scotland were united when Parliament met in May 1661 and refused either toleration or comprehension within the renewed state church and passed instead a series of acts, known as the Clarendon Code, although in fact, Clarendon was not the originator of the legislation.

Confessions of Faith

The desire to affirm where Baptist Christians stood, not only in regard to baptism, but also on all matters of doctrine and church practice, encouraged General Baptists to issue a series of *Confessions of Faith*. John Smyth, in Holland,

[4] Anne Laurence, *Parliamentary Army Chaplains*, 1642–1651, 1990, p.84. For details of the Clarendon Code, see chap.7

had made a personal statement of his faith in 1608 and again in 1611. Thomas Helwys did the same. General Baptist Confessions were issued in 1651, 1660, 1679, 1691 and 1704, clarifying General Baptist beliefs at critical times. Thirty Midland General Baptist congregations issued a statement of faith in 75 articles in 1651, adding a postscript that said a 'just parliamentary way' had to be found for the governance of England, an interesting comment as Cromwell was contemplating taking the title 'Lord Protector'. But this Confession obtained no permanent recognition among other General Baptist churches.

A 1660 confession was published as all Dissenters were adjusting to the restoration of monarchy and the established church in Britain. Two Messengers, who affirmed Baptist loyalty to the crown and denied that General Baptists had been involved in armed insurrection, presented a copy to King Charles II.

The 1678 *Orthodox Confession* was by far the most substantial statement of General Baptist beliefs yet published. It was issued at a time when state and Anglican authorities were persecuting all dissenters, when Roman Catholicism was resurgent, and when the unorthodox theological views of the Kent and Sussex General Messenger, Matthew Caffyn, were troubling the larger General Baptist community. The full title indicates the purpose: *AN ORTHODOX CREED or a Protestant Confession of Faith being an Essay to Unite and Confirm all true Protestants in the Fundamental Articles of the Christian Religion, against the Errors and Heresies of Rome.* It held that the Apostles', Nicene and Athanasian creeds ought to be both received and believed. The Confession reflects on the attributes of God, relationships between the persons of the Trinity, the nature and offices of Christ, predestination, reprobation, justification and sanctification. The doctrinal emphasis within the Confession defended 'the fundamental Christian doctrines of the Trinity, the Incarnation, and the Atonement against those within their own fold who would have replaced the common faith of Christendom by a cobweb of private fantasies and ultimately a barren Unitarianism'.[5]

There was a deep desire among Baptists to re-create the apostolic understanding of the Church. Fundamental to this was an understanding of the nature and authority of Scripture. Among Baptists an adequate Scriptural answer to the question: 'What is the Church?' is always prior to any discussion about the nature of New Testament baptism.

Article 37 of the *Orthodox Creed* declared: 'The authority of the holy scripture dependeth not upon the authority of any man, but only upon the authority of God, who hath delivered and revealed his mind therein unto us, and containeth all things necessary for salvation.' The Article continues: 'We do believe, that all people ought to have them in their mother tongue, and diligently and constantly to read them in their particular places and families for their edification and comfort; and endeavour to frame their lives, according to the direction of God's word, both in faith and practice, the holy Scriptures being of no private interpretation, but ought to be interpreted according to the analogy of faith, and is the best interpreter of itself, and is sole judge in controversy.'

For General Baptists, whether in church meeting, Association gathering or

[5] A. J. Baines, *The Signatories of the Orthodox Confession of 1679*, (revised) 1960, p.3

national Assembly, the final court of appeal is the mind of Christ as revealed in Holy Scripture. It is the magnetic north to which all discussions of belief and practice for individuals or churches constantly turn. It provides the authority and pattern for the ministry of Word and sacrament and the motivation for Christian mission.

A disciplined people

General Baptists would often ask members to stay after Sunday worship to deal with matters of polity and discipline and for these Scripture was profoundly important.

The *Orthodox Creed* established a discipline procedure, based on Matthew 18.15ff, but urged that an offender be tendered 'an admonition of repentance … with gravity, love and authority, and all this without hypocrisy or partiality, praying for the sinner.' Church discipline among Baptists was corrective but rarely vindictive. Discipline was motivated by love. It was first of all necessary to determine whether the conduct alleged was contrary to Scripture. Hearsay evidence was never enough—the church meeting required incontrovertible evidence of the offence in question and would send its leaders to establish the facts with the people concerned. The church dealt differently with those who succumbed to sudden temptations and those who were persistent transgressors.

The *Orthodox Creed* acknowledged the covenant idea held a central position in General Baptist thought. The new covenant is the basis for humanity's acceptance before God, since the old covenant has failed. The new covenant in Christ is the foundation for a new relationship between God and humanity, and it is on this that the Church is built. This new covenant is of God's 'free grace and love to fallen man' and is freely and fully offered to all men on the terms of the Gospel, viz. repentance and faith.

For General Baptists the relationship between churches was deliberately connexional because 'there is only one invisible catholick Church of Christ … Nevertheless, we believe the visible Church of Christ on earth, is made up of several distinct congregations, which make up that one catholick church, or mystical body of Christ. And the marks by which she is known to be the true spouse of Christ, are these, viz. Where the word of God is rightly preached, and the sacraments truly administered, according to Christ's institution and the practice of the primitive church; having discipline and government duly executed by ministers or pastors of God's appointing and the Church's election, that is a true constituted church, to which church, and not elsewhere, all persons that seek for eternal life, should gladly join themselves.'[6]

The General Baptist understanding of the power of the national Assembly comes in Article 39:

> General Councils or Assemblies, consisting of Bishops, Elders and Brethren, of the several churches of Christ, … and the churches appearing there by their representatives, make but one church, and have lawful right, and suffrage in this general meeting, or assembly, to act in the name

[6] W. L. Lumpkin, *Baptist Confessions of Faith,* Judson, 1969, pp.318–9

of Christ; it being of divine authority, under heaven to preserve unity, to prevent heresy, and superintendency among, or in any congregation whatsoever within its own limits, or jurisdiction.[7]

Appeals concerning any injustice, schism or heresy in a particular congregation were dealt with by a majority vote in the Assembly, and in the final analysis it could excommunicate an offender.

It is worth noting an interesting development among General Baptists when the Orthodox Creed was adopted. Some wished that a more Scriptural basis for the Assembly had been found, rather than the ancient creeds of the Church. A small group proposed the adoption of a brief Scriptural formula, based upon Hebrews 6.1–2. The formula contained repentance from dead works, and faith towards God; the doctrine of believers' baptism and the laying on of hands; the resurrection of the dead and eternal judgment. The proposal found significant support and the result was the Assembly had two parallel statements of its orthodoxy, the Orthodox Confession and the Six Principles.

The Richard Haines story

The reality of an individual taking a complaint to the General Baptists Assembly is well illustrated by Richard Haines (1633–1685), a member at the Horsham church, who had a dispute with his pastor, Matthew Caffyn. The dispute was about an application by Haines for a patent relating to improving seed. It illustrates how the General Assembly could, as a court of appeal, redress a local church decision, even if it was against a pastor and Messenger of the Assembly.[8]

When Haines became a Baptist, he joined the Horsham church, on 12 June 1656. He was a man of wealth, a farmer, an inventor, and a manufacturer, with influential London friends, none of which helped in his relationship with Caffyn. After years of experiment Haines had evolved a method of successfully cleaning hop clover so that the crop's quantity and quality were significantly increased. When he applied to patent his method Caffyn first tried to dissuade him, and then attacked him in church meeting. Caffyn regarded patentees as covetous and a cause of offence to weaker brethren in the church. Haines tried to reply at a later church meeting but was interrupted and insulted by Caffyn, and then excommunicated on the grounds that Haines' greed was causing scandal in the countryside. A lawsuit followed over the matter, in which Caffyn was not directly involved, that resulted in a complete vindication of Haines. A friend tried to achieve reconciliation between Haines and Caffyn, by inviting five London Particular Baptist ministers to adjudicate. They upheld Haines, but the Horsham church simply said the Particular Baptists had no authority among them.

Haines first lodged an appeal with the General Assembly in 1673, but the issue came before the Assembly year after year, with both sides publishing broadsheets and tracts seeking to justify their position. It was only in 1680 that the Assembly

[7] *Ibid.*, p.327

[8] W. T. Whitley, ed., *Minutes of the General Assembly of the General Baptists*, 1909–10, ii, pp.xii–xv

finally found in favour of Haines, and ordered that Haines' excommunication be reversed and Caffyn must rescind it, which he promised to do.

Haines in a final summing up challenged the Assembly to be what it had always claimed to be, and not to pretend the churches are independent. He asked what an Assembly was for: 'Are you nothing but ropes of sand, and are you not gross hypocrites and jugglers not to tell me so before?' He pressed the Assembly hard, either to decide the appeal or dissolve the Assembly and own they are independents like the Particular Baptists.

The marriage question

Individual cases were inevitably rare since it required strength of character to take matters to an Assembly. One theme the Assembly discussed time and time again was the issue of marriage. The Assembly took the view that the Pauline restrictions on marriage in 2 Corinthians 6.14–18 meant that an unbeliever is anyone who 'is not a member of the visible church of Christ'. This meant that those who married partners who were not General Baptists were often excommunicated, although locally leniency was used so justice could be mixed with mercy. This drove many General Baptist Christians out of their churches, and it also turned Association gatherings into occasions for matchmaking! It was 1744 before the Assembly relaxed this harsh view, when in answer to a query from the Bessels Green church, Messenger Matthew Randal, at the Assembly's request, wrote a private response on behalf of the Assembly, stating that exclusion was not expedient. The letter continued:

> Now since among us in this nation women are not permitted to lookout for themselves; and when they have no offers from among the men of their own community, what must they do? **Must** they, on pain of excommunication, refuse every sober, virtuous, christianlike person merely because he has not happened to be baptized by immersion on profession of faith? Is this consistent with Christian charity and forbearance? Yea, as to both sexes, 'tis scarcely possible not to transgress: the accidental sight or conversation of strangers; their agreeable mien, complexion, or deportment, often create such mutual liking and affection, as shall render marriage almost necessary and unavoidable.[9]

Hymn singing disputed

Another matter that constantly plagued the General Baptists was hymn singing, which began as a concern about psalm singing. The objection reached back to John Smyth, whose belief in the essential spiritual nature of worship led him to conclude 'it is unlawful to have the book before the eye in time of singing a psalm.' Later Thomas Grantham wrote:

> This new device of singing what is put into Men's Mouths by a reader is foreign to the sincerity and simplicity of this holy service. The Holy Scripture is a stranger to it; none of the Apostles used to do thus that we read of … nor is there any reason … that all should be tyed to one man's Words, Measures and Tunes in so great an Ordinance.

[9] Underwood, *op.cit.*, p.124

He laid down a rule which said that Psalms could only be sung in public worship by a single voice, interpreting the 'one by one' of 1 Corinthians 14.31, literally. As the prayer of one in the church is the prayer of the whole church, so the singing of one in the church is the singing of the whole church'[10] was Grantham's argument and he strongly opposed the singing of men's 'own composures in a mixed multitude'. The matter dragged on until 1733 when the General Baptist Assembly finally voted to allow local congregations to determine their attitude to singing in churches.

General Baptists and Ministry

It was Thomas Helwys who held '... the officers of every church or congregation are tied by office only to that particular congregation whereof they are chosen'. The Separatist covenant theology emphasised the independence of each congregation, and in consequence a minister was limited to the church that called him, and of which they were normally first a member. The ministry was not an absolute necessity for the existence of the church, since, as John Smyth wrote: 'The brethren jointly have all the power both of the kingdom and priesthood immediately from Christ ... and that by virtue of the covenant God maketh with them.'

The recognition of the broader relationship between the ministers and churches was evident at the regular meeting of General Baptist churches in regional gatherings and annual Assembly. It was the breadth and depth of relationship discovered in them, which strengthened the conviction that isolationism was a denial of fellowship and that unity at regional and national level would advance Christ's cause.

Fit persons

On the status and authority of the ministry among the General Baptists the *Orthodox Confession* states: 'The visible Church of Christ, being completely gathered and organized, according to the mind of Christ, consists of officers and members; and the officers, appointed by Christ, to be chosen by his church'. Early Baptists used passages from the Pastoral Epistles to define the type of person fit for the ministry. The relationship between education and ministry is clearly stated in an addition made to the General Baptist *1691 Confession.*

> We believe that learning the languages, to whit, Hebrew, Greek, Latin, etc. is no qualification so absolutely necessary to the being of a minister, or Elder, but that a person may very possibly be sufficiently qualified without it; though we readily grant that the learning of languages may be useful in its place, and as a servant to help, etc., but to make it a qualification, absolutely necessary to the being of a minister, we dare not.

Functions

The functions of ministers were described in terms of their tasks, the *Orthodox Creed,* Article 31, giving three types of church officers:

> The visible church of Christ, being completely gathered and organized, according to the mind of Christ, consists of officers and members; and the

[10] W. T.Whitley, ed., *Minutes of the General Assemblyof the General Baptists, 1909–10*, i., p.27

> officers, appointed by Christ, to be chosen by his church, for the peculiar administration of ordinances, and execution of the power and duty Christ hath enjoined them to the end of the world, are these three, viz., Bishops (overseer or shepherd), or Messengers; and Elders, or Pastors; and Deacons, or Overseers of the poor.[11]

Throughout the decade 1650 to 1660 the term Messenger was used by both General and Particular Baptists to denote anyone who was commissioned by one church to preach the Gospel and form new churches, or sent by one church to another to settle a dispute or discuss matters of common concern. Among the general Baptists in the Midlands and Kent the word, by 1654, was also used of a specific office separate from that of elders. The General Baptist Messenger was chosen by the churches gathered in Association meeting and with the consent of their local church. The Messenger was essentially an evangelist, planting new churches, advising them in their early development and offering advice to the churches that had appointed him. The Messenger by 1670 was an itinerant preacher among the churches, 'strengthening both pastors and churches' by teaching new Christians, and opposing any who would promulgate false teaching.

The General Baptist Elder or Pastor, chosen 'by common suffrage of the particular congregation', was to 'feed the flock', which meant attending 'the service of Christ in his Church, in the Ministry of the Word and Prayer, with watching of their souls as they that must give account to him'

The functions of deacons, who were ordained, were based on Acts 6, namely, 'to relieve the necessity of the poor and impotent brethren concerning their bodies'.

Thomas Lambe

The life of Thomas Lambe, a native of Colchester who by 1645 was pastor of the Bell Alley church in Coleman Street, London, typifies General Baptist life in this period. He was almost certainly the author of *The Fountain of Free Grace Opened* (1645), a summary of General Baptist beliefs at that time. It was based on the Arminian critique of Calvinism, affirmed that Christ's atoning death was for all people, and gave considerable emphasis to individual human responsibility. Lambe understood church authority to be derived directly from Scripture, not the congregation, and that leaders operated within the whole 'Church of Christ', not just individual congregations.

Lambe spent much of his time in evangelistic activity, developing a whole range of techniques to match the times. His roving missionary tours through large parts of England were like those journeys made by George Fox, the Quaker, and his companions. He welcomed public disputes with the clergy and claimed his right to enter parish pulpits as an ordained pastor of a Christian congregation.

[11] W. L. Lumpkin, *op.cit.*, pp.319–20. See J. F. V. Nicholson, 'The office of "Messenger" among British Baptists in the Seventeenth and Eighteenth Centuries', BQ, 17, pp.206ff, and 'Towards a theology of Episkope among Baptists', BQ 30, pp.265ff and 319ff. Also G. G. Reynolds, *First Among Equals, A study of the basis of Association and oversight among Baptist Churches,* 1993

His church was unique among independent congregations in that its meetings were regularly open to the public. Murray Tolmie writes:

> It rivalled the theatre in its capacity to draw crowds, 'especially young youths and wenches' and on Sundays 'many people, some of other separate churches, and some of our [parish] churches', wrote the Presbyterian Edwards, 'will go to this Lambe's church for novelty, because of the disputes or wranglings that will be there upon questions, all kinds of things started and vented almost, and several companies in the same room, some speaking in one part, some in another.' It was the custom of the congregation for two or three men to preach successively, and, when one hath done, there's sometimes difference in the church who shall exercise next, `tis put to the vote, some for one, some for another … and strangers who come thither will make a cry, and cry out for whom they like best as well as the church … Sometimes the meeting broke apart in sections, and there was 'such confusion and noise, as if it were at a play; and some will be speaking here, some there'.[12]

The General Baptists had several itinerant evangelists in the 1640s, and Lambe's church attracted and trained some of the most effective. Henry Denne, a former Anglican clergyman, Samuel Oates, a Norwich weaver, and Jeremiah Ives, a cheesemonger and box maker of London, were all baptized by Lambe and retained strong links with the London church. Between 1641 and 1646 Lambe can be 'traced, usually with a companion, in Gloucestershire (with Clement Wrighter, who was briefly a member of Lambe's church before achieving notoriety as one of the leading sceptics of London), in Norfolk, in Essex (with Timothy Batt), in Surrey and Hampshire (with Samuel Oates), in Kent (with Henry Denne) and in Wiltshire (with Jeremiah Ives). Of his associates, Denne was the most important.[13]

Lambe had a deep social conscience that was partly reflected in his support of the Leveller's 'large' petition in the spring of 1647. Levellers were opposed to the monarchy, advocated the complete removal of state control from religion and called for all adult males to have the vote. They had considerable support in the Parliamentary Army, where John Lilburne led them. H. Wheeler Robinson called Lambe a Baptist reformer on the basis of his four page tract, *An Appeal to the Parliament concerning the Poor, that there may not be a beggar in England* (1660) which opens with the sentence: 'In the midst of the many and great Undertakings, let not a settlement for the *Poor* be forgotten' which has almost a contemporary ring about it.[14] It contained proposals for a Labour Exchange, a kind of parish Council, recognises the need to draft labour to places where the work is, 'since the idle will not come for it', and the need to bring new industry to places where the industrial centre has decayed. This small tract is a good example, even if not a common one, of the social action of a Baptist congregation that sought to demonstrate the hallmark of the Christian Gospel.

[12] M. Tolmie, *The Triumph of the Saints* 1977, p.76
[13] *Ibid.*, p.77
[14] H. W. Robinson, *The Life and Faith of the Baptists*, 1927, pp.34–36

Edward Barber

Barber led a very different London General Baptist church from a house in Bishopsgate. Unlike Lambe, Barber hated publicity, nonetheless, the Presbyterian minister Thomas Edwards was given a significant account of this church as it met on 12 November 1645:

> When the company was met together they began with prayer; after prayer, everyone of the company kneeled down apart; and Barber, with another of their way, went to each of them one after another, and laid both their hands upon every particular head, women as well as men, and either in a way of prayer, prayed they might receive the Holy Ghost; or else barely to every one of them used these words, *Receive the Holy Ghost*.' After this ceremony was finished, the meeting of the church sat down to supper, 'which was dressed for them by a cook'. When the meal was over, and before the cloth was removed, the Lord's Supper was administered to the congregation. Thereafter a question was proposed, whether Christ died for all men, and the meeting was still discussing this when Edwards' informant left the meeting at eleven o'clock in the evening.[15]

The ceremony involving the laying on of hands marked a new departure for Edward Barber's congregation and introduced a matter that would divide General Baptists for several decades to come. Some members of Lambe's church adopted the same view and under the leadership of John Griffith eventually formed a separate church, where all members had to receive the laying on of hands. Lambe and his associated evangelists opposed it, but they were in the minority, and eventually Griffith persuaded all General Baptist churches to make this a distinctive mark of the church.

Henry Denne

Henry Denne offers another cameo of General Baptist life. He was ordained by the Bishop of St David's about 1630 and became a curate at Pirton, Hertfordshire, for most of the 1630s. He was baptized by Lambe at Bell Alley in 1643 and from there was sent out as an evangelist to East Anglia, working in Bedfordshire and Cambridgeshire. The parliamentary committee of Cambridgeshire disliked Denne and he was imprisoned briefly, but eventually he became the minister of the Eltisley church. He joined Lambe on an evangelistic tour of Kent in 1645–66, preaching in Rochester and Canterbury. He was preaching in Spalding, Lincolnshire, the following June, when he was arrested for baptizing local people during the night.

Between June 1646 and May 1649 Denne joined the Parliamentary Army, not as a chaplain, but as a soldier. He was tried at Burford after the Army mutiny in May 1649, as one of four Leveller leaders and sentenced to be shot. He alone was pardoned and afterwards wrote a pamphlet *The Levellers' Design Discovered* (1649). It throws little light on the incident, beyond his admission of guilt for neither giving obedience 'unto that authority under which we are placed' nor telling the Council of War his grievances before taking the extreme step of mutiny.

[15] M. Tolmie, *The Triumph of the Saints*, 1977, p.78f

Denne's earlier preaching activity had led to the formation of the Cambridgeshire churches at Warboys and Fenstanton by 1647. He remained linked with the Fenstanton church—though never called as its pastor—evangelising in Cambridgeshire until 1653. He drew up some formal doctrinal statements about pressing faith issues of the time, which he judged to be: the extent of the atoning death of Christ, believers' baptism, whether God was the author of sin and whether believers could fall from grace. In November 1654 Fenstanton reluctantly accepted a request to let Denne become the minister of some Baptists not yet formally organized into a church at Canterbury.

In the Fenstanton church there was an ongoing dispute about the 'laying on of hands', as to whether it was essential for all seeking membership of the local church. Many members began to set aside Scripture and the ordinances of the Lord's Supper and baptism, claiming they were unnecessary since they had direct access to God through the Holy Spirit. Fenstanton practised foot washing and observed the Lord's Supper at the end of a church meal. The church regularly helped 'poor' members of their own and other churches. A typical case was John Wilson, who lost his barns, outhouses, grain and hay through a fire. Church members discussed his situation and agreed he should not, initially, go to the 'justices of the peace for the county' but that local congregations should be made aware of his need. A letter invited representatives to a meeting at the home of Arthur Hinds in Cambridge, at which Fenstanton promised £6 towards the £30 reparation needed.

It is improbable that many Baptists were among the new Puritan merchants. R. C. Walton is probably correct when he notes:

> Most Baptists were poor men and, moreover, poor men of the villages. Whitley, in his introduction to the *Minutes of the General Assembly of the General Baptists,* prints lists of leaders up to 1689 and, where known, their occupations. He also lists the places where General Baptists Churches are known to be established. From these lists it is clear that most of the churches were village causes and most of the occupations rural—yeoman, farmer, blacksmith, husbandman, thatcher, maltster, labourer.[16]

Thomas Monk

Monk, a farmer and theologian, was elected Messenger for the General Baptist churches in Mid-Buckinghamshire and Hertfordshire from 1654 onwards. He is best known as one of the so-called 'Twelve Confessors of Aylesbury', probably the last English Protestants to be sentenced to death for their faith. In May 1661 Thomas Monk and six others had issued *Sion's groans for her distressed,* a moving and dignified plea for universal religious toleration. It remained unanswered and was followed by growing persecution. In July 1662 the Bishop of Lincoln began a visitation and demanded that local parishes give him information concerning any 'Anabaptists'. Monk was denounced, along with others, by one of the Bierton churchwardens. The local magistrates decided not to wait for the process of the ecclesiastical courts and invoked a 1593 act demanding they conform immediately or be exiled to a foreign country. Monk and the others

[16] R. C. Walton, *The Gathered Community*, 1946, p.77

threw themselves on the mercy of the court, but almost unbelievably, after a few magistrates left the bench, the chairman sentenced the twelve to death. Monk's son, also Thomas, rode to London to get help from the Particular Baptist leader, William Kiffin, who urged the case be brought to the attention of King Charles II. The King was genuinely distressed and a pardon was issued, but the prisoners remained in gaol until the next Assizes, when the pardon arrived and they were released. When Charles II in 1672 announced a Declaration of Indulgence for those Dissenters who would register themselves and their buildings with the authorities, Monk and his colleagues did not apply for Licences.

As the persecution deepened so divisions began to appear in General Baptist ranks, particularly over the doctrine of the Trinity, and the opinion that Christ's natural body was not made of Mary's flesh. Thomas Monk became a leading protagonist among the General Baptists of those who encouraged local churches to adhere to the orthodox Christian position. He was dismayed at the views and influence of Matthew Caffyn, the General Messenger from Horsham, Sussex. Monk put his orthodox views in *A Cure for the cankering Error of the New Eutychians … who erred … saying that our blessed Mediator did not take his flesh of the Virgin Mary* (1672), which was highly prized among orthodox General Baptists for a long time. He repudiated the Hoffmanite heresy 'that our blessed mediator did not take his flesh of the Virgin Mary, neither was he made the seed of David according to the flesh'. Monk tried on a number of occasions to persuade the Assembly to adopt unambiguous declarations on the Trinity and the Incarnation, but was unsuccessful. Monk died probably in 1685 but his widow and son maintained his orthodox concerns in the Assembly.

Matthew Caffyn

Matthew Caffyn (1628–1714) was born of farming stock at Horsham, Sussex. While at Oxford during the first Civil War he adopted Baptist views and was expelled from the University. He returned to farm in Horsham where he became pastor of the local General Baptist church and a Messenger of the General Baptist Assembly with responsibility for evangelism in Sussex and Kent.

Caffyn's geographical base in Kent suggests a link with those earlier Anabaptist exiles who had testified to their faith, some of them to the point of martyrdom. General Baptists in the Midlands and Buckinghamshire had different roots going back to the much older Lollard tradition. A. J. Baines states:

> In the coastal counties from Norfolk round to Sussex the General Baptist churches were closely related to the Mennonites of the Low Countries, particularly as related to their Christology. In the inland counties, including Buckinghamshire and Hertfordshire, the General Baptists were the successors and descendants of the Lollards … A manuscript summary of the history of the church of Ford or Cuddington says very correctly 'The soil had been prepared in the district by the Lollards …'
>
> The General Baptists of Bucks and Herts remained 'stiff in their mode of faith'; they preserved the three creeds, the three-fold order of the ministry and the historic structure of the Christian year. They did not share the Mennonite scruples about warfare, judicial oaths and participation in civil government and the doctrine of the being of God and the person

Horsham Meeting House

of Christ, was that of the Fathers and the Councils. By 1654 their Bishop or Messenger was Thomas Monk, one of the Twelve Confessors (1664), a formidable scholastic theologian. For a generation he led the struggle against Matthew Caffyn, whom the Kent and Sussex churches cried up 'as their Battle Axe and Weapon of Warre ...'[17]

This is a significant distinction that underlies continuing General Baptist divisions between 1670 and 1730.[18]

Certainly Caffyn was strongly attracted to the Christological views of Melchior Hoffman. With equal vigour the Midland General Baptists and Thomas Monk repudiated these views. Monk's beliefs were shared by most of the General Baptist Messengers who gathered in Assembly in 1679 when they published *An Orthodox Creed or a Protestant Confession of Faith,* which sought to minimize differences with Calvinists and specifically repudiated the Hoffmanite teaching. Christ, they stated, is both 'coequal, coessential and coeternal with the Father' and was 'formed of the only seed, or substance of the Virgin Mary'. The 'denying of baptism is a lesser evil than to deny the divinity of Christ' they affirmed.[19]

Caffyn retained his unconventional ideas, despite the division it created in the General Baptist community. After the 1689 Toleration Act the General Baptists had two parties in direct conflict. The 1693 Assembly tried to compromise by condemning the heresy while at the same time affirming that Caffyn did not hold these views. At the 1696 Assembly the Western Association of General Baptist churches tried to re-open the matter, but was unsuccessful. The result was a division that meant there were two General Baptist gatherings each year. The Kent and Sussex churches, supporters of Caffyn, were known as the General Baptist Assembly; the others who came from London, the Midlands and the

[17] A. J. Baines, in Roger Hayden, ed., *English Baptist Records,* Vol.i, *Chesham, Bucks,* BHS, 1985, pp.vii–viii
[18] M. Watts, *The Dissenters from the Reformation to the French Revolution,* 1978, 1, pp.1–14
[19] W. L. Lumpkin, *op.cit.,* pp.295–334

West, were known as the General Association. The Assembly continued to meet in London; the Association, often meeting at the same time, but usually in Stony Stratford. The two groups re-united in 1731, on the basis of the so-called 'six principles' of Hebrews 6.2, seventeen years after the death of Caffyn. But he was always in the background of the arguments that existed within General Baptist life.

Thomas Grantham

Thomas Grantham (1634–93) was a most gifted leader among the General Baptists, a tailor by trade who became a farmer, his own life exemplified his central conviction that 'The most glorious and worthy work to be done by God's people is to advance his truth, and to seek the salvation of the world by all possible means … all is but trifles in comparison.'

He was baptized in Boston in 1653; three years later he became the pastor (elder) of a church near Spilsby, Lincolnshire, where his evangelistic success was evident in the planting of several Lincolnshire Baptist churches. In 1666 he was ordained a General Baptist Messenger. He later moved to Norwich and founded a new church there, afterwards opening new congregations in King's Lynn and Great Yarmouth. His reflections over the years were gathered together in *Christianismus Primitivus* which became the touchstone of General Baptist orthodoxy.

In a small book, *The Successors of the Apostles*, (1674) Grantham argued that Messengers were a God-given ministry for the Church, though inferior to the Apostles, and was in succession to them 'in such things as were ordinary and fixed to that office'. He indicated the main purpose of Messengers was: 'to preach the Gospel where it is not known; to plant churches where is none; to ordain Elders in churches remote, and to assist in dispensing the holy Mysteries.'[20]

General Baptists were connectionalists rather than Independents. They had a three-fold ministry—Messengers, Elders and Deacons. The Messengers, although the last office to be developed by the General Baptists, were officers of the church at large; the Elders and Deacons were pastors and administrators only in a local congregation. Messengers were patterned on the New Testament work of Timothy or Titus. Grantham explained it:

> … as God hath given to His Church a fixed ministry of Bishops, Elders, Pastors, etc., to take care of particular churches, so He hath given to her a travelling ministry, unfixed in respect of particular societies, to whom it pertains … to take all occasions to cause the light of the glorious gospel to shine unto such as sit in darkness, to plant churches, to confirm or settle them in the faith, to comfort and visit those who have believed through grace.[21]

Frustrated hopes: 1689 and after

A noticeable phenomenon among the General Baptists during the reigns of Charles II and James II was the steady movement of some ministers from a General to a Particular Baptist stance in their ministerial leadership, although it

[20] Quoted in Underwood, *op.cit.*, p.120
[21] Quoted in Underwood, *op.cit.*, p.121

was not a significant feature among ordinary church members. Benjamin Keach came from Winslow, Bucks, to Southwark in London, and under the influence of William Kiffin and Hanserd Knollys joined the Particular Baptists in 1668. Mark Key, also under Kiffin's influence, left the General Baptists and joined Kiffin's church. When the six principles were asserted in the Assembly, Richard Allen of White's Alley, London, withdrew, and became a Particular Baptist pastor. Richard Adams of the Shad Thames church in London persuaded his church to send delegates to the 1689 Particular Baptist Assembly, which caused a disruption in his church. He relinquished his ministry and joined Kiffin's church although his church remained in the General Baptist Assembly. There was virtually no traffic in the other direction.

Grantham's vision that 'The most glorious and worthy work to be done by God's people is to advance his truth, and to seek the salvation of the world by all possible means' was not realised. The work of the General Baptists declined, as it became harder and harder to persuade churches to offer elders and deacons for service in the wider work of Messenger. The predominant General Baptist view of a minister as one who ministered solely within one congregation, for his whole life, also frustrated the calling of Messengers and therefore the work of mission.

The local Baptist churches were linked together in district Associations. The Associations were joined in a national General Assembly that dealt with such matters as were referred to it by local churches, pastors and Messengers from the churches that comprised the Assembly. By contrast with the Particular Baptists, whose national Assembly did not meet between 1692 and 1813, the General Baptist Assembly met almost year on year from 1654 onwards.

The power of the Assembly within a local church was strengthened over the years. The early Assembly decisions were referred by the Assembly to churches for them to test and accept as they determined within the local congregation. The Assembly Minutes for 1656 recorded that

> The Messengers and Elders being met together having obtained mercy of the Lord do desire to present to the congregations ... that you would seriously consider and examine them by the Scriptures of truth ... and as you find truth here so own, and entertain and practice it'.[22]

By 1696 the Assembly was of a very different mind. It had before it the issue of 'Independence' which delegates agreed was 'very dangerous and detrimental to the churches'; and it was further noted that local churches were not free to depart from agreed assembly decisions 'without the consent and approbation of an Assembly'.[23]

On another Assembly issue, D. M. Himbury comments,

> It was the contemporary emphasis upon the *reasonableness* of the Christian faith which led many of the General Baptists to seek, as many had done in the early centuries of Christian history, for a more rational explanation of the central doctrine of the Trinity. In 1692, the General Assembly had

[22] W. T. Whitley, ed., *Minutes of the General Assembly of General Baptist Churches*, 1909–10, i, p.9
[23] *Ibid.*, p.42

> answered a complaint made by the church at Shrewsbury, that some were holding views contrary to the articles of faith, and advised it to seek the help of sister churches in combating Socinianism. The main division arose, however, when Matthew Caffin, pastor of the Horsham church and its 'Messenger', was accused by Joseph Wright, of Maidstone, of holding heterodox views concerning the person of our Lord ... In 1697 the Assembly decided that all who debated matters relating to the doctrine of the Trinity should use 'Scripture Words' and no other terms. The following year the doctrines attributed to Caffin, 'that the Son of God or the Word was not of the Uncreated Nature and Substance of the Father, neither of the Created Nature and substance of his Mother' were condemned and Caffin ordered to appear for trial before the next Assembly, but he was again protected from censure ... There was constant suspicion of one side by the other, and there was some doubt in the minds of certain men whether a credal statement made in non-scriptural terms was a valid expression of Christian truth.[24]

The General Baptists, the smaller of the two Baptist groups, were reckoned to have in 1718 about 19,000 'hearers' regularly in attendance at their 120 churches. Relatively strong in Kent, Sussex, Buckinghamshire and Cambridgeshire, with outposts in Lincolnshire and the West of England, they had little work elsewhere and were weak in the urban settings of London and Bristol. They were fundamentally a rural people, who often did not build chapels, choosing instead to meet in barns, farmhouses and private dwellings. This was possible while the owners lived, but when they died, a congregation might just disappear overnight, literally having nowhere to meet.

The fact that, unusually, the Amersham Church had a building was not the result of a conscious decision to pursue that option, but to avoid paying a fine under the Coventicle Act. Prior to 1677 the church had bought a burial ground, and they erected on the same piece of ground a house for the congregation to meet in, but in which nobody lived. The aim was to avoid the fine on a resident, but by accident they ensured the permanence of their meeting. This was definitely the exception that proved the rule among General Baptists who did not generally build chapels for themselves.

Long ministries in one church, an untrained ministry, a Biblicism which did not encourage thought and action, and a policy of marriage only within the General Baptist community, all spelt out a recipe for decline rather than growth. Add to this the passing away of elderly, but strong, leaders at the turn of the century, without their replacement, and decline was almost inevitable.

[24] D. M. Himbury, *British Baptists, A Short History*, 1962, pp.64–66

4

General Baptists in the Eighteenth Century

AFTER a century of political upheaval and religious revolution the nation yearned for peace. Thomas Gray's *Elegy,* a bestseller, caught the spirit of the age. Goldsmith and Sheridan brought wit and humour to the English stage. Artists captured the glories of rural England, Gainsborough pictured the elegance of the fashionable world, and Hogarth, with his biting, satirical cartoons, depicted the manner of life of the vast majority who lived in the middle of violence, vice and poverty.

Henry Cavendish at Cambridge University explored the separation and identification of gases and experimented with electricity. Joseph Priestley, a political and theological radical, isolated oxygen and discovered the law of inverse squares in physics. Adam Smith's *Enquiry into the Wealth of Nations* (1776) established political economy as a social science. Gibbon's *Decline and Fall of the Roman Empire* (1776), a breakthrough in historical writing, was careful in its scholarship and confident in its judgement.

The monarchy became more thoroughly constitutional, the King depending on Parliament for funds to pay the armed services. He appointed ministers of the Crown at his personal will and pleasure, but the Ministers so appointed were answerable to Parliament.

The Trinity Questioned

The eighteenth century has been called 'the age of rationalism' and there emerged in English Christianity two forms of anti-Trinitarian thought: Arianism and Socinianism. Both taught a subordinationist view of Jesus in relation to God the Father. Arians acknowledged the pre-existence of Christ, thought him in some sense divine and retained the idea of the atonement in respect of Christ's death. However, they regarded Christ as different in essence from God. These views were first propounded by the Alexandrian priest, Arius, and then rejected by the Council of Nicaea in 325 AD. Socinians completely rejected the idea of God's pre-existence, together with the Trinitarian formulations of the fourth-century Councils of the Church. They believed Christ was a man whom God made worthy of adoration, a modern day Unitarian view of the person of Christ. In 1687 Stephen Nye, an Anglican priest, published A *Brief History of the Unitarians, called also Socinians,* which disseminated anti-Trinitarian views. Certain measures were adopted to curb the spread of these views, such as the Blasphemy Act 1698, which made those propagating them liable to three years

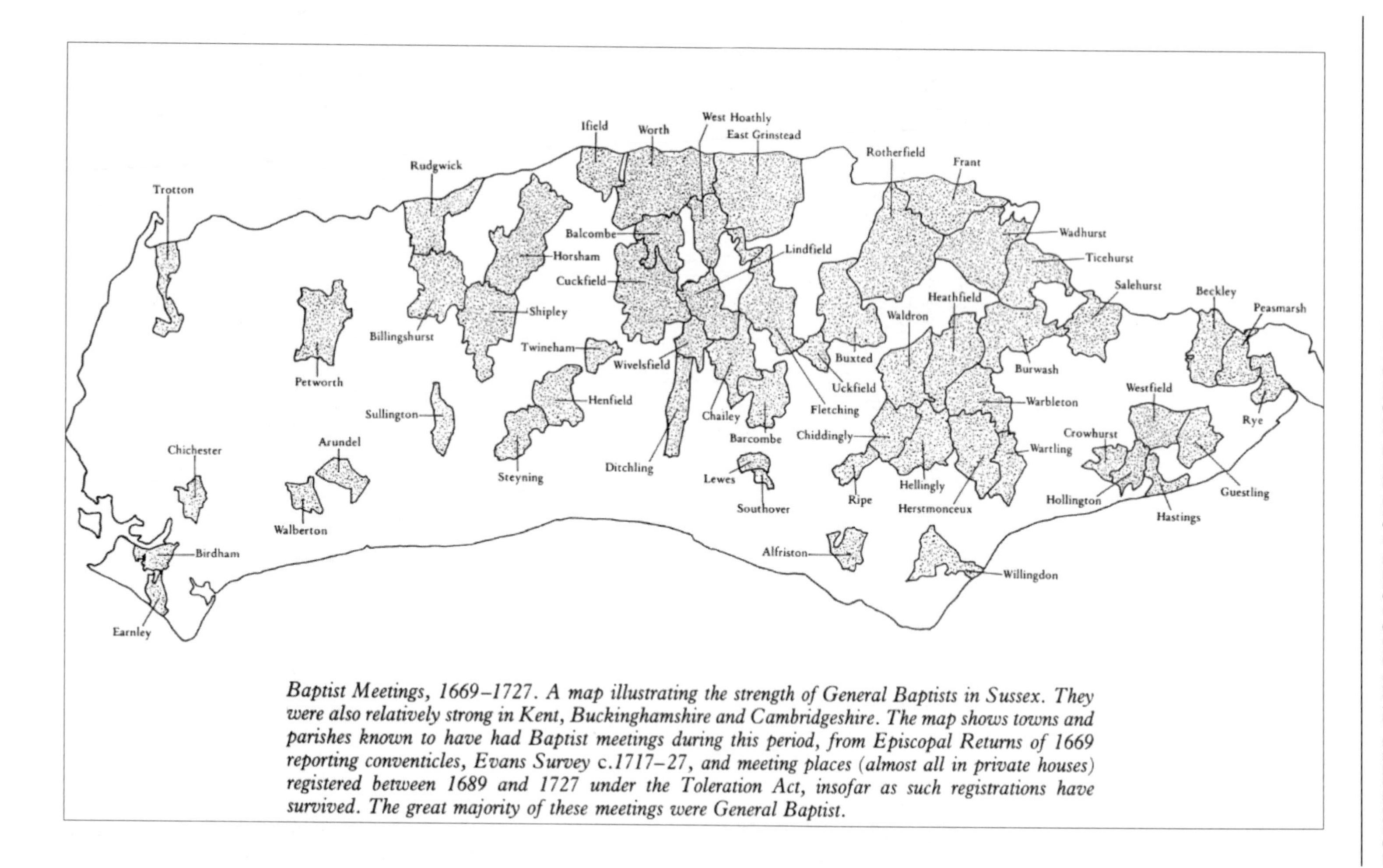

Baptist Meetings, 1669–1727. A map illustrating the strength of General Baptists in Sussex. They were also relatively strong in Kent, Buckinghamshire and Cambridgeshire. The map shows towns and parishes known to have had Baptist meetings during this period, from Episcopal Returns of 1669 reporting conventicles, Evans Survey c.*1717–27, and meeting places (almost all in private houses) registered between 1689 and 1727 under the Toleration Act, insofar as such registrations have survived. The great majority of these meetings were General Baptist.*

imprisonment. But the heresy gained ground. William Whiston, a Cambridge Professor of Mathematics, published in 1710 a book called *Primitive Christianity Revived,* which set out an Arian interpretation of Christianity, and for this he was deprived of his post at Cambridge.

The Salters' Hall Meeting

In the dissenting world the Christological issue came to a head when London ministers were asked to give advice about views which were then being propagated by two Exeter Presbyterian ministers. The meeting was convened in 1719 at Salters' Hall, London, an important centre of Dissent. The question at issue was whether the matter could be resolved by an appeal to Scripture only, or was it right also to appeal to the creeds of Christendom? The creeds drew upon the Trinitarian understanding of God as inferred from the Scriptures.

The majority of Presbyterian and General Baptist churches took their stand on the sufficiency of Scripture alone. Most Congregational and Particular Baptist churches also appealed for subscription to Trinitarian creeds. Within a century many Presbyterian, and General Baptist churches connected with the original General Baptist Assembly, became Unitarian. The Congregational and Particular Baptist churches not only remained Trinitarian but also espoused the theology of John Calvin.

The attitude of the General Baptists to this issue was established when, in dealing with the Caffyn dispute, the Assembly claimed in 1697 that if members debated the Trinity they 'must do so in Scripture words and terms' and 'in no other'. In the Bible, however, Trinitarian thought is implicit, not explicit. Alongside this, the philosopher John Locke was encouraging Dissenters at large to test revelation by reason, not by the theological schemes of Athanasius or Calvin - and when they used that method they frequently ended up with unorthodox answers! General Baptist literalism in regard to Scripture, which led them into the practice of foot washing and anointing with oil, also led them to suspect doctrine not based on explicit Scripture references. The predilection of early General Baptists for Arianism, encouraged a more liberal theology among them, until finally many became Unitarian.

In the eighteenth century, religion was commonly approached through reason. Religious certainties of previous generations became a confusing complex of probabilities arising out of human thought. God was the divine watchmaker who had put the world together, wound it up, and now left it running without need for further intervention. Matthew Tindal, a leading Deist, claimed in 1730 in *Christianity as old as Creation*, that 'the religion of nature is absolutely perfect'. John Tillotson, Archbishop of Canterbury under William III, believed that 'with charity and mutual forbearance the Church may be peaceful and happy without absolute unity of opinion'. Those who held so-called 'Latitudinarian' opinions saw themselves as champions of orthodoxy against the encroachments of the 'Deism' of Tindal. They engaged in an elaborate rational defence of Christian revelation but often seemed lax about precise Christian formulations of dogma, leaving as much room as possible for individual judgement.

Hillesley Baptist Church

Requests for new chapels

There was a steady call in the Assembly for finance to help with the building of much needed new meeting houses. Hillesley, in Gloucestershire, which began its witness in 1730 with Joseph Mason (d.1738) as its first pastor, in 1731 asked for financial help from the Assembly. Similar requests over the years came from congregations in Yarmouth, Wendover, Barnet, Peterborough and Wadsworth (Yorkshire).

An intriguing Assembly decision in respect of new buildings related to the need to find a new permanent home for the White's Alley church, which rented property in the Barbican, London. In 1777 Daniel Noble reported that the lease on the Barbican meeting house would soon expire. The Assembly asked all its churches, including the 'country brethren', to raise funds so that a new lease could be negotiated. In 1778 'the committee for providing a meeting house for the use of the churches in London and the Assembly' thanked all the churches that had funded the proposed new permanent lease of the Barbican premises. The negotiations became protracted, and finally the Barbican landlord declined the terms of the proposed new lease. In 1779 an alternative piece of freehold land was bought in Worship Street, near Bishopsgate, where a new meeting house was built. It opened in 1781, housed the annual Assembly and the White's Alley, Glasshouse Yard, Horsleydown and Artillery Lane congregations. The churches subscribed £1700 and the Ramsgate church covered the £300 outstanding.

The Ministry

Hillesley church again contacted the Assembly for advice about its ministry in 1760. Following the death of its pastor, Mr Benge, it enquired whether it should appoint a minister of 'unexceptional Moderate principles' who had been known to them for some time or 'a person of learning at Bristol who now offers himself' and was commended by Hugh Evans. The Assembly advised Hillesley to take the former and ask Hugh Evans to offer the minister to another General Baptist church. The man of 'moderate principles' was William Hitchman, a member of Natton, near Tewkesbury, whose ministry began on 6 March 1762 and which he sustained until 1802. This was an incident which indicated that General Baptists might be 'lowly in social status … simple, even sombre, in their religious forms. But the history of Christianity, Catholic as well as Protestant, reminds us that penny plain has its own virtue'.[1]

The Bristol Academy connection is worthy of note because the first wife of the orthodox Particular Baptist, Caleb Evans, a tutor at the College, was Sarah Jefferies, the daughter of Joseph Jefferies, acknowledged as the Socinian General Baptist minister of Taunton. It was in 1772 that Dr Joseph Jefferies, Sarah's brother, was admitted a member of the Assembly without any credal or other test being applied. It marked a new departure for the Assembly and opened the door for the reception of a new leadership that in the nineteenth century was Unitarian rather than General Baptist. It is worth noting that a few Bristol students moved towards Unitarianism after leaving the Academy, among whom were Job David, William Richards, Anthony Robinson and the highly influential Robert Aspland.

The Assembly was concerned to promote informed congregations and produced a number of catechisms during the century. The need for a new catechism was noted in 1749 and when the work was not in hand for the 1750 Assembly, it was given to Joseph Morris. Ten years later Samuel Edwards sent the Assembly a revised catechism for its approval and this was accepted at the next Assembly. One of the most significant General Baptist books published in the period, was concerned with the doctrine of baptism, written by London General Baptist minister, John Gale.

Christological and Trinitarian controversies divided the churches and the Assembly for many years, and after the Salters' Hall debate of 1719 an increasing number of General Baptist ministers came to doubt the orthodox Christian understanding of the Trinity and the deity of Christ.

Contacts beyond the Assembly

Contact between the Particular Baptists and the General Baptists was generally very limited and there was not much cross fertilisation between them. In 1768 the Assembly received to its meeting the Revd Morgan Edwards, a Particular Baptist trained at the Bristol Academy, who had migrated to the American Colonies, and was now raising funds for a Baptist College in Providence, Rhode Island, which later became the prestigious Brown University. The goal was £2000 and churches were asked to send donations either to Joseph Jefferies, the minister at Taunton, or Daniel Noble in London. The Assembly also agreed in 1774 to help Josiah Thompson, a Particular Baptist, with his research in the history of all Baptist congregations, a hand-written document, still available in the Dr Williams's Library, London. In 1789, as Robert Robinson, the Cambridge Particular Baptist pastor drew towards the end of a long life, he was invited to preach to the Assembly and did so, with great acceptance, from 2 Peter 3.18,

[1] E. G. Rupp, *Religion in England 1688–1791*, p.137

which urges all to 'continue to grow in grace and knowledge of our Lord and Saviour Jesus Christ'.[2]

There was an active American connection during the whole century. In 1737 and 1738 there was an exchange of correspondence between the Assembly and American General Baptists in South Carolina. In 1756 the Charleston General Baptists sought a minister from England, the details were given in the Assembly and the next year it was reported that Daniel Wheeler had gone to fill the post. In 1773 the Assembly sent Daniel Dobel to minister in South Carolina. In 1795 there was substantial correspondence between the Assembly and American General Baptists handled by Dan Taylor and John Evans on a range of topics.

The General Baptist Fund

In 1737 six congregations met with two aims: to meet the financial needs of poorer ministers and to provide funds for ministerial training. The General Baptist Fund was initiated to benefit any congregation that had contributed a minimum of £20 for poorer ministers and £5 for ministerial training each year. The donations had to be in by 25 March each year and the monies were allocated in May each year. Those contributing at this level had one Fund manager to represent them. The churches' representation increased *pro rata* according to the level of their donation, to a maximum of three. The Assembly treasurer used the money raised by churches for this central fund, for the financial support of the poorest ministers.

The churches were also expected to raise money annually for the payment of the Messengers' expenses, which were paid each year when the Messengers came to the Assembly. A reminder of this arrangement was given in the 1774 Assembly, but it seems clear from the *Minutes* that many, if not most, of the churches failed to support their local ministers adequately, let alone Messengers.

The unwillingness on the part of the churches to finance appropriate ministerial training, combined with inadequate ministerial leaders, meant that although the funding was sought it was not until 1792 that a start was made with actual training. Initially Stephen Freeman of Ponders End, Middlesex, was asked to train ministers and his first student was Benjamin Austen. Five years later John Evans, a General Baptist student of Bristol Academy, and a relative of the President, Caleb Evans, took over the training. He was the second Ward scholar from Bristol who went on from Bristol to study at Aberdeen and Edinburgh universities. He was ordained at Worship Street in May 1791, by Job David, and also kept a school, was a prolific author, and received an honorary doctorate from Brown University in 1819. However, the Assembly in 1803 noted that although there were churches needing ministers and students waiting to be taught, the programme was still greatly hampered for lack of funds. Evans was a convinced Socinian, who openly advocated these views in the pulpit and to the students under his care, and became a powerful force in taking the Assembly towards a thoroughgoing Unitarianism. Some General Baptist churches, confronted with these views, joined the New Connexion of General Baptist churches led by Dan Taylor. Others went theologically further, as did

[2] For Robinson, see Chapter 9, below

John Stanger, the minister of Bessels Green, who finally persuaded his church to become part of the Particular Baptist community.

The unwillingness to debate the diversity of doctrinal issues in the Assembly weakened denominational life and many individual churches declined. Raymond Brown recounts how

> Thomas Brittain in 1749 went to preach at Caldcot, and recorded in his diary: 'when I came thither there was none to hear me, so I returned home that night, quite disappointed, sadly tired and sorely vexed. A few years later the same thing happened again, this time at Leighton Buzzard: '1755, Feb 23 ... On that day I went to Leighton, and when I came there was nobody to hear me. So I came home sorely disappointed'.[3]

The Evangelical Awakening

In mid-century the Evangelical Awakening led by the Wesley brothers, John and Charles, proved significant for some General Baptists, particularly those in Lincolnshire. The Assembly viewed Methodism's 'faith and practice' as contrary to the Bible and warned against the new movement in 1745, which in the light of its own long controversy about hymn singing was perhaps only to be expected. The other key figure in the revival was George Whitefield, who came from a Calvinistic theology, though he shared the Wesley brothers' missionary vision, first in America and then Britain. Dan Taylor, a Yorkshire convert of Whitefield's, was to become the one through whom many General Baptists re-discovered their evangelistic purpose. This final twist in the General Baptist story will be recounted later where it is more properly related to the Revival in Yorkshire, than a major change in direction of the existing General Baptists.

The slave trade question

Although regional Particular Baptist Associations expressed their opinion on national issues, it was the strength of the General Baptist Assembly to express at a national level its concern, for example, about the social evil of the slave trade. It passed a powerful condemnation of the slave trade and quickly gave its support to the abolitionists. In 1788 the Assembly affirmed that 'the slave trade is inconsistent with every rational and humane principle.' It gave its support to the abolition proposal before Parliament and appointed four of its members to wait upon the abolition committee 'to let them know of our approbation and readiness to assist in defraying the expenses of such an application'. A decade earlier the Assembly had supported those in the Anglican church who had wished to abolish the law which required all schoolmasters and college tutors to subscribe to the *Thirty-Nine Articles* and General Baptists were among those who joined in the agitation which resulted in the successful bill to that effect of 1779.

A growing Unitarianism?

As the century closed the doctrinal journey of the Assembly became clearer. First an American, Elhanan Winchester, began propounding universal restoration, a view which found a ready welcome in the Assembly and among its churches

[3] Raymond Brown, *The English Baptists of the Eighteenth Century*, BHS, 1986, p.66

and ministers. Next the 1801 Assembly agreed to admit William Vidler, an avowed Unitarian, to the Assembly, a decision that led Dan Taylor of the New Connexion of General Baptists to withdraw in 1803. In a few years Vidler came to play a leading role in the Assembly. Robert Aspland who, as already noted trained initially at Bristol, was another leading exponent of Unitarian views. Although he had been baptised at the Particular Baptist Devonshire Square church, in London, and went for his first ministry to Soham Baptist Church in Cambridgeshire, he asked John Evans for his help. With Evans' assistance he became minister at Newport, Isle of Wight, and once there declared himself a convinced Unitarian. He soon accepted the Hackney pastorate where he remained for 40 years. Aspland became associated with William Vidler in the production of the *Universal Theology Magazine*, which was widely canvassed among the churches and commended by the Assembly. As Raymond Brown writes:

> In 1815 an Assembly committee reported on 'the success of Unitarianism which, with the exception of baptism, may surely be called the cause of the General Baptists.' John Burgess, a General Baptist from Ditchling, Sussex, accurately reflects the Old General Baptist churches at this time when he wrote to a friend: 'I think the doctrine of the Trinity one of the greatest corruptions in the Christian Church. The doctrine of the pre-existence of Jesus Christ I have entirely given up … The doctrine of original sin … of atonement, are to me doctrines absurd in the extreme.'[4]

The Old General Baptist story

Whitley concluded his researches with the close of the second General Assembly minute book in 1837, and it is all too often assumed the Old General Baptist story concludes there. However, the churches continued with many adopting Unitarian views. It was Gilbert Boyce (1712–1800), the Messenger of the Lincolnshire General Baptists, who had taken on the challenge of the Wesleys, although as Underwood commented, reading Boyce's tract 'gives the modern reader the impression that he was more concerned to save the Baptist flag than to win religion's battle'.[5] Boyce had welcomed Dan Taylor, the founder of the New Connexion of the General Baptists,[6] at the Lincolnshire Assembly of the General Baptists in 1763 and ordained him in Yorkshire the following July. Boyce tried to keep the New Connexion and the Old General Baptist together after 1770, but with his death in 1800, those attempts ceased. The point of no return was reached with the admission of William Vidler in

John Wesley

[4] *Ibid.*, p.109
[5] Underwood, *op.cit.*, p.149
[6] For New Connexion details, see Chapter 5 following

1801, and was beyond recall with Dan Taylor's withdrawal in 1803. However, the formal break came when the New Connexion in 1813 received and accepted a resolution to its national Assembly, sponsored by many of its ministers, condemning the 'baneful poison of Socinianism'. Many formally closed their pulpits to all who held such views. Formal separation between the two groups came when the Old General Baptist Assembly of 1815 passed a resolution that affirmed, 'Unitarianism, with the exception of baptism, may be surely called the cause of the General Baptists'.

Some growing churches

Nonetheless, the decline of the Old General Baptist churches was by no means immediate. In Kent and Sussex there was some growth and development. Brighton and Northiam were founded by Vidler. Hammond Hill, Chatham, built a new chapel in 1802, as did Cranbrook in 1808, and Headcorn in 1819. Benjamin Martin built a new chapel at Adrian Street, Dover, for his 400 strong congregation in 1820 and as late as 1834 a new work was begun in Biddenden. On the other hand, the Smarden congregation abandoned its chapel to meet in a house; Chichester was in difficulty; and Turner's Hill suffered inroads from the new Free Thinkers. London had four causes: Glasshouse Yard, now meeting in Worship Street; Church Lane, Deptford, which had absorbed Horsleydown; White's Alley; and Parliament Court where Elhanan Winchester's congregation met. Elsewhere in the country the old General Baptist cause was in a parlous state. Godalming, Surrey; Saffron Walden, Essex; and Brentford, Middlesex were the only three churches in the Home Counties. In Lincolnshire, only Lutton and Fleet remained; York acquired a new chapel in 1816; and there were three Unitarian churches in Hull; and one in Newcastle upon Tyne.

As the Unitarian element grew more confident, they attacked the 'Baptist' element of the Old General Baptists, but John Evans fiercely defended it and used his control of the General Baptist Academy in this regard. Although he was a vigorous Unitarian in theology, he was not prepared to let the Baptist position be displaced.

Unitarians were politically very radical, condemning the Monarchy and Aristocracy outright, campaigning for the abolition of capital punishment, and even promoting legislation against cruelty to animals.

Joseph Means' leadership

For fifty years, between 1823 and 1875, it was Joseph C. Means who sought to defend 'the good old cause' against Unitarianism. He was baptised at Deptford, trained by John Evans, and was a teacher, pastor and poet, as well as editor of the *General Baptist Advocate,* and belonged to the 'reticent school' of high Arians. He became the minister at the key Worship Street church, then meeting at Trinity Place. Means was dismissed from the editorial chair of the *Advocate* after about five years, many believing he used the paper as a personal tool in the affairs of the denomination. He then withdrew from the mainstream for a while to write a book advocating the atonement. Returning to leadership, he led in the development of the 'institutional church', with its proliferation of Sunday Schools, sick clubs, chapel libraries, all of which seemed to be so much more effective than obsolescent theology.

Unitarian disapproval of the Old General Baptists increased markedly in the 1850s. In 1870, because of growing alienation from Unitarianism, the Old General Baptists, under Means' leadership, made an approach to the New Connexion, to see whether there could be reconciliation. This split the Old General Baptist Assembly in three ways. Three churches stood with Means; others affirmed their Unitarian theology; and some looked for the Assembly to become a new 'forum' for those of a General Baptist persuasion. The arguments raged for three years, but in the end it was the strong opposition within the New Connexion that ended the possibility of such a move in 1875. In 1887 the New Connexion and Old General Baptists were again having conversations. This time the discussions were frustrated when the Baptist Union, which was in unity talks with the New Connexion, found itself having to deal with other doctrinal issues raised by C. H. Spurgeon. However, the matter was finally resolved when the New Connexion General Baptists and the Particular Baptists joined to become the Baptist Union in 1891. The Old General Baptist denomination, according to Ian Sellers, 'now meets for legal purposes only as a rather picturesque appendage to the annual Assembly of the Unitarian Free Christian Church'.[7]

[7] Ian Sellers, 'The Old General Baptists', BQ 1971, pp.84–5

5

The New Connexion of General Baptists

WHEN the English General Baptists, after forty years of division, were reconciled in 1731, the denominational unity achieved was on the basis of a scriptural formula at the expense of doctrinal agreement.[1] As the General Baptist churches declined in the eighteenth century, many becoming Unitarian in doctrine, the effect of the Evangelical Revival was to remind the churches remaining orthodox of their origins in a lively evangelistic community. One aspect of the Evangelical Revival was the meeting of new Christians in people's homes for mutual support and further evangelistic outreach. In Leicestershire one of the Revival's preachers was David Taylor, a servant in the household of Selina, Countess of Huntingdon. Among the converts he gathered in the villages around was Samuel Deacon, a Leicestershire farm hand, who later became a leader among the General Baptists of the New Connexion. In 1745 a meeting house was built for Deacon's congregation at Barton Fabis, despite much local opposition. By 1755 this congregation had adopted the rite of believers' baptism without any direct contact with regular Baptist churches. As the work expanded into the adjacent counties of Nottinghamshire, Derbyshire and Staffordshire, new meeting houses were built to accommodate the emerging congregations. Within twenty-five years the combined membership of these churches was almost a thousand.

Formation of the New Connexion

At the same time, but completely unrelated to Deacon's work, a young Yorkshireman, Dan Taylor, began preaching among the Wesleyan Methodists around Halifax. Taylor became unhappy with some of the pastoral care aspects of Methodism and left the local Society. Dan Taylor was himself a child of the Evangelical Revival, but was not prepared to accept the 'dictatorship which Mr Wesley then assumed over the conduct and faith of his preachers'.[2] He formed an independent congregation at Wadsworth, near Heptonstall, Yorkshire. He used the newly built chapel as a day school during the week. By a study of the New Testament he enabled the congregation to discover the nature of church order and persuaded them to adopt believers' baptism. Local Particular

[1] See earlier, p.42
[2] Adam Taylor, *Memoir of the Revd Dan Taylor,* p.9

Dan Taylor

Baptist ministers refused to baptise Taylor and his members because of their Arminian theology. They advised him to go to Leicestershire to seek baptism from a General Baptist minister. Taylor undertook the journey with a friend and on the way called at Gamston, in Nottinghamshire, where there was a General Baptist church. The minister, Joseph Jeffries, baptised Taylor in the local river and introduced him to the General Baptist churches of the Midlands.

In May 1763 Taylor attended the Lincolnshire General Baptist Association meetings and soon after was ordained a minister by Gilbert Boyce. The next year Dan Taylor met Samuel Deacon, the convert of David Taylor, whose churches had adopted believers' baptism but were unwilling to join the Lincolnshire General Baptist Association because of its tendency to move towards Unitarian theology. The relationship between Dan Taylor and Deacon developed quickly and as a result Taylor realised that the old General Baptists were not evangelical as he understood that word. He concluded that it required a completely new beginning.

Therefore, in 1770 Dan Taylor called together a number of colleagues who all shared his evangelical Baptist sympathies and they formed the New Connexion of General Baptist Churches. Taylor recognised in those who comprised the New Connexion churches people who were 'strenuous advocates' for what he considered the 'essential truths of the Gospel'. Their stance was a protest against the formality, introversion and lack of missionary zeal among the old General Baptists. The essence of the New Connexion was a deep desire to offer God's grace to all, and when they finally separated from the original General Baptists they took as their name, Free Grace General Baptists. The Six Articles drawn up by the New Connexion clarified their position on the primary issues of debate between themselves and the old General Baptists. The Articles sought to restore 'primitive Christianity' among the churches and to 'revive experimental religion'. 'They rejected all Arian or Socinian tendencies on the one hand, and the antinomianism of High Calvinism on the other. The Connexion put the experience of personal conversion, sealed by believers' baptism and continuing regeneration and renewal by the Holy Spirit at the centre of their life together, making their membership essentially spiritual not structural'.[3]

The National Assembly

'The Assembly of the New Connexion of the General Baptists', or, the Connexion for short, had three strands within it. There were the independent Midland churches led by David Taylor and linked with Samuel Deacon's church, which numbered eight of the original 18 churches in 1770. The second strand was the original General Baptist churches from Lincolnshire, Essex, Kent and London that had remained orthodox. The smallest strand was the Yorkshire Baptists led by Dan Taylor.

Two of the three groups that formed the Connexion had no ties with basic Baptist organisation or tradition. It was Dan Taylor's 'Methodist' experience within the Evangelical Revival that was at the root of the 'experience meeting', with its emphasis upon personal salvation, which became a regular feature of the Connexion. The Barton group held regular 'conference meetings' at which the spiritual development of members, and the affairs of the congregations, were encouraged and conducted. The laity ultimately ran these meetings, which were at first led by ministers. The Connexion was shaped, and power shared within it, by a national annual Assembly, regional conferences held quarterly, and monthly meetings for members. The two distinct issues for the Connexion were, a rejection of the High Calvinist doctrine of election and a conscious organisation of the churches in a national Assembly, while allowing considerable congregational autonomy. Local churches often united in 'conferences' of ministry and laity, to resolve both theological and practical issues, particularly the need to station ministers who could help new or ailing causes.

Basis of membership

The first national Assembly of the Connexion agreed that all present should give 'full evidence, not only of the soundness of each other's faith but the genuineness of each other's piety' and that at the next Assembly 'every minister do give an account of his religious experience that they may be satisfied concerning the reality of each other's conversion'. Initially membership of the Connexion was open only to individuals who gave evidence of a personal spiritual experience;

[3] R. W. Ambler, quoted by F. Rinaldi, in his Glasgow PhD thesis, 'The Tribe of Dan', p.27f. Dr Frank Rinaldi provides the most recent account of the New Connexion of General Baptists between 1770 and 1891, and I am grateful to him for permission to use some of his extensive original research

it was 1777 before churches, as such, were admitted. It was only in 1795 that the Assembly was constituted as a delegated gathering.

Very much in the spirit of the period the Connexion developed a wide range of societies, formed on a voluntary basis, to meet specific needs. The Aged Ministers' Fund was begun in 1808, a Tract Society in 1810, and in 1816 a Missionary Society was formed, with a raft of periodicals following in their wake, all reflecting the haphazard nature of the New Connexion's denominational growth in the early years. Another significant factor in the development of the Connexion's churches at a national level was its leadership structure, which consisted of a committee of ministers and laity throughout the whole lifetime of the Connexion. It never made a full-time appointment to guide its life and work.

Local congregations

The baptism of believers created a closed church community that could only be entered through submission to this indispensable rite and such a baptism was obligatory for admission to the Lord's Supper. This strict position meant there were difficult relationships in a grouping whose evangelical roots were primary, and by the early nineteenth century there was a growing dissolution of this close relationship between baptism and membership. By 1882, J. C. Jones' Circular Letter, *The conditions of church membership*, argued that 'separate local societies are but functional parts of the One Universal Church' and that membership of the 'Universal Church' was 'the voluntary and hearty surrender of a penitent and believing soul to the government of the risen and exalted Saviour'. Baptism, while 'a duty and a privilege', was an ordinance 'attended to as a personal duty, independently of the recognition of the Church'. John Clifford gave his considerable support to the 'open membership' position, arguing that baptism is 'a question of the soul and Christ, not the soul and the Church'.

The debate about the Lord's Supper continued to centre upon conditions for admission to the Table. By the 1850s the General Baptists were engaging in 'open communion'. A test case at St Mary's Particular Baptist Church, Norwich, in which the Master of the Rolls adjudicated in favour of the 'open communion' position, together with C. H. Spurgeon's determination to form new churches which allowed a profession of faith as sufficient basis for membership, were non-General Baptist decisions that encouraged the New Connexion towards the 'open' position.

The Connexion's Conference

A distinctive mark of the Connexion churches was the local 'conference'. It was most prominent among the Midland churches and those originating through Dan Taylor. The conference had a spiritual and evangelistic role in the Connexion's congregations, being the centre of the planning and organisation of local mission work. However, when the numerical strength of the denomination increased, the emphasis moved from mission to the maintenance of an increasing number of congregations. The 16 churches in 1770 were 220 seventy years later, but there was less growth of churches between 1840 and 1891, when a final total of 275 New Connexion churches joined the Baptist Union.

The Connexion's constituency

The constituency of the Connexion was unusual and at first extremely narrow. The main supporters were found among the rural lower classes, although they were not agricultural labourers, as might be thought, but framework knitters of the small Midland villages and country towns that suffered an appalling recession early in the nineteenth century. The experience of the Hinckley church was typical: 200 members left in the eight years between 1812 and 1820, with many emigrating to the United States and others moving to neighbouring towns for work. The church book records that several of the members did not have 'clothes decent to appear at Meeting' and many experienced extreme poverty as well as 'want of decent rayment'. The Connexion had to wrestle with the practical outcome of the industrial revolution, but was also caught up in the social revolution of Victorian society. J. G. Pike, Secretary of the General Baptist Missionary Society from 1816, believed that what held back the 'genteeler part of society' from joining General Baptist churches was not their rural roots, but believers' baptism and he strongly advocated open membership churches. He also criticised the low level of ministerial pay, complaining that working class members, or 'poorer friends', simply did not understand the 'extra calls and expenses' associated with 'the middle sphere' of life which ministers led. 'A hundred a year' was altogether inadequate, he complained, at a time when the 258 members of Castle Donnington Baptist Church offered a prospective minister just £80 a year. John Clifford, in 1868, believed some churches had succeeded only too well in being 'genteel' and 'highly respectable', with the result they were frigid, formal and lifeless to such a degree, 'we should not marvel men will not enter into our ice house'.

John Clifford's leadership

The leader of the New Connexion of General Baptists in the second half of the nineteenth century was John Clifford, whose life spanned almost a century. Clifford, the son of a factory worker, was born in 1836 at Sawley, Derbyshire. By the age of twelve he was working in the local lace factory. Seven years later he entered the New Connexion College to train for the ministry and at twenty-two he settled in London as the minister at Praed Street, Paddington.

His thirst for knowledge was insatiable, and a condition of his acceptance at Praed Street was that the church allowed him to continue his studies. In those early years he took degrees at London University in Arts, Science and Law, but the studies never interfered with his commitment to the pastoral and evangelistic needs of the church. In his first year 73 people joined the membership.

John Clifford

In 1877 the chapel was enlarged and took a new name, Westbourne Park, where C. H. Spurgeon was one of the earliest preachers in the new chapel. Clifford ministered here until 1915.[4]

His interpretation of evangelicalism was Arminian, his appreciation of the new Biblical scholarship acute, and his adherence to the New Testament and its idea of the church unshakeable. He opposed blind conservatism and repudiated the antagonism between science and religion which was beginning to be so acute in this period. It was Clifford who took the New Connexion fully into the Baptist Union in 1891. He was twice President of the Baptist Union, the first President of the Baptist World Alliance in 1905, and President of the National Free Church Council. He was made a Companion of Honour in 1921.

He was the 'uncrowned King' of militant Nonconformity. He epitomized the Nonconformist Conscience and this resulted in attacks on his moral character in *Punch* and other weekly journals. He was an unrivalled platform speaker, an outspoken supporter of Liberal Party politics, and always entirely Christocentric in his outlook. He never tired of saying, 'Our first business is to make men see Christ'. Clifford, closely identified with the working classes in Paddington, was an unashamed member of the Fabian Society.

Haven Green, Ealing, London

One General Baptist church that began in this time of growing together, and had its origins in the work of the London Baptist Association in 1881, was Haven Green, Ealing.[5] Planted by the London Baptist Association as part of its programme to plant a new church each year, it was founded under the leadership of John Clifford. Typically, C. H. Spurgeon preached at its opening, and John Barran, MP for Leeds, presided at the welcome tea, commending the 'aggressive church work' of the Association and its wisdom in responding to

'Parsons in the pulpit'

[4] J. Marchant, *Dr John Clifford*, 1924, pp.44–5

[5] See Roger Hayden, *Haven Green, Ealing, 1881–1981*, published by the Church, 1981

the recently published rail traffic returns for West London suburbs. In 1882 Charles Clark became the first minister on an annual salary of £500 p.a. He was a Londoner with great personal charisma, having begun as a successful 'street preacher' in the East End. After ministerial training in London, and two years at Maze Pond Chapel, London, he went for three years to Broadmead, Bristol, where 'he did great work in reviving and inspiring with fresh courage and hope what was a declining congregation'. He left Bristol for Australia, where he ministered in Melbourne for eight years. He returned to London, aged forty-three, and was appointed to Haven Green. With his wife Jane, a brilliant musician who frequently played the organ at worship services, Charles Clark brought eloquence, breadth of experience, and popularity to his new task.

When Clark left in 1887, the church secretary wrote:

> As a pastor and lecturer he is remembered with hearty regard and admiring satisfaction. It is chiefly as a lecturer that he is known beyond the bounds of Baptist churches. He rendered Dickens with marvellous power, and made scenes painted by that master live and move before his audience. Many have confessed they never reached the soul of Dickens' work till they listened to his representations, with their deep pathos and rollicking fun, irresistible humour and tender humanity.

Haven Green church at this time had many large Victorian families who rented pews so all could be seated together in worship. In fact, 'pew rents' were the secret of financial stability for the infant church. In 1884 the nine deacons each rented a family pew, jointly mustering sixty adults and children, all usually present each Sunday.

By 1887, however, church income was not matching the costs of paying the minister and repaying the building debt. A motion was proposed and carried, to cut the minister's stipend to £300 p.a., which not surprisingly led to his resignation in June that year. The problem was that those who rented pews far exceeded membership. The membership only slowly rose to 100 by 1887, but there were 300 pew rents coming in. An average of twenty-seven members attended the monthly church meetings during Clark's ministry. When in 1888 an invitation was given to W. Thomas Adey to become minister, fifteen members were present and a further forty-nine postal votes were accepted. Adey had held pastorates in Leeds and Scarborough before London. For the previous two years he had been working in a predominantly Jewish area of London, seeking unsuccessfully to revive the Commercial Street Baptist Church.

Adey changed the church committee, which had originated the Haven Green cause, into an elected diaconate; passed all business through the church meeting; and kept a careful scrutiny of all the church funds. In 1889 there were two 'missions' in the church which resulted in thirty-two new members that year and twenty more the next. There was a doubling of the number of those subscribing to pew rents. Then the minister of the newly opened Presbyterian chapel began to 'poach' the pew renters from Haven Green. By 1892 the gains were wiped out and Haven Green was struggling to survive.

Adey was forced to resign and in 1893 was followed by the Evan Thomas, formerly of Mare Street, Hackney, who began what was to be a ministry of over

Haven Green, Ealing

twenty years. At the height of his ministerial powers, Thomas was noted as a 'poet preacher' with Celtic fire and mystical depth, a lover of liberty and personal friend of David Lloyd George, MP, who could often be found worshipping at the church.

Baptists hesitating

The Evangelical Revival that gave birth to the New Connexion was also the movement that brought a theological realignment among the Particular Baptist churches. After the initial impact of the New Connexion, many General Baptist churches found a place within the Baptist Union which was created in 1812–13. However, it was in 1830 that a writer to the *New Baptist Miscellany*, a Particular Baptist publication, suggested that Christians gave too much time perpetuating separation rather than devoting themselves to unity in fellowship and mission. Another reader of the same journal provided details of the New Connexion which suggested it had 11,000 members in 109 churches with 82 full-time ministers. The argument continued that Particular Baptist resources should be made available to General Baptists, consideration being given to such matters as the joining of missionary societies and uniting of periodicals. The correspondents noted that one difficulty was the different ecclesiology that existed: the partial Presbyterianism of the New Connexion stood in sharp contrast with the vaunted independency of Particular Baptists. In the *General Baptist Repository*, 1830, a Congregationalist had asked 'why the Orthodox General Baptists … and the Moderate Calvinistic Baptists did not unite as a denomination as their creeds appeared to be rapidly approximating'.

It was against this background that the reconstruction of the Baptist Union in 1832 was made. The doctrine set out in the 1689 Particular Baptist Confession was set aside as the foundation of the Union and it was agreed that both Baptist ministers and churches would unite upon the basis of those who agreed upon those 'sentiments usually denominated evangelical.' John Briggs comments: 'Thus was the breach between free-will and pre-ordained election boldly spanned and a first step taken to enable Baptists to walk in harmony.'[6] Evangelicalism at home and the powerful missionary drive towards overseas mission were primary forces that carried forward the desire for greater Baptist unity within the Union. E. A. Payne contends that the Union's workmanlike and new constitution 'presented in summary form and very different from the elaborate Confessions of Faith drawn up in the seventeenth century' and closely followed most of the contemporary Particular Baptist Association declarations.[7]

By 1860 there was hesitation about the initial move towards Baptist unity. Only one third of General Baptist churches had joined the Baptist Union. In 1864 Dr William Underwood reckoned there were 21000 members in 150 New Connexion churches served by 100 ordained ministers, of whom 75 had been college trained, with 20% of them from other traditions, principally the Particular Baptists. As New Connexion people moved about the country in search of work and climbed the social and economic ladder they increasingly did not bother to found New Connexion congregations. Instead they joined either Independent or Particular Baptist churches that had a more able ministry and more attractive buildings. One General Baptist minister, J. B. Pike, claimed in 1862 that it was Particular Baptist independency that prevented them having 'a denominational mind' on the matter. 'To speak of them as a body is a misnomer', he continued. 'They are a multitude of independent churches—in many instances isolated churches.' The meetings of the Baptist Union possessed no ecclesiological authority, they were a series of subscribers' meetings for the different Baptist Union agencies, not a representative assembly of all the churches.

In the 1870s the General Baptist Jabez Burns noted sadly that New Connexion congregations had far too many people in them who knew nothing of Baptist origins and development. Very few convinced Baptists of any kind were to be found among the new churches being founded, especially in London. The whole issue was also set within a wider debate between Baptist and Congregational churches seeking closer union. It was Clifford's view that baptism was in no way a condition for admission to the church. 'Uniformly and exclusively it is prescribed as a solemn transaction between the soul and the Saviour—nowhere a portion of church government or as indispensable in order to enter upon a church state.'[8] When baptism was viewed in this way, and Congregational churches welcomed people into membership on the basis of a confession of faith, the argument for Baptist and Congregational unity was compelling. Clifford's views enabled him to 'anticipate a time when Congregationalist churches of the

[6] J. H. Y. Briggs, *The English Baptists of the Nineteenth Century*, BHS 1994, p.106
[7] E. A. Payne, *The Baptist Union: A Short History*, 1958, pp.23–5
[8] J. H. Y. Briggs, *The English Baptists of the Nineteenth Century*, BHS 1994, p.135

land shall so completely understand baptism that it shall cease to be a divisive element.'[9]

Why was it, then, that the New Connexion's initial growth slowed? Clearly there were some very effective churches, like that in Ealing, planted in various places. However, on the wider English scene it is evident that when evangelism was no longer the prerogative of local General Baptist church members, and the task was perceived as a job for 'professional' ministers, serious problems emerged. Another major element in its decline was a subtle change in Sunday School recruitment. Initially the Sunday School was in touch with children from unchurched families; then it became concerned primarily with children of church members, which were perceived as the hope for the next generation of the church. John Clifford did some calculations on available figures between 1870 and 1890 by which he estimated that only 12 per thousand children in London General Baptist Sunday Schools ever became church members, rising to 14 per thousand in the provinces. Unfortunately, these huge Sunday Schools absorbed disproportionately large number of members as staff. Added to this there were constant power struggles within churches for control of the Sunday School. These struggles all kept members from their primary missionary task of sharing the Gospel with the unchurched. Clifford further felt that 'one man ministry' had much to answer for in respect of the churches decline. He urged the denomination to 'war against the tendency to centralisation of spiritual functions' and encourage churches to become 'congregations of ministers', a view which found expression in the planting of Haven Green by John Clifford in 1881.

Other factors converged to move the Connexion towards the Baptist Union. Faced with a growing culture of secularisation, finding allies to help overcome an alien culture was far more important than church differences. Doctrine is less significant than heredity, particularly when a small struggling community aspires to be part of a respectable, Protestant, and Evangelical denomination. By 1891 both the Particular and General Baptists of the New Connexion had abandoned any semblance of a credal definition of faith as a basis for fellowship. At this time both Baptists and Congregationalists were aware of the limitations of their inherited independency as a principle of organisation, which led to the demise of the concept of the Church as a covenanted community. It was no longer a gathered local body of true believers, covenanting with God and each other to seek the Kingdom of God, obeying Christ's ordinances and committed to God's mission. The impact of Evangelicalism meant that shared life in Christ gave way to the individualism of salvation, with church membership a personal option, not a necessity, for those in the Body of Christ. 'Church' no longer defined the community of Christ, it simply met an individual's spiritual need. By 1891 many perceived the way forward was to be found in the words Evangelical and Baptist, not General or Particular.

Generals and Particulars uniting

While the larger Free Church denominations were developing appropriate national structures, the New Connexion faced changes within the industrial

[9] *Ibid.*, p.122

and social structures of society as a relatively small group, and a growing recognition that the future was with the common Baptist heritage, so as the century closed, many looked towards unity within the Baptist Union. When Joseph Winks addressed a special meeting in 1869 to consider the lack of growth among Connexion churches, he told it that their three great universals, God loves all, Christ died for all, and the Holy Spirit strives for all, were in fact now accepted by the Particular Baptists and there was no longer a reason for separate Baptist communities.

In 1870 William Underwood noted that a sixth of all General Baptist churches had Particular Baptists as pastors, and suggested ordinary members either could not tell, or did not feel strongly about, the difference. The practical uniting of 1891 was not so much because the General Baptists of the New Connexion abandoned their distinctives, as that Particular Baptists had moved closer to the Generals.

What actually happened in 1891 was the dissolution of the General Baptist Associations and the redistribution of the member churches among existing Particular Baptist Associations. This was not too difficult an exercise, since many already shared in local matters. The two missionary societies united and special arrangements were made for uniting funds held by the various trust bodies. The final meeting of the General Baptist Association Assembly took place in Aenon Chapel, Burnley, where after a four-hour debate the resolution in favour of amalgamation with the Baptist Union was carried. The Baptist Union was now ready for a considerable expansion of its role as the national body representing the mainstream English Baptist churches.

Part Two:

The Particular Baptists

6

Particular Baptist Origins

Roots

THE roots of the first known Particular Baptist church grew out of the same soil as that of the General Baptists. The Separatists' 1596 *Confession* was the foundation document of an Independent (Congregational) church that stated a church should only have the officers described in the New Testament, and Christians should covenant together within such a congregation. The seat of power in the church was with the whole congregation, as it submitted together to the guidance of Scripture through the work of the Holy Spirit. In the Church those covenanted together in Christ had authority to accept or reject members, to discipline both pastors and people, and in case of difficulty to seek the advice of other congregations. All members were committed to the civil powers, but if a conflict of interest arose, then God must be obeyed and non-resistance was the method of protest.

In England Henry Jacob led such an Independent Calvinist church in 1616. It was a 'half-way' Separatist community whose members occupied a middle position between Puritans who conformed to the Church of England and those Separatists who totally repudiated the state church as false. Organised as a covenanted fellowship of believers they were unwilling to reject entirely the concept of a state Church.

By 1630 however, when John Lathrop was pastor, many in the congregation were urging a complete repudiation of the state church. On 12 September 1633, ten members of the congregation, after very lengthy debate, were given a formal release from the fellowship. They established a fully Separatist group because they were no longer able to accept that parish churches could in any way be reckoned as 'true' churches. In this group Samuel Eaton, at that date certainly baptised as a believer by effusion, became a member and leading figure, and by 1638 was probably the pastor.

There is a link between the General Baptist churches of the John Smyth and Thomas Helwys tradition and the Calvinist Independent churches that came into existence around the 1640s. The Arminian, Smyth, gave considerable space to the Kingship of Christ in his understanding of the Church, a theme to which the Calvinist Separatist, Henry Burton, gave specific support in 1641. He believed that 'the act of entering a congregation of visible saints was to enter

Christ's "kingdom" not in a metaphorical but in a literal sense ... Henry Burton ... spoke of Jesus as "the sole nominated king of his church" and as "the one and only king of the saints".'[1] Tolmie continues:

> By transferring the headship or kingly office of Christ from the mystical body of the universal church to the immediate local congregation of saints on earth, the Independents eliminated all intermediaries—whether the royal supremacy or papal, episcopal or presbyterian hierarchies—between Christ as the head of the church and the individual saint. The saint could thus enter Christ's kingdom immediately, and on this earth, not in a future life or in a future millennial age; and could do so without worrying unduly about those details of church order which preoccupied the clergy. Further, he was advancing Christ's kingdom on earth by swelling its ranks, and thus playing a part in the divine plan for human history.[2]

By 1641 the leading English Independents were committed to the non-parochial gathered church of the 'Jacob' tradition, rather than a parochial congregationalism. However, in England at this time, the overwhelming majority of those who called themselves Puritans were looking for a single state church, whose uniform worship and work could be found in every parish in the land, and open to everyone in the parish. The idea of a 'gathered church' which brought together Christians of a common mind, regardless of residence, that in place to place manifested many different patterns of worship and work, was essentially unacceptable in Protestant England.

Henry Burton insisted that a future new church would be 'properly a congregation of believers, called out from the rest of the world' who would have the freedom to inaugurate churches or congregations 'where Christ's ordinances are administered in their purity and so where none are admitted members of the congregation but such as are approved of by the whole assembly for their profession and conversations', such churches being 'peaceable members of the civil state, and subject to all its good and just laws'.[3]

How were such churches to be established without alienating those already in the English parishes? Some in England believed the way forward was to bring an already existing 'new' church from exile back to England. This would avoid the criticism of those English Puritans who resented their parishioners moving out of their parish congregations to join a 'gathered' congregation. But it did allow the possibility of a parochial congregation, to be a 'gathered church', and become the norm across the country.

John Goodwin's experiment

John Goodwin, a returned exile from Geneva, attempted this when the parishioners of St Stephen's, Coleman Street, London invited him to become their minister. The congregation included people from beyond the parish as

[1] Henry Burton, *The Protestation Protested,* quoted in Murray Tolmie, *The Triumph of the Saints: The Separate Churches of London, 1616–1649*, 1977, p.85
[2] *Ibid.,* 1977, p.86
[3] *Ibid.,* p.91

well as those within it, and took a significant decision to limit its membership to those who were 'visible saints'. Such visible saints were each admitted only after declaring their Christian experience to fellow members, who would then affirm, or not, whether they were those in whom God's grace had wrought salvation. The parochial congregationalism of Goodwin had three clear strands. First were those visible saints who comprised the Independent 'gathered' church, including some from outside the parish boundary. Second were members called the 'known godly' who, though eligible for membership, had decided not to join the 'gathered' church, for whatever reason. The final group comprised the remainder of St Stephen's parishioners whom Goodwin regarded as neither fit for membership of the gathered church nor capable of receiving the Lord's Supper.

This founding of a 'gathered' church within the parish system was at first successful, but by 1645 the experiment had failed. The parish vestry contained a significant majority of the 'known godly' and ordinary parishioners, who voted to remove Goodwin from office. He and the 'gathered church' continued to meet in his home at Coleman Street, and in 1649 were successful in persuading the nearby parish vestry of St Mary's to rent them rooms.

Problems began to emerge when Goodwin ceased to administer the Lord's Supper in his parish church, although he continued to offer it in the gathered church that probably met in his own house. The heart of the problem was the classification of those not members of the gathered church as 'outsiders'. They included the 'known godly' of the parish who, when they failed to join the actual gathered church for whatever reason, found themselves unchurched as effectively as the vast majority of parishioners, to none of whom was Goodwin prepared to offer the Lord's Supper. The godly of the parish found that their church membership and enjoyment of the sacrament in their own parish depended upon strangers from outside and they were not prepared to accept this. From Goodwin's point of view these godly members of the parish were guilty of separatism because they failed to take up the church membership in the gathered church for which they were qualified, and their separation deprived them of the sacrament. Tolmie writes

> Goodwin's congregation is the clearest, and perhaps the only, example of the evolution of a gathered church out of a parochial congregation. Goodwin began not with a covenanted congregation but with his parish vestry, and his intention was to implement a congregationalism on this foundation that could admit saints to membership from beyond parish boundaries. The experiment failed ... when the vestry reasserted its control of the parish by securing the removal of Goodwin as vicar, Goodwin's gathered church became as completely a separate church as the original Jacob church. In the revolutionary upheaval of the next few years it was to be the most important separate church in London.[4]

A Church outside the parish?

John Goodwin was not successful, but many believed the way forward was through a gathered church, albeit working outside the parish system. On 8 June

[4] *Ibid.*, pp.115, 116

1638 the original Jacob congregation, now led by John Lathrop, dismissed a further six from its number to join another former member, John Spilsbury, with whom the mother church had retained links. It was noted that they were 'of the same judgment with Samuel Eaton', that is, convinced that 'baptism was not for infants but professed believers'.

In May 1640 the original Spilsbury congregation was divided in two for administrative reasons. 'Praise God' Barbone led one part of the congregation, and Henry Jessey, who had been converted in the early 1620s while at Cambridge University, led the other.

The baptism question

In 1641 a discussion took place within the whole congregation, on the motion of Richard Blunt, a member of Eaton's group, about the correct mode of baptism: should it be by affusion or total immersion? Hearing that the Collegiants (a splinter group of the Mennonites) in Holland could advise on the matter, Blunt, who spoke Dutch, was sent over for consultations. One issue was who should actually baptise, and was baptism invalid if the wrong person performed it? These were not new questions: the Helwys group had raised them in Amsterdam thirty years earlier and the same answer was given as before, that the correctness of baptism did not depend on a succession of baptisers.

Blunt returned from Holland unbaptised and reported his discussions to the London church. In January 1642 Blunt and a Mr Blacklock apparently baptised each other by immersion and then each baptised a number of others. There were fifty-three baptisms all together.

Praise God Barbone resisted this move. He disliked self-baptising and claimed that some had now been baptised three times: once as an infant, once by sprinkling when a believer, and now by immersion as a believer. Thomas Killcop, another member of the baptised congregation, replied to Barbone in print, claiming every Scripture that gave Barbone the right 'to erect a Church-State, gives us the same warrant to erect baptism'. John Spilsbury further argued that the church had power under Christ to appoint people to a task, including the administration of ordinances such as baptism.

Believers' baptism by total immersion, in the name of the Triune God, upon a personal confession of repentance for sin and avowed trust in Christ as Saviour and Lord, dates from this period. It was specifically commanded in the Particular Baptist 1644 *Confession of Faith* and thereafter became the only valid form of believers' baptism in all Baptist congregations. William Kiffin joined Eaton's congregation about 1637–38, began to preach among them, and eventually became pastor. By October 1642 Kiffin had accepted the Baptist position and in that year, at Southwark, on 17 October, debated the issue of believers' baptism for about five hours with Dr Daniel Featley. Featley's reply was afterwards published as *The Dipper Dipt* (1643).

Discussion about baptism continued in the Jessey congregation and in 1643 some joined Kiffin's congregation. A Quaker source claims that the first baptised believer in Kent was Anne Stevens of Canterbury, who was 'Dipped into the Belief and Church of William Kiffin' in 1643–44. The Bristol *Broadmead Records* state that when that congregation moved to London after Bristol fell to Prince

'The Dipper Dipt'

Rupert on 26 July 1643, 'those professors that were Baptized before they went up, they did sit downe with Mr Kiffen and his Church in London, being likewise Baptized'.[5]

Baptists during the Commonwealth

Under Cromwell, when the traditional relationships between church and state were widely debated, Baptists faced a number of awkward questions. For example, should Baptist ministers take payment from the state, when it offered to finance godly ministers who would preach the Word faithfully? Particular Baptists generally answered negatively. Once the Commonwealth period was over, however, the conviction that the Lord's people should support the Lord's work took hold and became the norm for Baptist churches. Should Baptists pay the tithe that provided the state with money to pay for godly magistrates, and should Baptists accept the office of magistrate? This was a more difficult issue, but many Particular Baptists believed the answer should be 'Yes', since they did not wish to be involved in civil disobedience.

During Cromwell's rule and later, contemporary apocalyptic and millenarian thought challenged many Baptists, a debate that was intensified by the republican political sympathies, of a few Particular Baptists in this period. The

[5] Roger Hayden, ed., *Records of a Church of Christ in Bristol, 1640–87*, Bristol Record Society, Vol.27, 1974, p.98

issue centred on the so-called Fifth Monarchy movement, whose supporters were convinced of Christ's imminent return and that it would be to England that he came. The execution of Charles I in 1649 was seen as the end of the fourth monarchy spoken of in the book of Daniel. It was only, some believed, a matter of months, a year or two at most, before Christ came to reign and establish 'the Fifth Monarchy'.

When Cromwell summoned 'the Parliament of the Saints' in 1653 many Fifth Monarchists believed it heralded the return of Christ and the inauguration of the Millennium. The nation was to be governed by the godly alone. When Cromwell dismissed the 1653 Parliament and eventually agreed to receive the title Lord Protector, the reaction was intense. Cromwell was flying in the face of Christ's return. Was not his acceptance of the title Lord Protector the act of Anti-Christ? Until this point Cromwell had seemed to be on the side of King Jesus. Vavasor Powell, a Welsh Baptist minister and evangelist from Radnorshire, sent his London congregation home saying: 'Let us go home and pray, and say, "Lord, wilt Thou have Oliver Cromwell or Jesus Christ to reign over us?"' and he was in no doubt about the answer God would give.

Many people, a small number of Particular Baptists among them, called for intervention, including the overthrow of Cromwell, to hasten and help bring in the Millennium. They were concerned to secure the freedom for worship, which Cromwell had promised, and freedom from the obligation to contribute to the financial support of the state ministers. They conscientiously withdrew from a church in which 'New Presbyter was but old Priest writ large' as John Milton aptly put it.

Some historians believe there was a continuing link from the 1630s underground Independent churches to the Fifth Monarchists of the 1650s. B. R. White claims that 'while the majority of leading Calvinistic Baptists were probably republican in their political sentiments there must have been many who hardly had any political opinions at all'.[6] When the Levellers under the leadership of John Lilburne posited republicanism, it was Kiffin, his former friend and supporter, who encouraged leading Baptists to withdraw their support. He recognised that violent action to 'force' the return of Christ was not only theologically inept but also politically fatal for Baptists.

Particular Baptist beliefs

The Particular Baptist leaders in the early 1640s were of strong intellectual ability, several having received a university education, and they provided the basic framework for the seven London Particular Baptist Churches' beliefs in the 1644 *London Confession*, and travelled widely exercising a personal ministry among Baptist churches across the country. The Glaziers' Hall church, London, sent John Myles to Wales in 1649 and by 1652 five Baptist churches had been planted, beginning at Ilston, Swansea. Thomas Patient, an original signatory of the *Confession*, and John Vernon, also both members of London churches, founded churches in Ireland in the 1650s.

The *Confession* provided a basic framework for the Particular Baptist

[6] B. R. White, *The English Baptists of the Seventeenth Century*, 2nd edn., BHS 1996, p.87

understanding of the church and mission in this period. It was the theological basis which enabled them to withstand all kinds of pressures, not least those presented by the Society of Friends (the Quakers) which were to take over some General Baptist churches in the 1660s and 1670s.

The 1644 *Confession,* widely acknowledged and used by the churches, was revised and reprinted on several occasions, but its terminology shows clear dependence on the English Separatists' 1596 *Confession,* which it modifies in two ways. First, it adopted the distinctive five-point plan of Calvinism accepted at the Synod of Dort in 1619. Second, it fully supported the growing belief that baptism in the New Testament was the total immersion of believers who repented of sin and personally professed the Lordship of Christ.

The 1644 *Confession* deals with the doctrine of God, the life of believers and the church. The church comprised only professed believers; its ministry is placed firmly in the control of the local independent congregation; and the separation of church and state is total, although obedience to the magistrate is commanded without ambiguity. The relationship between local independent churches is similar to the interdependence that characterises fellowship between Christians in a local church. The *Confession* says:

> And although the particular Congregations be distinct and several Bodies, every one a compact and knit Citie in it selfe; yet are they all to walk by one and the same Rule, and by all meanes convenient to have the counsell and help one of another in all needful affaires of the Church, as members of one body in the common faith under Christ their only head.[7]

W. T. Whitley believed that Particular Baptist churches began a life of associating together by a conscious copying of the organisation of the New Model Army, in which many Baptists had served during the Civil Wars. But the word 'association', though widely used by Parliament and its army, was a late arrival among the Particular Baptists. They preferred the term 'General Meeting' for the periodic gatherings of their 'Messengers', who were not summoned on a county basis, but came as congregational representatives drawn from large regions that included several counties. The Western Association at this period included messengers of churches from Bristol, Gloucestershire, Somerset, Devon, Cornwall and South Wales.

The people who composed the Jacob-Lathrop-Jessey congregations had strong fraternal relationships. In 1638, for example, Samuel Eaton was arrested while worshipping in Jessey's congregation. In 1640 Richard Blunt, from Eaton's group, discussed the mode of baptism with both halves of the Jessey congregation. In 1642–43 William Kiffin, who was probably never a member of Jessey's church as such, was deeply involved in lengthy discussions with them on baptism.

It would appear that the Independent minister John Cotton's *The Keyes of the Kingdom of Heaven* was significant for the Particular Baptist understanding of relationships. Cotton deals with Christ's power in an individual congregation and among neighbouring congregations 'in association with it'. Cotton considered 'an association or communion of churches, sending their Elders and

[7] W. L. Lumpkin, *op.cit.,* p.169

Messengers into a Synod', an ordinance of Christ on the basis of Acts 15.

Typical of such a General Meeting was that held by Particular Baptists at Tetsworth, Oxfordshire, which brought together independent churches from a wide geographical area. In March 1653 the Messengers and ministers signed an 'Agreement' which was ratified later in the year by each church, so that each congregation's proper independency and interdependency was affirmed. This 'Agreement' outlined the doctrinal basis of the union between the independent churches, pledged loyalty to the churches' common programme in mission and affirmed contact with similar London Baptist churches. As each new independent church was admitted to the Tetsworth gathering it was asked to confirm acceptance of the 'Agreement'.

Thomas Tillam in the North

Thomas Tillam, who describes himself as 'minister and messenger of one of the seven churches in London', was a member of Hanserd Knollys' church, in Swan Alley, Coleman Street. He had an unusual background having been 'born a Jew and trained a Roman Catholic' according to Whitley.[8]

In 1650 Parliament established a Commission for spreading the Gospel in the north of England, which had to face the strength of the Presbyterian and Independent ministers whose Puritanism dominated the scene. The Commission was looking for men to appoint and accepted Tillam. The background of this 'charismatic and volatile figure' as Stephen Copson describes him is obscure.[9] He may have been for a while in the American colonies; he was an elder at Wrexham with Morgan Llwyd but left under a cloud. By 1651 he was in the Coleman Street church, a member with Hanserd Knollys, and they commissioned him as their 'messenger'. By July 1652 he had baptized eleven men and five women and formed them into a Baptist Church. It was not entirely successful but Tillam stuck to the evangelistic task despite disagreeing about other issues of church life. He engaged in evangelistic preaching tours in the north of England and Cheshire between 1652 and 1653 and in July he was involved in the formation of the church at Stokesley, Yorkshire. He left the north in 1655, his state appointment having concluded and Coleman Street having withdrawn their support, and went to minister in Colchester, Essex.

Thomas Collier in the West

A similar programme was developed among churches in the Midlands and the West Country. The Western Association, with Thomas Collier as one of its leading evangelists, stood off a little from the London group, perhaps for reasons of trade.

Collier, born at Westbury, Wiltshire about 1613, was a powerful evangelist and apologist in the west of England. He was a tenant farmer by 1634, was married in 1640, and in the ferment of the Civil Wars and the Commonwealth found himself active on the national scene as an evangelist. By 1644 he was a member of Kiffin's church for a time, as Hanserd Knollys acknowledged in a

[8] W. T. Whitley, *A History of British Baptists*, p.81

[9] S. L. Copson, in Roger Hayden, ed., *English Baptist Records*, Vol. iii, *Association Life of the Baptist Churches in the North of England, 1699–1732*, BHS 1991, p.13

Preface he wrote for Collier's *Exaltation of Christ* in 1646. Collier had been on an evangelistic tour of Kent with Kiffin and Thomas Patient in 1644 and two years later was working Guernsey, Portsmouth and Poole.

In 1674 Collier published his *Body of Divinity* in which it became clear that he still held to the view that salvation was only possible by grace through faith in the sacrifice Christ on the cross, but he had abandoned orthodox Calvinism in regard to its doctrine of election. He claimed the bible taught both particular election and general grace. The doctrines of the perseverance of the elect and justification by faith alone without works, he reckoned 'to be both alike dangerous, to the power and life of religion, and to the souls and bodies of men.'

Collier's changed theological views caused considerable concern in the West Country; the national nature of its fellowship resulted in a request to certain London Baptists to arbitrate in this dispute. The London Baptists initially responded by sending an open letter to West Country Baptist churches in which they named Collier a heretic and proposed to refute his views in a book. Collier's members at Southwick Baptist church, near Trowbridge, in 1676 called five Baptist ministers, Kiffin, Deane, Fitten, Cox and Moreton to settle the disputed issues in their church. Kiffin claimed Collier was still a member at Devonshire Square, which Collier refuted by asserting that the London membership ceased when he had joined the Wells church. Cox then refuted the heretical views of Collier and Kiffin concluded the meeting by calling on Collier to return to orthodox doctrine. Collier did not do so and a spate of tracts followed from both sides. Those at Southwick who disagreed with Collier then called on two of the Western Association Messengers, William Penn and Richard Clay to discipline Collier. At this point the Southwick church refused to surrender their church authority to the Western Association Messengers, who confirmed the London delegation's view, Penn asserting that the Devonshire Square church was 'representative of all the churches in the nation'. The debate over Collier continued for many years, and in the meantime he continued his work of planting new churches in the West Country.

William Kiffin, Devonshire Square, London

William Kiffin's long life, 1616–1701, covers one of the most revolutionary periods in English history, and it typifies the kind of personal involvement that was exhibited by a number of Particular Baptist leaders in this period. When he was at the height of his powers and influence in the 1650s, his importance can be easily stated. When Particular Baptists initially met at Tetsworth, in Oxfordshire, in June 1653, it was to Kiffin that the newly appointed messengers of the General Meeting wrote. A month later Kiffin received a letter from ten Irish Baptist churches giving information concerning their arrangements for caring for each other. On 24 July Kiffin wrote to the Welsh Baptist churches, on behalf of the seven London congregations, commending to them the Irish pattern of care. When Daniel King, in 1655, wanted to pass on information about the Midland Association, it was Kiffin he corresponded with in London. In 1657 Kiffin was a delegate to Devizes and gave advice from London on the matter of Baptist ministers receiving money from state funds. A year later, in May, he

William Kiffin

attended a meeting of the Western Association at Dorchester, where he used his considerable moral authority to argue against the adoption of Fifth Monarchist policies. Kiffin was a prime mover in organising Particular Baptists in this period, one of a number leaders who were concerned for the unity of the churches, cooperation between congregations, and the spread of Calvinistic, closed-membership, closed-communion Baptist churches, across the country.

Kiffin was born in London and survived the plague of 1625 but as an orphan. He was apprenticed to a London brewer as was his friend of many years, the future leader of the Levellers, John Lilburne, who was an enthusiastic republican that wished to abolish both the monarchy and the House of Lords. Kiffin at one point thought of leaving his apprenticeship, but early on the morning of his intended departure, saw people flocking into a London church, and following them in, found himself listening to a Puritan preacher, Thomas Foxley, who made a deep impression on him. He remained in his apprenticeship and over the next two years went to hear a number of different Puritan preachers, John Norton, John Davenport and most significantly John Goodwin, of St Stephen's, Coleman Street. As the young Kiffin compared various puritan preachers and writers with Scripture he came to the conclusion that God's sovereign grace was the key to the Christian life, baptism must be by immersion of believers only in the name of the triune God, and such baptism was a necessity before a believer was able to come to the Lord's Table. Kiffin adopted Baptist views in 1642 having first attended for a while Jessey's open communion congregation. He then joined the Spilsbury group at Wapping, before becoming the pastor of the Devonshire Square congregation until his death.

Kiffin was initially sympathetic to the Levellers, and wrote an introduction to *The Christian Man's Trial* (1641) in which John Lilburne claimed that Christ gave his kingly power 'not to a Hierarchy, neither to a National Presbytery, but to a Company of Saints in a Congregational way.' In a printed sermon of 1642, issued from the 'White Lyon' prison, Kiffin stated his own position in respect of legitimate state powers:

> Though I am accused and condemned for being at a coventicle, truly if praying for the King and Parliament and edifying one another in our most holy faith be keeping conventicles, then I am guilty. But if a coventicle be such a meeting as in the least measure is against any of these, then I detest it and abhor it.

Kiffin thereafter held this position all his life, never a rebel against King, or Parliament, even though he had been an MP under Cromwell. In 1645 a short tract by a Presbyterian merchant, Josiah Ricraft, was published, *A Looking Glass for the Anabaptists,* in which Kiffin was called 'the author and grand ringleader of that seduced sect'. In Thomas Edwards, *Gangraena,* Kiffin receives similar abuse from a Presbyterian minister, and is reckoned 'to be a mountebank'.

After his apprenticeship Kiffin spent some time as a glover, but then went into trade on his own account and under the peculiar trading circumstances prevailing in the 1640s made a personal fortune in 1643 through trade with Holland. He championed the cause of religious liberty and often spoke in defence of Baptists in London, and in Parliament, when he was the member for Middlesex from 1656–1658. At the time of Thomas Venner's insurrection it was Kiffin who made it clear that neither he, nor his Devonshire Square church, were involved.

In his mature years Kiffin was supported in the pastorate first by Thomas Patient, who died in 1666, then by Daniel Dyke, and then, after Dyke's death in 1690, by Richard Adams. Such support must have been crucial, not least when Kiffin was trying to secure the release of his two grandsons, William and Benjamin Hewling, who had supported the unsuccessful rebellion of the Duke of Monmouth. He was unsuccessful and Judge Jeffreys ordered William, aged 19, to be hanged at Lyme Regis on 12 September, 1685, and Benjamin, aged 22, at Taunton on the 30th. Their sister, Hannah, in 1686 married Henry Cromwell, Oliver's grandson, and died in 1732.

Henry Jessey

Another long-lived and influential Baptist leader was Henry Jessey, a man of great individuality who advocated open-membership, open-communion, Particular Baptist churches, such as those at Broadmead, Bristol, or at Bedford. Although they differed profoundly, Kiffin and Jessey knew and valued each other greatly.

Jessey was born in Yorkshire in September 1601, and it was while at St John's College, Cambridge, that he arrived at Puritan views in 1622. Ordained in June 1626, he was curate at Assington, Suffolk by January 1627. It was while in Suffolk that he first met the Winthrop family with whom he corresponded over the years, when they were in New England.

Jessey returned briefly to Yorkshire in 1633, found employment with Sir Matthew Boynton, and moved with that family to Uxbridge in 1636. A year later Jessey was in touch with the congregation founded by Henry Jacob in 1616, which following John Lathrop's migration to New England in 1638, was without a pastor. Invited to become the pastor, Jessey wrote to John Winthrop, junior, in August 1637, that the Lord had convinced him he should experience 'the necessity and beauty of being under Christ's government' by leading a gathered church. In 1642 Jessey was still baptizing babies, but by immersion. By 1644 the issue was again before the church when Hanserd Knollys, returning from New England, joined Jessey's church for a while. In 1645 Jessey finally asked for believers' baptism and it was Hanserd Knollys, who now led a new congregation, who baptised him on 29 June 1645.

Jessey and the Independents

Jessey was not part of the missionary programme organised by the Particular Baptists who drew up the 1646 *Confession,* choosing to retain close links with the Independents of the day. His church was certainly in correspondence with Thomas Tillam, the evangelist, who founded a church at Hexham, that Newcastle Particular Baptists disowned, because Hexham 'owned unbaptized churches and ministers, for churches of Christ and ministers of Christ'. Jessey also had links with the Llanvaches congregation, which left Wales to join with Broadmead, Bristol, during the Civil War. In 1654 Thomas Ewins and Robert Purnell both sought baptism at Jessey's hands, and in 1655 Purnell and Ewins were glad of Jessey's contribution in opposing the 'pernicious doctrine of the Quakers' confident that 'his endeavours were not successless in this thing'. Although Jessey, with his willingness to accept churches that had both Baptist and Paedo-Baptist members, would not have been welcome in many Particular Baptist churches in the west of England, he certainly visited towns where they existed at this time, in Wells, Cirencester, Chard, Taunton, Honiton, Exeter, Dartmouth, Lyme, Weymouth, Dorchester, Southampton and Chichester. Perhaps, as there is no record of his visits in Baptist records, he visited Independent churches in these places as A. G. Matthews suggests in *Calamy Revised.* He certainly visited during 1653 a number of like-minded congregations in Essex, Suffolk and Norfolk, accompanied by John Simpson from All Hallows in 1653.

Jessey as author

Jessey wrote a number of books, ranging from *A storehouse of provision* in 1650, concerned with questions of churchmanship, to a child's *Catechism,* in 1652. He possessed an enthusiasm for mission because of his conviction that Christ's return was not far off, even though he knew from his Bible that before this could happen the fullness of the Gentiles had to be gathered in and God's people, Israel, must be saved. His delight in the successful work of the 'Apostle to the Indians', John Eliot, in north America under the sponsorship of the Society for the Propagation of the Gospel found expression in his sending some literature to Eliot for distribution among the Indians. He published information each year in his *Scripture Calendar* about a wide range of events that pointed towards the return of Christ and noted, for example, the numerous conversions in Taiwan as a result of evangelism undertaken by Dutch ministers in the area. The *Calendar* noted the instability of the times and published the view that the restoration itself was just one step along the way to return of Christ and his rule for a thousand years. It is not surprising to find Jessey, a political republican, taking the Fifth Monarchy movement, in which he played a moderating role, seriously.

Jessey and the Fifth Monarchists

Jessey's particular friend in London from 1647 to 1661 was John Simpson, the minister of All Hallows. Simpson was far more committed to the Fifth

Monarchy movement than Jessey, but it was Jessey who successfully negotiated the withdrawal of the movement's hard-liners from the All Hallows church in early summer 1656. Jessey championed the return of the Jews to England at this time, because he saw in it a sign of the coming rule of Christ as King. He was among those who petitioned Cromwell against accepting the throne since this could only delay the coming of Christ's kingdom on earth. Jessey signed a Fifth Monarchy petition to parliament in September 1657 which expressed some hostility about the Protectorate, opposed government by a single person, or by any unrepentant person, whether politician or member of the armed services, and urged government by the 'godly', and laws intelligible to all, in line with Scripture. In 1659 Jessey also signed a *Declaration* made by twenty Particular Baptist ministers which sought to state their obedience to the state, hostility to the Quakers and Roman Catholics, and their tolerance of episcopacy and Presbyterianism. They clearly feared a popular reaction against Baptists, because some were also clearly aligned with the Fifth Monarchy and Venner. Jessey finally fell foul of the authorities in 1661 when he contributed material for publication in *Annus Mirabilis* which laid great stress upon the portents of the times that indicated divine displeasure with the restored monarchy. He was arrested, admitted his interest in the material, and was released from prison in the spring of 1663, but died in September that year.

> It is clear throughout his sectarian career he moved easily and co-operatively among the gathered churches and their leaders, especially the Independents. For, although he became a Baptist in the formal sense and published his Baptist opinions, neither he nor his church was actively involved with the nationwide programme and organization of the closed-membership Calvinistic Baptists. Rather they were close to those who held Fifth Monarchy opinions during the 1650s, whether moderate or violent, both Baptists and Independents: there are signs also that they sought to build a pattern of formal co-operation in 1653 with other churches which practised 'mixed' communion … but he expected neither the Protectorate nor the restored monarchy to last and he believed steadfastly in the coming of King Jesus.[10]

Broadmead Bristol

The Baptist church in Broadmead, Bristol, originated in the Puritan Separatism that characterised the Commonwealth period, but its story is intertwined with that of Jessey over the formative years. As early as 1613 a Puritan minister at Bristol had gathered a group of interested lay people around him. By 1639 this group centred its activities on a newly arrived minister at St Ewen's, Bristol, Matthew Hazzard. He married a widow in the group, Dorothy Kelly, and it was in the Hazzard's home that Broadmead was first formed.

The disturbances of the times brought a Welsh influence to bear on the Broadmead congregation. The congregation at Llanvaches, near Chepstow, first under the leadership of William Wroth and then Walter Craddock, came to Bristol

[10] B. R. White, 'Henry Jessey in the Great Rebellion', in R. B. Knox, ed., *Reformation Conformity and Dissent*, 1977, pp.132–153

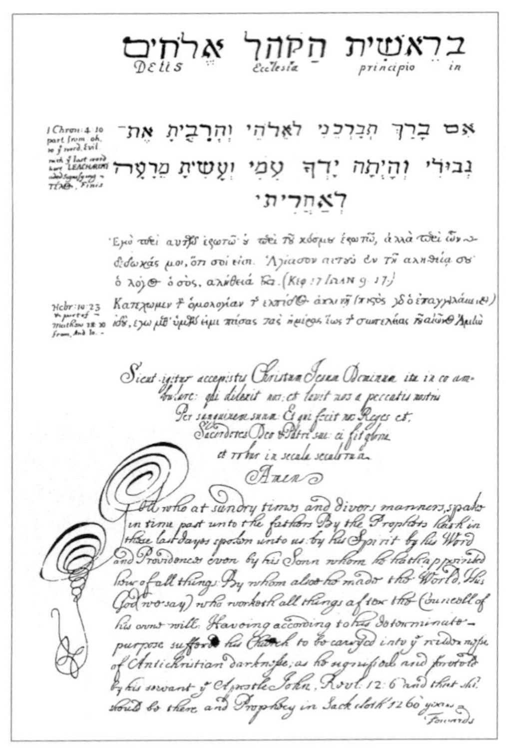
בְּרֵאשִׁית הַקָּהָל אֱלֹהִים
Deus Ecclesia principio in

אִם בָּרֵךְ תְּבָרְכֵנִי לֵאלֹהַי וְהִרְבִּיתָ אֶת־
גְּבוּלִי וְהָיְתָה יָדְךָ עִמִּי וְעָשִׂיתָ מֵרָעָה
לְאַחֲרִיתִי

Sicut igitur accepistis Christum Jesum Dominum ita in eo ambulate: qui dilexit nos: et lavit nos a peccatis nostris
Per sanguinem suum: Et qui fecit nos Reges et
Sacerdotes Deo & Patri suo: ei sit gloria
et robur in secula seculorum.
Amen

God who at sundry times and divers manners, spake in time past unto the fathers By the Prophets hath in these last dayes spoken unto us: by his Spirit by his Word and Providences even by his Sonn whom he hath appointed heir of all things: By whom also he made the World, this God (we say) who worketh all things after the Councell of his owne will: Having according to his determinate purpose suffered his Church to be carryed into ye wildernesse of Antichristian darknesse; as he signified and foretold by his servant ye Apostle John, Revel: 12:6 and that she should be there and Prophecy in Sack cloth 1260 years
Towards

Broadmead Records Page

in 1642, and the two groups met for worship under Craddock's leadership at the Dolphin Inn, on James' Back. When Bristol fell to Prince Rupert in 1643, this whole group migrated to London, where some joined Kiffin's congregation, while others went to Jessey's church.

With the return of Bristol to Parliamentary control in 1645, some of the Bristolians returned and met under the leadership of an Anglican Puritan, Nathaniel Ingello. They were a 'church within a church'. Eventually this group fell out with Ingello who was a little too worldly for them. They called Thomas Ewins, then pastor at Llanvaches, formerly a member at Jessey's London church, to be minister. He was appointed the City Lecturer in Bristol and remained at Broadmead till his death in 1670.

Baptism first became an issue at Broadmead in the early 1650s when one or two members left to join 'the other baptised congregation' in Bristol, that is Henry Hynam's Particular Baptist congregation at the Pithay. Eventually it was decided that baptism was a matter of individual conscience, and that both baptised believers and paedo-baptists would be admitted to full membership of the church and to the Lord's Table. Thomas Ewins and his Elder, Robert Purnell, were baptised by Henry Jessey in London in 1654, after which others who requested it were baptised in Bristol.

Robert Purnell at Broadmead

There is very little about the layman Robert Purnell in the *Broadmead Records,* written later by a lay Elder, Edward Terrill, who recorded Purnell's appointment as Elder in 1654. However, he makes no mention of Purnell's substantial writings published during the Commonwealth period. Yet when Terrill recounted his own conversion experience and his hesitation about believers' baptism, it was Purnell's *Good Tydings for Sinners, Great Joy for Saints* (1649), containing a 'short prophecy on the downfall of Anabaptism', which was influential in persuading Terrill to become a Christian and join Broadmead.[11] Purnell's book critically evaluated various forms of church government and ends with Purnell's concept of the 'true church state' as a 'communion of saints arising from a cleare apprehension of their union with saints', who must stand together in the Spirit and offer spiritual worship to God.

[11] E. B. Underhill, *The Records of a Church of Christ, 1640–1687,* Hanserd Knollys Society, 1842, p.61

Robert Purnell, who had this irenical Christian spirit, was a carpet weaver who lived on James' Back, Bristol. At the end of his life, Purnell, in *A Little Cabinet Richly Stored* (1657), offered a summary 'of all that I have learned, all I have gained this four and twenty years by reading the Scriptures, hearing of sermons, conferring with Christians, and pursuing their writings, together with several things God hath immediately darted in upon my heart ...' He wrote of the way a church should be gathered initially:

Thomas Ewins preaching from prison

> Let seven, eight, nine or ten or more of those men that are most sound in the Faith, and most unblameable in their lives, appoint one day to fast and pray together, and earnestly seek unto God for his direction therein ... Toward the end of the day, let them one by one give an account of the work of grace upon their hearts, and of the hope that is in them and then give up yourselves to one another by the will of God, with no other covenant than this, to endeavour as God shall enlighten and enable you, to walk together in the appointments, ordinances and institutions of Christ, the head of the Church, exprest, implied and contained in the Scriptures of truth, which you take to be your rule.

Once this has been done he advises people to

> appoint your next meeting, both time and place, expecting the presence of Christ with you to assist and teach you. You having proceeded thus far, you may look upon yourselves as a Church of Christ in its infancy... Let the brethren call a meeting to confer with them about the time when, the place where, the manner how, the Lord did first appear to them in a powerful conviction, conversion and regeneration or something equivalent thereunto, and if they give such an account of the work of grace upon their hearts, as doth satisfie the brethren ...

Then all that are admitted

> must put themselves upon the test, and be received by consent, for the Church is Christ's Kingdom; now the matter or subjects of Christ's Kingdom, they are believers gathered out of the world by the preaching of the Gospel and the powerful ministry of the Spirit ...

His opening remarks *To the Reader*, in *Good Tydings for Sinners, Great Joy for Saints* (1649), describe the 'true Church state' that he believed in, and worked hard to achieve in Broadmead:

> The ground of this communion shall be spiritual union: and when the day is dawned, and the daystar risen in our hearts, Ephraim shall not envy Judah, nor Judah vex Ephraim, Presbyterians shall not bitterly cry out against Independents, nor Independents have such hard thoughts of Presbyterians. Yea, they shall be ashamed to own one another by their fleshly titles, but look upon and love one another as Christians, members of the same body, heires of the same promise, children of the same father: having all the same spirit, all clothed with the same robe, inclined to the same work; ruled by the same Word and Spirit. And so their love of each other shall arise from union in the same Spirit. And against this church-state the gates of hell shall not prevail.

Preaching was fundamental in the life of the church for Purnel, and he wrote of it: 'The business of preaching is to make new creatures, to turn Lions into lambs ... so Preachers and preaching is but instrumental in the hand of the Spirit to make you Christ's ...' Closely linked to this was the reformation practice of prophecy:

> In the exercise of prophecie such as are not in office in the Church, may exercise their gifts to speak unto edification, exhortation and comfort after the publick ministry by the teachers and under their direction and moderation, whose duty it is, if anything be obscure, to open it; if doubtful, to clear it; if unsound, to refute it; if imperfect, to supply what is wanting ...

Purnell was a freeman of Bristol, voting in the 1654 Bristol Parliamentary election, a member of Broadmead Baptist Church, Bristol, from its beginning, and its first and 'eldest Ruleing Elder' when he was elected in 1654, the year he received believers' baptism from Henry Jessey in London.[12] Purnell advocated reconciliation between all the church groups of the Commonwealth period and it was Purnell who put his belief in to practice as he united the Broadmead church after Dennis Hollister, a former Broadmead leader, split the congregation over his adoption of Quaker views.

The title page of *A Little Cabinet Richly Stored* (1657), has a full statement of the 'true Christian religion' presented for catechetical use in any congregation who 'are in love sweetly united, or that have their spirits too much embittered' (title page). Although a Baptist himself Purnell typically warns his co-religionists: 'You that have taken up this ordinance, beware of laying more stress upon it, than ever God appointed you, viz, it was never appointed to break love and communion, and to quench the Spirit, and to jostle out some other ordinances, nor to shut out the weak in faith ... are all blind that doth not see by our eyes?

Purnell's distinct contribution was in his advocacy of a wide measure of toleration between all Christian communities. Among Baptists he argued strenuously for a middle way between Particular and General Baptist views. With Henry Jessey and John Bunyan he urged that all Christians should recognise all other Christians, treating 'saints as saints'. He insisted that Broadmead must never allow its advocacy of believers' baptism to create a barrier to communion

[12] Bristol Record Society, Vol 13 (ii), p.180; and Vol. 27, pp.111, 122

with Christians of a different persuasion. Gifted laymen like Purnell and Edward Terrill often led Baptist congregations in these years. Though Calvinist in theology, each were marked by a catholicity of spirit that was not common in this era.

Seventh Day Baptists

Further, there was a much smaller group of Baptists who using the bible as their only source of teaching and doctrine, came to the conclusion that a strict disciplined observance of Sunday was an appropriate part of Christian discipleship. In the process they also came to believe that Christian worship should be held on the Sabbath, that is, Saturday, not Sunday.[13] The most important writing on the Sabbath during the reformation period was Nicolas Bownde who in 1596 published *The Doctrine of the Sabbath,* and provided biblical grounds for a strictly disciplined observance of Sunday.

James Ockford, in the 1650s, was the first Baptist to support the seventh day position in *The Doctrine of the Fourth Commandment, Deformed by Popery, Reformed and Restored to its Primitive Purity.* He saw the Sabbath as a delight and a joy, stating: 'happy shall the Church be, that worshippeth God according to his Law, and giveth him his due, by placing on the seventh day, the honour which God requireth to be performed on it' (p.59). The mayor of Salisbury viewed the book differently, and referred it to Parliament, because it challenged Sunday observance. It was publicly burned and only a single copy escaped. Some construed it as encouraging Jewish views, although Ockford made it clear: 'I am no Jew, nor inclined to any Jewish opinions; I seek not righteousness by the Law, but by faith in the Son of God, according to the Gospel'.

By 1653 the first Seventh Day church was probably that meeting in Mill Yard, London, under the leadership of William Saller. This was probably the W. Saller, who published the tract *Sundry Queries tendered to Ministers for clearing the doctrine of the Fourth Commandment and the Lords Sabbath Day,* and wrote eleven more books arguing his case in various ways. Thomas Tillam certainly knew of Saller in 1657, for he received a letter from a London Seventh Day Church, probably Mill Yard, while at Colchester. Henry Jessey personally came to Seventh Day views, but for a long time kept them to himself. He and a few friends would sometimes meet on Saturday, and then continue on Sunday. In Jessey's *Scripture Almanack,* on each seventh day the word 'Sabbath' was printed.

There was a debate at Stone Chapel, London, near St Paul's in 1659, when Jeremiah Ives spoke against the Saturday Sabbath, and Peter Chamberlen, Thomas Tillam and Matthew Coppinger spoke for it. Ives published his account of the debate in *Saturday no Sabbath* and addressed it to the Colchester Baptist church led by Tillam. Tillam had requested from Cromwell a place to meet in Colchester and was given a parish church for the purpose in May 1657. In 1660 Tillam wrote that the Sabbath Church in Colchester met in a 'steeple' house. *The Seventh Day sought out and celebrated,* written by Tillam, was published in 1657. He began from the position of preferring Sabbath observance yet allowing

[13] A recent study of Seventh Day Baptists is D. A. Sanford, *A Choosing People: The History of Seventh Day Baptists*, Broadman Press, 1992

people to worship on Sunday, through to advocacy of Saturday, and was especially concerned that the Lord's Supper be celebrated only on Saturday. By 1660, in *The Temple of Lively Stones*, he concluded it was time to withdraw from those who did not accept the Seventh Day position. Tillam, a Fifth Monarchist, became increasingly legalistic in his practice and grew intolerant of others. In 1662 using the name 'Mallit' he headed a community in Heidelberg, Germany, where he set up a church that was free to follow the biblical teachings that he felt were required of all Christians.

In 1667 a document was signed by a number of leading Seventh Day Baptists, including one of the Stennetts, disavowing Tillam's legalistic beliefs and practices. A letter from John Davis of London to Samuel Hubbard in Rhode Island, written in 1674, confirms Tillam's death in Germany, and comments that the Sabbath Day view had been brought into disrepute by Tillam, not helped forward.

Much more important for the continuance of the Seventh Day Baptist views was Peter Chamberlen (1601–83). He was of Huguenot extraction, educated at the Merchant Taylors' School in London and Emmanuel College, Cambridge. After further study at Heidelberg and Padua universities he became a Fellow of the College of Physicians in 1628. As a doctor he provoked much opposition by his proposal that London midwives should be organized into a sisterhood. His reputation in midwifery was built upon the use he made of certain secret forceps invented by an earlier member of his family. He was an advocate of public baths as a means of eradicating disease, and a public bank to help the poor. He was 'physician in ordinary to three Kings and Queens of England', namely James I, Charles I, and Charles II, as well as to some European princes whom he met in his travels over the years. Early in life he was a member of the Lothbury Baptist church that under his leadership adopted Seventh Day views before migrating to Mill Yard. A tireless advocate of Baptist and Seventh Day opinions, Chamberlen's social position made him a significant help to a despised minority group of Baptists.

Particular Baptists were carefully organised as closed membership, closed communion, missionary congregations, in association across England, effective in church planting in a variety of situations. Among them were a minority of Particular Baptists who were open membership, open communion; and the smallest group of all were the Sabbatarian or 'Seventh Day Baptists'.

7

Baptists Persecuted

WHEN Charles II returned to the English throne he was prepared to offer a compromise on the religious issue, but he came under great pressure from the now restored Church of England to enforce a religious conformity based on the *Thirty-Nine Articles* and the *Book of Common Prayer*. He wished to provide a measure of toleration for Roman Catholics, under the guise of similar relief for Dissenters. Edward Hyde, Charles's Lord Chancellor (created Earl of Clarendon in 1661), skilfully presented legislation that would have allowed for such comprehension and toleration. However, a rising of Fifth Monarchy men, led by Thomas Venner, in January 1661, encouraged the spread of growing alarm about the political intentions of religious dissenters prior to the May 1661 Parliament. The political and church leaders in England and Scotland united to refuse both toleration and comprehension within the re-born state church.

The Clarendon Code

Dissenters did not always have those who could keep a record of what was happening to set alongside the official reports of the ecclesiastical and secular courts. The significant commentary of Edward Terrill and his successors in the Church of Christ in Bristol, meeting in Broadmead, provides a rare first hand account of this particular situation for Baptists, not in a remote location, but in the second city in the nation.

1 The Corporation Act

The first part of Clarendon's Code was this act, passed in May 1661, and it was as much a political as a religious measure in its intention. It required all persons holding municipal office to renounce the *Solemn League and Covenant*, an agreement made between Scotland and the English Parliament to maintain Presbyterianism in Scotland, and to work towards the adoption of Presbyterianism in England, and thus remove 'popery' and episcopacy. All future holders of municipal office had to swear an oath of non-resistance to the established government in both church and state, thus excluding republican sympathisers from office. Before any could take municipal office they had first to receive the Sacrament according to the rites of the Church of England. This provision, intended to exclude all Roman Catholics, effectively prevented Dissenters from holding office. Presbyterians were, for the first time, made part of the Dissenting community, and as Whitley rightly observes: 'From this moment the storm of persecution was directed to the new, wealthy, influential class which for more than a century had been at home in the Church of England ...'[1]

Thomas Ewins, the pastor of Broadmead, Bristol, at this time, and a city lecturer (or preacher), was turned out of his lectureship by this Act, but continued to minister at Broadmead. Under this Act he was imprisoned for a month for preaching during the summer of 1661. The following extended extract from *The Records of a Church of Christ in Bristol* indicates the effects of such persecution on the Broadmead congregation.

> When King Charles II was brought from his Exile again into the Nation and to the Crown, Then Sathan stirred up adversaryes against us, and our Trouble or Persecution began. And then our friends of the Presbyterian party were turned out of their Publique Places as well as we. Then those who had preached against us for meeting in Private houses, they were faine to meet in Private houses as we had, and did doe. For then, when our Pastor, or Teacher, Mr Ewins, was turned out of those Publique places called Nicolas and Christchurch, (then) we first met every Lord's day at our Pastour's house in the Castle, and there we continued a long time; but being straitened for room, we took a large Place or Hall, towards the end of Broadmead, called the Fryars, which formerly had been some Chapel; and there we Continued, holding forth the Gospel of God's Free grace by our Lord Jesus Christ.
>
> And in the 10 month 1660, Orders come that all above 16 years of age must take the Oaths of Allegiance and Supremacy; which many scrupled to doe, because of the Extensiveness of some words in the Oath of Allegiance; as the words Whatsoever and otherwise. Whereupon the Brethren only of our and Brother Hynam's congregation met together, and discoursed our judgments, and searched the Scriptures, concerning our dutie and subjection to Magistrates; in which we all agreed, Concerning Civil matters they ought to be reverenced and obeyed. And to give them some assurance of it we drew up in Writing our sense, and in what terms we could engage ourselves; which was Consonant to the Scripture, and we did judge it as full as the Oath of Allegiance; which we sent by two messengers to the Mayor of the City, who then was Sir Henry Creswick. He sent the same writeing up to the King and Council, and ordered us to be left alone for some time, until he had answer from above; which within a month came, and was that we must take the Oath according to the letter of the Law, and not in other words. But Sir Henry telling us they did not require us to oblige ourselves no further than the Scripture did require of us, whereupon divers members of both congregations took it. But some others, though they held an Oath for the end of Controversie to be lawful, yet were not then satisfied to take a Promissary Oath. And so in Peace we bare one with another, them that did, and them that did not. So that trouble passed over.[2]

[1] W. T. Whitley, *A History of British Baptists,* 1923, p.113

[2] Roger Hayden, ed., *The Records of a Church of Christ in Bristol, 1640–1687,* Bristol Record Society, 1974, p.115

2 The Act of Uniformity

Charles II delayed signing the next piece of legislation, *The Act of Uniformity,* for three months in 1662, but Parliament declared it would not tolerate any indulgences proposed by the King to allow religious diversity.

The 1662 Act had the effect of identifying those who would not conform or who dissented from the measures. *The Book of Common Prayer* issued in 1662 was to be read by each minister on a given Sunday in August. The minister was then to give publicly his own unfeigned assent and consent to all and everything contained within it. Failure to do this would deprive the minister of his 'living'. In the future all ordinands would be required to do the same.

All the ejected ministers, afterwards known as Nonconformists, or Dissenters, stood by their conviction that the church's authority over matters of faith and order was distinct from, not subordinate to, the state. All questions of faith and order must be brought to the touchstone of Scripture. Further, the historic episcopate was neither an essential mark of the church nor a necessity for effective ministry. The orderly public worship of God could not be contained within the liturgy of a single book. The effect in Bristol was to throw Baptists and Independents, Presbyterians, Quakers, together as 'the persecuted' until 1690. Thomas Ewins felt the sting of the now Anglican and Royalist City Council's implementation of the Act, as one Council member in particular, Sir John Knight, made repeated and often violent attacks on the several dissenting communities.

3 The Conventicle Act

This Act began by re-imposing the provisions of an act of Elizabeth I that required regular attendance at the parish church. It was an actively persecuting measure and went on to outline legislation against 'the growing and dangerous practice of seditious sectaries ... who under the pretence of tender consciences, do at their meetings contrive insurrections.'

Any person aged sixteen or over, present at a meeting of five or more persons, other than those of the household, who shared in a service in any other form than that allowed by *The Book of Common Prayer,* could be convicted on proper evidence and sent to prison for at least three months, and also fined £5. A second conviction meant six months in prison and a £10 fine. A third arrest could lead to trial at the Quarter Sessions, where conviction would mean transportation for seven years, probably to the West Indies. Payment of £100 could secure release from transportation. Penalties were imposed on law enforcement officers who refused to apply the law.

The Broadmead congregation had supported pastors who might be imprisoned, but now this could happen to any worshipper. Transportation was no empty threat. An existing letter from Ewins underlines this point. He said that all the members have a duty to bear witness at least once, though then the prospect of banishment should make them careful, remembering their family responsibilities.

> But when may we say, Our testimony is finished? I answer, when you have witnessed against this late unrighteous act, or law of man, which is directly and so highly against the prerogative of Jesus Christ; or, when

you have suffered the first penalty either by fine or imprisonment, then, I conceive, you have borne your testimony ... Why should any fear or draw back, upon the account of the first penalty of this Act? It is not worth mentioning. You may redeem yourselves out for a shilling; if not they will turn you out in a week or two.

But some will say, They will do that but in policy, that they make take us again and hasten our banishment. I answer, let their ends be what they will, if you be out, you may then confine yourselves to private family meetings, and so escape banishment; having borne your testimony so fully, you may comfortably rest, and leave the work to those that have not yet been taken.[3]

4 The Five Mile Act

This 1665 Act was aimed at former ministers, who might be ministering to congregations that were now classed as Dissenters. It prohibited ministers from coming within five miles of any place where they had formerly carried out religious duties, or where they had been convicted of taking illegal dissenting worship.

5 Second Conventicle Act, 1670

The Act dispensed with transportation and introduced instead the possibility of limitless fines. The penalty for a first offence was a fine of five shillings with all subsequent offences carrying a ten shilling fine. The fines could be obtained by 'distress and sale of the offender's goods and chattels'. If this did not produce enough funds, then the belongings of another person convicted at the same meeting could be sold to make up the deficit! The fines were divided in three ways by the court: a third to the Crown, a third to parish poor relief, and a third to the informer.

A preacher or teacher at a conventicle could be fined twenty pounds and the congregations' goods sold to meet the bill. Appeal to the Quarter Sessions against such a conviction was permitted but if lost, all the fines were trebled. A parish constable could break down the doors of a meeting on the receipt of information that a conventicle was being held. Refusal to act meant he would be fined £5; justices who refused to act on information received would be fined £100, and half of this would go to the informer. The Act was, in its own words, 'to be construed most largely and beneficially for the suppressing of conventicles, and for the justification and encouragement of all persons to be employed in the execution thereof.'

It is at this point that Terrill's records talk of 'our persecutions'. The Bishop of Bristol urged the Act on his clergy pointing out its great advantages for Anglicans, and himself appointed informers to visit most nonconformist gatherings over four consecutive weeks beginning May 10, 1670.

The first Lord's day ... Informers from the Bishop, (that was then one lronsides) came upon us and because we did not know which way they would begin upon us, we shut our Publique Meeting-house door when

[3] *Ibid.*, p.62

> we understood they were coming. Then they fetcht Constables and brake open the door, came in and took our names, for which some of us were brought before the Magistrates and Convicted. Then, against the next Lord's day, we brake a wall up on high for a window, and put the speaker in the next house to stand and preach, whereby we heard him as well as if in the room with us. The Bishop's Informers come in again, take our names, for which we were again brought before the Mayor, and Convicted. So they did the 3rd Lord's day. And the fourth Lord's day, the Mayor himself, with his officers and some Aldm came upon us, and turned us out, but seeing they could not make us refrain our Meeting they Raised the Trained Bands every last day of the week in the Evening, one band to keep us out of our places, and Nailed up our doors, and putt locks upon them; so they kept us out by force and power, That we were faine to meet in the Lanes and highways for several months.[4]

The Bristol harassments eased in 1671 when a mayor, sympathetic to Nonconformity, was in control of the city. Charles II issued an Indulgence in 1672 to Dissenters who registered their meeting places. Many did so, including Broadmead, but some did not comply. The peace was short-lived because Parliament was in no mood for measures that would allow Roman Catholics freedom under the guise of accepting Dissenters.

The 1673 Test Act

This Act specifically excluded Roman Catholics from all national and local offices, including commissions in the army and navy. Holders of such posts had to take the oath of allegiance and receive the Lord's Supper according to Anglican rites. The parish minister who gave communion had to provide evidence, supported by the priest's warden and two other witnesses.

'Our Persecutions'

From 1672 until 1689 continuing persecution dogged the Bristol dissenters. John Hellier, a constable for the parish in which Broadmead met, Ralph Olive the Mayor and landlord of a public house in Broadmead, with encouragement from the new Bishop of Bristol, Guy Carleton, together launched an attack on Bristol Dissenters, with Broadmead and the Quakers suffering considerably. The attacks were encouraged by the fact that a third of the fines went to the local parish's poor relief fund, and a third to the informers themselves.

Thomas Hardcastle, the Broadmead pastor at this time, was imprisoned for a considerable period. Some of the most eloquent expressions of Christian faith in a time of persecution are contained in his twenty-two letters written from prison to the congregation. They were read, instead of the sermon, each Sunday afternoon. Hardcastle believed that persecutions would not only deepen faith and patience, but eventually bring about the conversion of many. He did not see a quick end to the persecutions and believed greater troubles would come: 'these are but the footmen you have been running with; these are but the little figures of Anti-Christ'.

[4] *Ibid.*, p.128

Thomas Hardcastle

In these 'sermon letters' Hardcastle discusses the deep nature of Christian faith, recognising the gift of faith in God as a veritable shield in danger, the kind of faith by which the just shall be able to live: a faith which brings a deep and lasting joy. This faith takes seriously the warnings that God's judgment provides, looks upon life as a pilgrimage to God, and is capable of overcoming the world. When Christians are obedient to Christ, then despite all outward factors, they will enter into the very presence of God. It was teaching of this calibre that sustained the church in persecution and particularly after 1680 when the most severe persecutions broke out.

> On the 22nd, being Ld's day, we met at Br. Terrill's, at the upper end of Redcross Lane, about 6 and 7 in the morning. But while Mr. Enoch Prosser, a Gifted Br. belonging to Mr. Keech of London, who came to our Fair, was preaching, about ten, Hellier, Sheriff Knight, Bp's Register, and Constables came, to the number of about 20. The Sheriff and Hellier with others knock at the Street Door, but none answered. And they sent to Tilly's for an Iron Crow, wherewith they broke some Battens, but could not enter after much Labour. Others of them laboured hard with a Bar at the Back door, but could not get in. Then Edw. Summers, a vile young man, a Butcher, with others, got into Capt. Vaughan's Orchard behind the House, but neither they, nor those at the Street Door, could get in. They behind broke a Window and its Shutter, driving the Bar into the Room where Several people were. Br. Terrill offered to open the Doors if they would stay till he had tyed up his mastiff dog, but they would not. So he let them alone, till, after much fruitless Labour, they were willing to accept his offer. He opened the Back door, and they that came in there let in their Gang at the Street door; and one of them threatened to shoot the Dog, which they saw tied, and strove to come at them. Then Jno. Hellier arrested Mr. Terrill in the King's Name.[5]

Particular Baptists Associating

In the mid-seventeenth century Baptists met in regional Associations to share their common life as churches. When the West Country churches met as the Western Association it was through their appointed Messengers. The gatherings often lasted three days or more. After opening prayer a Letter was read from each church by the Messenger to the assembled company. Queries from the

[5] *Ibid.*, p.236

churches were received and answers propounded were written down by each delegate and sent to the churches for their consideration. When the Association met at Bridgwater in 1656 the first query was:

> Whether it be an absolute duty now lying on several churches speedily to send forth persons fitted for the great and good work of the preaching the Gospel to the world?

The answer was unequivocal:

> We judge it to be a duty and at this time much to be laid to heart and performed to send forth such brethren as are fitted to the work of preaching the Gospel to poor sinners that they might be saved. 1.That it is a duty appears by the commission of Christ, Mat. 28.18f., and by the churches that first trusted in Christ according thereunto, Acts 11.22, 13.1ff, 1:15–23.2.That it's now to be performed appears by the open door that God hath set before us, Acts 16.19f, the fields being white to harvest, Jn. 4.35, Mat. 9.37f., and the abounding also of the mystery of iniquity.[6]

At Wells in 1659 a query rose as to whether evangelising 'were a hasty conclusion or whether it be the churches' neglect in not sending?' The answer was as precise and positive as it had been at the opening of the decade: 'It was then the sense of the assembly and still is, that according to the capacity that the churches are in they ought to send their ministers to preach the Gospell to the world'.[7]

In the West Country the *Somerset Confession, 1656,* had an article not found in the 1644 *London Confession,* which revealed this clear evangelistic emphasis of Baptists churches joined together in the Western association, which stated:

> That as it is an ordinance of Christ, so it is the duty of his church in his authority to send forth such brethren as are fitly gifted and qualified through the Spirit of Christ to preach the gospel to the world, Acts 13.1,2,3; Acts 11.22 and 8.14.[8]

The 'general meeting' or Association of Particular Baptists in the west was just one of a number of national Baptist groups across the country from the 1650s onwards. The Associations that met in the West, the Midlands, the North, around Abingdon, as well as in Ireland and Wales were spokes issuing from a central group of London particular congregations who signed a *Confession* in 1644. There was a common theology and shared concern to plant new churches. The Associations provided advice on controversial issues that individual congregations were unable to resolve; gave an opportunity for financial support and practical care between needy congregations; and the possibility of planning joint action by the wider fellowship of the churches. The evangelistic initiatives were a crucial factor among these Associations, the London leadership sending various people to begin work in different parts of the country. Benjamin Cox, John Miles, Thomas Patient, Daniel King, Thomas Tillam, Nathaniel Strange and Thomas Collier all made it their business to supply the cement of their

[6] B. R. White, *Association Records of the Particular Baptists of England Wales and Ireland to 1660,* BHS, 3 vols., ii, p.64
[7] *Ibid.,* p.102
[8] Lumpkin, *op.cit.,* pp.212f

John Bunyan

personal concern to a national programme. The programme was based on local congregations commissioning chosen members to organize new Particular Baptist churches, all holding the principle of 'closed communion'.

John Bunyan: Christ's prisoner

One of the most famous of those imprisoned for conscience' sake during the Restoration period was John Bunyan, the Bedford tinker, who during his incarceration composed the classic description of Christian pilgrimage through this world, *The Pilgrim's Progress*. Both Baptists and Independents claim him. The church he joined in Bedford, like others at Llanvaches in Wales, Broadmead in Bristol, and Jessey's London congregation, initially included both Baptists and those who practised the baptism of infants. Bunyan personally accepted the doctrine of believers' baptism, but found the position of the Particular Baptists, as enshrined in the 1646 *Confession,* unacceptable. The Bedford church was gathered in 1650, largely as the result of the efforts of John Gifford. Its covenant indicated membership was on the basis of 'Faith in Christ and holiness of life, without regard to this or that circumstance or opinion in outward or circumstantial things'.

Bunyan joined in 1655 and the following year began to preach. In his autobiographical book *Grace Abounding to the Chief of Sinners* he told how he was led to Christ by three or four older women as one day they sat talking about the things of God in a way which profoundly challenged him and led to his conversion. On 25 March 1658, prayer was offered in the church, on Bunyan's behalf, seeking divine guidance as he was to be indicted at the Assizes for preaching. After the restoration of Charles II, on 12 November, 1660, he was arrested and spent the greater part of the next twelve years in prison. Such a prison sentence is difficult to explain, some suggesting he was believed guilty of association with the Fifth Monarchists. The severity of persecution during this period can be judged from the fact that there are no entries at all the in the Bedford *Church Book* between 1663 and 1668, the church knowing little peace until the barn in which they worshipped was licensed in 1672.

Rye House Plot

The persecutions experienced in Bristol were intensified at various times as national events brought pressure on Dissenters who were thought to be plotting political anarchy in their 'Conventicles'. A good example of such intensification came with the discovery of the Rye House Plot in 1683. Three Baptists took part in the Plot who had each been former officers in Cromwell's Army. One, Colonel Richard Rumbold, had been one of the scaffold guards at the execution of Charles I, and served at the battles of Dunbar and Worcester. He was now a maltster at the Rye House in Hoddesdon, Hertfordshire. Not far from the Rye House the narrow Newmarket road passed between high banks. When the King returned from the Newmarket races he often passed that way. It would be easy enough to block the road and seize the King. It would require swords to be used, in case the King resisted, which made it a dangerous ploy.

On the day when the King was to be seized, a fire at Newmarket burnt down half the town, and the King came through earlier than expected. Three months later one of the conspirators revealed the plot to the authorities. Rumbold escaped, as did Colonel Abraham Holmes who had encouraged Baptist work in Leith in 1654. Holmes, who had already spent three years in prison since 1660, survived to join the Duke of Monmouth at the battle of Sedgemoor, but afterwards was taken prisoner and executed. The third Baptist, Captain Thomas Walcot, who had served in Ireland and was licensed to preach in Bungay in 1672, was executed along with others.

Monmouth's Rebellion

The Earl of Shaftesbury was at the centre of political intrigue in 1680 when he advocated putting the illegitimate, but Protestant, Duke of Monmouth on the throne, when Charles II died, instead of the Catholic James, Duke of York. The discovery of the Rye House Plot in 1683 meant that Monmouth had to flee the country.

In 1684 the Lords Lieutenant of each county were ordered to seize the arms of those disaffected to government. The list of arms seized in Bristol has survived. It reveals massive dissenting support for Monmouth from Baptists across the west including Broadmead, Bristol.

After Monmouth's abortive rising in the West, the infamous Judge Jeffreys severely punished Dissenters. By his orders seventy-four were hanged in Dorset, and two hundred and thirty-three in Somerset. Eight hundred and forty were transported to Barbados. Congregations assembled in the countryside to avoid arrest. Two of William Kiffin's grandsons, Benjamin and William Hewling, who had come over in Monmouth's personal bodyguard and were members of Lyme Regis Baptist church, were hanged, one on the quay at Lyme, the other at Taunton.

In Bristol, Thomas Hardcastle's successor, George Fownes, was kept in prison for over two years and died in Gloucester prison in 1685. When James II came to the throne in 1685 as an avowed Papist, the country again experienced considerable unrest. The laws against Dissenters were ferociously applied. Courts were crowded with victims, worshippers pursued through the countryside, and many prisons overflowed with Nonconformists.

An interesting development produced by these experiences, was a willingness among Dissenters to raise funds for the defence of those prosecuted under the Clarendon Code. Once, when Broadmead worshippers were being chased through the woods, Mr Ford, the dissenting minister from Taunton, was drowned. The matter was pursued through the courts and brought to a successful conclusion, and the Constables responsible punished. Terrill and others enlisted the support of various attorneys and pointed out defects in the warrants and other legal documents that made them invalid.

Many suffered abuse at the hands of informers, being ridiculed in court, and put in overcrowded prison cells where heat, cold, filth and disease made conditions intolerable, and where a bribed or vindictive gaoler could make matters even worse. Several prisoners died, but most were released with their health permanently impaired. For the majority the seizure of goods, added to imprisonment, spelt financial ruin. But in it all, a strength of character was shown that brought new lustre to Dissenters.

The 'Glorious Revolution'

Eventually King James II recognised the futility of such ferocity and in 1687 issued a Declaration of Indulgence allowing a liberty of conscience that effectively nullified the Test Act, and gave liberty to Catholics and Dissenters to worship in public. He appointed several Roman Catholics to office in government and the armed services. He also attempted to set up a commission to assess the damage caused to dissenting meeting houses and property during the last ten years, with a view to making reparations. Most Dissenters recognised that James' true objective was to advance Catholicism and refused co-operation.

However agents for the Crown did their best to secure the 'thanks' from a number of 'loyal' Dissenters that would demonstrate support for the Catholic King James. A few reputable Baptists responded, including William Collins and Nehemiah Coxe of the Petty France church, Plant of the Barbican and Dennis of Bow. On the other hand the aged Kiffin and Joseph Stennett, while advising the churches to re-open their premises, said none should publicly thank King James, whose action was illegal and whose motives deserved none.

Dissenters and Anglicans, united for a brief time in opposition to a Catholic King, and worked to enthrone James II's daughter, Mary, married to the Protestant William, Prince of Orange. In May 1688 James tried to enforce the reading of his Indulgence in all the London parish churches, but the bishops petitioned the King not to make alterations in religion without the sanction of Parliament. The bishops, who were for a time imprisoned in the Tower, were eventually tried and acquitted, and received by the London populace with great acclaim.

Eventually, without further bloodshed, James II fled the country and William and Mary were established on the throne by act of Parliament. A Toleration Act, passed in 1689, allowed freedom of worship to Dissenters, but the Test Act remained in effect and effectively barred all Catholics and Dissenters from public office.

Baptists in National Assembly

After the passing of the Toleration Act in 1689 Baptists in the West country began to meet together again and were encouraged in this by a letter from seven London Baptist ministers, including the venerable William Kiffin of

Devonshire Square, Hanserd Knollys of Broken Wharf, and Benjamin Keach of Horsleydown. More than 150 Baptist ministers and messengers met together from 3 to 9 September, 1689, in London, when the historic 1689 *Confession of Faith* was signed and became, in its various editions, the Particular Baptist doctrinal standard until 1832. *The Narrative* of these proceedings disclaimed any power over local churches, leaving each church 'their own liberty to walk together as they have received from the Lord'.

Among factors leading to the 'decay of religion', the neglect of 'the worship of God in families' was believed by many to be uppermost. To this end the 1689 *Confession* was to be used 'to catechise and instruct the young'. The failure to ordain pastors and deacons meant that churches lacked a proper authority. The lack of adequate financial support for ministers meant they were too busy in secular occupations to fulfil 'their holy calling in preaching the Gospel and watching over their respective flocks.' A public fund was proposed, that would be administered by nine leading London Baptist ministers, to strengthen the ministry through the education and training of new ministers. Small churches in close geographical proximity were encouraged to share public ministry whenever possible. Worship was to be held on Sunday, not Saturday, which was a deliberate exclusion of Seventh Day Baptists, a small minority group among English Baptists. It was agreed that when it was absolutely necessary an Elder in one church could administer the Lord's Supper in another. Finally it was recommended that Benjamin Keach's *The Ministers Maintenance Vindicated* (1688), which argued for a paid ministry, 'be dispersed among all our respective congregations'.

However the national assembly was short lived, some arguing that the arduous nature of travel kept delegates away, others that it was the Baptist laity's pride, covetousness and worldly-mindedness which killed it off, and some that Baptists, now in a civil and social backwater, preferred to evade questions of organization, neglected the need for an educated ministry, and this in turn led to the demise of a national assembly.

A document of proceedings, called *The Narrative,* at this period listed twelve Associations across the country including two in Wales. An attempt was made in 1692 to hold two annual national meetings in Bristol and London, at Easter and Whitsun respectively, with two messengers from each General Assembly, attending the next Assembly, to maintain 'General Communion' between the two. Unfortunately a furious pamphlet debate on the propriety of singing in worship raged in London from 1690 to 1698, in the first phase of which congregational hymn singing was the issue, and in the second, psalm singing was the main topic of discussion. After 1693 there was no London Assembly as such, but the Western Association kept meeting in various venues together with a number of the Welsh Baptist churches.

8

The Challenge to Mind and Heart

We are a garden wall'd around
Chosen and made peculiar ground

Isaac Watts

WATTS'S view of the people of God enclosed by grace, has been thought by some, to be an apt contemporary view of Dissent in the early eighteenth century. Certainly, the legal and social disadvantages imposed by the constitutional settlement of 1689, effectively removed Dissenters from national life. Thus Whitley wrote Baptists were 'now in a backwater, well off the main channel of national life. Whether in State Papers or private correspondence, they simply disappear henceforward, or at most appear as obscure satellites, to be discerned occasionally, amongst the "Dissenters"'.[1]

H. S. Skeats, another Dissenting historian, claimed Baptists lacked gifted leaders and that most Baptist ministers were also in secular employment. The zeal of the Baptist community was 'to a very considerable extent, consumed in contentions amongst themselves and with other denominations ... What they gained in sectarianism they lost in spirituality.'[2] He reckoned Joseph Stennett to be the 'head of the denomination' in Queen Anne's reign and Little Wild Street, London, the leading Baptist congregation.

H. W. Clark, writing half a century later, said 'democratisation' had caused eighteenth-century Baptists problems and encouraged them to promulgate the issue of believers' baptism as a distinguishing or foundation idea of religious fellowship. To maintain their witness on the question of baptism was in Baptist estimation the main issue. Clark also quoted Joseph Stennett, who in a sermon on the decay of the Dissenting interest, 'lamented that religion had come to mean little for many who professed it, and was taken as only making small claims and was offered lip service alone.'[3]

Clark reckoned that Baptist advocacy of believers' baptism, discussion of the practice of open or closed communion, and the desire to maintain the doctrines of hyper-Calvinism, were the core of Baptist beliefs, and enabled them to survive

[1] W. T. Whitley, *A History of British Baptists*, 1923, p.163
[2] H. Skeats, *History of the Free Churches of England, 1688–1851*, 1869, pp.260–262
[3] H. W. Clark, *History of Nonconformity*, 1913, ii, pp.120, 132

the doctrinal attacks of the Enlightenment. But Nonconformity generally 'had lost its inspiring power, its compulsion, its greatness, its thrill and the garden ... was becoming weed-grown and bare.'[4]

Duncan Coomer claimed that Presbyterians were Dissent's 'cold intellect', Independents its 'clamorous voice', but Baptists its 'untutored heart'. It was more difficult to get an idea of Baptists than the other two denominations, because there is 'both a lack of outstanding names and an obscurity about many of their churches which at times baffles the enquirer. This is so, even in London, where it is the exception for a church to have a permanent place of meeting ... And there is still greater elusiveness in some of the country districts.'[5]

Coomer's ignorance of Baptist church books, printed Confessions and covenant documents led him to make a demonstrably false claim that 'the Church Covenant was unknown to them.' He believed Baptists were impelled by 'strong-minded laymen to adopt extreme theological views' and the average Baptist church consisted of a comparatively few people and those very obscure.[6] To challenge such views it is important to give full weight to the evidence of Baptist life outside London.

The Western Baptist Association

The joint meetings of London and provincial Baptists in the early 1690s soon ceased, as London Baptist ministers preferred to meet in London Coffee Houses, as ministers, rather than as churches, in association. In Bristol the Association continued to meet regularly, and issues that divided London Baptists were handled more adeptly in the provinces.

For example, in the west, the affirmations of Seventh Day Baptists and the use of hymns in worship became not a cause for division, but an issue for personal decision. Much more important was the adoption of the 1689 *Confession*, (3rd edition) as the fundamental doctrinal basis for all churches of the Association and for the Association itself. By 1735 the only churches in Association were Calvinistic Baptists, the Arminian General Baptist churches having been successfully excluded.

Western Association Baptists were more determined than those in London to retain their Association life, despite geographical distance and theological diversity. Association meetings were held at Frome in 1692, and at Westbury, Wiltshire, in 1693. The *Letter* to the Churches issued at Bristol in 1694 urged those who had not attended to do so at the next opportunity. Those attending 'were grieved, because you, who some years ago did zealously promote such association for the general good of the churches and the glory of Christ have declined it.'

The *Letter* commented how the previous gathering, when it had considered the need for new pastors, had been able to remove

> jealousies and misapprehensions that divers person and some churches had, concerning our designs in bringing several young men, who were

[4] *Ibid.*, pp.199, 200
[5] D. Coomer, *English Dissent*, 1946, p.20f
[6] *Ibid.*, pp.23, 25

gifted brethren, to the knowledge of the tongues in which the Holy Scriptures were written: a work for God, in our generation, which we hope not only the churches in this day will have cause to bless God for, but also the generation to come.

An educated ministry

All Baptist leaders identified the need for an educated ministry in Baptist churches as a key issue at this time, but the case was made and carried not in London, which would wait for half a century before having its own institution, but in Bristol and the Western Association.

The resistance to 'humane learning' was as strong in the west as elsewhere, Thomas Collier opposing it in 1651 when he said 'it is the Spirit of Anti-Christ that seeks after humane help … and having gotten it they grow proud of it, are self-conceited in it, make it their idol and dare reproach the Spirit and power of the Lord and His saints.'

However, in Broadmead, Bristol, a very different attitude prevailed through the vision and resources of a wealthy layman, Edward Terrill. He made a deed of gift in his 1679 will which left money to support a second minister at Broadmead who was to be skilled in the Biblical languages and prepare young men for ministry in Baptist churches. When the 1689 London meeting advocated support for training new ministers, the Pithay, Baptist church, Bristol, sent £30. Broadmead's initial attempt to fulfil Terrill's hopes proved abortive. Caleb Jope who joined Peter Kitterell, did not train any pastors and left in 1707. It was left to Bernard Foskett in 1720, to put Terrill's wishes into action.

The question of Dissenting Academies in general came under the spot-light in 1707 when a pamphlet written by Samuel Wesley in 1690, was re-printed. It urged Anglicans to use their power 'to suppress utterly and extinguish those private, blind, conventicling schools or academies of grammar and philosophy set up and taught secretly by fanatics here and there all over the Kingdom.' Henry Sacheverell, a High Church priest and Oxford don, added fuel to the fire in 1709 with a sermon before the Lord Mayor of London, *The Perils of False Brethren*, in which he declared Dissenters and their academies a national peril. 'Atheism, Deism, Tritheism, Socinianism, Regicide and Anarchy' were, he claimed, all being taught within these institutions. Sacheverell went further: English Dissenters were 'monsters and vipers in our bosom … miscreants begat in rebellion, born in sedition and nursed up in faction.' As he came to trial for a seditious sermon, Sacheverell's supporters raised a riot in London on the night of 1 March 1710 inciting supporters to attack the Bank of England and six Dissenting meetinghouses. The results of the rioting echoed round the country for several years.

A common doctrine

Doctrinal issues came to a head in the Western Association, which had included General and Particular Baptists, when John Sharp of Frome was sent to the Salters' Hall conference, which had been called to adjudicate on differences about the Trinity.[7] When Sharp reported to the Western Association at Trowbridge his views were conveyed through the *Letter* to the churches.

[7] See above, chapter 4, pp.45ff

Bernard Foskett

> We have great cause to rejoice that though it is a perilous day, wherein many other denominations depart from 'the faith once delivered to the saints' particularly in that great article of the Christian religion—the deity of our Lord and Saviour Jesus Christ; denying or calling into question his eternal Godhead; suggesting it is not of the same nature with the Father … though it is thus with others, we rejoice that none of the churches, or ministers belonging to this Association, hold any such pernicious doctrine.

Unfortunately this was not true. The elderly minister of Frome, John Davisson, was soon to be succeeded by Thomas Lucas who within seven years would take his church into just such a doctrinal understanding of Christ's person. In Taunton, Thomas Whinnel, who had attended the 1689 London meeting was followed by Joseph Jefferies, who by 1733 had taken the church to a General Baptist position, and by the end of the century the church would adopt Unitarian doctrine

The doctrinal issue in the Western Association was brought to a head by the Broadmead church, through its pastor from 1720, Bernard Foskett. In 1723 Foskett called for an article to be added to the Association's *Preliminaries*:

> Seeing that many errors have been broached, and ancient heresies revived of late in the world, no messenger shall be received from any church whose letter don't every year express, either in the preamble, or the body of it, that they of the Church do approve the Confession of Faith put forth by above a hundred Baptist churches, (Edit. 3d. A.D. 1699) and do maintain the principles contained therein; such letter being signed at a church meeting, in the name and by the consent of the whole church.

For seven years Broadmead failed to get its resolution carried in the Association, a stalemate only broken when a major fire at Tiverton in 1733 prevented the Association gathering. Caleb Evans' manuscript account of the Western Association some years later began the story with the following paragraph.

> The Western Baptist Association was for many years kept up by the Baptists as such without any regard to their different principles in other respects. The consequence of this was, these annual meetings were found to be rather pernicious than useful; as there was scarcely a meeting of the kind but some unhappy differences arose betwixt the Calvinistic and Armin:n Ministers. In the year of 1733 their annual meeting was to have been held at Tiverton but an awful fire abt that time, which consum'd most of the town, prevented it. The next year it was not revived. But in the following year an Invitation was sent to the respective churches by the church in Broadmead, Bris:l desiring them to renew their former annual Meeting upon the foot of their agreement in the Baptist Confess:n of 1689.[8]

The Northern Baptist Association

Baptists in Yorkshire, Lancashire and Cheshire originated through links with Cromwell's New Model Army that visited York (1647), Stokesley (1653) and Horton in 1655, two of their leaders corresponding with Cromwell. At Frodsham in Cheshire James Cockayne was the 'Anabaptist' leader, but it was Hill Cliffe, near Warrington, that was known as 'the Church of Christ in Cheshire'. Manchester Baptists, led by Colonel Wigan, an officer in the Army, leaning towards Fifth Monarchy views date from 1649. The Northern Baptist Association, with churches first formed in the 1640s by London Baptist ministers at Hexham and Newcastle, was based on the 1644 *London Baptist Confession*. In the Restoration period these northern churches retained an evangelistic cutting edge. William Mitchell and his cousin David Crossley, initially not Baptists, experienced revival with churches in the Rossendale Valley, on the Lancashire –Yorkshire border. Soon there were over 20 meeting places, centred upon Bacup, where one meeting house was erected in 1692, and another at Goodshaw. By this time both Mitchell and Crossley had become Baptists, and between 1692 and 1705 established further congregations in the Calder, Wharfe and Aire Valleys of Yorkshire.

Mitchell was very reliable, but Crossley was 'a rolling stone' who 'lacked the grace of settlement' and having been refused ordination by the Presbyterians, was baptized at Bromsgrove, Worcestershire, in 1692. He returned north to missionary work at Tottlebank, near Morecambe Bay, and at Barnoldswick. After a spell in London, when his 'sexual peccadillos' led to his dismissal from his London pastorate in 1710, he was back in Lancashire, and settled at Goodshaw as a schoolmaster and preacher.

After the 1689 London Assembly, attended by delegates of over a hundred Baptist churches, including some from Newcastle-upon-Tyne and Derwentwater, the Northern Association was revived and was functioning again in 1691. It was never strong and more than most Associations depended upon the leadership that the larger churches gave to the wider work.[9]

[8] Transcripts of each year's Western Association Meetings, 1734–1812, in a manuscript book held at Bristol Baptist College

[9] Ian Sellers, ed., *Our Heritage: the Baptists of Yorkshire and Lancashire, 1647–1987*, Yorkshire Baptist Association, 1987, pp.9–11

One strong leader in the North was George Braithwaite born in 1681 at Hawkshead, who graduated from Oxford and was baptised by David Crossley, then minister at Cripplegate, London. In 1713, returning to the north, he ministered at Bridlington until 1733. He then went to London to minister at Devonshire Square until his death in 1741. In the Bridlington church covenant document, re-affirmed in 1746, the 1689 *Confession* was regarded as the true statement of Baptist belief and polity and the church gave its willing adherence to it.

In the Association there were many queries concerning anti-nomianism, the view that Christians are by God's grace set free from the need to observe any moral law. The issue was debated actively between 1701 and 1704. When the Association accepted a new constitution in 1723 the *Preamble* affirmed Particular Baptist doctrines and declared the aim of the Association was that

> churches may be improved in their usefulness and better supported, that order and unity may be obtained, faith advanced and encouraged, and error detected and rooted out.

The Northern Baptist Association, as other Associations at the time, was politically aligned with the Whigs, and acknowledged that continued toleration depended upon loyalty to the Hanoverian monarchy.

Membership of the Association was through the four delegates each church was entitled to send to Association gatherings, the local church bearing the costs of delegates attending. The worship at each Association gathering was presided over by the minister of the church where the meetings were held. The Moderator kept the Association 'in order' during its meetings and a clerk kept a formal record of the proceedings each year. The questions raised were answered only on the basis of advice to the questioner, the Messengers 'not pretending to infallibility or setting themselves up as Lords over God's Heritage or as having dominion over the Faith of others'. An annual collection was taken at the Association meeting to be at the disposal of Messengers for helping either ministers or congregations in need.

Stephen Copson comments on the Northern Association's evangelistic concern at this time:

> The question about the spiritual condition of the churches raised in 1701 followed on the question and answer given in 1700 about the form and content of a strategy necessary to gain new converts. The answer to this had spoken of the responsibility of members to maintain the witness to Christ through the church, by giving liberally to uphold the ministry of the Word, and by the continuing use of gifts in ministry, through the family and their own personal testimony.[10]

The Northern churches were not immune from disputes about Calvinism as initial enthusiasm faltered at the opening of the eighteenth century. The intellectual and theological niceties of London Baptists did not impinge on the local churches who were more concerned to maintain their worship and witness while conducting themselves in a manner honouring to Christ.

[10] S. L. Copson, in Roger Hayden, ed., *English Baptist Records 3: Association Life of the Particular Baptists of Northern England, 1699–1732*, BHS, 1991, p.75

New *preliminaries* were drawn up, now thirteen in number, not seven, but with the significant omission of the original clause which allowed Baptists, General or Particular, with antinomian and high Calvinist tendencies or even Arian views, to share in the one Association. Clause thirteen read:

> That we join together in Association as agreeing on the Confession of Faith put forth by the Elders and Brethren of our denomination in the city of London in year 1689 as being we think agreeable to the Scriptures. And we expect that every associating church do in their letter every year, signify their approbation of the said Confession.

The Midland Baptist Association

The Midland Association, like those in Wales and the West Country, was formed in 1655.[11] When it was re-formed in 1690 at Warwick, it took the 1689 *Confession* as its doctrinal standard. It issued a five-point guide about advice and consultation procedures, to be adopted by the churches for the good of their common life. Association delegates each year wrote out the *Letter* and *Breviates* (minutes) by hand and reported to their church. In 1733 an Association Minute Book was bought and a standing record of Association principles and proceedings kept. In 1759 the printing of the annual *Association Letter* and *Breviates* enhanced the accuracy of reporting and provided a useful means of disseminating the information among the churches.

In the yearly *Letter* the Association commented on national events as well as church business. The war with France over Nova Scotia in 1756 brought the comment: 'Several churches take notice of the War' and the churches were urged to be 'very humble and importunate with God for Great Britain and Ireland, and the colonies pertaining thereto, and for the Church of Christ; because, though we have a considerable army and fleet wherewith to oppose our enemies, yet, if we trust in these our strength may soon be turned to weakness ...'

The Association had nine member churches in 1690, by 1800 there were twenty-two. The doctrinal stance of the Association on the 1689 *Confession* was never in doubt. It developed similar practices to other Baptist Associations, which was to be expected, since a number of the ministers were Bristol trained, while Bernard Foskett had himself ministered at Henley-in-Arden till moving to Broadmead, Bristol in 1720.

Association Meeting, Birmingham, 1777

In a letter from James Turner, minister at Cannon Street, Birmingham, to his long time friend, John Sutcliff of Olney, written on 29 May 1777, there is a lively account of a Midland Association meeting in Birmingham.

> I have so many things to say I scarce know where to begin or end. Our Association was a very blessed one indeed! more so than any I ever attended. We borrowed Carr's Lane, but afterwards altered our mind, and I went and borrow'd the New Meeting which was readily granted, and well fill'd. Dr Ash came on Friday and was with us on the Lord's Day. He pleased our people much. He is an affable, good natur'd man

[11] W. Stokes, *The History of the Midland Association*, Birmingham, 1855; and J. M. G. Owen, *Records of an Old Association*, 1905. Both are required to document the whole story

as ever liv'd. Have you seen his 'Sentiments on Education'? 5s in boards, 6 in sheep and ye calf.gilt and gold lettered—I spent my time in his company very agreeably. On Tuesday friends began to pour in. At the reading of the Letters we had, I suppose 2000 people. Messrs Medley and Clarke of London (who called on me the week before in his way to Salop ordination) Sandys and H. Butterworth all came together just before we began. The time was spent delightfully. Next day the ministers seemed to have much of God with them. Little Dore (do you know him?) preached a most excellent sermon. Everybody spoke of him very highly. My own soul was fed to the full. Mr Hiller preached well. He has a good presence and a good voice; and, as I told him, he spoke as one having authority. Mr Medley filled up the basket in the evening. O How did the good man talk! On the last clause of his text he was excellent, every eye upon him most of the time. I was not very happy a while at first, but the case alter'd. It was a truly blessed day. Messrs Hawkes and Blyth attended in the morning and again at night; together with Mr Belcham of Daventry, Mr Schofiled and many others. Persuaded I am they must feel something. They could not help it. God follows his word with blessing! In short, everything went so charmingly that it was truly delightful. We had somewhere about 4 or 5 and twenty Baptist ministers, may be more. Messrs Poynting, Carpenter, Whitmore and Blackshaw were not with us. Mr. Lucas of Walsall dined with us. Mr Passfield did not, tho invited. The two Presbyterian ministers I invited but they were pre-engaged. We were fourscore and four at Dinner. The Ordinary 2s 6d. The Landlord was well pleased and so were his guests. Nothing to be seen but friendship, harmony, etc … [12]

The sheer excitement and spiritual vitality of the annual gathering is evident, with a large number attending to hear preachers from other parts of the country, and to share the social fellowship of like-minded people.

London Baptists Associating

In London, by 1727, Particular Baptist ministers were consciously organized around a strong, strictly Calvinist, ministers' meeting, held in various coffee houses, that excluded all laity and admitted only Calvinistic Baptist ministers. The London Particular Baptist Fund was distributed, as its minutes clearly demonstrate, among churches and ministers who encouraged Calvinist and Trinitarian orthodoxy.

In the capital it was the influence of the *Committee of the Three Denominations* that encouraged London Particular Baptists to adopt a strongly ministerial dominated pattern of church life, and this brought them into conflict with the London Baptist laity. Dr M. D. MacDonald, who has researched London Calvinistic Baptists between 1689 and 1730, notes that Dissenters generally shared a decline in spiritual vitality towards the close of the reign of George I. For a while Dissenters suffered a loss of nerve, and London Calvinistic Baptists were no exception. Baptists responded by adopting 'a defensive posture of

[12] File of original letters written to John Sutcliff in BMS archives, Oxford. This letter dated 29 May 1777

rigour, symbolized by the creation of the particular Baptist Fund in 1717 along strict lines and the publication in 1722 of Skepp's *Divine Energy*. They showed a heightened interest after 1717 in specifically theological issues. This rigorous posture and increased interest in theology set the stage for the triumph of the exaggerated Calvinism of John Gill and John Brine in the eighteenth century.'[13]

MacDonald commented:

> This was not the most obvious form of corporate life for Calvinistic Baptists who had tended since the 1650s to organize in local associations that involved pastors and members of the churches. London's failure to organize in this way was atypical of denominational life generally.

Arianism at Paul's Alley, London

Whitley reckoned only four Particular Baptist churches succumbed to Arian theology, a heresy that denied the true divinity of Christ. Paul's Alley, in the Barbican, was certainly the most significant Baptist centre of this. The members were strong intellectually, progressive, wealthy, with access to a fine church library, as well as the first purpose-built baptistery north of the Thames. The 'Society for Promoting Catholic Christianity', formed in 1715 to promote the discussion of anti-Trinitarian theology, followed the lead given from Cambridge mathematician, William Whiston. John Gale, a Baptist minister at Paul's Alley, though not its pastor, chaired the Society from the beginning. He had been trained in Dr John Ward's school and took a doctorate from Leyden University at the age of 19. He was called to ministry at the Barbican in 1706. In 1711 he published a wide-ranging critique of Wall's *History of Infant Baptism*, which stayed in print for over a century. Whitley said of him:

> No other Baptist minister of the time could compare with him for learning, or for preaching power; and as he took every morning service at his church he must be held chiefly responsible for its decided transformation, so that at the foundation of the Particular Baptist Fund in 1717 its co-operation was declined and on his death the pastor replaced him with James Foster.[14]

Foster, who had received a first class academic training in the west of England, came to London and, at the age of 27, became pastor at the Barbican. Here he won the praise of Alexander Pope as the best preacher of his age. He became a leading champion in the fight against the Deistic school in theology. Perhaps it was the hypnotic effect of the discussions of Christology and ethics that mesmerised both church and minister. Under Gale and Foster and two other learned ministers, the Barbican so declined that when its lease on the building expired in 1768 the congregation simply disbanded.

Protestant Dissenting Deputies

Presbyterian, Congregational and Baptist lay people came to a growing realisation that there was a need to fight for more civic freedom for dissenters and in 1732 every dissenting church in the London area was invited to appoint

[13] M. D. MacDonald, 'London Calvinistic Baptists 1698–1727: tensions within a Dissenting Community under Toleration', unpublished D.Phil, Oxford, 1982

[14] W. T. Whitley, *A History of British Baptists*, 1923, p.200f

two deputies to a committee which would direct political action.

Clyde Binfield well describes the situation for Dissenters after 1689 and during much of the eighteenth century:

> By excluding Dissenters from the full rights of citizenship the Clarendon Code recognised their existence. The fact of a Uniformity Act is a testimony to the lack of uniformity. The fact of a Conventicle Act testifies to the existence of a dissident Christian community. Those whose lives were affected by such acts were indelibly stamped by them, but they were not stamped out and in 1689 the Toleration Act set them apart as a legally recognised entity, an almost second-rate establishment ... tolerated provided that their meeting houses were licensed and their services held behind unlocked doors. They were thus accommodated *within the system*; their freedom of action was effectively restricted to a freedom of re-action to whatever initiative the establishment took ... 1727 saw the first of a series of Indemnity Acts to suspend the invocation of the Test and Corporation Acts. But it was suspension, not repeal. The plural society which emerged from the restoration Settlement, although based on law and upheld by statute, was neither equal nor just.[15]

The Protestant Dissenting Deputies met to challenge just such a situation in 1744, when London City Councillors passed a bye-law which meant that a man elected to civic office who declined to fulfil it would be fined £600. Many Dissenters could not conscientiously pass the Test required of those holding public office, and paid the fine. It was claimed that the costs of the London Mansion House, some £15,000, were largely met from the fines imposed![16]

In 1754 the Dissenting Deputies found one of its leaders, Allen Evans, and two others, were caught in this situation. Evans, a Common Councillor and a wealthy member of the Wild Street Baptist church, was elected Sheriff but refused to pay the fine. In 1762 he took his case, with the support of the Deputies, through the City courts to the House of Lords, and won the case. When the Lord Chancellor, Lord Mansfield, finally decided in Evans favour in 1767, Evans was 82 but he did live long enough to hear the Chancellor declare:

> It is now no crime for a man to say he is a Dissenter; nor is it a crime for him not to take the sacrament according to the rites of the Church of England: nay, the crime is if he does it contrary to the dictates of his conscience.

However, the repeal of this legislation waited until the next century despite the best efforts of the Protestant Dissenting Deputies in which both General and Particular Baptists were actively involved.

High Calvinism

Richard Davis, Independent minister at Rothwell, Northamptonshire, was thought to be the father of high Calvinism (sometimes referred to as hyper-Calvinism). Yet he also regarded vigorous evangelism as essential for a church, and was a successful exponent of this in the early eighteenth century. The three

[15] C. Binfield, *Pastors and People*, 1984, pp.16f
[16] B. L. Manning, *The Protestant Dissenting Deputies,*, 1952

primary exponents of high Calvinism were Baptist ministers, all originally from Northamptonshire, but none of them known as evangelists.

John Skepp, Baptist minister at Curriers' Hall, London, expounded his views in a posthumously published series of sermons in 1722. In these he established, at least to his own satisfaction, that it was wrong to use moral persuasion in presenting the Gospel. In this he echoed the teaching of his mentor, an Independent minister, Joseph Hussey, of Cambridge. Hussey's own book of 1707 summed up his position in its title, *God's operations of Grace; but no offers of Grace.*

John Brine, minister at Cripplegate, London, entered the debate in 1743 with a book which refuted the principles of Richard Davis's successor at Rothwell, Matthias Maurice. Maurice's book, A *Modern Question Modestly Answered* (1737), asked whether it was not the duty of the unconverted to believe in the Gospel of Christ. He answered his own question in the affirmative and claimed it would be a failure in any preacher not to offer the Gospel. Support came from Alvery Jackson, a Baptist minister, who published *The Question Answered* (1752), and argued that a balanced evangelical theology demanded that preachers offer the Gospel for all to receive.

John Gill was the third and most influential of the three London Baptist ministers. He came from Kettering to settle as the pastor of the Southwark Church following Benjamin Stinton. Gill was a close friend of Skepp and developed his views in some depth.

Gill had attended Kettering Grammar School until he was eleven and had a quick, disciplined mind. He came to faith and was baptised in November 1716, aged 19. In 1719 after further theological education under John Davis at Higham Ferrers, he was invited to the Southwark pastorate. Some thought he was too young, others did not like his preaching style and pulpit mannerisms. Gill accepted the call but some of those who had dissented urged him to withdraw. After six months the congregation split and Gill assumed pastoral leadership of those who had given him the call, and was ordained in March 1720, when John Skepp and John Noble preached.

Gill's problems were not over as Thomas Crosby, the Baptist historian and then a member with Gill, brought scandalous and slanderous reports against the pastor and his wife. When these were refuted, Crosby was excluded from the church.

Gill considered his own Calvinistic system to be the only true faith but his first venture in theological writing was a polemical exposition of *The Song of Solomon*. Over the years he touched upon all the major theological issues of the day: the Trinitarian controversy, the threat from Deism, and the tensions between Calvinism, Antinomianism and Arminianism. Gill was a very competent Biblical exegete and a number of his friends founded the Great Eastcheap Lectureship that allowed people from many denominations to benefit from Gill's biblical expositions on Wednesday evenings from 1729 until 1754. His nine-volume *Expositions of Scripture* preceded his *Body of Divinity* and was the basis for his considerable reputation among Baptists as well as others.

Gill reasoned that since not all people responded to the Gospel, some were

Baptism at Southwick, Wiltshire

never intended to respond to it, and he was convinced this was the sovereign will of God. He rationalised his experience into his theological system where, by God's eternal decrees, every person was destined either to salvation or exclusion from it, and the highest virtue was willing submission to their destiny for the greater glory of God. This theology became accepted orthodoxy among many Baptist churches for many years. As late as 1786 William Clarke could write:

> The offers of salvation and overtures of mercy are the weak and wicked inventions of unsound Teachers. To bring Christ to Market, is, in my view, an indication that the Teacher stands in need of being taught … Christ's Gospel is only to be taught to regenerate children.

Even fifty years later, two Wiltshire men were dismissed from membership of a church because they had been preaching in the neighbouring villages. The issue was not that they had done this without proper church authority, but that they were theologically wrong to do so. The church book recorded the Church

> could not show friendship to those who held that invitations of the Gospels were general and indefinite, addressed to sinners of every description.

John Rippon's view of his predecessor in the Southwark pastorate was that Gill was, like the Saviour, 'hung up between two robbers: Antinomianism, which robs God of his grace, and Arminianism, which robs him of his glory.'

Gill and Brine were ministers with great influence in the middle years of the eighteenth century and they profoundly disagreed with Alvery Jackson's answer to the 'modern question'. Their books were on the shelves of all orthodox

Particular Baptist ministers. They often preached at ministerial ordinations and inductions. For almost fifty years their teaching, concentrating almost exclusively on the quality of life within the church, robbed many Particular Baptists of evangelical preaching.

Baptist Churches: luke-warm or growing?

Eighteenth-century Baptists were considerably concerned about what Isaac Hann of Loughwood near Kilmington, Devon in 1740, called the 'sleepy professors' of religion, and Benjamin Francis of Nailsworth, Gloucestershire, in 1765, termed 'the lukewarm and careless' in the churches who had become 'formal and indolent in the service of God'. However, a closer examination of the information provided by the churches to the Association each year paints a more encouraging picture.

When the Western Association met at Salisbury in 1769, for example, the *Letter* deplored that 'many churches within the circle of this Association continue still in a drooping and almost dying condition, having from year to year very few if any added to them, and complaining that they have but little power of religion among them'. Yet in the very next paragraph it is stated 'we have not been without our joys. The churches are all at peace—all enjoy the means of grace—all express a desire for being revived—and blessed be God, in some instances the increase in visible converts the past year has been considerable.'

In the *Letter* Robert Day wrote for the Western Association in 1772 concern was expressed that there had been only 44 baptisms that year, the lowest since 1744 when there were 35. This was correct but the figure for baptisms in the years either side of 1771 reveal the steady growth of converts in the churches. There were 110 in 1766; 112 in 1767; 124 in 1768; 69 in 1769 and 75 in 1770. After the 1771 figure of 44, there were 110 in 1772, 150 in 1773, and 122 in 1774. If any Association Messenger had studied the trends for the period they would have been considerably surprised. Between 1736 and 1758 the churches in the Association recorded 1326 baptisms, with a further 31 additions by transfer from other churches. In the same period 740 members died and 25 were excluded for disciplinary matters. The result was net gain in membership of the churches of 592.

In the period 1758 to 1791, when the Foskett and Evans leadership and training of new ministers began to be effective in the churches, there were 3547 baptisms and 261 additions by transfer from other churches. In the same period 1723 deaths of members were noted together with 297 transfers out and exclusions. This means there was a net gain in the period of 1788 members in the Association churches, with an average of 110 baptisms per year and an overall annual increase in the Association membership of 47.

Two years later John Kingdon's Association *Letter* of 1774 better caught the optimism of these figures:

> Parts of your Letters have been to us like cold water to thirsty souls, in as much as they tell us of a general enjoyment of peace, of your regard for the fundamental truths of the Gospel, and of many poor perishing sinners having felt the quickening influence of divine grace on their hearts, so

> that they thereby have been brought back home to the Lord Jesus Christ, the good and chief shepherd of souls, and have entered by him into his sheepfold.

Strength in Association

Outside London the Particular Baptists reveal a considerable concern for evangelisation and a deep desire that church life should be centred in a personal religious conversion experience rather than an empty subscribing to a formal credal statement. This did not mean there was a neglect of doctrine, quite the opposite, as churches and Associations made the 1689 Confession a vehicle for unity and church polity. Through the Confession, Baptist catechisms, and shared fellowship at Association level, Baptists discovered how to defend their doctrine from Socinian, Arian and Arminian challenges, and at the same time resist the extremes of London Baptist hyper-Calvinists. The Association was the place where problems were raised and answered; where action on a common date by prayer and fasting about specific issues was encouraged; where concern for an intellectually able yet evangelical ministry was being met through the Bristol Academy.

The life of churches meeting in Association gave good expression to the outcropping of the invisible universal Church of Christ while allowing for the independency of each gathered fellowship of believers as an accountable community of Christ. James Turner's description of the Midland Association gives the lie to those who claimed the Association meeting was simply a gathering of the ministerial elite. That was so in London, where the wider life of the churches was expressed through elitist coffee house groups of ministers only, but not in the provinces, where a very different style appertained.

The *Confession*, catechisms and local church covenants were common agencies for nurturing new Christians. The Association meeting was not afraid to tackle the larger issues of civil and religious liberties, as evidenced by recurring attempts to repeal the Test and Corporation Acts, sympathy with the American Colonists, and at the close of the century with the anti-slavery campaign. The picture of a lively, evangelical Calvinism at the heart of the Associations and the churches in the eighteenth century, and the training of 172 able and evangelical ministers for the churches by the Bristol Academy, makes the atypical nature of London Particular Baptist life clear, despite the attempt by some previous Baptist historians to suggest otherwise.

9

The Evangelical Revival and Particular Baptists

EARLIER Baptist historians had a marked tendency to tell the Particular Baptist story in the eighteenth century from a London Baptist perspective, often ignoring the vitality of the other twelve Baptist Associations that, unlike London Baptists, kept on meeting throughout the century. This led to an emphasis on High Calvinist Particular Baptists, and writing predominantly about High Calvinist London Baptist ministers, who had specifically excluded laity from their Coffee House meetings. The fact that nearly two hundred trained Baptist ministers from the Bristol Academy were supplied to Baptist churches, of whom less than a handful went to London churches, is largely ignored. Most of the Bristol ministers went to provincial Baptist churches, and several to America, Ireland, and Wales.

Among London Baptists the early part of the century was riven with controversy over hymn and psalm singing, and the place of the minority Seventh Day Baptists in the larger Baptist community. It was not until 1754 that the London Education Society, under the tutelage of Thomas Llewellyn, a Bristol trained lay theologian, attempted a semblance of ministerial education. It was in the provinces that Evangelical Calvinism was retained, although there were many discouragements. These Associations based their fellowship within churches and the Association, specifically on the third edition of the 1689 *Confession*. This determination in the Western Association, for example, was spearheaded by Bernard Foskett and Hugh Evans, both of Broadmead, Bristol, and meant that the Association was purged of the General Baptists and their incipient 'Unitarian' views by 1740, leaving the way clear for a slow, but early response to the challenge of the Evangelical Revival, particularly its manifestation under George Whitefield.

W. T. Whitley expressed the conviction that the denomination at this time was 'uncultured and had no aspiration after culture. The fallacy gained ground that God set a premium on ignorance, that piety and education were barely compatible.'[1] However, the growing concern for an educated ministry among Particular Baptists came not from London, but from churches of the Western Baptist Association. An educated ministry had become a possibility through

[1] Whitley, *A History of British Baptists,*, p.184

Edward Terrill, the Elder at Broadmead, Bristol, who by his deed of gift in 1679, endowed a programme for the theological education of such potential 'able and evangelical' Baptist ministers. Also in Bristol, three generations of the Gifford family, who were members at the Pithay, the first Bristol Baptist church, played a significant part in sustaining evangelical Calvinism, as well as encouraging an educated ministry. Andrew Gifford, Snr., pastor at the Pithay in the seventeenth century, rivalled Thomas Collier to be known as the 'Apostle of the West' because of his evangelistic preaching and church planting ministry. Andrew Gifford's grandson, also Andrew, was trained for the ministry under Samuel Jones at Tewkesbury, before becoming minister at Eagle Street, in London. There he was one of the founders of the British Museum and left his own considerable library to the Bristol Academy when he died in 1784. He often went to hear George Whitefield preach, claiming that he would be glad to light his 'farthing rushlight' at the evangelist's 'flaming torch'.

Robert Robinson

Robert Robinson

Robinson typifies a small, but significant number, of Baptist ministers at this time.[2] He found faith under the influence of the Evangelical Revival but it was through the ministry of George Whitefield, a Calvinist evangelical, rather than John Wesley. Robert Robinson became the minister of St Andrew's Street Baptist Church in Cambridge. Robinson was a radical in theology and in politics, who sought to promote 'rational religion', foster free enquiry and establish liberal sentiments. Rational Dissenters, as such ministers were often called, had outstanding ability and stood for reform and toleration, arguing for equal liberty and justice for all.

'Power in the people'

Robinson had a passionate concern to remove the social and political disabilities, which shackled Dissent in his day. In 1778 he published a series of lectures he had given at the Eastern Baptist Association, under the title *The Principles of Nonconformity*. They were approved by the Marquis of Lansdowne in the House of Lords, attacked by Edmund Burke in the Commons, and defended by Charles James Fox. The result was that the book went through many editions. Robinson's book was admired by Dissenters and reviled by their enemies, since it argued that *people* are the origin of power in Government. Benjamin Flower,

[2] See Graham W. Hughes, *With Freedom Fired: the story of Robert Robinson, Cambridge nonconformist*, 1955

Robinson's friend and editor of the *Cambridge Intelligencer,* reviewed the book thus: 'Few ministers of religion have been so well acquainted with foundation principles of good government or have inculcated such sentiments of civil and religious liberty as Mr Robinson.' A later publication by Robinson, *Political Catechism,* revealed his interest in political matters. In its preface he hoped for 'the everlasting death of toryism and the joyful resurrection of honest men'.

Robinson was a founder member of the Cambridge Constitutional Society, which was concerned with electoral reform. Among other Baptist ministers who shared his concern were Mark Wilks and Joseph Kinghorn, both in pastorate at Norwich. Robinson had deep sympathy with French Revolutionary thought and translated into English the *Paris Revolutionary Magazine.* He was more deeply attached to the Republicans' cause in the American Colonies and openly campaigned for them in their struggle for independence.

Robinson as author

Robinson held firmly to the view that God revealed himself in history and that God's will and purpose for mankind were best understood in this context. His two major historical works, *Ecclesiastical Remains* and A *History of Baptism,* were the fruit of years of historical research in which he used the past to illustrate themes of God's action in the present.

Robinson's book A *Plea for the Divinity of our Lord Jesus Christ* (1776) went through four editions in the year of its publication. It was a response to Theophilus Lindsey, an Anglican priest, who in 1773 became a Unitarian Dissenter and opened the first Unitarian chapel in 1774. Lindsey's decision brought many literary attacks, but Lindsey reckoned that Robinson's book was one of the very few that required an answer.

Robinson as Pastor

Robinson was known primarily as the pastor of his church. There is an interesting note in the Cambridge Baptist Church book for 1769 in which Robert Robinson, the pastor, argues that the worship is specifically in his control and he is unwilling to yield his responsibility to anyone else in the congregation. On November 18 that year the church book records:

> The pastor this day complained that, whereas the manner of conducting the public worship of the assembly was a branch of the duty which belonged to his office, he had been interrupted in this part of his work by certain heady people. They had not only found fault with certain tunes, which the best judges of music in the assembly had approved as proper church-music; but had done this at a lecture on a Lord's-day evening, a service which the church did not require, and over which they claimed no authority. A service which the pastor began and continued by desire of the gown and town. That his aim in diversifying the manner of worship in lectures was the good of his hearers in general, and the growth of the church in particular. That for these purposes he sometimes indulged even the prejudices of his hearers, by introducing a sprightly tune, and by preaching in another language and in another manner than he did in the CHURCH'S WORSHIP. That he devoted the Thursday evening lecture

> to the church, the Lord's-day evening lecture to the gown and town, and the monthly lectures in the country villages to the country-people, and thought it his duty to vary them all as well as he was able. He begged the church to believe the goodness of his intentions, to claim no jurisdiction over his lectures, but to leave him an entire liberty of conducting them as he judges most conducive to the public edification. All this was allowed. And indeed, what sort of discipline has that church, which, having no confidence in its pastor, submits his office to the control of every disaffected brother, however destitute of pastoral responsibilities he might be?[3]

Robinson is quite clear as to his role in worship and how that worship must be varied to meet the needs of diverse groups not only within the church but also in the local community. Hymn singing amongst Baptists caused great controversy for a good number of years. Eventually the impetus given by Isaac Watts encouraged Particular Baptists to pursue this with enthusiasm, and the thrilling songs of the evangelical revival under the Wesleys secured the tradition in the churches.

The Cambridge church book, during Robinson's ministry, also records the four types of monetary collections, which were made each year in the church. It illustrates the pastoral care and concern of all through the pastor. Money taken at the Lord's Supper was for church members. They took a second collection at Christmas to help their own members and those in the congregation. A third collection was taken at Midsummer to help with the expenses relating to the upkeep of the premises. Fourthly, there were occasional collections for other ministers in need, or for churches which had building repair programmes, although the latter were usually confined to one a year. The collection each Lord's Supper, Robinson recorded, was approximately a guinea each time. He then outlines how the money for the church's poor was spent.

> I find by the Poor's Book that from Jan 1st to June 24th 1774 there has been distributed among the poor of the church and auditory, in money, clothing, firing, etc., twenty five pounds one shilling ... Last Christmas the deacons purchased 40 ells of hemping at 1s.4d. per ell, which they distributed in shirting, shifting, etc., 45 yds of baize at 1s.1d. per yard for petticoats., beside stockings, handkerchiefs, and flannel waistcoats ... Two children of the widow Nottage and one of Will Johnson's have been taught to read and write by the deacons' allowance. Two old men and two widows have weekly payments ... The whole of the last six months is about £25.[4]

This was all part of the work of the church, which flowed out of its regular commitments in worship and was not uncommon among churches of the period. There was great variety in worship and undoubtedly much depended on the pastor's leadership, but there was a wholesome, caring concern in many Baptist congregations that is not always evident from the records.

[3] Roger Hayden, ed., *English Baptist Records, 2, St Andrew's Street Baptist Church Book, 1720–1832*, BHS, 1991, pp.45f

[4] *Ibid.*, pp.107ff

Hugh Evans

Bristol and Evangelical Calvinism

The Bristol Baptist Fund founded in 1717, though without the London insistence on ministerial control, was a West Country counterpart to the London-based Particular Baptist Fund. It was used alongside the provisions of Terrill's will to support ministers in training with the Broadmead pastors. It fell to Bernard Foskett, during his pastorate at Broadmead from 1720 to 1758, to put on a sound footing Terrill's scheme for ministerial training. In those years he trained over eighty ministers in equal number from Wales and England. John Rippon said of Foskett: 'some good scholars and several of our greatest ministers were educated by him'.

Hugh Evans

Foskett's associate minister, Hugh Evans, a Welsh minister whom he had trained some years earlier, followed Foskett as pastor and teacher at Broadmead. His son, Caleb Evans, who had grown up under Foskett as a boy at Broadmead, followed him. Caleb recalled hearing his father preach at Broadmead: 'Hearing the awful terrors of the law and the astonishing grace of the Gospel I was brought in very dust before the throne of a Holy God, and enabled to magnify the riches of free grace.' This Calvinism with an evangelical heart gripped the soul of Caleb, as his own personal *Confession of Faith* reveals. He begins by affirming the right of private judgement in religious matters as the undoubted and inalienable privilege of every rational, intelligent creature. 'I am accountable to God' he claimed, 'I cannot deny the doctrine of election ... this is the deepest lesson I learn from it ... with the deepest humility every believer ought to say "by the grace of God I am what I am".'

The Baptist Academy in Bristol at this period was the only effective Baptist training institution for ministers in England. Andrew Gifford, Jnr., of Eagle Street, London, together with Dr Thomas Llewellyn, who taught students of the London Education Society, were both evangelical Calvinists from Bristol, and it was to the Bristol Academy that both left their libraries in the 1780s. As had always been the case, individual ministers took students in to their own homes for training.

Caleb Evans

Caleb Evans (1737–91) had wide interests. He was educated at Mile End Academy in London and it was while in London that he was baptised at the Little Wild Street church in 1753. He assisted Josiah Thompson at Unicorn Yard until he was called to assist his father at Broadmead, Bristol, in 1759. He became Principal of the Academy and Senior Pastor of the church when his father, Hugh, died in 1781. Together they had put the Academy on a sound financial basis with the founding of the Bristol Education Society in 1770, which enabled individuals and churches to support the training of 'pious candidates for the ministry' and 'the encouragement of missionaries to preach the Gospel'. Evans himself undertook evangelistic preaching tours in the company of his students, the first in 1773 to Cornwall.

Caleb Evans

Politically, Evans though a Hanoverian loyalist, also expressed the opinion that the 'American question' of the Colonies and their independence was intricately interwoven with the British constitution and British liberty, and the American's resistance was 'one of the best causes in the world'.[5] Evans, while an advocate of radical political reform, nonetheless refuted republican ideals. Evans disagreed, publicly, with John Wesley when he contended the king had power to tax his subjects without their consent. Evans celebrated annually Guy Fawkes' night and the landing at Torbay on 5 November of King William.

Evans was involved in founding day schools at Downend and Broadmead. His Association sermon in 1775 urged the repeal of the Test and Corporation Acts and appealed for 'constitutional liberty'. A decade later he was to be found supporting Bristol's Anti-Slavery Group. When Caleb died in 1791 it could be rightly said that Foskett, Hugh Evans and himself had contributed significantly to the renewal of the Particular Baptists. In 1734 they had put the Western Association, which up till then had General and Particular Baptist in it, on a purely Calvinistic basis, rather than accept the growing General Baptist tendency towards Unitarian views. Outside London and the south-east, they had encouraged a vigorous evangelistic strategy through a programme of planting new churches, which they and the ministers they trained put into effect. To sustain this growth they trained over two hundred ministers of whom the vast majority worked in England and Wales, while some went to Ireland and America. They fuelled and welcomed the evangelical theology that led to renewal of the churches and the founding of the Baptist Missionary Society, which took the Gospel to the ends of the earth.

The first Baptist Hymn Book

Provincial Baptist churches were often divided over the issue of singing psalms and hymns, but for Particular Baptists, hymn singing was here to stay. As the

[5] Caleb Evans, *Political Sophistry Detected* Bristol, 1776, pp.14, 35

College Lane Baptist Church, Northampton, in the record of its 'Singing Society' for 1762 notes, it was agreed that 'Dr Watts's version of the inspired Psalms of David shall always have the honour to stand above every other book of divine poetry ...' and that the collection of tunes of Caleb Ashworth, from nearby Daventry 'shall be the standard book of this Society—not excluding at proper times any other Tune Book.'

Five years later the first specifically Baptist hymn book was published when Caleb Evans, with his friend and fellow student John Ash, of Pershore, produced *A Collection of Hymns Adapted to Public Worship*. It was the first Baptist compilation of hymns by different Baptist authors, although Watts and Doddridge still predominated, but it included many Baptist hymns from collections published by earlier Baptist hymn writers. Among them were the first published hymns of Anne Steele (1717–78), from Broughton in Hampshire, whose hymns became widely used in Britain and America, and others by Benjamin Wallin, Benjamin Beddome, Benjamin Francis, and Joseph Stennett.

Wallin's *Evangelical Hymns and Songs* (1750) was an earlier but intriguing publication because of his family connection with the Maze Pond church in London. This church had originated in a group from Benjamin Keach's church who opposed congregational hymn singing, where he had first introduced it in the late seventeenth century. Wallin's father Edward ministered to the Maze Pond church from 1703–30 confining public worship to the reading of Scripture, preaching and prayer. His immediate successor was Abraham West who made it a condition of his acceptance of the pastorate in 1736 that singing be allowed. If there were some in the church who hoped that the appointment of Edward Wallin's son, Benjamin, would mean a return to his father's ways, they were to be disappointed.

Benjamin Beddome, minister at Bourton-on-the-Water, for over fifty years was trained at Bristol Academy. Beddome prepared a few verses each Sunday to be sung after his morning sermon, quite a common practice among Baptist ministers at the time. Horton Davies describes Beddome as '... the indefatigable sermon summarizer in verse' who 'was only taking a leaf from Philip Doddridge's book.' The hymns began life as verses to follow a specific sermon Beddome had preached. Beddome allowed thirteen of these to be used in the Evans and Ash collection, and some years later thirty-six more were published in John Rippon's *Selection*. Julian, the hymnologist, realistically evaluated Beddome when he noted in 1907 that six of these hymns were still widely in use in Great Britain and America. Robert Hall, Jnr., who after Beddome's death edited 830 pieces for publication, wrote:

> The variety of the subjects treated of, the poetical elevation of some, the simple pathos of others, and the piety and justness of thought, which pervade all the compositions ... will we trust be deemed a valuable accession to the treasures of sacred poetry.[6]

Dr. Karen Smith has noted the particular contribution of Anne Steele, and

[6] Robert Hall, in *Preface* of Benjamin Beddome's *Hymns adapted to public worship or family devotion*, 1818

believes that among Particular Baptist congregations,

> Although the ministry of the Word was always intended for private application, it was in hymn singing that personal faith was given expression in corporate worship … It provided a means for preserving and communicating doctrine, and at the same time it allowed believers to rejoice together in their personal faith as they responded to God in corporate worship.[7]

When Ash and Evans published their Bristol collection in 1769 another Bristol student was beginning his training, John Rippon, from Devon. He published his own first *Selection* in 1787, recognising that most congregations wanted, by then, to supplement, not relinquish, Watts hymns and that was the secret of his success as a hymnbook publisher. It was Rippon who presented hymns in a stated order for use in public worship. He added hymns on certain themes, which he believed had been missed in earlier books, such as election, perseverance in the Christian life and the Holy Spirit. He also reflected the moderated Calvinism of the Particular Baptists in the early nineteenth century, adding to his selection hymns from the Wesleys. *The Comprehensive Rippon* was published shortly after his death, comprising 1174 hymns, which became the standard nineteenth-century Baptist Hymn Book, and was the precursor of contemporary Baptist hymnody.[8]

Influence of Jonathan Edwards

It was amongst some ministers of the Northamptonshire Baptist Association, which included self-taught and Bristol trained ministers, that a renewed Evangelical Calvinism emerged in the last third of the eighteenth century. The 'modern question', as it was termed, had first been under discussion among the Independents. Richard Davis, of Rothwell, Northamptonshire was so vigorous in his evangelistic ministry that it caused some of his Calvinistic colleagues to ask 'Whether it be the duty of all men to whom the Gospel is published, to repent and believe in Christ?'[9] In the ensuing years there was a lively exchange of views in tracts by Presbyterians and Independents. Among Baptists, Alvery Jackson, the Baptist minister at Barnoldswick, Yorkshire, answered the question affirmatively.

Initially it was the account by Jonathan Edwards of the revival in the American Colonies, at Northampton, Massachusetts, in 1735, that was a critical turning point in Baptist thinking. In his first major work Edwards wrote *A Faithful Narrative of the Surprising Work of God in the Conversion of Many Hundred Souls in Northampton and the neighbouring Towns and Villages.* (1736). The first copy known to be in the hands of an English Baptist minister was a copy of the 1741 edition that arrived in Benjamin Beddome's hands in 1742. It was in Edwards' pulpit at Northampton, Mass., in 1740, preaching on four occasions, that George

[7] K. E. Smith, 'The community and the believer: a study of Calvinistic Baptist Spirituality … 1730–1830', unpublished Oxford D.Phil, 1986, p.241

[8] Ken Manley, *'Redeeming Love Proclaim': John Rippon and the Baptists*, Paternoster, 2004

[9] J. Ryland, *Life and Death of Andrew Fuller*, 1816, pp.6–11; also G. F. Nuttall, 'Northamptonshire and the Modern Question: A turning point in eighteenth-century Dissent', *JTS*, xvi, pp. 101–123

Whitefield first felt the fires of revival burning, and took the experience back with him to England and so made his own lasting contribution to the Evangelical Revival.

In 1747 Jonathan Edwards had sought to rekindle the flames of revival and wrote *An Humble Attempt to Promote Explicit Agreement and Visible Union of God's People in Extraordinary Prayer for the Revival of Religion and Advancement of Christ's Kingdom on Earth.* It was this that John Sutcliff, of Olney, published in an English edition in 1784, and commended to the Association. It soon had Particular Baptists Associations round the country praying for revival, at monthly prayer meetings, held in most churches on the first Monday of each month.

It is almost impossible to exaggerate Jonathan Edwards' impact on eighteenth-century Particular Baptists. Out of his personal experience of revival and through his theological and narrative writing he demonstrated that Evangelical Calvinism could stand shoulder to shoulder with the Arminianism of the Wesleyan movement. He produced the theological keys that unlocked the closed doors of hyper-Calvinism, yet with absolutely no concession to Arminianism or Antinomianism. He fired the English Particular Baptist imagination with his own involvement with the revival and with his story of the remarkable missionary endeavours of David Brainerd among the American Indians. The Association *Letters* of the period are redolent with longing for revival, and it was through Edwards that the true heart of the old Puritan evangelical Calvinist fervour was once more kindled and released into the world.

John Sutcliff of Olney

John Sutcliff was a member with John Fawcett at Wainsgate, Hebden Bridge, and in 1772 he entered Bristol Baptist Academy for ministerial training.[10] He settled at Olney, Northamptonshire, in 1775 and soon became a close friend of the Olney Rector and one-time slave-ship captain, John Newton. Newton's diaries testify to their close relationship and in 1776 Newton provided hospitality at his rectory for the Baptist ministers meeting at the annual Association gathering.

By 1780 Sutcliff was in trouble with some among his hyper-Calvinist congregation who felt that he did not properly or sufficiently teach true Calvinism. At an Association gathering in 1783 Sutcliff affirmed that any person who did not know Christ as Saviour was the neighbour with whom Christians needed to share the Gospel. Sutcliff had been introduced to the writings of Jonathan Edwards by his Bristol tutors and it was Edwards who provided the theological and philosophical resources to overcome the problems he faced. Among many Particular Baptists, the views of John Wesley were suspect owing to his Arminian views, but Jonathan Edwards, as a thorough Calvinist was warmly welcomed.

A Call to Prayer 1784

When Sutcliff issued through the Northamptonshire Association, a *Call to Prayer*, which pleaded for concerted prayer for the general revival and spread of religion, it was set out in the following terms:

[10] M. A. G. Haykin, *One Heart and One Soul, John Sutcliff of Olney,* Evangelical Press, Durham, England, 1994, is a good modern account of Sutcliff

> The grand object in prayer is to be that the Holy Spirit may be poured down on our ministers and churches, that sinners may be converted, the saints edified, the interest of religion revived, and the name of God glorified. At the same time remember, we trust you will not confine your requests to your own societies; or to your own immediate connection; let the whole interest of the Redeemer be affectionately remembered and the spread of the Gospel to the most distant parts of the habitable globe be the object of your most fervent requests.

Sutcliff was moved by the journal of David Brainerd, Jonathan Edwards' son-in-law, who had died of the privations experienced while preaching the Gospel to the Red Indians in the so-called American 'wilderness'. In 1785 William Carey was a member of Sutcliffe's church and from that time both became deeply committed to the missionary task facing the church. Sutcliffe's challenge to pray each month for the revival of religion around the world was taken up across Britain by Baptist churches and was a significant factor in the founding of the Baptist Missionary Society in 1792.

In the seventeenth and eighteenth centuries, Protestantism in general had lacked a concern for the vast non-Christian world. Many at the Reformation would have argued that the Apostolic mandate was addressed to the apostolic age and was fulfilled then. The promises in the New Testament concerning the 'Gentiles' belonged to those nations who received and held fast the Gospel and were now part of the Christian community. Islam and other pagan religions were such as had, under one dispensation or another, rejected the light of revealed truth and sinned away their day of grace. Also many believed that the world would shortly come to an end.

Robert Hall, Snr., of Arnesby, another Northamptonshire Baptist minister, in 1779 had preached the Association sermon on Isaiah 65.14, and this was later published as the book *Help to Zion's Travellers* (1781). It began the process of challenging the hyper-Calvinism of the day and urged a new involvement in mission. William Carey, minister at Moulton, Northamptonshire, wrote to the friend who had given him a copy, 'I do not remember to have read any book with such raptures'. Thereafter he would walk twenty miles to hear Hall preach, and when Carey died in India many years later, among his few possessions was a well-thumbed, worm-eaten copy of Hall's book, with Carey's own notes made over the years, on almost every page.

Founding the Baptist Missionary Society

The Baptist Missionary Society had its origins in the *Prayer Call* of John Sutcliff to the Northamptonshire Association in 1784. It began a decade of serious re-thinking concerning the missionary task of the churches. The theology of Andrew Fuller, the self-taught Baptist minister at Soham expressed in his book *The Gospel Worthy of all Acceptation* (1785) was the next outworking of this new thinking. The burden on Carey's heart for the unevangelised millions of his day was detailed in *An Enquiry into the Obligations of Christians to use Means for the Conversion of the Heathens* (1792). As the Particular Baptist churches took up the prayer-call, the expectation of revival was uppermost in the minds of the ordinary church members, as month by month they sought it from God in

Andrew Fuller

prayer. The high Calvinism of John Gill, which had resulted in arid, dry, 'non-invitation' preaching, was superseded by the neo-Calvinism of Fuller, which clearly laid on Christ's disciples the responsibility for taking the Gospel to spiritually destitute men and women. The formation of the Baptist Mission presented a challenge to Carey to answer his own prayers and go himself halfway across the world to Asia to share the Gospel.

Andrew Fuller and the 'Modern Question'

The theological root of the matter was this: Have the unconverted a duty to believe the Gospel? In *The Modern Question ... examined* (1742), a tract by Abraham Taylor, an Independent minister, it was argued that 'the eternal God does by his word make it the duty of poor unconverted sinners, who hear the Gospel preached or published, to believe in Jesus Christ'. The book had a catena of texts demonstrating that John the Baptist, Christ and the Apostles *did* offer grace and salvation to the unconverted. It was a study of this book that led Andrew Fuller to attempt a modification of the high-Calvinism of his day. Fuller wrote thus of his early reading:

> The principal writings with which I was first acquainted were those of Bunyan, Brine and Gill. I had read pretty much of Dr Gill's *Body of Divinity,* and from many parts of it had received considerable instruction. I perceived, however, that the system of Bunyan was not the same as his; for that while he [i.e. Bunyan] maintained the doctrines of election and predestination he nevertheless held with the free offer of salvation to sinners without distinction. These were things which I could not then reconcile, and therefore supposed that Bunyan, though a great and good man, was not so clear in his views of the doctrines of the Gospel as the writers who succeeded him. I found indeed, the same things in all the old writers of the sixteenth and seventeenth centuries that came my way. They all dealt as Bunyan did, in free invitations to sinners to come to Christ and be saved, the consistency of which with personal election I could not understand.[11]

Fuller presented his reasoning over the issue in *The Gospel Worthy of all Acceptation, or the Duty of Sinners to Believe in Jesus Christ* (1785), which was rested largely on Jonathan Edwards' specific distinction between the natural and moral

[11] A. Fuller, *The Complete Works of the Revd Andrew Fuller,* 5 vols, 1,pp.xxix–xxx

abilities of men. Its publication launched him into a sea of controversy for the rest of his life, but 'Fullerism', as it came to be known, or 'moderated Calvinism', proved to be the significant theological factor in establishing the principle of world mission among the Particular Baptists.

William Carey

Fuller's thesis proposed it was the duty of all who hear the Gospel to believe in Christ with such a faith as issues in salvation. What is this saving faith? It is a real belief of God's report or record concerning his Son (Mark 6.15–16; John 20.31), which includes personal acceptance of Christ's promises. Later in his life Fuller wrote: 'I was not aware that any poor sinner had a warrant to believe in Christ for the salvation of his soul, but supposed there must be some qualification to entitle him to do so.' It was this which held back Fuller in his youth from full Christian commitment. 'If at that time I had known any poor sinner might warrantably have trusted Him for salvation, I conceive I should have done so, and found rest to my soul sooner than I did ... When I thought of the Gospel way of salvation, I drank it in, as cold water is imbibed by a thirsty man ... I thought I had the joys of salvation before: but now I knew I had found them and was conscious that I had passed from death unto life.'

The second part of the book comprised arguments to prove that faith in Christ is the duty of all who hear the Gospel. Unconverted sinners are commanded, exhorted and invited to believe in Christ for salvation. The Gospel requires obedience and such obedience includes saving faith. Scripture ascribes the want of faith in Christ to men's depravity and God has threatened and inflicted the most awful punishments on sinners for not believing on the Lord Jesus Christ. Whatever the Biblical doctrines of election, particular redemption, and human inability properly express, Fuller claimed the duty of preachers was clear:

> I believe it is the duty of every minister of Christ plainly and faithfully to preach the Gospel to all who will hear it ... I therefore believe free and solemn addresses, invitations, calls and warnings to be not only consistent, but directly adapted, as means, in the hand of the Spirit of God to bring them to Christ. I consider it as part of my duty which I could not omit without being guilty of the blood of souls.

Fuller was a self-taught man, but when he came into the Northamptonshire Baptist Association he was introduced to a remarkable ministers' meeting which included the Rylands, father and son, John Sutcliff, Robert Hall, Snr., and William Carey. It was Hall who introduced Fuller to the works of Jonathan Edwards, which was to prove crucial in meeting the charge of antinomianism that would be made against his new theology. It was John Sutcliff who introduced him to *An Address to the Serious and Candid Professors of Christianity* (1772) by Caleb

AN

ENQUIRY

INTO THE

OBLIGATIONS OF CHRISTIANS,

TO USE MEANS FOR THE

CONVERSION

OF THE

HEATHENS.

IN WHICH THE

RELIGIOUS STATE OF THE DIFFERENT NATIONS OF THE WORLD, THE SUCCESS OF FORMER UNDERTAKINGS, AND THE PRACTICABILITY OF FURTHER UNDERTAKINGS, ARE CONSIDERED,

BY WILLIAM CAREY.

For there is no Difference between the Jew and the Greek; for the ſame Lord over all, is rich unto all that call upon him. For whoſoever ſhall call on the name of the Lord ſhall be ſaved. How then ſhall they call on him, in whom they have not believed? and how ſhall they believe in him of whom they have not heard? and how ſhall they hear without a Preacher? and how ſhall they preach except they be ſent?

PAUL.

LEICESTER:

Printed and ſold by ANN IRELAND, and the other Bookſellers in *Leiceſter*; J. JOHNSON, St. Paul's Church yard; T. KNOTT, Lombard Street; R. DILLY, in the Poultry, *London*; and SMITH, at *Sheffield*.

[Price One Shilling and Six-pence.]

MDCCXCII.

The title page of Carey's 'Enquiry'.

Title page from an 'Enquiry'

Evans, and from which Fuller made an extensive and telling quotation in his book. Something of the impact the Northamptonshire ministers were about to make is reflected in the fact that Andrew Fuller was so apprehensive about the effect of his book that for four years after completing it he could not summon up the courage to deliver it to the printer!

William Carey and an 'Enquiry'

William Carey was closely identified with Hall, Fuller and Sutcliff in their search for a new understanding of the Gospel and was soon affirming that it was the duty of sinners to have faith in Jesus. This meant that all mankind must be presented with the Gospel by the Christian church. Carey's *Enquiry*, which he began while minister at Moulton, near Northampton, was published in 1792 at Leicester. He wrote in the Introduction:

> As our blessed Lord has required us to pray that his kingdom may come, and his will be done on earth as it is in heaven, it becomes us not only to express our desires of that event by words, but to use every lawful method to spread the knowledge of his name.[12]

Carey recognised that individual efforts were being made: 'but they are inconsiderable in comparison of what might be done if the whole body of Christians entered heartily into the spirit of the divine command on this subject.' The first section of the *Enquiry* argued that Christ's commission to his disciples was still binding on the Church, a position now so generally accepted that it is difficult to appreciate how revolutionary a view it appeared in 1792.

> It seems as if many thought the commission was sufficiently put in execution by what the apostles and others have done; that we have enough to do to attend to the salvation of our own countrymen; and that if God intends the salvation of the heathen, he will some way or other bring them to the gospel or the gospel to them.[13]

There then followed a wide-ranging view of missionary endeavours from the New Testament period to his own day. It contained a survey of the countries of the world, with their religious allegiance shown as either Christian, Jewish,

[12] W. Carey, *An Enquiry into the Obligations of Christians, to use Means for the Conversion of the Heathens* … 1792, reprinted 1991, p.31
[13] *Ibid.*, p.35f

Baptist Missionary Society house at Kettering

Islamic or pagan. He estimated the world population at 731 millions, of whom about 420 millions were pagan. The challenge is obvious 'to Christians, and especially to ministers, to exert themselves to the utmost.' A number of impediments prevented more being done for 'the conversion of the heathen' and Carey listed these as their distance from us, their barbarous and savage manner of living, the danger of being killed by them, the difficulty of procuring the necessities of life, or the unintelligibleness of their languages.

Carey was impressed by the efforts of traders and comments:

> It is no objection to commercial men. It only requires that we should have as much love to the souls of our fellow-creatures and fellow-sinners, as they have for the profits arising from a few otter skins, and all these difficulties would be easily surmounted.[14]

Carey then suggested a way forward: 'The first, and most important of those duties which are incumbent upon us, is *fervent and united prayer*.' He mentioned the Association *Prayer Call* of Sutcliff, and recognised that 'our monthly prayer meetings for the success of the Gospel have not been in vain'.[15] However, 'we must not be contented … with praying, with-out exerting ourselves in the use of the means for obtaining those things we pray for.' He put forward a 'society' idea, with a competent committee to administer its affairs.

> I do not mean … to confine it to one denomination of Christians. I wish with all my heart, that every one who loves our Lord Jesus Christ with

[14] *Ibid.*, p.95
[15] *Ibid.*, pp.103, 105

> sincerity, would in some way or other engage in it. But in the present divided state of Christendom, it would be more likely for good to be done by each denomination engaging separately in the work, than if they were to embark in it conjointly ... Surely', Carey concluded, 'it is worth while to lay ourselves out with all our might, in promoting the cause and kingdom of Christ.[16]

Within thirty years the theology of Fuller, linked with the 'society' method of Carey, transformed the face of Baptist church life in England. Responses to social and organisational factors undoubtedly contributed to the transformation, but as Dr L. G. Champion has suggested, there was at this time a 'renewed theology' that led to a 'rediscovery of mission and the creation of organisations for the fulfilment of mission'.[17] The willingness of Carey to translate his vision into reality by sailing with Dr John Thomas in 1793 assured the successful launching of the Baptist Missionary Society. The whole venture centred in a Biblical and theological understanding of the church's task. Only one thing needed attention—the financing of the object in view.

Getting Started

The *Periodical Accounts* recorded the developing life of the Missionary Society, and make it quite clear that the way forward was through the voluntary support of those who supported the project.

> As such an undertaking must needs be attended with expense, we agree immediately to open a subscription list for the above purpose, and to recommend it to others. Every person who shall subscribe ten pounds at once, or ten shillings and sixpence annually, shall be considered a member of the society.

The reason for this method was the impossibility of raising support from the whole Church of Christ, or even from every Baptist church, so finance was raised on the voluntary principle. It was a matter of expediency. The second resolution passed at the foundation meeting of the Society in October 1792 reads:

> As in the present divided state of Christendom it seems likely that each denomination, by exerting itself separately, is most likely to accomplish the great end of a mission, it is agreed that this society be called, The Particular Baptist Society for Propagating the Gospel among the Heathens.

It was now for the individual churches, and their members, to decide whether they would support the mission or not. Many did so generously, and it succeeded. The 'voluntary' principle was not a vital theological, nor even an historic Baptist, principle. It was simply the most convenient expedient for the financial support of the venture.

Within five years the need to evangelise at home as well as overseas was recognised with the formation of the 'Home' mission society in 1797, following a missionary tour of Cornwall, undertaken by the Baptist Missionary Society. 'Home' mission sprang from a conversation between two Plymouth ministers,

[16] *Ibid.*, pp.109, 112
[17] L. G. Champion, 'Evangelical Calvinism and the Structures of Baptist Church Life', BQ, 28, p.206ff

Philip Gibbs and Isaiah Birt, and John Ryland the Principal of Bristol Baptist College. Ryland wrote to Andrew Fuller, who invited John Saffery and William Steadman, both of Salisbury, to conduct an iterant preaching tour through Cornwall in 1796. A Baptist Society for 'the encouragement and support of Itinerant Preaching', formed in 1797, was the precursor of The Home Missionary Society.

10

Particular Baptists in a Changing World

WITHIN Particular Baptist churches, as the nineteenth century opened, there is no doubt that preaching was regarded as a powerful and formative influence in society. The period produced some ministers who were primarily powerful as preachers, within society at large and among their peers. A copy of an old print, which used to hang in chapel vestries, was a composite etching of Baptist worthies at the opening of the Victorian period, gathered round a vestry table. The group included the advocates of overseas mission, Carey, Fuller, Ryland, and Knibb, the essayist John Foster, and Joseph Kinghorn, the advocate of closed church membership and communion. But one man, standing in front of them all, dominates the scene. He is Robert Hall Jnr., an acknowledged 'prince of preachers', a vigorous social reformer and a champion of religious

Baptist Leaders

liberty. Throughout the nineteenth century preachers predominated in churches, and as far as Baptists were concerned, Robert Hall was the great pulpit orator when it opened. As the century progressed, John Clifford, who dominated London together with Charles Haddon Spurgeon, were well matched by Alexander McLaren in Manchester and John Fawcett at Hebden Bridge, Yorkshire, who were equally as popular and effective.[1]

Robert Hall junior

Robert Hall junior

Hall brought to the ministry a devotional spirit, a brilliant intellect and a profound grasp of philosophy, theology and public affairs. Primarily a doctrinal preacher on faith's fundamentals, Hall's sermons were firmly rooted in events. *The New York Observer* once commented: 'The springs of political government have also felt the touch of his unobtrusive but mighty hand. There is not perhaps a man living ... of whom the English politicians stand so much in awe. He explains to them the British Constitution, points them to the path of duty, arraigns them before the tribunal of the public, sifts all their proceedings, and dares even to speak against Mr Pitt!'[2]

One such sermon was delivered at short notice when he was called on unexpectedly to preach at Broadmead, Bristol. It was October 19, 1803. In the chapel a large congregation containing many servicemen in uniform waited for the 'public fast day' service to begin. The fast had been called as Napoleon stood poised to invade Britain. The oratory was superb as Hall concluded that 'the intoxication of his greatness is the omen of his fall'. *Sentiments Proper to the Present Crisis* became a best seller.

Another sermon attracting wide interest was *Modern Infidelity Considered* (1800). It went through many editions, was quoted at length by Sir James Mackintosh during his law lectures at Lincoln's Inn, and brought many to hear Hall during his ministry at St Andrew's Street, Cambridge. The sermon attacked the irreligion which was rooted in the philosophy of the French Revolution. 'Atheism is an inhuman, bloody, ferocious system ... its first object is to dethrone God, its next to destroy man.' Hall contrasted the moral results of irreligion and the ethical fruits of Christianity.

More typical of his preaching is this series of brief extracts from an evangelistic sermon, which appealed direct to the person.

[1] For a comparison of the McLaren and Facwett, see Ian Sellers, 'Other times, other ministries', BQ, 32, 1987, pp.181–198

[2] Graham W. Hughes, *Robert Hall*, 1943, p.84

> To be a partaker of Christ is to be at peace with God; to have peace of conscience, to possess a beneficent interest in all things, and an assured hope of everlasting life. He came that you might have life, and more than life. He came to give rest to your souls, to afford you strong consolation under the sorrows of the world, support in the hour of death, and an entrance when your mortal course is ended into the glory to be revealed ...
> While the bare possession of Christianity will bestow neither profit nor delight, the possession of it in reality will be replete with both ...
> Is the Saviour, the Lord of his Church, wooing your souls? Is he asking leave to come in? ... Open the door and let the King of Glory come ...

Social Reformer

An appeal on the subject of the Framework Knitters' Fund appeared as an anonymous tract in 1819. War and industrialisation made the period after the Napoleonic wars desperate. The government pursued a repressive policy against all who tried to organise workers in defence of their basic pay. Flying in the face of the Combination Acts, the tract argued for a workers' 'Union' among the stocking-makers of the Midlands area to prevent starvation and raise basic wages. The workers would contribute to a central fund from which fellow unemployed workers would be paid. The problem was that the stocking-makers already lived on starvation wages. To be out of work was even worse, so many workers would accept lower wages, a position which manufacturers exploited to the full to reduce overheads. The *Appeal* sought capital for the proposed central fund. It would benefit workers by supporting the unemployed and thus remove a cause of low wages. It would help by relieving the already over-strained parish poor-relief. Local tradesmen would benefit because the purchasing power of the workers would be increased and debts reduced.

The pamphlet called down the wrath of William Cobbett, author of *Rural Rides,* and it was at this point Robert Hall revealed that he was the author of the pamphlet and replied on behalf of the workers. Hall viewed Cobbett as 'shrewd, intemperate, presumptuous, careless of the truth of his representations and indifferent to their consequences.' Cobbett claimed employers could not afford to pay their workers more and the whole scheme would encourage idleness. Hall replied that already many employers in three counties had seen the wisdom of his suggestion and responded with gifts for the capital of the union.

Champion of Liberty

Hall opposed the slave trade, as had Caleb Evans and Robert Robinson before him, long before Knibb went to Jamaica with the Baptist Missionary Society. He said the slave trade 'degrades human beings from the denomination of persons to that of things ... The sale of human flesh is the most atrocious of social crimes.' He opposed the trade as 'most iniquitous in its origins, most mischievous in its effects, and diametrically opposed to the genius of Christianity and the British Constitution.'

One of Hall's most enduring publications, *An Apology for the Freedom of the Press* (1793), came early from his pen: and was reissued, largely unchanged, in

1822. From the beginning of his ministry Hall believed that Christianity was consistent with a love of freedom. He reasoned that fellow ministers should be involved in civil affairs, to cherish freedom, to work for it and when it was secured to maintain it. The *Apology* demanded universal adult suffrage, annual parliaments, and the independence of the House of Commons from the paralysing control of the rich. He asserted the need of a free press, a free church and a free state in which people governed themselves.

Itinerancy and rural Baptist growth

In the nineteenth century the Baptist community in Britain grew in size and significance particularly in the rural areas during the first half of the century. Dynamic village preaching by both ministers and lay people was responsible for this remarkable growth. The move among Particular Baptists into a moderate Calvinism was important and the influence of itinerancy among Methodists showed a way forward, but for Baptists the most powerful factor was the creation of the Baptist Missionary Society.

Soon after the founding of the Society, at a general meeting held in Birmingham in 1795, the challenge of 'the heathen at home' was accepted by setting aside funds for the mission at home. Two preaching tours organised in Cornwall in 1796 and 1797 were led by William Steadman of Broughton, Hampshire, helped by a Bristol Academy student, Francis Franklin, who was eventually to become the pastor at Coventry. Help provided by the fund met various ministers' expenses, which were incurred when they engaged in local village preaching. For several years Thomas Wastfield, a schoolmaster from Imber, Wiltshire, was enabled to itinerate in the Vale of Pewsey and the upper Avon Valley. By 1810 every English county had a dissenting itinerant society of some sort, many of them Baptist, which was a positive force in breaking down the isolation of independent churches, and encouraging a deeper Association life.

It also produced a change of emphasis on what it meant to be a Baptist minister. It challenged the static concept of ministry as the ministry of Word and Sacrament and the pastoral care of the people of God. It encouraged a new relationship between ministers and members who engaged in village preaching. It created an expectation of evangelistic pastors, like John Saffrey of Salisbury, who supported both home and overseas mission and also itinerated regularly in the villages round Salisbury. In the year 1796–1797 twenty-six members were added to the Salisbury church with nineteen more the next year, and of these, nine were from the surrounding villages in which the Salisbury Baptist itinerant preachers had been at work. The adoption of itinerancy by Baptists marked a transition from relative obscurity in the eighteenth century to their prominence in the next.

Itinerancy made striking progress in this period and one major contributory factor was that first the Bristol and later the Bradford Academies provided a number of ministers who were trained in village preaching and convinced of the need for aggressive evangelism.

The success of the initial phase of itinerancy meant the Gospel penetrated new communities, with a considerable accession of hearers and a lesser number of members to the new Baptist churches. The place of adherents in these churches, as distinct from members, produced an increasing breakdown of Baptist churchmanship. Itinerancy concentrated on the principal gospel themes but lacked an emphasis on the obligations of church membership, encouraging the development of a rural chapel culture, conscious of its Nonconformity rather than specific denominational allegiance.[3]

Baptist Home Missionary Society

These results were not so evident at the time and Baptists were pleased to co-ordinate their efforts in the work of the Baptist Home Missionary Society which was founded in 1797. By 1820 Baptists were employing some full-time evangelists with success, to supplement local ministries. Typical was the missionary to East Kent, who each week travelled some seventy to eighty miles, preached in five villages, ran a Sunday School for fifty children and conducted two prayer meetings; every fortnight he exchanged loan tracts and sold copies of the Bible; in addition he preached frequently in the open air in various unevangelised villages. By 1825 the Baptist Home Missionary Society supported twenty-five such missionaries, and in 1835 there were a hundred working across the country. After 1835 the Society increasingly turned its attention to the rapidly expanding population in the north of England. By 1850 one third of its three hundred stations were in urban situations, many of them in Lancashire. The Society also began to direct some evangelists to revive established churches through special 'protracted meetings', rather than planting new causes.

The word *revival* is a clue to much thinking about mission in the nineteenth century. Charles Hill Roe, the robust secretary of the Baptist Home Missionary Society in 1835, spent five years reviving existing 'feeble' churches. The revival services he conducted were based very much on the American model of Charles G. Finney in *Lectures on Revivals of Religi*on. Roe's health collapsed under the strain of work, and Thomas Pulsford took over the itinerating work in the north of England in 1839. Pulsford's 'flame of Pentecostal fire' was carried with vigour through the churches for a decade.

A growing tide of criticism, the deterioration of the Society's finances in the later 1840s, and the departure of two committee members to America were too much for the evangelist system. Criticism focused on the pressures that itinerant evangelists put on those who were unqualified and unprepared, to accept baptism and church membership, so that new converts, inflated with a sense of their own importance, lost confidence in their pastors whom they compared unfavourably with dynamic evangelists. The emphasis on revivals did damage to the Home Mission Society's task of 'extension'; and evangelists were increasingly asked to cultivate new areas, not to revive old ones. The result of such criticism was the termination of Pulsford's appointment. Baptists continued to benefit from the revivals but their commitment was cautious and often uncertain.[4]

[3] For a full discussion, D. Lovegrove, *Established Church, Sectarian People: Itinerancy and the Transformation of English Dissent, 1780–1830,* 1988

[4] R. Cawardine, 'The Evangelist System: Charles Roe, Thomas Pulsford and the Baptist Home Missionary Society', BQ, 28, pp.209–224

John Hinton on Evangelism

John Hinton

J. H. Hinton was typical of many Baptist ministers who stirred his members to take up personal evangelism. *The Means of a Religious Revival* (1828) began as a sermon on Matthew 5.13, given to his Reading congregation. Hinton complained that far too many Christians left evangelism to the minister and called for a new commitment to personal evangelism by all members.

> This cherished feeling of exemption on the part of Christians at large … is one of the greatest evils of the present age. There is no hope for a revival of religion, until this vast slumbering body is aroused to throw off the incubus, and to bend its energies to the effort. The Church has become a refuge from the world's trials. It should be as a fortress from which the soldiers of the cross are continually issuing, to assail the Kingdom of darkness, and rescue the captives of Satan. Hence, finally, it arises that even the ministry of the divine word has undergone a most injurious modification. The pastoral character in great part absorbs the ministerial. The edification of the Church takes precedence over the conversion of the world … its main address no longer to sinners but saints.

Hinton followed the printing of the sermon with two series of lectures in 1830 and 1831. The first, *Individual Effort for the conversion of sinners enforced* revealed Hinton's 'moderate Calvinism' as he argued all Christians are responsible for the condition of fellow men and women and must exert themselves to convert sinners. He discussed direct and indirect means of conversion, and the close connection between prayer, labour and success. *The Active Christian* published a year later is a straightforward guide to personal evangelism. Subsequently the two series were published under a joint title *Individual Effort and the Active Christian.* Another popular work of Hinton's provided a theological basis for such practical books on personal evangelism. It was called *The Holy Spirit's Work in Conversion.* Writing an introduction to his collected works in 1865, Hinton said these books: 'are to me an affecting memorial of a period of general religious excitement—too transient, alas! and unproductive—to which they owed their origin, but the topics treated of are not temporary or of an evanescent interest'.

Baptists Mid-century

When the census of 1851—the only official census of religion ever taken in Britain—was carried out, it revealed the considerable growth among Baptist churches. It reported that about 366,000 Baptists were spread across 1374 Particular Baptist chapels in England, the new Connexion of General Baptists met in 179 chapels, while the Old General Baptists, which were predominantly, though not entirely, Unitarian had 93 chapels.[5]

This was a significant advance compared with seventy years earlier. What had transformed the situation? In part it was the difference in ethos between the dullness of Brine and Gill, and the vigour of Fuller and the younger Robert Hall. Hall's description of Gill's eighteenth-century classic, *Body of Divinity*, as a 'continent of mud' typifies the mood swing. The theological shift was of Copernican proportions, but much more was at stake. Association life across the country had been stimulated and was advancing. Itinerant preaching, Sunday Schools, overseas mission, and an expanding programme of ministerial education as new colleges were founded in Manchester, Leeds and London, all strengthened Baptist advance.

Many 'Fullerites' believed themselves to be living in a new era for the denomination, in which there was a conscious return to evangelical roots. This was expressed in the moderation of Particular Baptist Calvinism to such an extent that by the close of the century integration with General Baptists of the New Connexion seemed logical, despite doctrinal differences. It was the spirit of the times to subsume doctrinal distinctives in a common *Declaration of Principle*, because since 1832 Baptist churches of both persuasions were united by a common loyalty to those sentiments 'usually denominated evangelical'.

An increasing range of literature presented the new spirit of the times. The theme of missionary advance and endeavour, at home and overseas, as the century opened, was presented each year in the pages of John Rippon's *Baptist Annual Register*, published from 1790 to 1802, together with historical themes which reminded the Baptist family of its glorious past. The *Periodical Accounts* of the Baptist Missionary Society and its successor, the popular *Missionary Herald*, were telling the story of missionary advance round the world.

There was a new engagement with problems facing communities around the world as well as at home. Carey was appalled by the custom of widow burning in India and actively campaigned against it. Two Bristol trained ministers, Grigg and Rodway, who were sent by the Baptist Missionary Society to Freetown, were unable to accept the conditions for black people in Sierra Leone, Rodway coming home for health reasons, Grigg choosing to go to America, where he spent his life opposing slavery in the South. William Knibb faced a similar political dilemma working in Jamaica, as he had been specifically told to stay out of the politics of the island. When he came back to England he declared that he was prepared to walk barefoot and penniless through the land with his wife and children rather than withhold the story of the appalling treatment of Jamaican Baptist slaves. All this contributed to a growing concern in English Baptist consciousness for liberty, physical and spiritual, personal and political, at home and abroad.

Baptists and Education

Education in England at the end of the eighteenth century was not available to all, and what primary and secondary education there was, reached only a tiny minority of the population. Initially the Sunday School movement

[5] E. A. Payne, *The Baptist Union: A Short History*, 1958, pp.78f, J. H. Y. Briggs, *English Baptists of the Nineteenth Century*, BHS 1994, pp.253–257 for a discussion of Baptist 'number, class and gender' at this time

offered education cheaply, but it depended upon voluntary labour. The non-denominational British and Foreign School Society, benefiting from the Quaker Joseph Lancaster, used senior scholars as monitors to teach the younger pupils. This nonconformist initiative soon produced a reaction from the Church of England, which founded the National Society in 1811 as its agency for educational development. The *Baptist Magazine* of 1811 was astounded that leading churchmen should so relentlessly attack any attempt to teach poor children to read the Bible. Joseph Fox, a surgeon and dentist at Guy's Hospital, and a Baptist deacon at John Rippon's Carter Lane Church supported the British and Foreign School Society with an endowment of £2000 and accepted office as one of its administrative secretaries. Until the 1870 Education Act most Baptists supported this Society in preference to a denominational school of any kind.

After the passing of the 1832 Reform Bill, a new parliament offered grants to the two voluntary institutions, such grants to be matched by each Society. The issue was not so much between church and dissent, as between an Anglican catechetical and credal education and the non-denominational Bible teaching of the other. Funds were distributed equitably at the start, but before long Dissenters were properly objecting to the majority of the grants going to Anglican schools.

In 1843 Peel's government announced a scheme for the compulsory education of pauper and factory children and this proposal was annexed to what was essentially a Factory Bill. This meant the public funding of Anglican education, since the new schools were to be funded by Government grants, money from the Poor Rates, and voluntary subscription. The Baptist Union strongly objected, viewing the new schools as 'high church nurseries' as against Baptist churches, which they perceived as 'nurseries of freedom'. The Union organised from within its constituency 13,600 petitions, containing over two million signatures, and shared in the rejoicing of Dissent at large, when the bill was abandoned in the summer of 1843. It was a nonconformist shot across the bows of the established church, which at this time was espousing a revival of Catholicism in its own ranks. The Baptist Union thanked the churches that had helped defeat the Factory Bill and warmly commended the British and Foreign School Society to the constituency.

Prior to W. E. Forster's Education Act of 1870, Church Rates had been abolished in 1868 and the Anglican Church had been disestablished in Ireland. Were the abolished church rates now to re-appear as educational rates in support of church schools? Education in the proposed new Board Schools was to be publicly funded, but by an alteration, the Temple-Cowper amendment, provided for non-sectarian religious education. By 1874 most Baptists were accepting the new situation provided by the School Board system. John Clifford was one Baptist leader who remained uneasy, claiming 'State Education is from first to last a question of citizenhood and not of Churchmanship or creed.'[6]

By 1902 the educational needs of the nation required radical restructuring. Balfour's Education Bill created a new system of secondary schools, abolished

[6] J. Marchant, *Dr John Clifford*, 1924, p.120

the School Boards, and made county and borough councils the local educational authority for all schools, elementary and secondary. Rate-payers would now be paying for Anglican, Methodist and Roman Catholic instruction. To many, if not most Nonconformists, this was a direct challenge: it meant: 'Rome was on the rates.' Balfour's Education Bill saw the launch of the so-called 'Passive Resistance Movement' led among Baptists by John Clifford. In 1907 it was noted that of 190 Passive Resisters sent to prison, 48 were Baptists, and they were reckoned to be the most active group among nonconformist resisters. Between 1902 and 1911 almost 5000 voluntary schools transferred to the local education authorities. The Government had won by establishing free universal elementary and secondary education as the civil right of all.

The search for religious liberty

Religious liberty was a constantly recurring theme in the nineteenth century and Baptists played a full part in the various societies that sought to remedy such grievances. The Anti-State Church Association was formed in 1844 to secure the disestablishment of the Church of England. In 1853 the Society became the Society for the Liberation of the Church from State Patronage and Control, or The Liberation Society.

Church Rates were a particular problem for Dissenters. They disliked paying these rates that could be levied in any parish by a decision of a majority of the parishioners and then used for maintaining the fabric of parish churches. Only Church of England clergy could celebrate marriages. Even burials in a churchyard had to be conducted according to the *Book of Common Prayer.* The taking of degrees at the universities of Oxford and Cambridge remained closed to Dissenters. Nonconformists at Cambridge were able to matriculate but not graduate; at Oxford they could do neither. The failure to remedy these and similar grievances, plus a rising sense of power among all Victorian Dissenters, led to a head-on clash in the mid-nineteenth century.

Test and Corporation Acts repealed

Like most Dissenters, Baptists were fully supportive of the House of Hanover, and ministers like Caleb Evans and Robert Hall Jnr, as well as Robert Robinson of Cambridge, celebrated each 5 November by preaching special sermons recalling the landing of King William at Lyme Regis on that date in 1688. As the centenary of the royal landing approached, events in France began to give a new content to the word 'revolution'. Dissenters had been beneficiaries of 1688, the Toleration Act of 1689 suspended enactments of the Clarendon Code, which had denied them freedom of worship, now allowed them to register their churches as places where dissenting worship could take place as a legitimate form of worship. In 1787 a move was planned to obtain political, as well as religious freedom, by the Repeal of the Test and Corporation Acts that had for so long hampered Dissenters' participation in the political life of the nation. However, in the light of the French Revolution (1789) and the subsequent threat of a French invasion, Dissenters found themselves under suspicion of revolutionary designs. It was Baptist minister John Martin, of Keppel Street, London, who openly voiced the fear that, should the French invade, many Dissenters would join with the French to achieve their full civil liberties. London Baptists, who excluded him from their Jamaica Street Coffee House meeting, disowned him and he was also barred from future meetings of the Protestant Dissenting Deputies.

Martin's view, however, was not entirely without foundation in respect of his fellow Baptists. Robert Robinson, as already noted, gave vigorous support first to the American Colonists and then to the French Revolutionaries. Morgan J Rees, a Welshman trained at Bristol Academy, was ordained in Wales in 1787 and was so fervent in support of the French Revolution that he went to Boulogne and opened a meetinghouse that was used as base for New Testament distribution. He rejoiced at having been present when the Bastille fell to the revolutionary forces. Returning to Wales, he was identified as a French sympathiser, and only survived arrest by taking passage to America in 1794. He lived the rest of his life there in the Welsh speaking Baptist community in Philadelphia, and he died there in 1804.[7]

Joseph Kinghorn

In Norwich, Joseph Kinghorn, the newly appointed young minister at Norwich, reading of the fall of the Bastille in the Norwich papers, wrote to his parents: 'I rejoice in my very heart at the destruction of that most infamous place, the Bastille, which the populace are regularly demolishing without any interruption from government who evidently dare not meddle with them.'[8] In Norwich the Revolution Society was founded in November 1789, at which Dissenters in the city

> declared themselves loyal subjects of the House of Brunswick but considered that every member of a civil society was entitled to participate in all its rights and privileges unless he had done something to forfeit them. They therefore regarded it as a most unmerited indignity that they were excluded from places of trust and profit under the government and they once more sought the repeal of the Test and Corporation Acts.[9]

Another strongly political minister was William Winterbotham, Baptist minister at Shortwood, Nailsworth, in Gloucestershire, who was imprisoned for allegedly preaching four sermons in support of the French Revolution. It was this mixture of loyalty to the throne, an active campaign for political and

[7] G. A. Williams, *The Search for Beulah Land*, 1988
[8] M. H. Wilkin, *Joseph Kinghorn of Norwich*,1855, p.163
[9] C. B. Jewson, *Jacobin City: a portrait of Norwich 1788–1802*, (1975) p.17

civil equality, which when mixed with the French Revolution and its notorious excesses, prevented progress towards repeal.

It was in 1811 that the Home Secretary Sidmouth tried unsuccessfully to amend the Toleration Act, not least because the Dissenters themselves disliked it. Dan Taylor chaired a meeting of the Ministers of the Three Denominations at Dr Williams' Library that lodged five objections to the proposals. In the next few years a number of changes took place, which forwarded the removal of Dissenters' political disabilities. In 1812 the Conventicle and Five Mile Acts were removed from the statute book and in 1813 toleration was extended to the Unitarian denomination. In 1814 the Chancellor proposed to make chapels exempt from local rating. Ivimey notes that 'in this 'arduous struggle' against the Test and Corporation Acts, 'the Baptists took their part.'[10] The Acts were finally repealed in 1828 and four years later the passing of the Reform Bill opened the way for Dissenters to appear in the House of Commons. The first Baptist to be elected to Parliament since Cromwellian times, was Morton Peto, a Baptist builder and railway contractor, who was elected for Norwich in 1847. The next year Robert Harris, a hosiery manufacturer, and a member of Harvey Lane, Leicester, was elected MP for Leicester.

The Liberation Society

'It is difficult to exaggerate' writes John Briggs, 'the way in which, from the 1840s onwards, a tremendous amount of Baptist energy ... was involved in campaigning against dissenting disabilities and ecclesiastical abuses...The most important aspect of the work ... was the campaign for the abolition of Church Rates for the upkeep of the fabric of a Church whose doctrine, liturgy and establishment they rejected.'[11]

Alexander McClaren

The activities of the Protestant Society, which monitored these happenings, were published regularly in the *Baptist Magazine,* which reported when dissenting worship was disturbed, or internment or marriage was refused, or an incorrect assessment of 'poor rates' made.

Baptist involvement in the Liberation Society can be judged by the fact that three leading Baptist ministers were among its active supporters. John Clifford, minister at Westbourne Park, Paddington, for fifty years, was a supporter of the Society. C. H. Spurgeon was identified with the Liberation Society throughout much of his life, and

[10] J. Ivimey, *History of the English Baptists,* 1811–1830, 4 vols, iv, p.117
[11] J. H. Y. Briggs, *The English Baptists of the Nineteenth Century,* BHS 1994, p.385

though he finally repudiated it, its Annual Meetings were held sometimes at the Metropolitan Tabernacle. Even the quiet and retiring Alexander McLaren of Manchester, was a member of the Society from the days when Edward Miall, his neighbour in Southampton, encouraged him to join. When McLaren was President of the Baptist Union in 1901, he apologised to the Secretary of the Liberation Society for non-attendance at the Society's Spring Meeting and assured the meeting that the Baptist Union would be fully supportive of the Liberation Society's objectives.

Abolition of the Corn Laws

After the abolition of slavery in the British Empire by the 1833 Act, slavery remained in the American South. However, the 1828 Corn Laws passed to stop imports of grain cutting the price on the home market, coincided with a series of bad harvests, and resulted in very high prices for grain in England. In 1835 two British Baptist ministers, F. A. Cox and James Hoby, were sent to make a 'friendly expostulation' with American Baptists about slavery in the South, but they were unsuccessful. They returned to England, convinced that the Corn Laws were keeping the American slavery system in place. The Americans argued that:

> ... if England desires America to be freed from slavery, England must receive the products of our free labour instead of the products of our slaves. Let then every abolitionist consider that view and strive in every lawful way to open your ports to the corn of our country which grows upon free soil, and is cultivated by free men.[12]

To struggle against the Corn Laws was, for Baptists, to continue the battle against slavery and for religious freedom and human dignity. The list of the Baptist members of the Anti-Corn Law League was almost a Victorian *Who's Who* of the denomination. William Brock of Norwich and Bloomsbury, Benjamin Evans of Scarborough, and J. H. Hinton of Reading were all supporters of the League, as was Thomas Price, editor of the *Eclectic Review* and personal friend of William Knibb. When Cobden called a meeting in Manchester in 1841 to urge that the Corn Laws were opposed to God's law, the Scriptures and Christ, 650 ministers were present. Of these, 182 were Baptists (more than would attend a Baptist Union Assembly for several years yet). The main speaker after Cobden was J. E. Giles, Baptist minister in Leeds, and a known Chartist sympathiser.

Religious liberty and human freedom have been essential principles of Baptists, arising from their understanding of the Gospel. As H. Wheeler Robinson once described it:

> There is, in fact, an unachieved liberty *within* faith as well as *for* faith, and its best safeguard is found in the dominating principle of Milton's *Areopagitica:* 'Give me liberty to know, to utter, and to argue freely according to conscience, above all liberties.'

The risk involved in honestly following such programmes of liberty was well put in the next century, at the Baptist World Alliance Congress in Atlanta in 1939.

> No man, no government nor religious institution, religious or civil, social or economic, has the right to dictate how a person may worship God or

[12] See K. R. M. Short, 'English Baptists and the Corn Laws', BQ, 21, pp.309–320

Charles Williams

whether he shall worship no God at all. In the continuance of our consistent Baptist practice we are imperatively constrained again to insist upon the full maintenance of religious liberty for every man of every faith and no faith.

Baptists in the North

In the north of England, Charles Williams of Accrington became a superb builder of the denomination. Williams was liberal in temperament, methodical in conduct, evangelical in experience, Baptist by conviction, and professional in training. He represented a new, and hitherto unknown, type of minister. When Williams was called to the Accrington Baptist church, whose previous pastor had been a Strict Baptist, there was a breach in the Association. A Strict-Communion Baptist Association was formed in 1860. By 1876 Williams had won it back into fellowship with the Lancashire and Cheshire Association. In doing so, he secured the commitment of the Association's churches to evangelism as a vital way of life for Baptist churches.

From 1876 onwards aggressive evangelism, church extension and the advance of God's kingdom became paramount. During a long ministry at Accrington, Williams led the church from a membership of 224 in 1850 to 625 in 1901. A new chapel was built in 1874; a Day School with 1575 children attending was opened in 1894; and at its height there was a Sunday School where 1154 children were taught each week by 133 teachers.

Williams was a great advocate of the Baptist Union. He was its President in 1886, and for many years he helped J. H. Millard, Secretary after Hinton, to develop the Union's role. He was responsible for establishing a Pastors' Income Augmentation Fund which within five years was distributing £1500 a year to augment the income of the lowest paid ministers. In 1875 Williams took responsibility for raising an Annuity Fund for sick and aged pastors and their dependants and by 1877 he had raised capital of £50,000. As if this was not sufficient, he was also fully involved in Association life, being the Secretary of the Lancashire and Cheshire Association for eight years from 1871. He epitomized Victorian evangelical Dissent and was a Baptist whose leadership inspired many in the Union. He said of himself:

> I profess to be a denominationalist. I hope to God I may never be a sectarian. I love the Baptists, as well I may, but I love them more for what I see of Christ in them than I do because they are Baptists, and when I see Christ in others I try to love them equally well, because the love of Jesus demands that we love all alike.

Personal example, theology, Nonconformity at its best, political or social affairs were all subject to one grand end as far as Charles Williams was concerned: that all people might discover a deeper faith in Christ and in the Bible. It was not only highly capable ministers but also churches in this period that showed great vigour and concern to make the social application of the Gospel a reality.

Independency and mission at Bacup

Just across the hills from Accrington is the Rossendale Valley where there had been Baptist work since the late seventeenth century. In Bacup, at the head of the Valley, there was one Baptist church in 1820, but by the end of the century there were nine. In Lancashire the fierce independency of local Baptist congregations was evident at every turn. Following personal differences in the Ebenezer Baptist Church in 1821, a new church was formed just across the town square at Irwell Terrace. There were then doctrinal disagreements at Irwell Terrace in 1854, which led to the formation of Zion Baptist Church, and in 1900 a dispute over the doctrine of 'conditional immortality' led to the formation of Mount Olivet Baptist Church.

The Valley was the centre of the newly industrialised cotton trade and the source of the River Irwell, just above the town, provided good water for dyeing and the power which turned the mill machinery. At the Irwell Springs Print and Dye Works the small village of Weir developed. It was here that the local dye works owner, out of his own personal funds, provided Doals Baptist Chapel for his workers, as well as supporting the Ebenezer congregation. Mr Shepherd, another local Baptist industrialist, gave £850 to build a chapel and Sunday School for the workers living around his Whitworth Mill, along the road towards Rochdale. The chapel community was decimated during the cotton famine of the 1860s, but in 1887 Mr Shepherd provided a further £1700 towards the cost of enlarged premises. The Waterbarn Baptist Church was commenced in 1838 at Orchard Hill, Stacksteads, to the south of Bacup, when members of the Irwell Terrace church living in the area gathered for worship in a local house. The chapel and schoolrooms were built at a cost of £2000, a 'penny' day school was opened, and, under the remarkable leadership of the Revd John Howe from 1851–1887, the church grew quickly. At his farewell he noted that during those years he had baptised 428 members, and of these, 70 were young people who had all been baptised in 1869. He recalled the contribution of Robert o' th' Moss, one of the so-called 'Deign Layrocks', as the local Lancashire dialect termed this company of Christian musicians and preachers. Robert would ascend the pulpit, give out the first hymn, then descend to the singing pew where he had carefully placed his violin-cello, start the tune, conduct the hymn, then re-ascend the pulpit and continue the service. He would bring his lunch with him, wiling away the time by playing his 'cello until it was time for the next service.

He also remembered with affection one of his deacons, James Cox, a printer and bookseller who had come to Stacksteads from Haddenham in Cambridgeshire about 1848. He was an educational pioneer in Day and Sunday Schools. It was he who carried on the 'Penny Day School' for 25 years and taught nearly 200 adults to read and write at his weekly night school. He started the Mutual Improvement Society, where on three nights a week he taught a class of 24 men to read, as well as writing, arithmetic, dictation, essay writing and biblical instruction, all of which, stated the Fifth Annual Report, 'creates mutual

Henry Howarth

love towards one another, a love which cannot be obtained at the ale-bench, or the gambling table, or the foot race, or the theatre, where young men may be trained up to all sorts of infamy and wickedness.' There were also others in the church of distinctive character and considerable spirituality; people like Henry Howorth who lived up on the hill and 'would always take the prayer meeting if they would put him down for a moonlight night'.

A group of out-of-work cotton spinners came to Bacup from Heptonstall Slack, Yorkshire, in 1852. They were seven families of General Baptist persuasion and as all the Baptist churches in Bacup were Calvinist, they formed their own church and built a chapel in 1872.

Bacup was typical of towns across the United Kingdom where the industrial revolution brought many people together for work. Baptist churches were strongly independent and they multiplied because of industrial growth, personal and doctrinal disputes, and also because several of the churches had a genuine concern to meet the spiritual and social needs of the people.

Industrial Revolution in Burnley

Burnley, to the north of Accrington, presents a similar pattern of Baptist independency and growth. In 1801 it had a population of around 4000. Fifty years later it had become 20,000 and by the end of the century it was just short of 100,000. An obscure Lancashire hamlet had become a significant manufacturing town. Burnley Baptists originated in the work of Dan Taylor, of the New Connexion of General Baptists, with their Ebenezer Chapel in Colne Road opening in 1787.

The small village of Sabden, just outside Burnley, also had Baptist work begun as the nineteenth century opened. It was founded by John and James Bigy who owned the calico-print works there. Richard Cobden remarked on the way they cared for the work force, when he worked there, as a light to the surrounding countryside. The Padiham Church founded this village cause in 1840.

The Colne Road members started Sion Baptist Church in 1828, when a Sunday School was formed. In 1831 a chapel was built and in 1884 a complete new suite of Sunday School buildings was erected. Aenon, a General Baptist Church, was begun in another part of the fast growing town in 1852, and it was in this chapel that the historic decision was taken in 1891 to merge with the Particular Baptists in the Baptist Union. Aenon itself started new work in a smithy in the High Street in 1884 that became Broughton Street Baptist Church with its own chapel in 1892.

Even C. H. Spurgeon had a hand in Baptist advance in Burnley. After correspondence between some Burnley Baptists and himself, he sent C. W. Oldring, from the 'Pastor's College' to begin a new work that was to become the Mount Pleasant Baptist Church.

There were also in Burnley, unusually, three so-called 'Scotch Baptist' churches at Haggate, Angle Street, and Brierfield. They were Baptists who maintained Calvinistic doctrine and ordained lay elders to lead the community.

In this microcosm of Baptist life in the nineteenth century there is ample evidence of the vitality of the independent churches as they sought to meet the challenge of the new age. The evangelistic task of the church was tackled aggressively through a wide range of educational and social programmes, in a fearless and buoyant spirit typical of the age. It was also typical of the Victorian period that the differences between Calvinist and Arminian were progressively eroded until the merger of 1891 seemed the appropriate way forward.

11

The Baptist Union and C. H. Spurgeon

AS the nineteenth century progressed the importance of a national agreement between those with Baptist views whether Calvinist or Arminian required some kind of formal organisation. Baptists, like other Nonconformists, were experiencing a growing self-awareness. Methodism in its several manifestations, Wesleyan, Primitive and New Connexion, had reasonable levels of national organisations, as did the Society of Friends (Quakers) through its annual London Meetings. Congregationalists were caught up in these centralising pressures and eventually created a voluntary union of churches to meet the national situation.

For Baptists, the movement towards a national organisation sprang from the demands of support for overseas missionary work. It was following a London-based meeting in 1812, where sermons were preached in aid of the Baptist Missionary Society, that a group of ministers met in Carter Lane chapel. They were concerned with 'the promotion of the cause of Christ in general, and the interests of the denomination in particular with a primary view to the encouragement and support of the Baptist Mission.'

When they met again in 1813 it was as a company of Particular Baptists who still accepted the doctrine of the 1689 *Confession of Faith.* John Rippon was a prime mover in the formation of the Baptist Union and recognised that it could have a wider place in the life of the British churches. He hoped its annual Assembly would consider 'whatever relates to the real issues of the denomination at home or abroad'. The constitution stated that the Baptist Union's first task was the support of 'our missions'. In its origin the Union was a voluntary fund-raising arm of the Baptist Missionary Society. Any attempt to superintend or guide the life and work of local churches, or to impose anything on their faith and order was specifically disclaimed. The original title of the organisation was 'The General Meeting of the Particular (or Calvinistic) Baptist Denomination' and remained so until 1873 when it became the Baptist Union of Great Britain and Ireland. By then, however, it was known by the brief title, The Baptist Union.[1]

Not surprisingly one of the first treasurers of the infant organisation was Mr Burls, then the treasurer of the Baptist Missionary Society. The Baptist Union was

[1] E. A. Payne, *The Baptist Union: A Short History*, 1958, pp.15–42

run from the homes of its secretariat until 1849, after which rooms were rented in the Mission House, Furnival Street, Moorgate. The Union recommended the forming of 'Auxiliary Societies in aid of the Mission', as well as collections for other Baptist philanthropic and educational interests. It was not until 1903 that a specific national headquarters, Baptist Church House, was opened in Southampton Row.

Re-organisation and development

The Union was re-organised in 1832. It was felt sufficient to describe it as a union of Baptist ministers and churches who 'agree in the sentiments usually denominated evangelical'. This opened the door to co-operation with the New Connexion General Baptists. What actually happened in 1891 was the dissolution of the General Baptist Association and the redistribution of its member churches among existing Particular Baptist Associations. In fact, this was not too difficult an exercise since many already shared in local matters. It was this aspect which deeply affected some of the more rigidly Calvinistic Baptist churches and led to the organisation of Strict and Particular Baptist structures outside the orbit of the Baptist Union.[2]

One main purpose of the Union was to encourage growing denominational awareness and mutual help between ministers and churches. It was to 'promote unity of exertion in whatever may best serve the cause of Christ in general and the interests of the Baptist denomination in particular'. To this end it was agreed to collect 'accurate statistical information' from the denomination's churches, societies, colleges and institutions, both in Britain and abroad. An annual report of the proceedings of the Union and the state of the denomination was published, and this helped the struggling Union to be known in the constituency and to grow. Joseph Belcher, minister at Chelsea, produced a statistical survey, which demonstrated that the denomination in England had trebled in size since 1790. It revealed considerable denominational strength in the West of the country, growth in Yorkshire, but very little progress in London.

Between 1832 and 1873 the Union struggled to find its place in Baptist life, but with the firm leadership of Edward Steane, from Camberwell, and J. H. Hinton, from Devonshire Square, its work gradually developed. The graph of Baptist numerical growth dipped slightly at the end of the 1840s but produced an upward curve in the next two decades.

In 1855 *The Freeman* appeared, a weekly Baptist newspaper, and a forerunner of today's *Baptist Times*. The paper was launched by a Leeds printer at the suggestion of the Revd Dr Benjamin Evans of Scarborough and was soon a considerable influence among Baptists nationwide. In the same period the Stepney College for training Baptist ministers moved from the East End to Regent's Park in London, to be closer to the new London University.[3]

[2] For the life of these churches, see K. Dix, *Strict and Particular: English Strict and Particular Baptist Churches in the 19th Century*, BHS, 2001; and Geoffrey Breed, *Particular Baptists in Victorian England*, BHS, 2003

[3] E. A. Payne, *The Baptist Union: A Short History*, 1958, pp.59–90. R. E. Cooper, *From Stepney to St Giles, The Story of Regent's Park College, 1810–1960*, 1960

Unity with diversity

In 1863 J. H. Hinton, aged 72, reflected on the state of the Union from its Presidential chair, albeit pessimistically:

> Denominational union among Baptists has been slow in manifestation, and difficult of cultivation ... The Baptist denomination, while in name one, is in *fact* many ... it is divided into two by a difference of doctrinal sentiment, some churches holding the Calvinistic system, some the Arminian ... Of these two bodies the larger, or the Particular Baptists, is itself divided by a doctrinal diversity, according as the Calvinistic system has been found capable of being modified into two forms, which have been called High and Moderate Calvinism ... The Particular Baptist body is further divided by a practical diversity on the subject of communion. It contains churches which restrict fellowship at the Lord's Table to persons who have made profession of their faith by Baptism, and churches who admit to Communion professed believers in Jesus, although unbaptised. These are called respectively Open-Communionists and Strict-Communionists. We have then six parties.

Hinton, though cautious about the Union's future and usefulness, had himself contributed significantly to its increasing effectiveness, and the work grew rapidly in the next thirty years.

The Spurgeon Century

One person dominated nineteenth-century Baptist life like a 'Colossus' and was born in 1834 at Kelvedon, Essex, into the family of a Congregational minister, the first of ten children. Charles Haddon Spurgeon was largely brought up by his grandparents, his grandfather also being a Congregational minister. As a child he read Puritan writings like Richard Baxter's *Call to the Unconverted* and Philip Doddridge's *Rise and Progress of Religion in the Soul* (1745). He was converted through the ministry of a Methodist lay-preacher when snow forced the young Spurgeon unexpectedly into a local chapel. Spurgeon was baptised in his early teens at Isleham Ferry in Cambridgeshire, about eight miles from his Newmarket home.

Isleham Ferry

Waterbeach Chapel

He began work in a Cambridge school and joined the St Andrew's Street Baptist Church, serving as a Sunday School teacher. He began preaching in his early teens and became pastor at Waterbeach, Cambridgeshire, when only seventeen.

In November 1853, he was invited to preach at New Park Street, Southwark, in the city of London. He preached, was invited to accept the pastorate, and at the age of twenty became the minister who was soon known in London as 'the boy preacher'. He was an orator and an elocutionist, dramatic to the finger-tips, whose imaginative, lively preaching soon filled the chapel each Sunday.

At his recognition service (he did not favour ordination), Spurgeon said:

> I am not ashamed to avow myself a Calvinist, although I claim to be a Calvinist according to Calvin rather than after the modern fashion. I do not hesitate to take the name Baptist ... but if I am asked to say what is my creed, I think I must reply, 'It is Jesus Christ' ... who is the sum and substance of the Gospel, who is in himself all theology, the incarnation of every precious truth, the all-glorious embodiment of the way, the truth and the life.

The New Park Street Chapel was soon replaced with the Metropolitan Tabernacle, which could seat five thousand people and was usually full each Sunday during Spurgeon's ministry which lasted till 1892.

Spurgeon's widespread influence

Spurgeon was a great philanthropist who encouraged others in their work, people like John Groom working for disabled people and Charles Montacute who worked in London for forty years among destitute slum children. Spurgeon's particular concern for children was reflected in his founding of the Stockwell

C. H. Spurgeon

orphanage, which eventually became Spurgeon's Homes, now Spurgeon's Child Care.

Ten years later he began a Colportage Society that took books, pamphlets and tracts to people around the country and offered a personal ministry of care to the sick and the bereaved. There were soon fifty men doing this work with an annual turnover of £3000 from sales. Spurgeon was himself a prolific writer, publishing well over a hundred books, and each week his Sunday morning sermons were printed and sold throughout the country for a penny each.

Spurgeon contributed to Baptist national awareness in a number of ways. He was first and foremost, for over forty years, one of London's greatest and most popular preachers. This drew thousands of new members into Baptist churches, not only at the Metropolitan Tabernacle but nationwide. When in 1856 he founded the 'Pastor's College', now Spurgeon's College, he contributed significantly to the growth of the denomination. In the College many men from the working classes, who possessed ministerial gifts, were encouraged to become better equipped for the work of Christian ministry. With the help of these new ministers, Spurgeon was responsible for founding many new churches, most of them in London and the Home Counties.

When a new cause started, Spurgeon's lawyers at the Metropolitan Tabernacle drew up the Trust Deeds. As the work achieved independence the property was invested in individual trustees, appointed by the new church itself. In a letter written to one such church at its opening, Spurgeon expressed his own understanding of being Baptist in Victorian London. 'Cherish full sympathy with the great denominational movements and seek association with sister churches that you may take your part in the work to be done.'

Spurgeon threw the denominational principle of believers' baptism into the arena of public debate with other evangelicals in the Evangelical Alliance in 1865. He made an outright attack on infant baptism, especially as it was expressed in the rites and ceremonies of the Anglican *Book of Common Prayer.* By 1875, William Landels, minister at Regent's Park chapel and President of the Baptist Union that year, rejoiced that baptism, 'our distinctive principle' was recognised as 'the very essence of Christianity'. Spurgeon, Brock and Landels were three leading ministers in the formation of the London Baptist Association in 1865. It had as one of its

Metropolitan Tabernacle

primary objectives the formation of at least one new Baptist church each year.

Spurgeon was active in his support of this part of the programme. At the opening of the new London Baptist Association chapel at Haven Green, Ealing, in 1881, which had been sponsored during his year of office by the Association President, John Clifford, Spurgeon preached at one service and Clifford at the other.

The origins of 'Down-grade'

It was in 1873, at a meeting of the Baptist Union Council, that Charles Stovel, a prominent member since 1832, successfully moved that there be a further change in the Baptist Union's Constitution. It was proposed that a Declaration of Principle replace all previous formulations.

> In this Union it is fully recognised that every separate church has liberty to interpret and administer the laws of Christ, and that immersion of believers is the only Christian baptism.

The assertion of liberty meant Victorian individualism dominated much Baptist thinking at this time. Doctrinal statements were unfashionable, and *Confessions* of the previous 250 years were set aside. Open or closed membership and communion issues were put into the background and Baptist unity founded solely on congregational independence and a mode of baptism.

However, among some Baptist ministers of the period there was a move towards Romanticism, and this expressed itself in the pulpit and public worship as a fashion for quoting poetry, especially Wordsworth, and in the elevation of feeling at the expense of doctrine. The embodiment of these aesthetic and cultural influences was S. A. Tipple, the Baptist minister at Upper Norwood Baptist Church, a mile or so from Spurgeon's private residence.

> The services at Central Hill started at five past eleven to allow the train to arrive with the more influential members of the congregation from the West End: the church was closed for the summer when the minister was not there ... The tone of Tipple's mysticism may perhaps be indicated from the following titles (in a book of prayers): 'Union Amidst Many Differences in Prayer and Praise' ... 'The Intimate God, Whom Seeking to Express in Our Creeds, We Leave Even Unexpressed', a delicate statement of the superiority of spiritual over credal religion; 'Through All and In All', a summing up of Tipple's concern to see the universality of God: there is no word more frequent in the title of his prayers than the word 'all'.[4]

In April 1887 Spurgeon attacked such aesthetic preaching in his church magazine, *The Sword and Trowel.*

> Those who hold the eternal verities of salvation and yet do not see all that we believe and embrace, are by no means the object of our opposition: our warfare is with men who are giving up the atoning sacrifice, denying the inspiration of Holy Scripture, and casting slurs upon justification by faith: we care far more for the central evangelical truths than we do for Calvinism as a system.

Spurgeon also led Baptist reaction against the Biblical criticism which dominated this period. He saw the change to the Baptist Union's basis in 1873 as a final repudiation of doctrinal unity among the churches and urged the adoption of the Evangelical Alliance's credal statement. He was increasingly unsympathetic towards those ministers in the Baptist Union who accepted the results of Biblical criticism. Typical of such ministers would be Richard Glover of Tyndale, Bristol, who was frankly interested in Darwin's researches and did not see why that barred him from keeping company with the New Testament. F. W. Gotch, Principal at Bristol Baptist College, was one whose modern critical approach was recognized by his appointment to the translation panel of those producing the 1884 Revised Version of the Bible.

'Downgrade'

The denomination was clearly surprised by the public controversy, which followed the publication of two unsigned articles in Spurgeon's magazine in the spring of 1887, under the title 'Downgrade'.[5] They were written by Baptist minister Robert Shindler and attacked the spiritual declension of the day. In August, September and October 1887 Spurgeon wrote three further signed articles on the issue. They contained pointed references to certain ministers, not named, whose beliefs were 'no more Christianity than chalk was cheese', who 'derided Scripture', who 'degraded the Holy Spirit into an influence' and who turned 'the resurrection into a myth'. Yet Spurgeon claimed that in the Baptist Union, 'these enemies of our faith expect us to call them brethren and maintain a confederacy with them.'

On 25 October 1887, Spurgeon wrote to the Baptist Union Secretary, Samuel

[4] J. H. Y. Briggs, 'Image and Appearance', BQ, 23, p.26
[5] E. A. Payne, *The Baptist Union: A Short History,* 1958, pp.127–143; J. H. Y. Briggs, *The English Baptists of the Nineteenth Century*, BHS, 1994, pp.175–189

Harris Booth, resigning and complaining that these 'so-called Christian Unions ... begin to look like Confederacies in Evil'. The news made national headlines; a special meeting of the Baptist Union Council was called, and in January 1888 Booth, the Union's President (John Clifford), and a Council member, James Culross, (President of Bristol Baptist College) met Spurgeon privately, but to no avail. The resignation was accepted and a vote of censure was passed on Spurgeon for making allegations against individuals whom he repeatedly refused to name.

Spurgeon's death commemorated

It fell to John Clifford to handle this matter in the Assembly meeting of 1888. In the morning his Presidential address, titled *The Great Forty Years: The Primitive Christian Faith, its real substance and best defence,* had been masterly. It made clear how he would handle the business of the afternoon, for the address had as its thesis that 'the history of Christianity is the history of controversy', which he illustrated from the New Testament. 'The evils of controversy are all temporary and its benefits are all permanent', he argued. He concluded by addressing the 'modern questions' that faced young people.

> We shall not save or help them by the clashing of our creeds ... Worse than useless will it be for us to ban thinking and denounce enquiry ... [The divine vocation is to be] steadfastly resting on the FACTS, joyously experiencing the FORCES, clearly teaching and powerfully embodying the IDEAS of the Great Forty Years of the Christianity of Jesus Christ.

At the afternoon session a Declaratory Statement of Faith was read and approved by the Assembly, which affirmed that the Union is:

> an association of churches and ministers, professing not only to believe the facts and doctrines of the Gospel, but to have undergone the spiritual change expressed or implied in them, [a change which is] the fundamental principle of our church life.

It then listed and briefly explained six facts and doctrines commonly believed by the Union's churches. They were

> the divine inspiration of Scripture,
> the fallen and sinful state of man,
> the person and work of Jesus Christ,

> justification by faith,
> the work of the Holy Spirit,
> the resurrection and judgement at the Last Day.

The aftermath of the controversy

The Baptist Union survived both the theological reductionism that characterised the nineteenth century and the withdrawal of Spurgeon from its ranks.[6] For Spurgeon the immediate safety of those who love the Gospel was:

> in the isolation of independency, tempered by the love of the Spirit of Christ which binds us all to the faithful in Christ Jesus ... [where] we think the lovers of the Gospel will for the present find their immediate safety.

Such isolation was soon tempered for Spurgeon by his membership of the Surrey Baptist Association. Ministers who supported Spurgeon, many of them trained at the Pastor's College, realised that such isolation was impossible for them. As Ernest Payne noted:

> The pastor of the Metropolitan Tabernacle might speak like this. For the minister of the average Baptist church the situation was different. The Augmentation and Annuity Funds, Home Mission and the Board of Introduction were drawing together and supplementing the resources of the individual churches, carrying out tasks they could not otherwise fulfil. The necessity of union had to be balanced against any desire for complete uniformity of doctrine.[7]

The churches, as well as the leaders of the Baptist Union, were determined to maintain the corporate life that had been established. Despite changing ways of thought and expression, all believed the fundamental loyalty of the denomination was to evangelical Christianity. The Baptist Union emerged from 'Downgrade' shaken but not shattered. Various addresses at the Baptist Union meetings that followed 'Downgrade' reveal a growing concern to explain the way in which working ministers might relate to the challenge of the new approach to Scripture.

In statements issued after 1888, the Baptist Union itself firmly asserted the centrality of the Scriptures. In that year, replying to the Archbishop of Canterbury's letter concerning fuller organic Christian unity, the Union agreed that: 'The supreme authority of Holy Scripture in matters of religious faith and duty is a cardinal principle underlying our Church organization and individual life'. This scriptural emphasis led to the assertion in the same letter of the importance of 'non-sacerdotal religion', believers' baptism and church government.[8]

Particulars and Generals unite

'Starting from different theological and geographical centres, fed and nourished on a different theological diet,' General and Particular Baptists came together, said John Clifford, 'slowly, shyly and surely.' A further moderating of Calvinism

[6] E. A. Payne, *The Baptist Union: A Short History,* 1958, pp.144–155
[7] *Ibid.*, p.142–3
[8] *Ibid.*, pp.145, 272–274

among the Particular Baptists, the growth of open-communion churches in both bodies, and working together over thirty years on the common platform of the Baptist Union, made possible the formal uniting in 1891.

J. H. Shakespeare

The Union had left far behind the outdated eighteenth-century methods which it inherited in 1813 and in 1832 re-organised itself in such a way that Baptist ministers and churches recognised the potential of union for furthering the mission of the churches in a rapidly expanding industrial society. The churches realised the necessity of permanent officers if the Union was to succeed, and in this respect moved in a different direction from the General Baptists, who although nationally organised always ran the national network through a committee of ministers and lay people. Samuel Harris Booth served as the first permanent Secretary of the Baptist Union from 1883 to 1898. Increasingly both Particular and General Baptist wings of the denomination saw the Baptist Union as providing a place for working together and getting to know each other. The Presidential Chair of the Union became a place for leaders in both denominations to provide innovative and imaginative leadership.

John Howard Shakespeare was appointed to lead a united Baptist community in the twentieth century, as Baptist Union General Secretary in 1898. Shakespeare worked hard to create a new constitution for the Union and a number of departments to develop Baptist work nationally, and prepared the denomination for a new future within the national church scene in England. As the nineteenth century closed Baptist churches still had a rising membership, Sunday Schools were well attended, and the Liberal-Nonconformist alliance seemed to offer considerable political scope for the wider community of Dissenters. However, as John Briggs concludes his study of nineteenth century English Baptists:

> The denomination under Shakespeare was better organized and more coherent than that of earlier generations but it was already facing formidable sociological, intellectual and cultural problems before the carnage of the Western Front burst the bubble of liberal optimism with which modern dissent had too readily identified itself ... The world of 1918 offered as great a challenge to the churches as the turbulent world at the end of the Napoleonic Wars had done a century earlier.[9]

[9] J. H. Y. Briggs, *The English Baptists of the Nineteenth Century,* BHS, 1994, p.408

Part Three:
Baptists Together

Baptist Church House 1903–90

12

A National Baptist Community

WITHOUT doubt the Free Churches in general had more influence, prosperity and freedom in 1900 than they had known before. They came into the twentieth century with enthusiasm, even if a few among them lacked confidence, and Baptists were no exception. The Baptist Union, as it gathered various Baptist communities into its orbit, was assured. Its General Secretary, J. H. Shakespeare, brought 'the daring of genius' to his task, and with Baptist funds in place, moved the Union from its three or four rooms in the Baptist Missionary Society in Furnival Street, to Baptist Church House in Southampton Row. The very name made clear the future being sought by English Baptists. The Union's President in 1898, when Shakespeare was appointed was Samuel Vincent, who told the Autumn Assembly: 'Till we get such a house … there may be a doubt of its worth to us. Ten years after we get it we will be amused, if not amazed, that we were content to lodge … in the Mission House, that friendliest house in the world.'

As the Free Churches entered the twentieth century its preachers still had the ear of the populace. Opportunities for dissenters to be active in municipal and national politics were many, and at last, Oxford and Cambridge universities were open to Nonconformists. Money was in plentiful supply, Methodists and Congregationalists as well as Baptists raising extensive central funds. George White, the Baptist Union's President in his April 1903 Assembly Address, stated: 'If we make politics a part of our religion, as I claim we should, then in the conduct of our national policy, moral principles must be supreme'.[1] White had worked his way to the top and was a shoe manufacturer and civic leader in Norwich which he also represented in Parliament.

The political power Dissenters exercised together provided a legitimate way of encouraging Christian moral standards in every part of the nation's life. Baptists, within Dissent as a whole, in political terms, had not felt so involved or influential since Cromwell's time. In the previous hundred years most Baptists had initially played a minor role in local politics beyond the Meeting House, although they had expressed strong opposition to the Slave trade as early as 1780. After the Reform Act (1832) the politics of Nonconformity came to the

[1] *Baptist Handbook,* 1904, p.113

fore, as William Knibb returned from Jamaica and brought Baptists firmly into the abolition movement. Baptists began to air religious grievances about the registration of births, deaths, and marriages, closely linked to calls for the disestablishment of the Church of England. As Baptist people found a distinct place in national life, most expressed it through Gladstone's Liberal Party.[2]

'It is probable that Nonconformity reached its height of political power, was most representative of the temper of the English people round the beginning of this century', wrote Dennis Brogan. 'But in the generation that has passed since the great Liberal landslide of 1906, one of the greatest changes in the English religious and social landscape has been the decline of Nonconformity'.[3]

Yet it was the growing political diversity within Nonconformity, states James Munson, which in 1899 'brought the Nonconformist Conscience to grief'.[4] Specifically, it was the Boer War, which broke out in October 1899 when Britain tried to compel the Transvaal to concede the franchise to British gold prospectors. Baptists were not solidly against the war, and although the *Baptist Magazine* in February 1900 put all the blame on the Transvaal, in 1901 the London Baptist Association declined to debate the issue for fear of revealing the divided opinion in the churches. Baptist minister J. G. Greenhough might put the responsibility on the Transvaal, but in the early months of the war a majority of Baptist ministers, led by John Clifford, Alexander McLaren, and J. C. Carlile, opposed it. However, W. E. Blomfield, of Queens Road, Coventry, challenged the view of the *Daily News* in December 1901, when it published the names of 5,270 nonconformist ministers who signed its 'Peace Manifesto', that nonconformity was against the war. He pointed out that only a third of all Dissenting ministers had signed the manifesto, and among Baptists, only half its ministers had signed. 'In the 1870s most Nonconformists' comments David Bebbington, 'were among the sternest critics of the growth of empire; by the 1900s the majority were dedicated imperialists ... no longer little Englanders standing out against the national trend.'[5]

Balfour's 1902 Education Act which further supported Anglican schools in the state system, led to the Passive Resistance movement with many dissenting ministers being imprisoned, others had their goods taken and auctioned, and all because of their refusal to pay that proportion of the rates raised for education. The result was that in the 1906 General Election the Liberal Party swept into power and the new Parliament contained as many Dissenters as in the days of Cromwell.

Political dissenters secured the disestablishment the Church in Wales, strongly supported the curtailment of the power of the House of Lords, and hoped its education grievances would soon be remedied. The resulting constitutional crisis was at its height when, warnings unheeded, Britain found itself suddenly at war with Germany in 1914.

[2] D. Bebbington, 'The Baptist Conscience in the Nineteenth Century', *BQ*, 34, 1991, pp.13–24
[3] D. W. Brogan, in *The English People*, quoted by E. A. Payne in *The Free Church Tradition in the life of England*, SCM, 1944, p.121
[4] J. Munson, *The Nonconformists*, 1991, pp.234–238
[5] D. W. Bebbington, *The Nonconformists Conscience: Chapel and Politics 1870–1914*, 1982, p.106

The Baptist Union

Samuel Booth

Baptists had appointed John Howard Shakespeare, aged 41, to be the pathfinder for Baptists in the new century. He was an ecclesiastical administrator of the first order, who by powerful directive leadership drew Baptists together in the opening decades of the century and gave shape, purpose and hope to the national Baptist family. Shakespeare, elected Secretary of the Baptist Union in 1898, had first appeared at a Baptist Union Assembly in 1892, to present a challenging paper on Baptist church extension in large, new, urban areas. The stated purpose of the proposed scheme 'was an attempt to weld into a real and active unity the scattered or contending forces of the Baptist Churches of Great Britain' into 'a wise and sympathetic congregationalism.' His final words were these:

> God forgive us that we have been in the midst of perishing multitudes not like the compassionate Master, but enjoying our religious privileges, rapt in glorious memories and clutching at a dead idol, the brazen and deceptive serpent of an extreme and selfish independency.

Shakespeare, unanimously appointed as Samuel Harris Booth's successor, was noted by the *Baptist Magazine* as having

> qualities which have made him an able and efficient administrator ... He has both 'culture and go'. He is clear-sighted, bold in conception with a well-balanced judgment and something of the daring of genius. He has the power of initiation ... and the energy of enthusiasm.

At the 1898 Nottingham Assembly that elected him, Shakespeare told them:

> If in any way I can promote the extension of our churches in the towns, quicken the denominational conscience to play its part in the national life—that part which its past history and the present opportunity demand—and if I can lessen the burden of the humblest village minister, I shall have my reward.[6]

Later, as he outlined his proposals to a Committee of the Union, a senior member remarked, in a voice tinged with incredulity, 'And is that all that you propose?' Shakespeare believed that 'prophetic leadership had to challenge anything that smacked of congregational isolationism, and if that involved a measure of institutional centralization then that was a price that had to be paid and opposition had to be firmly countered.'[7]

[6] W. M. S. West, *Baptists Together*, BHS, 2000, p.38
[7] *Ibid.*, p.44

General and Particular Baptist had now found common ground in a Baptist Union coming together, not on the basis of a detailed *Confession*, but on the basis of 'that interpretation of the faith denominated evangelical' while holding to the conviction that 'each church has liberty under the guidance of the Holy Spirit to interpret and administer His laws'. His goal was the 'institutionalised interdependence' of 'independent and missionary orientated' Baptist churches.[8] Initially he won the day with his 'reconstruction' of the Baptist national family within the Baptist Union, but the issue of interdependence would surface several times, long after Shakespeare's death.

Eagle Street Chapel

The 'daring of genius'

Typical of the next twenty-six crowded years of his tenure of office, Shakespeare, within twenty-four hours of being appointed set about raising a significantly large fund for the Union, to implement his vision for Baptists in the twentieth century. The *Twentieth Century Fund* had a proposed capital of £250,000, the equivalent of about £14 million in 2000. Half the money would provide capital to erect seventy-five new churches in city locations where there had been no previous Baptist presence. £30,000 went to help ministers of village churches and a similar sum in the Annuity Fund would help retired ministers. A significant sum would provide for the purchase and building of a 'Baptist Church House', at 4 Southampton Row, London, on the site of the old Eagle Street chapel. To encourage a more able ministry, £6000 was used to establish a Scholarship Fund to give ministers opportunities for further training.

In the opening decade of the century much time was spent considering the recognition of ministers, how pastoral oversight for small village and inner-city churches could be sustained, and ways to ease difficult situations arising from ministerial removal and settlement. Shakespeare's answer was a second fund, the *Sustentation Fund*, launched in 1912 for a capital sum of £250,000. It was successfully completed two years later. The money, to supplement the stipends of the most poorly paid ministers, was accompanied by an elaborate and careful scheme for ministerial removal and settlement and the appointment of ten General Superintendents, employed by the Union, to implement it. As originally conceived the scheme also addressed the complete re-organization of ministerial training through the Colleges. However, this was not acceptable to the Colleges and was never implemented.

[8] *Ibid.*, p.35

Re-shaping the Baptist Union

As early as 1892 the Baptist Union Council had agreed to publish a weekly newspaper, and Shakespeare was successful in purchasing the privately owned *Freeman* that had built up a large circulation since its inception in 1855. Shakespeare edited *The Baptist Times and Freeman* with the help of his brother Arthur, and it became the official weekly journal of the Baptist Union. In 1910 the Union purchased *The Baptist,* edited by T. H. Stockwell since 1886, and amalgamated it with the *Baptist Times.* The paper remained the Union's official journal until the 1960s, when it reverted to an independent paper.

Shakespeare supervised the various departments created within the framework of the Union. The Baptist Tract and Book Society were amalgamated in a Baptist Union publishing project, the Kingsgate Press, and a bookshop was opened in Southampton Row. The Young People's Union was started in 1904, and a Baptist Total Abstinence Association in the same year. The latter had 2037 'Bands of Hope' in churches across the country. Closely linked to the temperance commitment in the churches was the abandonment of the use of fermented wine at the Lord's Supper in 2079 local churches. The Baptist Insurance Company opened for business in 1905 and in the same year Shakespeare was responsible for organising the first ever meeting of the newly created Baptist World Alliance, becoming one of its first secretaries. The *Baptist Historical Society* started in 1908, publishing first the *Transactions* and then the *Baptist Quarterly*, the latter still publishing a wide range of Baptist history and theology.

`The liberation of women'

In regard to the growing place of women within the life of the churches, Shakespeare wrote in 1918.

> I regard the liberation of women from the bonds of prejudice ... as the most helpful feature of our times. Only at its peril can the Church make itself the last ditch of prejudice in this respect ... In the new world, women will enter upon hitherto untried paths, they will assume added responsibilities and will advance in power, efficiency, and self confidence; prejudices will disappear, and the Church will be compelled to accept the principle that sex itself can be no bar to position or service.[9]

In 1889 and again in 1891 some women had addressed the Baptist Assembly in connection with women working among 'the social poor'. From this 'seed' a number of women with nursing training devoted themselves to visiting and social work in churches, and became 'Deaconesses' in various Baptist churches. Shakespeare, who was committed to extending the place of women in every part of the denomination, initiated through Mrs Isabel James, the daughter of a friend, the founding of the *Baptist Women's League* in 1910, of which she later became the national President. In the same year the Baptist Union Council allowed the election of up to ten more women than its 1904 constitution had previously allowed.

[9] J. H. Shakespeare, *The Churches at the Crossroads*, 1918, pp.10f. Also P. Shepherd, *The Making of a Modern Denomination*, 2001, pp.139–145

'Sisters of the People'

The first women ministers

In 1890 a London Baptist Association initiative resulted in the founding of a Baptist Deaconesses Home and Mission in the city. By 1894 it had become independent. The work grew and a report in the *Baptist Times* for 1917 commended it to the denomination as it came under the auspices of the Union. Shakespeare encouraged women in this 'social service' to the churches, and by 1918 there were 48 Deaconesses working in the churches. But it was 1910 before the Baptist Union received an enquiry about entry into the ministry. It came from a Miss Clark of Glasgow, but she did not proceed. In 1922 the Recognition Committee noted that Edith Gates had in 1918 become the minister of Little Tew and Cleveley, in Oxfordshire and as she fulfilled the requirements she was enrolled as a probationer with a recommendation she take further studies at Havelock Hall, Hampstead. Edith Gates received a grant of £33 per annum from the Sustentation Fund.

Violet Hedger was the first woman trained for ministry, and her name appeared on the list of Regent's Park students seeking settlement in 1924. After two years' hard work by the Superintendents' Board she settled at Littleover, Derby, and received a Sustentation Fund grant. The Union's Recognition Committee in September 1925 noted a third woman on its list, Mrs Maria Living-Taylor, BA, recommended by her Essex Association after 'two years of efficient pastoral work' and now working alongside her husband in the Sion Jubilee Church, Bradford, Yorkshire. From such spasmodic requests came the beginnings of women training for ministry. But the real development did not come until the last third of the century.

The Baptist family had arrived as a national body in England, with an increasing number of women among the new leadership, new headquarters, a new weekly newspaper, a new hymnbook, *The Baptist Church Hymnal,* and new funds to be administered for the benefit of ministers and churches through the various agencies of the Union, including the Superintendents' Board.

Building Society

Helping the ministers

All these measures brought into question the very nature of Baptist churches and a long discussion as to who would be recognised as Baptist ministers within the churches.[10] In 1906 the Assembly listened to two addresses on the 'Interpretation of Congregationalism'. Both the speakers agreed that the delegation of power to a central or Association body did not constitute the abandonment of Congregational principles. *The Baptist*, which at that time offered through its pages a platform to any who opposed Shakespeare, did not agree.

> One is fearful to anticipate, but can we detect the Ecclesiastical Baptist England, with its Provinces and Bishops, of Bristol, Rawdon, London, Manchester and Nottingham, the deeds of the churches in a 'strong room', the pastorates filled, adjusted and terminated by a committee and the 'Man of God' the puppet of a wire puller.[11]

The paper further asserted, probably correctly, that more than half of all the Baptist churches in the country were not in the Union and twenty percent of the two thousand ministers listed were not recognised by it.

At the 1907 spring Assembly it was proposed that ministers would be listed without distinction; training received at colleges other than those recognised by the Union would be accepted as sufficient; and ministers who had entered the pastorate prior to 1900, backed by their Association, would be accepted without submitting to any of the new procedures. The rules for those entering the ministry between 1900 and 1907 would be relaxed as necessary. These changes made recognition easier for existing ministers, provided a period of probation for new entrants, but required all applicants to pass at least one Baptist Union examination. The examination was the crucial element and by it the Union secured total control over entry to the recognised Baptist ministry, and it was to accredited ministers alone that the Union's funds would be available.

The co-ordination of the dispersal of the Union's increasing funds would result in the ministry being less and less rooted in the local congregation. Shakespeare openly criticised those who wanted to retain the 'aggressive liberty of the individual congregation', because ministers were victims of that 'system'. The system must be changed so ministers would not be frequently 'broken upon the wheel of life'. The Assembly vote was important, but Shakespeare's goal was to get it working in the churches.

The *Baptist Times* allowed two principle opponents of the scheme, Richard

[10] For a full account of the growth of 'accredited' Baptist ministry, see D. C. Sparkes, *An Accredited Ministry*, BHS, 1996

[11] *The Baptist*, 17 May 1906

Glover of Bristol, and J. Moffatt Logan of Accrington, to argue their position in its pages. Logan declared that Shakespeare's ambition was to create a national Baptist Church, that the 'voluntary' nature of the scheme would soon become compulsory. Glover had voiced his opposition at the 1909 Autumn Assembly. He believed it could split the denomination and contradicted the Biblical principle that the local church needed neither association with others, nor a minister, to be complete. It would lead to the imposition of a cumbersome administrative system. It would not solve the problems faced by ministers and churches, and could only lead to disappointment.

The Baptist leader of 2 December 1909, pondered 'the far-reaching mischief that a drastic officialism may unconsciously work, by its bestowal of preference, and privileges, towards turning a federation of Christian ministers into something nearly akin to a mere Trades Union organisation.'

In a long debate at the 1910 Assembly, a major turning point was Logan's admission that he had changed his mind and would now vote in favour of the amended scheme. The scheme was commended because it 'would make a real advance in Denominational usefulness and efficiency … mitigate many of the evils of our present system, while at the same time maintaining the unity which so happily prevails in our midst.' Only Richard Glover and eight others voted against it. However, it would take six years before the scheme was fully operational and it would be still further changed in the process.

The Union had formed a Ministerial Recognition Committee as early as 1896 to handle the delicate issue of who could properly decide, and on what criteria, what it meant to be recognised as a Baptist minister. Ministers were those whom churches chose to call to office, but many viewed this as 'irresponsible independency' which needed a 'restraining and controlling authority'. In 1900 the Baptist problem was a surfeit of ministers, many not properly trained, who deserved a better system for their settlement but in the process there would have to be a 'weeding out' of poor quality ministers.

Charles Williams had proposed the first criteria by which ministers would be accredited, and then admitted to the benefits, largely financial, of belonging to the Baptist Union. It became important that further criteria should be agreed. With the effectual uniting of Particular and General Baptist churches in the loose federation of the Baptist Union, the notion of a national Baptist ministry became a reality that many Baptists thought not only possible but also desirable.

The Sustentation Fund was raised by the close of 1914 and during that year there was much talk of a national Baptist Church. J. H. Rushbrooke said the Fund marked the recognition of the minister as a leader of the whole Christian Church, not just of a local community. The outbreak of the First World War changed everything, Baptists included. Nevertheless practical implications of the scheme were still addressed. The Associations met with Shakespeare and agreed that central stipends would be paid by the Union to aided churches. The local churches, with an Association endorsement, would send their contributions towards stipends to the Association Treasurer, who would forward them to the Union, and the Union would pay the ministerial stipends. The Associations would raise a total of £15,000 per year to support the ministry in the aided churches. In addition, once the Association's own running expenses had been met the surplus would be applied to the payment of ministers.

The General Superintendents

In 1915, Association officers were given plans for grouping of churches and the division of the country into ten districts that would have General Superintendents, appointed and paid by the Union, to supervise arrangements under the scheme. At no time previous to this had Superintendents been included in any of the proposals made by Shakespeare or anyone else.

The Assembly in 1915 was told of the indispensability of the Superintendents for the success of the scheme, and in seconding the resolution creating them, G. P. Gould, President of Regent's Park College, indicated that the Assembly would be approving the appointment of a 'new order of ministry'. These far reaching proposals were accepted, but after this date Associations, which until then had been the only meaningful regional Baptist grouping, were faced with 'Areas' of the national Union. Five of the ten new Superintendents were originally Association Secretaries, who after 1916 were paid by the Union and therefore no longer answerable to the Associations. In this way the Union increasingly gained control of the national corporate life of the churches.

The Superintendents were Shakespeare's legacy to Baptists who, perhaps because of the demands of the War, were simply appointed and started work. This suited Shakespeare, who having determined what to do, wanted to get on with the job in hand, since he was essentially a pragmatist. Peter Shepherd believes that if Shakespeare had a theory of the church, it was not Episcopal, Congregational, or Presbyterian as such, it was above all clerical; because he was convinced of Richard Baxter's dictum that 'All the churches either rise or fall as the ministry doth rise and fall (not in riches or worldly grandeur) but in knowledge, zeal and ability for their work'.

His frustration with Baptist independency was because it did not produce and sustain the ministry the Church needed. If Superintendents were the practical necessity for implementing the scheme, he would have them, regardless of the fact that he was introducing into Baptist congregational polity an unacknowledged and undefined form of episcopacy.[12]

An interviewer for the *Christian World* on 14 December 1916 writing of the 'revolution' at Baptist Church House since Shakespeare had become Secretary, suggested that the Union had become a 'powerful central authority'. Asked whether, 'practically the Baptist Union takes up a minister as soon as he is ordained according to your regulations, and to the end of his ministerial life, you guarantee him a minimum living wage, and when he retires from ministerial life, or is incapacitated, you guarantee him an annuity?' Shakespeare simply answered: that is so. The paper's headline writer was correct: if Shakespeare's reply was an accurate description of what had been happening, the about face in Baptist church polity was in truth, a revolution.

Shakespeare's considerable effort to raise ministerial standards was not simply so that ministers' status in society would be improved, but primarily to

[12] Peter Shepherd, *The Making of a Modern Denomination,* 2001, chapters 2 and 3 especially

carry forward the mission of the churches. This was a vital principle as Baptists considered the numerical and spiritual decline that dogged them for the whole of the twentieth century.

Accreditation

Each year in the *Baptist Union Handbook* it stated that:

> ... great care should be exercised to safeguard the right of churches to appoint their own pastors and not discourage any man who has received from the Lord the gifts and call which qualify for the work of a pastor and teacher; that the object of any rules or regulations which may be adopted should be (a) to prevent the unworthy or unfit from entering our ministry, (b) to assist those who God has called and qualified for service in the pastorate by commending them to the churches of the denomination, and (c) to secure to such pastors, among other privileges, eligibility to participate in the benefit of the Funds of the Union—and that, while gratefully acknowledging the varied and great services which many brethren, who had not had the advantage of a collegiate training, have rendered to the churches and to the Kingdom of our Lord, it should be regarded as highly desirable that any man 'seeking entrance to our ministry' should receive thorough and effective training in one of our Colleges or at some other seat of learning.

In 1903, when J. G. Greenhough addressed the Assembly on *The Condition of our Ministry*, he affirmed that the door to the ministry in the past had been too widely open. Anyone could enter that could get a church to call him. As he spoke, there were too many ministers, with at least 100 ministers out of pastorate. The number of ministers must be limited. The colleges deserved the respect of the denomination but it needed a central college committee to determine the number of admissions for each of the colleges. Shakespeare had expressed his personal opinion as early as 1902 in the *Baptist Times* (20 July). The Union was the proper body to 'guard the door' to Baptist ministry. He was concerned about the quality of ministry, particularly in smaller churches; he was ashamed that many good ministers were living in real poverty; and it was his belief that only a centralised programme for regulating the ministry would be able to address these issues. Shakespeare's own high standards led him to insist that only those who had matriculated at a recognised University be accredited.

'Professionalism' resisted

In 1903 Shakespeare produced a series of proposals about ministerial recognition, support, deployment and pensions. *The Baptist* attacked the proposals and advocated the Spurgeon's College approach that did not insist on educational qualifications for its students.

Three years later *The Baptist* was infuriated when the 1906 *Baptist Union Handbook* differentiated between ministers whom it recognized and 400 others it did not. It was one thing for the Union to keep such a list, but it was very different when the distinction was put in print.

> Our pastors ... complain of hardships and conditions of oppression ... Their friends whom they had themselves voted to high places have lifted up their heel against them. It was mortification indeed to find the Baptist Union Council refusing to 'recognise' and then seeking power to submerge them, and this not because of spiritual failures, but by reason of the accident of their non-collegiate training or unwillingness and possible inability to submit to a test of the schoolmen. And who shall yet deliver them from a form of tyranny so essentially opposed to everything Baptist?[13]

The attempt to 'professionalise' the ministry was deeply resented by many Baptists, and some felt it was the growing affluence of the Union that was responsible for this non-Baptist, unchristian and non-scriptural action.

Ecumenism

A united Free Church in England

At the very moment Baptists had discovered a way for the two major expressions of the denomination to move forward together, they were faced by the wider question of the unity of the Free Churches, and beyond that their relationship with the state church.

The emergence and rapid success of the Free Church Council movement in the last decade of the nineteenth century encouraged Evangelical Nonconformists towards a common programme of action against clericalism on the one hand and the rising tide of secularism on the other. Local groups of churches across the country met regularly to plan a variety of activities, which included functions like united evangelism and temperance campaigns, school board elections. Each year from 1892 a national Congress of evangelical Free Churches met whose resolutions embodied the Nonconformist Conscience. Free Churches became a growing force in politics, which the Government of the day would ignore at its peril.

The co-operation experienced in the Free Church Councils encouraged moves towards unity between the Free Churches, and there was a movement towards what W. T. Stead called the 'Civic Church', a non-creedal organisation which dealt with all aspects of poverty. Social concern and ecclesiastical reconciliation were both on the agenda for the first Free Church Congresses, each stimulating the other. But at the local level, the social issues dominated the scene. In the *Christian World* G. H. James, a Nottingham Baptist minister, wrote that his local Free Church Council:

> hoped to focus the convictions of their churches on the great social, moral and non-partisan political questions, such as the drink system, the opium traffic, gambling, peace and war, sanitation, capital and labour, and the religious alienation of the masses.[14]

United evangelistic action was also a prime objective, as in Bradford, for example, where the town was divided into Free Church 'Parishes' for the purpose of house-to-house visitation.

[13] *The Baptist*, 14 September 1905

[14] *Christian World*, 13 December 1894, p.931

A new brand of churchmanship appeared, which originated in the mind of Charles Berry, a Congregational minister. He claimed that the churches represented in the National Free Church Council were in a partnership that he described as 'Scriptural Catholicism', and these were the only genuine 'High Churchmen in England today'. It was an attempt to move from the negativism of the old title, 'Nonconformist', towards the positive affirmation of the inter-denominational nature of Free Churches. Among Baptists this idea was affirmed by J. G. Greenhough in a Baptist Union Assembly address in 1895, when he urged 'Dissenter' be dropped in favour of 'Free Churchman'.

These moves towards unity between the English Free Churches as the twentieth century opened put increasing pressure on Baptists to reconsider their understanding of the church, while yet remaining loyal to the congregational principle of the church as a gathered fellowship of believers.

From a different perspective there was a growing Anglican desire to seek a path towards re-union and its first manifestation had been in an early challenge to all other Christians, contained in a statement from the 1881 Lambeth Conference. It had stated the basis on which Anglicans would consider any form of united church. Known as the 'Lambeth Quadrilateral' there were four issues that Anglicans felt were an irreducible minimum for re-union. These were the centrality of the Scriptures, baptism and the Lord's Supper, the historic episcopate, and the Apostles' Creed as the baptismal confession with the Nicene Creed as the sufficient statement of the Christian Faith. The Baptist reply to this had been made under the stress of the Downgrade controversy. Although the need for organic union among Christians was accepted, the Baptist Union felt that a sacrifice of principle was asked that they could not make.

The growing pressures for Free Church unity before the First World War were considerable, but it was out of that crucible of suffering and change that in 1918 Shakespeare, as Secretary of the Baptist Union, wrote *The Churches at the Cross Roads*. It marked a watershed in Shakespeare's tenure of office since his appointment in 1898, and for him it was the moment when he felt personally that a United Free Church of England would not be sufficient for the missionary task which faced Christian people after 1918 and he committed himself to work a united church, even if that meant the Free Churches accepting episcopacy in some form.

Mission

As the twentieth century opened much was changing in society, even if the churches were slow to appreciate change. The growing segregation of the classes, as middle-class chapel goers moved out from the city to an expanding suburbia, meant that the working-classes were increasingly isolated from the churches. The opportunity to offer social welfare through community based congregations decreased as communities physically separated. The total community programme of a church like Haven Green Ealing, was impossible to sustain after the First World War, because the Liberal government reforms after 1906 had paved the way for the welfare state which really rendered church philanthropy ineffective as a means of outreach.

In Bristol, the Tyndale Baptist Church had employed a minister to work among the poverty stricken families down by the docks in the 1890s. His surviving diaries reveal a fever of activity and a number brought to faith and baptised. Those who made that spiritual journey had their membership not in the mission church, but at Tyndale itself, where this failure to encourage a local lay leadership to put deep roots into the local community meant the ultimate failure of the process as an effective missionary method.

T. E. Howe's diaries reveal his holidays each year, not surprising as one of Tyndale's leaders was Edward Robinson, a Bristol printer, who as early as 1889 was giving a week's holiday with pay to all who had been in his employ for a year. Robinson was one of the first to introduce a pension fund and a profit-sharing scheme into his business. On his golden wedding he gave a gift to the Bristol Corporation that enabled it to clear a slum into a permanent open space in the city centre, and also provided towards the cost of housing the dispossessed.

At the Tyndale mission centre there was a continual battle against the excesses of alcohol. Howe records with great satisfaction those who sign the pledge and escape the allure of alcohol. Many nonconformists, including Baptists, believed that drink was the cause not only of poverty but also resistance to Gospel claims. George White from Norwich had proposed that a 'Million Pledges Crusade' should follow the successful Simultaneous Free Church Mission of the early twentieth century. Bands of Hope taught children the virtues of temperance in many urban and rural chapels.

Some ministers also promoted what one leading Baptist, John Clifford, had called 'a social gospel', which challenged Victorian individualism and laissez-faire attitudes. But what was meant to be a strategy for mass evangelism, in the end allowed secularising forces to gain a foothold in many congregations.

Frank Buffard speaks of evangelism continuing to play a large part in the Kent and Sussex Association activities. 'Most of the churches joined in the Free Church Simultaneous Mission of 1901, and nearly every church in the Association was fostering a mission church in its neighbourhood.'[15] Dover Baptists opened a new church at St. Margaret's, where it had been working for over a hundred years. Deal Baptists were working in Walmer, and Folkestone in Cheriton. Worthing built a schoolroom for West Tarring and started new work at Bognor in 1899. In 1902 Eythorne was supporting eleven preaching stations and eight Sunday Schools in an area of 50 square miles. The so-called Pleasant Sunday Afternoon Movement was reaching men outside the churches with the Gospel, a small church like Battle attracting 150 men. At Ramsgate over a thousand came each Sunday evening to special services held in the local theatre. Nineteen new chapels and school halls were built in the Association before 1914, most with the help of the Twentieth Century Fund.

Numerical decline recognised

In 1908 readers of both denominational newspapers were surprised to find that in the previous year Baptist membership in England and Wales had seriously declined. The *Baptist Times* explained the new situation as a result of the short-

[15] F. S. Buffard, *The Kent and Sussex Baptist Association*, 1963, p.118

lived increases following the Welsh revival, and noted that in England there had been a small increase of Baptists. *The Baptist* quickly noted the inevitable discouragement of such figures and the 'depressingly slow' march of the Kingdom of God. A certain sense of failure now began to haunt Baptist Union debates. The Baxter dictum linking ministry and mission sharpened the argument for a systematic approach to ministerial recognition and sustentation.

Shakespeare spoke at the 1908 Assembly about 'The Arrested Progress of the Church', noting that in spite of more money, buildings, societies and machinery, the Church lacked confidence in its message. This derived from 'our defective Denominational system, which fails to use to the best advantage such resources as we have'; it was obsolete, encouraged selfishness, degraded the ministry, and made the advance of the Kingdom of God simply impossible. In the framework of changing national and social conditions, the decay of personal religion, and the break-up of external forms of religion among Christian people themselves, a bold remedy was needed.

He called for a return to Scripture, more effective preaching, and an aggressive policy of mission by the denomination. He wanted one Baptist Church in every town, rural churches grouped and led by a special order of Union ministers, committed to church extension and evangelism. He upheld the ideal of the Church as 'the pure and radiant bride of Christ', acknowledged the key role of ministers, and sought a re-birth of Christian piety in the churches.

The century had begun full of optimism about the advance of God's Kingdom through Baptists, but by 1921 this confidence had gone, and the churches were found to be substantially weaker and increasingly ineffective in mission.

13

A Vision of Unity in Mission

AS the First World War broke in all its horror on the British public, Shakespeare increasingly recognised that the future mission of the Church in England demanded a more unified and coherent approach than ever before, if the Gospel was to secure a hearing in the traumatised society that emerged after 1918.

Shakespeare had a friend who lost two sons during the War and recalled his colleague saying: 'the sects as such can do nothing at all. The things they stand for in their divisions may be true and good as far as they go, but they do not matter … they simply and finally do not matter in this tragic hour.' It was out of this that his book, *The Churches at the Cross Roads: A study in Church unity,* was born.[1] 'Advancing with the inevitableness of the dawn and the energy of the springtime is the growing conviction that the actual differences are not a sufficient ground for separation.' It was more important to establish the Kingdom of God in the world, to risk something in solving the ills of society, to transcend denominationalism, to step out into this new world on the offensive for the Gospel. Shakespeare described his own journey by saying, over the years 'I seem to myself to have travelled into a new country'.[2] He was correct. He did not suddenly arrive at these conclusions, they were with him from the beginning, perhaps more than he himself realised.

Shakespeare, unity and mission

At the beginning of his ministry Shakespeare saw himself as 'a Baptist of the Baptists and a dissenter of the dissenters'. In 1918 he recalled two events, which happened when he was minister of St Mary's Baptist Church, Norwich. The first was the success of a united Free Church mission in the town, the other was the coolness of his reception at the Anglican Church Congress held in Norwich. Of the latter he noted: 'It left on my mind at the time the impression that it was best for us to go our own way … the gulf was too wide for us even to shake hands across it.'[3]

In his speech to the Congress he noted: 'It is your inalienable glory that generation after generation you have maintained the use of common prayer

[1] J. H. Shakespeare, *The Churches at the Crossroads,* 1918, p.77
[2] *Ibid.,* p.79, 201
[3] *Ibid.,* p.204

and the regular reading of the word of God. In a secular age you have offered a persistent witness to the best things.' He acknowledged that continued disunity was a pressing problem, but that 'a new spirit is abroad, a weariness of strife and turmoil ... a very solemn feeling that division must mean mutual loss ... and concluded, 'Whether we are conscious of it or no, the realities which unite us infinitely transcend our differences, grave and serious as they are ...'[4]

The broader sympathies of Shakespeare are most clearly revealed in his 'grass roots' experience of and attachment to, the Free Church Council movement. He certainly supported the political involvement that the Free Churches engaged in and remained a loyal supporter of the Liberal political agenda all his life. The Yorkshire Baptist Association once reprimanded him for his support of Lloyd George. Through the columns of the *Baptist Times* his editorial reply made no concessions:

> We make no apology for our political notes. We have never attempted to write vapid nothings. We are supporters of Mr Lloyd George and the coalition and no one imagines that what we write is in an official capacity. Nevertheless we firmly believe that our official view is that of the immense majority of the Baptist denomination.[5]

Within the Free Church movement Shakespeare was a Congregationalist at heart, as his book for the series *Eras of Nonconformity* unashamedly asserts. 'It is entirely unhistorical and misleading to confuse the English Baptists with Anabaptists ... they were marked off from each other by differences of origin, doctrine, social and political ideas.' Baptist pioneers, according to Shakespeare, are the 'English Separatists, congregational in church polity and anti-paedoBaptist in practice, who gave rise to indigenous churches in this country'. John Smyth is, for Shakespeare, the founder of modern Baptist churches, who in his 'noble and historic confession' separated, 'like dross from gold', those 'elements of Anabaptism which would never have communicated themselves to the practical English mind'. [6] He also noted something contemporary historians have emphasised again recently: 'It is vital to note that the Puritans were within the Church of England. Many of them not only accepted episcopacy but believed in it'—a theme to which he returns when considering possible reunion with Anglicans.[7] 'Only by bad history' he wrote in 1922, 'can we cite our Puritan forefathers against episcopacy, for they believed in it and desired to remain under it within the Church of England'.[8]

At the 1906 Assembly Shakespeare asked Dr Wheeler Robinson and Dr W. Henderson to consider his dictum that 'Congregationalism interpreted as Independency was not only unequal to the solution of the problems which are before the denomination but was unscriptural' and in so doing they agreed with him.[9]

[4] *Report of Church Congress*, Norwich, 1895, p.27
[5] *Baptist Times*, 13 December 1918
[6] J. H. Shakespeare, *Baptist and Congregational Pioneers*, 1906, p.125
[7] *Ibid.*, p.10
[8] Shakespeare, 'Where the Renaissance must begin', in J. Marchant, ed., *The Coming Renaissance*, 1922, p.87
[9] E. A. Payne, *Henry Wheeler Robinson*, 1946, p.51

Shakespeare was deeply committed to the idea of a united Free Church in England, but the National Council of Evangelical Free Churches had failed to achieve that objective which seemed realisable in the 1890s. This was not a final goal, nor an ideal solution, as far as Shakespeare was concerned, but an intermediate step aimed at a reconciliation of autonomy with co-operation, liberty with order and unity with diversity. Free Church union depended on a shared understanding of Christian faith, and Shakespeare welcomed, as 'catholic, evangelical and positive', the Declaratory Statement agreed among the Free Churches, which he had helped to write. He looked to a situation after the War when there would be one Free Church in every village in England, when all Free Church ministers would receive common training, and when trans-denominational appointed Home Mission Superintendents would 'go with apostolic zeal through the land to cheer, to advise and to perfect in every parish the organization for bringing religion to the homes of the people'. He believed once the War ended the days of denominationalism would be over and that there was nothing more pathetic or useless than clinging to dead issues, worn-out methods and antiquated programmes.[10]

Churches 'at the crossroads'

Shakespeare had spent two decades giving a denominational shape to the Baptist family in Britain, but the impact of the First World War was such that he could no longer see one denomination as relevant to the changes which the war had brought about in society. 'No one could ever regard me as an indifferent Baptist' he wrote, 'I plan and toil for the church of my own faith, that when the grand festival of union comes she may be led to the altar in radiant beauty, a bride anyone may be proud to have.'[11] Shakespeare argued his case in a radical and controversial book, *The Churches at the Cross Roads* (1918). He considered that growing secular opposition and the quickening pace of life, with consequent demands on nervous energy, and the awakening of a social conscience determined to secure a better chance for the poor, the weak and disinherited, all demanded the churches unite.

Shakespeare knew the Church was no longer at the centre of the stage, not so much beset as disregarded. The new age needed a Church whose 'supreme function … is to know God, and to make its idea of God operative in human lives'. The Church

> must know God, with depths of humility and penitence, it must know Him for itself, not by tradition or in a creed, but with a vital, penetrating knowledge which dominates its worship, thought and activity, if it is to make its distinctive impression upon the world...The true objective of the Church is to establish the Kingdom of God in the world. [The question is whether the Church can find a] vital fund of spiritual creative energy for the immense new needs of the years which lie before it?'[12]

[10] E. A. Payne, *The Baptist Union: A Short History*, 1958, pp.275–278, for the full text
[11] J. H. Shakespeare, *The Churches at the Crossroads*, 1918, p.82
[12] *Ibid.*, pp.18, 22

The Church's place in the new order would depend on the strength and passion of the conviction at its heart. It must be ready to risk all, to venture everything on God. The Church must understand the attitude and temper of the age, look through its eyes, speak its vocabulary, wear the garb of the new age. It would not count for much unless it took its part in solving the ills of society and, particularly, transcended a narrow nationalism. Shakespeare wrote:

> Christianity is the religion of love and fellowship [but] organised Christianity does not strike the world in quite this way ... The churches place that which is divisive and distinctive in the very forefront. Their glory is apparently not in that which unites them to one another, but in that which separates them. The names do not witness to Christ but to some historical controversy.[13]

The gains of denominationalism were few in Shakespeare's view. In separation, a special emphasis was put on truth that had been obscured, forgotten or denied. Among the Free Churches, there was the strength of piety, and perhaps even the painful divisions of the Free Churches had added to the sacrificial activities of organised Christianity. However, the losses were obvious. The radical numerical decline in the churches indicated the denominations were bleeding to death. The divisions among the Free Churches were diverting energies from the spiritual to the material, with a consequent failure to secure the Church's goal. Denominationalism, in fact, no longer commended itself to the members of the churches or their adherents. 'The Free Churches: have reached a stage in the religious life of this country when, if they are simply a denomination and not a united Church, they are doomed.'[14]

What kind of unity?

The unity Shakespeare urged meant 'the different parts of the body working together in complete harmony of means and ends without any collision or frustration of the life force, each organ fulfilling its function and answering to its own type'.

Continuing would be disastrous: 'Unrelieved denominationalism will involve inevitable and increasing loss'.[15] Reunion without the Church of England was unthinkable to Shakespeare. 'It is no use concealing my conviction that reunion will never come to pass except upon the basis of episcopacy. I did not think so once, but that was simply because I did not understand it.' That one sentence was costly for Shakespeare in the remaining years of his Secretaryship at the Union. He had felt a profound change in the air and was not afraid to frame it in words and actions. He concluded his book:

> I passionately desire the goal of Church Unity, but it is an issue I can leave with God ... It is impossible—but the Church is always called to impossible tasks and there is no other national outlook for the world or the Church.[16]

[13] *Ibid.*, pp.41–43
[14] *Ibid.*, p.102
[15] *Ibid.*, pp.104, 117
[16] *Ibid.*, pp.178, 212

T. R. Glover

Baptists had given only a cautious welcome to the Archbishop of Canterbury's invitation to consider the possibility of corporate reunion on the basis of the so-called Lambeth Quadrilateral in 1888. Baptists were present at the World Missionary Conference (1910) and early in 1914 the Baptist Union Council expressed its willingness to share in a proposed World Faith and Order Conference. The Union was also represented at a series of unofficial Anglican-Free Church conferences held in Oxford between 1918 and 1920.

Response to the Lambeth Appeal

In 1920 the Lambeth Conference issued *The Appeal to All Christian People*, and this marked a new stage in relationships between churches in England. Shakespeare was correct—the Anglicans made it clear in a series of joint conferences held between 1921 and 1925 that they would regard a direct link with the episcopal succession of the past as essential to a united Church. Shakespeare was ready for this, but the elderly John Clifford and particularly the layman, Dr T. R. Glover, a classics fellow of St John's College, Cambridge, and the son of Richard Glover of Bristol, were definitely not. Shakespeare had moved far beyond the rank and file of the Baptist family in his thinking and he failed to take the denomination with him.

Glover led the denominational opposition by proposing a resolution, carried at the Assembly in April 1919, which noted:

> If the price of Ecclesiastical Reunion be the acceptance of episcopacy, in its historical sense or in some non-historical sense, with the implied necessity of regularizing our ministry by episcopal ordination or re-ordination, the Baptists of this country ... elect to stand by the priesthood of all believers and God's right to call and consecrate whom He will and how He will.[17]

Glover wrote a defence of the Free Churches in a series of articles in *The British Weekly*, later published as *The Free Churches and Reunion*, which carried a commendatory preface by the veteran John Clifford who, after a long silence, finally declared himself against the Secretary of the Union. Shakespeare told the Assembly: 'In leading this movement I have no intention of stampeding the Baptist denomination or doing anything dishonourable ... I am not at the crossroads. I have chosen my path and I shall follow it.'[18]

Shakespeare used his influence to persuade the Archbishop of York, Cosmo Gordon Lang, to address the 1921 Baptist Assembly on the *Appeal to all Christian People*. Shakespeare was thrilled with the event, a real ecumenical breakthrough,

[17] H. G. Wood, *Terrot Reavely Glover, A Biography*, 1953, p.153
[18] *Baptist Times*, 9 May 1919

and wrote afterwards to Lang: 'Your address was so persuasive that I said that if someone had risen and moved that we accept Episcopal ordination, it could have been carried. I think this is perhaps an exaggeration, but something very near it would have been reached.'

Lang's reaction was more down to earth as the cynicism of his diary entry reveals following his visit to both the Baptist and the Presbyterian Assemblies that month. 'In both cases the reception was very cordial to me personally, but I do not think these good people have any real care about a visible church at all. I am afraid they are still content if only they can preach at St Paul's and communicate at our altars'.[19] Whatever Shakespeare or Lang felt, it did not convince the delegates, and Shakespeare became increasingly isolated from the Baptist churches he was called to serve.

Shakespeare's final word

At the Baptist World Alliance 1923 meetings in Stockholm when he preached at a special service arranged in the Cathedral by Archbishop Söderblom, his text was 'No man having put his hand to the plough and looking back is fit for the Kingdom of God.' The sermon opens with the necessity of the ploughman to stay at his task despite every distraction, and it is clearly autobiographical.

> It is hard work to be God's ploughman and endure ... to maintain the first enthusiasm, the early devotion, sincerity of heart, purity of motive, unbroken courage and undimmed zeal ... We have almost envied the ploughman on the fields bathed in sunlight, breathing the fresh warm air. But watch him—he is in a lonely furrow, he must go straight and keep his eye fixed on the goal. He must plough deep and the share strikes stones which fling the handle ... he must press on. The essential task of God's ploughman is to penetrate beneath the surface ... All around as far as the eye can see, is the bare field. Not even the tiniest blade of wheat is above the surface. But the ploughman labours on ...

Shakespeare, who had never turned back on his walk with God ploughed on, committed to the task which had called him into ministry, enabling the Church to 'win the world to God', and as he did so he stated that the two great aims for the Church after the Great War must be first, international peace and then Church Union.

> The record of the Church in war and peace is a very bad one ... Nearly all the Christian nations have been engaged for five years killing one another—a strange spectacle for heathen nations to watch ... the Church must [now] throw its weight in the scales for peace. The other problem of our time is Church Unity. Indeed the two are very closely related, for men will only deride churches which desire peace everywhere else except among themselves. It is a hard field, full of stones and weeds and poisonous things ... At present we do not see which way God is leading us ... to realise the great spiritual fact of our oneness in Christ. We have put our hand to the plough and in spite of the opposition of foes, and what is harder to bear, the misunderstanding of friends, we must not look back.[20]

[19] J. W. Lockhart, *Cosmo Gordon Lang*, 1949, pp.271, 274
[20] K. W. Clements, ed., *Baptists in the Twentieth Century*, BHS, p.51

As Shakespeare walked to the pulpit to preach, the huge pulpit Bible fell over the edge. This caused him great consternation, and together with the constant interpolations of the interpreter, made for an uninspired service. Later that evening Shakespeare told J. C. Carlile, who had led the service in the Cathedral, that the Bible's fall was a sign: 'My work is done'. Nervous exhaustion and breakdown were suddenly in evidence as he cried uncontrollably like a child. He had a cerebral haemorrhage at the end of March 1925 and eventually died in 1928.

Assessing Shakespeare

Shakespeare expressed a wish that no biography of him should be written and that has been respected over the years. But Baptist self-understanding requires at least a recognition that Shakespeare's ecumenical vision must always be placed in the context of his deepest conviction, that the task of the Church is to win the world to God, and his deepest desire, that the Baptist family be effectively equipped for this task nationally and locally. He put his hand to the plough of Christian mission and unity, never looked back, as he planned and toiled for the Baptist Church in which he found faith and served Christ all his life.

Peter Shepherd believes Shakespeare's conviction was that centralised co-ordination of effort and resources was required, if evangelistic effectiveness was to be restored and a return to growth achieved. Shepherd comments: 'It seems unlikely, however, that a denomination which owed its past vigour and growth to the local and spontaneous could ever recover that vitality by means of institutionalisation.' Shakespeare shared the disdain found in other Free Churches for the new evangelical dissent emerging in groups like the Plymouth Brethren, Churches of Christ and Pentecostals, and movements like Keswick. But as he took the Baptist Union towards a respected place in national life his fascination with the Church of England increased.

His desire for Baptists to have a place within the church as a national institution, encouraged him to strengthen an educated ministry within the Union's churches. This ministry was increasingly supported financially by the Union in terms of stipend and pension, and by the Union's General Superintendents who would enable easier ministerial movement and thus free local ministers to engage in 'aggressive evangelism' in their areas.

It was Shakespeare's peculiar gift to use his own visionary organisational and leadership skills, to seize for the denomination at large the widespread desire for denominational cohesion, so powerful when he came into office. As the Union took on a comprehensive range of responsibilities for Baptists, its Secretary became an increasingly influential national figure among them, as Shakespeare's successors were quick to appreciate.

Shakespeare 'was motivated, not only by a desire to see ministers properly supported and the conviction that the churches' prosperity depended above all on the ministry, but also by a high, indeed almost priestly, concept of the ministry.' His determination to restore the status of ministers among Baptists resulted in his promotion of a denominational and clerical concept of ministry, which was something entirely new for Baptists. Until then Baptists had historically perceived the call to ministry to be worked out in a particular local church, rather than a call to ministry in the universal Church.

Shepherd is emphatic that Shakespeare's development of the Baptist Union was at the ultimate expense of Association life, which had been the historic heart of Baptist church life.

Melbourne E. Aubrey

> Twentieth-century Baptists owe to him the institutional framework of their denomination, and especially the central authority of the Baptist Union, which has enabled them to make a corporate contribution to national life and to co-ordinate their work at a national level ... His achievements were substantial and lasting. By not basing them securely on the ecclesiology that lay at the heart of Baptist denominational identity he institutionalised a sense of ambiguity and confusion about the nature of the relationship between the Union and the churches. He left Baptists without a clear sense of where responsibility for mission and ministry really lay. The institutional framework the denomination inherited from him has survived substantially intact, as has the uncertainty to which it gave rise.[21]

The Aubrey Years

Melbourne E. Aubrey succeeded Shakespeare in 1926 and held office until 1951.[22] The son of a Welsh Baptist minister at Zion, Pentre, Aubrey was sent as a boarder to Taunton School. He trained at Cardiff Baptist College from 1904 and won a Baptist Union Scholarship that took him to Mansfield College, Oxford, where he became a close friend of his fellow student, C. H. Dodd. His first appointment in 1911 was co-pastor with the renowned P. T. Thomson in Leicester, before he moved to St Andrew's Street Church, Cambridge, for twelve years. T. R. Glover, a member at St Andrew's Street, wrote to Aubrey concerning the invitation. 'If it were any other church you might stay where you are. But you can do what is needed in Cambridge and Cambridge calls you.' To Cambridge he went in 1913. It was Glover again who became involved in Aubrey's appointment as Secretary of the Baptist Union.

He came to the post when the denomination was in evident and serious numerical and spiritual decline, what E. A. Payne called a period of unusual

[21] P. Shepherd, *The Making of a Modern Denomination*, 2001, pp.185, 187

[22] For a discussion of Aubrey, see W. M. S. West, BQ, 34, 1992, pp.199–213, 263–281, 320–336, and W. M. S. West, *Baptists Together*, BHS, 2000, pp.48–63

difficulty.[23] When he was elected in 1925 the immediate post-war hopes of 'a land fit for heroes to live in' had faded. His first Assembly at Leeds in 1926 coincided with the General Strike. There followed years of economic depression and social unrest. Unemployment was rife and poverty common.

Aubrey knew that Shakespeare's key decisions of the past 25 years could not be reversed: interdependence was here to stay. Aubrey's task was consolidation and to this he turned. He sought to steer Baptists away from a pre-occupation with ecumenism after the firm rejection of Shakespeare's vision, although he was himself mindful of the need for ecumenical co-operation. He pursued a greater sense of relatedness within the Baptist family and continually asked churches to evangelise in a post-Christian society and meet the challenge of serious numerical decline. From the aftermath of the First World War through to the trauma of the Second World War, much was asked of Aubrey, and he provided steady, if unsensational, leadership, all the time searching for closer co-operation between churches in the Associations and the work of the Union. Awkward domestic and ecclesiastical issues in a time of recurrent crises in international and public affairs, called for courage, wisdom and inspirational powers of a high order.

Superannuation Fund

Soon after coming to office Aubrey successfully raised the capital sum of £300,000 needed to reorganise comprehensively the Superannuation Funds of the Union. This was a piece of business outstanding from Shakespeare's time as the denomination sought to raise the profile of the ministry to meet the known decline of the churches numerically and spiritually. Launched in 1926, the year of the National Strike, it tied the churches and ministers more deeply into the programme of the Union, since only accredited ministers in Baptist Union affiliated churches qualified for benefits under the scheme.

Ecumenical Concerns

As the third decade of the century advanced Baptists, like all other Christians, were faced with a decade of profound social crisis, poverty and deprivation, encapsulated in the 'slump' and the 'General Strike'. When the Baptist Assembly met in Leeds in 1926, just as the General Strike was called, J. H. Rushbrooke was the Baptist Union President. An emergency debate in the Assembly within twelve hours of the start of the General Strike urged all sides to negotiate a settlement. Telegrams were sent to Anglican and Presbyterian leaders but they failed to produce a united response from the Churches, and the Assembly concluded with telegrams to the Prime Minister and Trades Union Council urging both sides to resume negotiations immediately.

At the same Assembly a strong reaction was made to the ecumenical issue by Rushbrooke with his chosen theme: 'The Faith of the Baptists' and his keynote address, 'Protestant of Protestants'. Rushbrooke had been deeply involved with the official Baptist response to the Lambeth Appeal and his address drew attention to distinctive Baptist principles that had to be honestly addressed in the search for Christian unity.

[23] E. A. Payne, *The Baptist Union: A Short History*, 1958, pp.194–213

> We 'unchurch' no person or community because of difference from ourselves ... We claim no monopoly of truth; but rather thank God that our hold upon it is strengthened by the consensus of many brethren beyond our borders ... Our thought and life have been enlarged by teachers and saints of other churches, including not a few who strongly disapprove of us ... We cherish the catholic mind which would glorify God in all ... Indeed, it is our essential catholicity which shrinks from anything that would mar not only our freedom in Christ, but freedom of others.[24]

The Baptist Union Council had also decided that English Baptists would not be represented at the Lausanne Faith and Order Conference in 1927. When an *Outline of a Re-union Scheme* was published a decade later, the result of conversations between Anglicans and the Federal Council of Evangelical Free Churches, the suspicion of ecumenism had eased to the extent that three Baptists, including Aubrey, were on the Free Church team. The proposals received no significant support and Baptists had no desire to join a proposed scheme of union between Presbyterians, Congregationalists and Baptists. However, Baptists participated in the Oxford Conference on Church, Community and State in 1937.

Ministry

Shakespeare's concern for ministers and their effectiveness, unlike his ecumenical concerns, was firmly installed in everyday Baptist life. In 1920, A. E. F. Page, of Bristol, argued afresh that ministry belonged to the whole denomination, not just a local church, because all the churches share in shaping the ministry. His purpose in stating this was his conviction that the Colleges should be under the control of a central authority where denominational needs, rather than the Colleges' self-interest, would be uppermost. He pressed the desirability of a central entry process, with common standards being applied and students then sent to a college with an appropriate curriculum and staff. The number admitted would be based on projected known vacancies. Finally there should then be an annual act of ordination at the Assembly. The transfer of ministers to the accredited list at the Assembly was the only suggestion that was put into action.

Once the Sustentation Fund had been raised and the scheme was in place, increasing positive collaboration between the Colleges and the Union meant that most ministers were trained for work within churches now firmly based in the structures of the Union. The early years of three significant Baptist ministers show this process in action.

J. O. Barrett

When the First World War started, John Barrett (1901–78), the son of a Watford decorator, was thirteen and found a job in a local chocolate factory at six shillings a week.[25] In his spare time he learned shorthand and typing and secured a job as a booking clerk with the London and North Western Railway, based at Euston station, and quickly progressed in the company. As a lad he attended Leavesden

[24] B. Green, *Tomorrow's Man*, BHS,1997, p.140f

[25] E. A. Payne, *A 20th Century Minister: John Oliver Barrett*. Privately printed, 1979, p.3. I have drawn extensively on Payne's tribute to his personal friend for this material

Road Baptist Church, a new cause in Watford, where his parents were members. When the family moved to Holloway, they went to Upper Holloway Baptist Church, at that time a very large and flourishing church led by Sidney G. Morris (SGM). Miss Eva Wood, daughter of the former minister, J. R. Wood, led the Bible Class at Upper Holloway. John Barrett once said of her: 'She and SGM converted me'. John's mother was a political Liberal and he followed her convictions but like so many other Liberals in the 1920s he moved over to the Labour Party.

John Barrett

Training

When John Barrett felt the call to ministry, Sidney Morris spoke with Dr W. E. Blomfield, Principal of Rawdon. John did well in the new intellectual challenge that came to him at Rawdon. He graduated at Leeds in 1928 and took further study at Regent's Park College, London, where he met and became a life-long friend of Ernest Payne.

Barrett with Payne founded the Baptist Theological Students' Union in 1926, bringing together students from the eight Baptist theological colleges, which at that time included Dublin. John was a member of the Student Christian Movement while at College, an ecumenical experience that he built on in Oxford. He wrote to Ernest Payne, 'Oxford did a wonderful thing for me, it opened my eyes to the catholic nature of the Christian faith.' And it was there, in the Baptist John Bunyan Society, that he met his future wife, Gladys Hipkin of Somerville College, a Baptist from Peterborough.

Newcastle-upon-Tyne

In 1930 Barrett went to be minister at Westgate Road, Newcastle-upon-Tyne, and served there till 1939. Westgate Road was regarded in the neighbourhood at that time, as a kind of Baptist cathedral, with roots back into the seventeenth century. It was reputed to be rather exclusive and aristocratic. Under John Barrett's leadership in the thirties it became a natural home for those in the area who suffered 'grim and terrible poverty'. With 'rosy cheeks, open countenance, and glad welcome smile' Barrett 'looked more boyish than he actually was and North Country folk soon took him to their hearts'. Alan Richardson, an Anglican theologian and local vicar, and Leslie Hunter, who would become Bishop of Sheffield in 1939, were two of Barrett's regular colleagues at this time.

Ingli James

Ingli James

Ingli James was born in December 1889 at Ponthir, near Blackwood, Monmouthshire, a son of the manse. He grew up in the poverty of the Welsh Valleys and eventually went to Manchester University to read politics and economics, where Townley Lord, later minister at Bloomsbury, was his fellow student. From Manchester he went to Mansfield College, Oxford, where his dissertation was on the atonement in English theology.

In 1915 he went to assist for two years at Union Chapel, Manchester, where J. E. Roberts was minister, having followed the legendary Dr Alexander McClaren. James was known as a socialist, a Christian pacifist and a temperance advocate.

Accrington

After a brief spell at Stoneygate, Leicester, in 1919 he accepted the pastorate at Cannon Street, Accrington, in Lancashire, whose most illustrious pastor had been Charles Williams, for whom this 'nonconformist cathedral of the north' had been built. Williams's descendants were still among its members as was the family of Sir George McAlpine, a President of the Baptist Union and Chairman of the Baptist Missionary Society. The church had 700 members, and a thousand Sunday School children with 116 teachers. J. Moffat Logan, James's immediate predecessor, had died in post. As the 1920s opened, Accrington, at the heart of the Lancashire cotton industry, was about to be broken apart industrially and socially.

In the 1922 General Election Charles R. Buxton, from a Liberal family, was chosen as the Labour Party candidate for Accrington, and James supported him totally, both in and out of the pulpit. His deacons called James to account claiming that 'the public propagation both in and out of the Church of so-called Socialistic doctrines' was 'unacceptable to the great majority of the congregation.' James answered he was preaching the New Testament and would continue to support Buxton. Further complaints were lodged against his ministry claiming that he had spoken on a Labour platform, did not visit people as much as he should, gave too much attention to the young and too little to the older members, and his sermons were questionable. He made it clear the members would have to respond to such charges, as he had other churches wishing to call him to ministry among them.

Not surprisingly he left in June 1920 for Wales and took the pastorate at

Pantygwydr Baptist Church, Swansea. His ministry there involved him in local life, Labour politics, adult education, and attracted a huge student congregation from the University. He was called a Welsh John Clifford, preaching to the unevangelised, pursuing international peace, and working among the young, and in everything showing how the Gospel contains both the explanation of the present plight of humanity and the remedy for it. 'His stances are not to be separated from each other. He was too evangelistically passionate to be waylaid by the social gospel, too intellectually rigorous to be detained by mere evangelism, too reasonable to be a party man yet too sensible to be otherwise.'[26] In 1931 James accepted an invitation to the pastorate at Queen's Road Coventry.

Benjamin Grey Griffith

Born in Swansea in 1877 Grey Griffith came from a Welsh-speaking family, the eldest of five children. The family worshipped in a Welsh language chapel where his father as a deacon. Griffith senior had left school at 9, eventually became an accountant in a tin-plate factory, and then company secretary for a group of Temperance Hotels, and was at one time Mayor of Swansea.[27]

Grey Griffith entered Regent's Park College, London, in 1900 and four years later went to be pastor at Durham Road, Gateshead. As he arrived the 1904 Welsh Revival exploded on the scene, and he wrote of its impact:

> The week following the induction services I received newspapers from home, giving accounts of the meetings ... It had its excesses, it had its failures; but to have seen a whole countryside moved, to hear the untutored pray, to hear strong men in tears, to see enemies reconciled, to hear of old debts repaid—well, it taught me that it is not for man to limit the grace of God or determine his ways of working, nor to doubt the appeal of the Gospel. When the wind blows, new things come to birth, old things are renewed. It is spring-time.

Cardiff

In 1909 he moved to Tredegarville Baptist Church, Cardiff, an influential church in the Roath part of the city, with a membership of over a thousand. During his ministry three other churches were formed out of the Tredegarville congregation. In the First World Ward, unusually, his church agreed he should go with the YMCA for some months to the Western Front. When the Baptist United Fund was raised to help with the post War situation in the Baptist Union's churches, Tredegarville gave £4,060 in a month, the largest contribution made by any church in the United Kingdom. From 1921 he was a member of both the Baptist Union Council and the BMS General Committee.

In 1926 he led a commission for the Baptist Missionary Society which examined the funds and policy of the Society and addressed the £35,000 deficit it faced that year. In 1927, with Dr W. Y. Fullerton in failing health, Grey Griffith became the Home Secretary of the Society and left Cardiff for London, where he became a member at Ramsden Road, Balham. He saw the Society through the

[26] C. Binfield, *Pastors and People*, p.202–264

[27] This section uses E. A. Payne, *Veteran Warrior*, 1962

London Road Baptist Church, Lowestoft

150th celebrations of the BMS in 1942, and immediately accepted an invitation to become President of the Baptist Union. The Missionary Society in its Annual Report described him as

> possessed of firm convictions tenaciously held, of clear judgment combined with intuition which brings him surely to the heart of issues and with a grasp of the missionary situation allied to a sympathetic understanding of the condition of the home churches.[28]

Mission

Although there were ministers who led very large congregations, most ministers functioned in churches with a smaller number of members. For example, the Association statistics for Kent and Sussex in 1929 reveal that 23 churches had less than 50 members, 25 churches had between 51 and 150 members; 6 churches had between 151 and 250 members, 13 churches had between 251 and 400 members,

[28] *Ibid.*, p.58

2 had over 400 members and one over 500 members. Since 1900 the number of churches had increased from 60 to 77, membership had increased from 8168 to 10,209, and Sunday School scholars from 11,577 to 12,899. The annual number of baptisms, which had large variations over the period, went down from 464 in 1900 to 294 in 1929. There were some long ministries during this period, John Doubleday at Sittingbourne for 40 years, W. Blocksidge at Gillingham for 45 years and G. A. Miller at Rochester for 37 years. It should not be forgotten that alongside these Baptist Union churches, and with virtually no connection to the local Association, were the 110 Strict and Particular Baptist churches that comprised a loose Association of independent Baptist churches in the same geographical area.[29]

Douglas Brown

'A Forgotten Revival'

Throughout the whole century Baptists passionately pursued the elusive dream of mass conversions that would turn the relentless ebb tide of numerical decline, first noted in 1906. The new manifestation of 'revival' in Wales, 1904–6, puzzled many but people increasingly knew that local churches must get to grips with the evangelistic task facing them.

In 1924 the Baptist Union appointed Douglas Brown, minister of Ramsden Road, Balham, London, to be its Commissioner for Evangelism. The appointment was made in part as recognition of Brown's involvement with what has been called by its recent historian, Stanley Griffin, 'a forgotten revival'. Brown had become involved in this through Hugh E. Ferguson.

In 1920, although the effects of the First World War were still very evident in Baptist churches across the country, many still had substantial congregations who wanted to reach out with the Gospel. At London Road Baptist Church, Lowestoft, services were well attended and the choir, the Bible classes for men and women, as well as the Sunday School, were all strong, and at the heart of each week there was an energetic prayer meeting. On a free Sunday, the minister, Hugh Ferguson, went to hear Douglas Brown, minister at Ramsden Road, Balham, London preach. He stayed overnight and on the Monday afternoon visited Brown and invited him to take a 'mission week' at Lowestoft in March 1921.

Brown, a son of the manse, was born in Bow, London, on 13 March 1874, at which time his father, Archibald, was minister at the East London Tabernacle. His father had supported Spurgeon over 'Downgrade' and resigned from the

[29] K. Dix, *Strict and Particular*, 2001, BHS, pp.218–265, 279–294

Baptist Union over the issue. Douglas had ministries at Herne Bay (1895–7), Splott Road, Cardiff, (1898–9), Kensington, Bristol (1899–1907), and had been at Ramsden Road, Balham, from 1907.[30]

In 1929 Brown, then President of the Baptist Union, recalled Ferguson's visit.

> I refer to an experience of the authority of Christ in my own soul. It happened in the middle of the night, after weeks of mental and moral struggle. I awoke with a sense of the Royal Presence, I dressed and went into my study. Sitting at my desk I was conscious of a Divine Companion. He was in front of me, questioning, waiting for a verdict. For weeks I had admitted His authority. In humble submission I bowed to it. I assented to a task from which I had shrunk and excused myself. It was not a moment of conscious self-sufficiency, it was an indescribable moment of self-surrender.
>
> The sequel explains the surrender. The next day in my congregation was a minister from Lowestoft. As he sat in the pew, he felt authority to plead with me (a stranger to him) to come to Lowestoft to conduct evangelistic meetings for three days. I consented. The three days turned into three months of miracles, followed by four years of 'harvesting' in all parts of the United Kingdom. I was upheld and sustained by the 'quickening' of a vital experience of the authority of Christ in my soul. During that period I had an increased measure of health and an amazing freedom from all fret and care.'[31]

Brown had not easily undertaken the Lowestoft project. He claimed he had never seen himself as an evangelist. In another place Brown described his submission to the Lowestoft invitation in these words: 'God had waited four months for a man like me; and I said, "Lord Jesus, I know what you want. You want me to go into Mission work. I will, because I love you more than I dislike that!"'

Over the next eighteen months Brown addressed over 1,700 meetings. In September 1921, as in other years, hundreds of Scottish fishermen ended their pursuit of the herring down the east coast of Britain at Lowestoft, their wives coming over land, curing the herring as they went. One fisherman involved was Jock Troup, an open-air preacher, who found himself in the middle of the revival. Conversions spread through the fishing fleet and when they returned to northeast Scotland whole communities were changed. Jock Troup eventually became the Superintendent of the famous Tent Hall Mission in the middle of Glasgow, and the revival spread from there to Belfast within a year. Several thousands of people were converted through Brown's ministry in these years. His influence was brought into even sharper focus when he became President of the Baptist Union in 1929. Only Billy Graham Crusades had anything like a similar effect on twentieth century English Baptist churches.

In the twenties and thirties the evangelical heart of the Baptist family was stirred by such ventures and encouraged by some measure of success. The passion for mission was still intense, but effectiveness continued to elude the denomination at large.

[30] Stanley C. Griffin, *A Forgotten Revival,* Day One Publications, 1992, gives the detailed story of this revival

[31] D. Brown, *President's Address 1929,* p.4

14

Consolidation and Self-Awareness

WHEN Aubrey became the Union's Secretary his first task was one of consolidation. He began by providing full-time staff to handle youth and women's work. In 1934 a new lay leadership began a significant period of service for the Union, when Gordon Fairbairn was appointed Honorary Solicitor and Arnold Clark the Treasurer.

In the late 1930s there was a possibility that the Baptist Missionary Society might quit Furnival Street to make way for new Government Offices on the site. The Society's officers raised the possibility of a new joint headquarters in London for the Society and the Union. The Union's leadership did not wish to leave Church House but gave serious consideration to the proposal on the understanding that some measure of integration between the two bodies be agreed prior to the purchase of the new site. It was suggested that Publications, Youth and Women's programmes would be united in the proposed new premises for the Society and the Union, but anything beyond this was resisted by the Society.

At this time Benjamin Grey Griffiths was Home Secretary of the Baptist Missionary Society, a fellow Welshman and friend of Aubrey. Also at this time, the Treasurer of the BMS, H. L. Taylor of Bristol, was President of the Union for 1937–8. The layman, Robert Wilson Black, a financial supporter and advocate of the merger was in favour and found a site in Russell Square, available on a 200 year lease. It was the leasehold nature of the property, and also its size, which was double the requirement, that caused hesitations. The executive bodies of both Society and Union gave approval but the proposal was defeated at the 1938 Assembly.[1]

'Old for New'

One way to secure new resources for new church building was the sale of unwanted premises and using the funds in developing situations across the country. However, as Baptists increasingly co-operated nationally, it became clear that some revision of church trust deeds was required if a united Baptist programme of mission was to be developed from within the existing resources.

[1] W. M. S. West, 'The Reverend Secretary Aubrey', BQ, 34, 1992, pp.263–281

What should have been straightforward was frustrated by variations within the original trust deeds of Baptist properties. When the closure of a property was necessary, or a congregation needed its resources for use in a new work elsewhere, the ultimate trust in the documents was often inadequate to secure it legally for the use of the now united Baptist denomination within the structures of the Baptist Union.

For example, the doctrines set out in many old deeds were not exclusively Baptist. One way of resolving the difficulty was to name the Particular Baptist Fund or the Baptist Building Fund as beneficiaries, but this procedure left local trustees with no ultimate control of funds or property.

To resolve this the Baptist Union developed a model trust deed that placed trusteeship in the hands of the Baptist Union Corporation and the ultimate trust with the Union itself, which remedied most, but not all, the problems. The resistance of a very few church members, or technical legal reasons, often made it impossible for proceeds from the sale of property to be used elsewhere.

> Accordingly a clause was included in the Model Deed which made it possible for the Association and the Union acting together to close the church, sell the property and dispose of the proceeds as they thought fit. It also required that churches adopting the deed be in membership with both an Association and the Union and that the minister be on the accredited list.[2]

Initially the new Trust could only be applied to newly formed churches created as part of the 'Forward Movement', but increasingly many churches adopted it.

It was only in 1951 that an act of Parliament was passed which officially recognized the existence of the Baptist and Congregational Unions and gave them power to approve their own Trust Corporations for certain purposes, most importantly the power to accede to the request of a church to adopt the Model Trust in place of an existing one. The Unions were authorized to require changes as a condition of financial aid. E. A. Payne commented:

> This would seem to be entirely justifiable so long as the basis and organization of the Union maintains its fully representative character and is related to an adequate doctrine of the Church.[3]

Baptists and Scriptural Authority

Following 'Downgrade' the leaders of the Baptist Union had not shirked the need to address the issues relating to the authority of Scripture in the light of literary criticism. In 1889 Dr J. W. Todd had given an Assembly address on Higher Biblical Criticism. In 1894 'The spirit in which we should regard the present phases of Biblical Criticism' was tackled by the Revd S. Vincent. In 1909 H. G. Wood spoke on the 'Criticism of the Gospel' and J. T. Marshall addressed the Assembly on the 'Permanent Value of the Old Testament and Gospel'.

These issues related to a prior question: Where is authority to be found in the Christian religion? Dr H. Wheeler Robinson, who had become Principal of

[2] E. A. Payne, *The Baptist Union*, 1958, p.203f
[3] Ibid., p.254

H. Wheeler Robinson

Regent's Park College, London in 1920, was one Baptist who gave considerable thought to this issue. Robinson, born in Northampton in 1872, lived his early life with his devoted mother, and they shared the home of her uncle and aunt, effectively a 'one parent' family. Robinson started work at age 15, in the counting house of a wholesale leather merchant. He went to the College Street Baptist Church where he was greatly influenced by the associate minister, Henry Pollard, who worked alongside the legendary Turland Brown. Robinson was converted and baptized in his late teens, took an active share in church life, became a lay preacher, and was soon recognised as having gifts for full-time ministry.

He went to Regent's Park College, but was dissatisfied with what Dr Angus, the Principal, offered, and so moved to Edinburgh to take an Arts degree. This was followed by three years Mansfield College, Oxford, and a couple of years studying on the continent, the whole period decisive in his development. He married Alice Ashford in 1900 and held pastorates at Pitlochry, Perthshire, and at St Michael's Baptist Church, Coventry, before he joined Principal W. E. Blomfield, at Rawdon Baptist College.

He was appointed Principal at Regent's Park College, London, in 1920 as the College looked for someone

> at the height of his powers, who is willing to live for his post and who may be expected in the providence of God to give twenty years or so to the service of the College. He must be able in all directions to impress himself upon his men, a scholar, a University man, a Baptist, a saint, and with marked administrative ability. These exacting requirements were more than met in Henry Wheeler Robinson.[4]

Late in his life, Robinson gave a paper in Oxford in 1942 that addressed the authority issue. He asserted that in religion there must be a revelation, and this comes in three ways. First, there is history, the events of the early Christian tradition that are interpreted as the mighty acts of God and they become foundational for Christianity. Next, is the social dimension, the corporate organisation and fellowship of the Church. Finally, there is the individual, because every form of Christian faith demands some kind of personal response from its adherents.

[4] R. E. Cooper, *From Stepney to St Giles*, 1960, p.81

Robinson was aware that though many Baptists were still content with a simple appeal to Scripture, an increasing number were aware that Biblical criticism and the historical method had raised new problems, and of these the most important was 'authority'. The escape from obscurantism in regard to Biblical interpretation delivered Baptists into the entanglements of subjectivism.

The problem posed itself in terms of the competing claims of the 'Jesus of History' and the 'Christ of experience'. Keith Clements has noted how T. R. Glover and Robinson, both Baptists, one a historian and the other a theologian, faced this issue.

> Glover was not a theologian, but a historian with imaginative insight and an attractive pen ... He had a profoundly significant doctrine, though he would not have thought of it as such: the doctrine of the individual ... [but] Glover seems to have had no real concept of *community*.[5]

Robinson, at this time, had worked out his doctrine of 'corporate personality', as a vital clue in understanding Hebraic thought. It was this understanding of relationships that enabled Robinson to conclude that the subjective and objective aspects of authority must not be held in isolation. Consciousness always includes both, though the emphasis may now fall on one side, now on the other.

> God is really known, notwithstanding the inevitable symbolism of all human thought and language, in the bible, the tradition of the Christian community, the individual consciousness, and He is known in all these three realms by the intrinsic truth of the revelation, not by any claims which it makes for itself. To this intricate truth there is an intuitive response of personal faith. In all three realms the Holy Spirit is active partner and director.[6]

In an earlier book Robinson had dealt with the influence of the Holy Spirit, and gave a chapter to the Bible and the Spirit.[7] He commented that the Bible, open before a 'plain man' makes a double impression—it is both like and unlike any other book he has ever read. The literary and historical method of study pushes the whole problem of inspiration back to an understanding of the prophetic consciousness.

> Behind the literature there is history; within the history there are men who believe or are represented as believing that they are 'inspired' ... The issue as to the reality and the nature of inspiration of Scripture turns at last on the issue as to the inspiration of the prophetic consciousness, in other words, on a particular case of the fellowship of the Spirit and spirit.[8]

God's knowledge is mediated in and through religious experience, and this is as crucial for inspiration as it is for the doctrines of incarnation, Church and sacraments. God has made human experience the medium of this revelation.

[5] K. W. Clements, *Lovers of Discord,* p.127
[6] E. A. Payne, *Henry Wheeler Robinson*, p.178
[7] H. W. Robinson, *The Christian Experience of the Holy Spirit*, 1928. All quotes from Fontana edn., 1962
[8] Ibid., p.141

God is revealed, of course, because he is there. 'But He is there in the midst of human experience, and the revelation is *wholly* through that medium, not in the creation of the record alone, but also in the original form of the experience.'[9] Robinson developed the idea of the Bible as an organism—almost as the fruit of the Spirit in Christian experience:

> The authority of Scripture finds expression through the record of a rich and varied and extensive religious experience, within which we may discern the activity of God.[10]

It is important to recognize that revelation was mediated. The authority of Scripture and its inspiration depend on mediation through this human experience. God's revelation is a supernatural enrichment of an active mind. Despite the careful thinking of Robinson over the opening years of the century, Baptists remained ill-prepared to face these issues as the century progressed.

Baptists and Fundamentalism

The Fundamentals, 1910–1915, were a series of booklets written by both American and British authors that brought to the surface a strong defence of evangelical Christianity. Over these years Shakespeare had been deeply involved in preparing a Free Church doctrinal statement and when it came before the Baptist Union for ratification there were two main objections. The first was, that the statement on scripture said it contained the word of God, not that it was identical with it. Second, there was no affirmation of the essential deity of Christ.

At the 1918 Assembly the doctrinal basis for the projected Federal Council of Evangelical Free Churches was approved. It contained the following statement about the Bible:

> The Scriptures, delivered through men moved by the Holy Ghost, record and interpret the revelation of redemption, and contain the sure Word of God concerning our salvation and all things necessary thereto. Of this we are convinced by the witness of the Holy Spirit in the hearts of men to and with the Word; and this Spirit, thus speaking from the Scriptures to believers and to the Church, is the supreme Authority by which all opinions in religion are finally to be judged.[11]

The Baptist Bible Union

It was at this point that theologically conservative Baptists who disagreed with Shakespeare's declared intentions on Christian unity formed the Baptist Bible Union (BBU). It was at a meeting of the BBU in February 1922 that the attack was launched upon 'the modernist movement' as an agent of anarchy, revolution and Bolshevism. A year later its journal, *The Bible Call* had added to its title, *'and Fundamentalist Advocate'*. Some Congregationalists, Anglicans, and Wesleyan Methodists were also opposed to modern critical interpretations of Scripture and encouraged further Baptist action.

James Mountain was a key figure in the movement. He was a former Congregationalist minister, who had been baptized by F. B. Meyer in 1893. He

[9] Ibid., p.148
[10] Ibid., p.153
[11] E. A. Payne, *The Baptist Union: A Short History*, 1958, p.276

persuaded some members of his congregation to join him in founding St John's Free Church, Tunbridge Wells. Mountain vigorously opposed Shakespeare, and toured the north of England and South Wales to secure support for the BBU. 'Tunbridge Wells was ... where organized Baptist Fundamentalism was born'.[12]

The pastor at the Metropolitan Tabernacle, London, in the 1920s, H. Tydeman Chilvers, was a Strict and Particular Baptist who came to the Tabernacle in 1919. He published a sermon, *The Coming Conflict*, that urged his readers to be ready for a struggle which would require them to stand firm for the sound doctrine of former years. The echoes of Downgrade were heard in the *Baptist Times* from ministers trained at the Pastors' College who supported the BBU. One speaker at the annual conference of Spurgeon's ministers in 1923 spoke of the Baptist denomination as 'dying' and claimed only Spurgeon's men could save it from extinction.

Other supporters of the BBU came from the Bible League, a non-denominational body founded in 1892 to oppose higher criticism of the Bible. Of the twenty-two vice-presidents of the Bible League in 1923, nine were Baptists. The Bible League was a further stimulus to Fundamentalism among Baptists.

Challenge from individuals

An initial attack on Baptist Union ministers came from Principal McCaig of Spurgeon's College, against R. H. Coats of Handsworth, Birmingham. Coats, in his Sunday School notes published in the *Baptist Times* in December 1919, stated that the first chapter in the Bible 'was one of the last to be written, and it gives a priestly lawyer's account of the origin of all things, as believed by the Hebrews four or five centuries before Christ was born.' McCaig protested that 'the guesses of "higher criticism" were being presented to young people as "assured facts".'

The Keswick Convention, two weeks each year of 'Holiness' meetings, that had begun in 1875, invited Charles Brown, minister at Ferme Park, London, to speak on its platform. He had defended Coats' position in a sermon for the *Baptist Times* on 'How the Bible came to be'. However, Brown's more serious offence for Fundamentalists was his commendation of the A. S. Peake one-volume commentary on the Bible that advocated the results of higher criticism. James Mountain attacked Brown in an article, sent 'spies' to his church and to Keswick, afterwards attacking Brown and two other Keswick speakers in a pamphlet. Brown was never again invited to Keswick, which hurt him greatly. Four years later he made his own position clear by inviting the American Baptist liberal minister, Harry Emerson Fosdick, to preach at Ferme Park.

F. C. Spurr was another moderate Baptist minister pursued by James Mountain. He had succeeded F. B. Meyer at Regent's Park Chapel in 1914. He had also been invited to speak at the Keswick Convention. It was an unseemly affair with Spurr withdrawing from Keswick only a month before being due to speak for a second time. He made his position clear by accepting the Handsworth pastorate

[12] D. W. Bebbington, 'Baptists and Fundamentalism in Inter-War Britain', in Keith Robbins, ed., *Protestant Evangelicalism*, Oxford, 1990, p.303

when Coats left, and continued to affirm that the words of the Bible 'do not constitute the Word of God, which is "a living thing inside the words".'

Challenge to the Assembly

Dr T. R. Glover, son of the Revd Dr Richard Glover of Tyndale, Bristol, the Public Orator of Cambridge University, a classical scholar, deacon of St Andrew's Street Baptist church and personal friend of Charles Brown, was nominated as vice-president of the Baptist Union in 1923.[13] His book *Jesus of History* (1917) had been widely appreciated by theological conservatives, but his later books, *Jesus in the Experience of Men* and *Progress in Religion* had been built on higher criticism and were attacked. In his weekly column in *The Daily News*, he had attacked Fundamentalism as 'weak-headed', which gave great offence. However, Glover enjoyed substantial conservative support in the Baptist Union because he opposed Shakespeare on Church Union and was elected.

Fundamentalists began to organize quickly, claiming that the support for Modernism within the Baptist Union was widespread. A few churches withdrew from the Baptist Union. The Welsh wing of the BBU attempted to challenge Glover at the autumn assembly of the Baptist Union in Cardiff, but it was an anticlimax, his presidential address on the continuity and change within Christianity finding wide acceptance among the conservatives present.

Challenge to the BMS

An attack was simultaneously launched on the Baptist Missionary Society as the Bible Union of China called upon sending societies to confirm that their staff held to the full inspiration of Scripture. The BBU also published a book by W. Roberts, a former missionary to Assam, *The Ravages of Higher Criticism in the Indian Mission Field.* When the BMS refused to impose doctrinal tests on its candidates a Missionary Trust Fund was created to divert Baptist mission money. At the 1923 Assembly, where Glover was elected, W. Y. Fullerton of the BMS spoke of the Society's loyalty to the evangelical faith. The new Trust raised less than a thousand pounds in five years and 'once more a Fundamentalist campaign produced scant results except ill feeling.'[14]

British fundamentalists were less self-assured than their American counterparts and the movement did not make significant ground among the vast majority of Baptists in Britain. Subscribers to the BBU magazine were in hundreds, rather than thousands. In America a large network of Bible Colleges existed to challenge Baptist denominational colleges. In England Baptist colleges were firmly identified with the Baptist Union. Only Spurgeon's was unaffiliated to the Baptist Union in the inter-war years but under the leadership of its Principal from 1925, Percy Evans, it came closer to the Baptist Union. There was a further Fundamentalist challenge in 1930, when a ministerial student at Rawdon, W. E. Dalling, protested at the allegedly Modernist teaching of Principal A. C. Underwood was giving and resigned the Probationers' list.

The inherent aversion to extremism in the British temperament found

[13] For Glover, see, H. G. Wood, *Terrot Reavely Glover: A Biography*, Cambridge, 1953; K. Clements, *Lovers of Discord*, SPCK, 1988, pp.107–142

[14] Bebbington, op.cit., p.319

expression in Graham Scroggie, Baptist minister in Edinburgh, who in 1924 said after visiting America, 'Let us understand that the interests of Christ and His Word are not served by raw haste, violent denunciation, presumptuous ignorance, or uncharitableness of spirit.'[15] The legacy of the Fundamentalist debate was the Fellowship of Independent Evangelical Churches founded in 1922 by E. J. Poole-Connor who held to inerrancy as a primary doctrine. By 1935 there were 123 ministers and 22 probationers on its ministerial list. Within the denomination, those who were troubled by Modernism joined the Baptist Revival Fellowship, which emerged in the 1930s under the leadership of Theo Bamber, of Rye Lane Baptist Church, Peckham. It provided a focus in the 1960s for opposition within the Baptist Union to ecumenism, and growing Baptist centralization.

Ministry

The Ministry between the Wars

The ministry issues that had dominated the earlier part of the century for Baptists receded into the background in the next 30 years, to re-appear with a plethora of reports in the 1960s. Something of this acceptance of ministry in the Thirties is reflected in the lives of the three Baptist ministers considered earlier as part of a new generation of ministers. Alongside these must be placed the style and activity of the 'Essex Five', recounted later in this chapter who were typical of a large sector of Baptist ministry at this time. In 1932 Aubrey, in an exchange of views with his one time deacon at Cambridge, T. R. Glover, who had attacked the Spurgeon tradition in an article in *The Times*, went so far as to rebuke Glover:

> Remember that men like Carlile, Hiley, Evans, Hancock and the others of that great brigade—all of them stalwarts—don't like being told their training was 'amateurish'. Think of Luff and all the others whom Spurgeon compelled to face hard places filled with an enthusiasm that has never died. Contrast the half-warmed ineffective bunch that too many of our Colleges have been turning out in this last generation, with little moral or spiritual force and a lack of passion for saving men that have sustained Spurgeon's men through long, long, ministries—Wilson 54 years, Cuff a lifetime in Shoreditch, Carlile 30 odd years at Folkestone, Douglas Brown 25 years at Balham. It's a great story and the amateurs often beat the experts hands down.[16]

Aubrey's rebuke of Glover was properly made, but there were ministers who were College trained that had a considerable impact, an impact seen, for example, in the continuing stories of Ingli James and J. O. Barrett.

Ingli James

In 1931 Ingli James was called to Queen's Road, Coventry. In 1934 it was noted at Queen's Road that the church had 'always displayed a zeal for God, but always it has been a zeal according to knowledge—intelligent, sensitive and responsive

[15] Ibid., p.323
[16] W. M. S. West, 'The Reverend Secretary Aubrey', BQ, 34, 1992, p.203

to the changing conditions of a changing world'. Those who came to hear the 'communist' parson and those who came in rather larger numbers to hear the 'pacifist' parson, 'found that the pacifist was no communist, and that his passions for peace and social justice were always subservient to his witness for Christ. His sermons ended with a summons to the Cross and a call for decision at its foot.'[17] However, the Queen's Road church was an exception, not the norm, among Baptist churches of the day, with its combination of ministers from the liberal evangelical persuasion, its wide range of members from all strata in the local society, and its three centuries of being a leading Baptist church in the area.

In 1943 James was called to be East Midland General Superintendent and transferred to South Wales in 1947 until his retirement in 1956. His book on *Communism and Christian Faith* (1950) was 'written from the standpoint of evangelical Christianity' and aimed at Christian ministers and workers who often knew little of Marxism, but frequently came into contact with people who had fallen under its influence. He expounded Marxism, materialism, its ethic and view of history, and then offered what he termed a relevant Christian rejoinder alongside appropriate action for Christians in the Marxist Age. James was one of the few Baptist ministers who took the challenge of Marxist-Leninism seriously as well as offering a critique of its practical outworking.

J. O. Barrett

Fuller Baptist Church, Kettering, called Barrett to the pastorate, just as the Second World War broke out. It was here, particularly when the Baptist Missionary Society moved back to Kettering because of the London blitz, and celebrated its 150th anniversary in 1942, that Barrett came to the attention of a wider circle of Baptist leaders. He served twice as chaplain to the town's Mayor and started a new Baptist Church in Corby New Town.

He made his first broadcast service for the BBC in 1940 and thereafter became a member of the Midlands Religious Advisory Committee. Sidney Morris had drawn him into the work of the Baptist Ministers' Fellowship and he was involved with starting Summer Schools for ministers, the first held at Rhuddlan in 1945, with later ones at Oxford. He was also involved in establishing Probationer Ministers' Summer Schools.

As a member of the Baptist Union Council, Ernest Payne drew him into the founding of the 'Focus Group' in 1940. The group met regularly in London on the evening before the spring and autumn meetings of the Baptist Union Council, and then, in addition, once a year at longer meetings in Oxford where there was greater leisure and freedom to consider denominational matters.

From the group came future leaders of the denomination. The first members were William Bowie, Frank Buffard, Frank Bryan, Robert Child, H. Ingli James, J. B. Middlebrook, Guy Ramsay, J. C. Rendall, Ronald Bell, Charles Jewson, Ernest Payne, and J. O. Barrett. The two laymen, Bell and Jewson, occupied important public and business positions. The other ten were pastors, over the years, of more than a dozen of the most strategically placed Baptist churches,

[17] C. Binfield, *Pastors and People*, p.234

and from their ranks came a College Principal, four General Superintendents, and two General Secretaries, one of the Baptist Union and the other of the Baptist Missionary Society. Their original purpose had been to publish theological and practical papers, but that never happened. John Barrett kept the minutes of their meetings for over twenty years.

To M. E. Aubrey the Focus Group was an irritant without clear alternative policies rather than a creative force for meeting the challenge of the present times.

Barrett was approached at least four times to become a Superintendent but always declined, preferring the preaching ministry and valuing the theological liberty he enjoyed at Fuller. In 1947 he wrote a small commentary on *The Book of Revelation* at the request of J. B. Middlebrook, by then the Home Secretary of the BMS, as part of a series on the missionary message of the Bible.

Barrett was short-listed for the post of Deputy General Secretary of the Baptist Union, but the appointment went to O. D. Wiles, of Burlington, Ipswich. At the same time Henry Bonser indicated that he would retire from the Superintendency and it was then that Barrett finally agreed to serve, and was appointed to the North-East Area in March 1949.

It would be true to say that the Superintendency was still only cautiously welcomed among the 125 Baptist churches of Yorkshire, and the 38 of the Northern Association, situated in Northumberland, Durham and Cleveland.

John Barrett had two advantages: he had been trained at Rawdon and been a pastor in Newcastle. One of his first tasks was to implement Aubrey's 'Baptist Advance' and he was involved in persuading his churches to participate and in the preparation of literature. John Barrett was typical of a generation of Baptists who took modern Bible study very seriously, planned for a better ordering of Baptist worship and drank deeply at the springs of liturgical renewal before that was commonplace. Planning for a 'Holiday School' for deacons and young people near Scarborough in 1956 he told Ernest Payne in a letter:

> It needs on the one hand a deep down theological revival or renewal, and on the other a sense of our fellowship with the Church Universal and historic—perhaps the Ecumenical Movement will give us the latter—to put our worship and witness on right lines.[18]

Ecumenism

The Edinburgh World Missionary Conference in 1910 greatly stimulated missionary enthusiasm and resulted in various plans for working together. It inspired the 'Life and Work' movement which drew together world Christians in a search as to how best to present the Gospel in a secular age. Alongside this was the 'Faith and Order' movement that handled the theological and ecclesiastical divisions of Christianity. All of this came together in the plans for the World Council of Churches that was formed after World War Two in Amsterdam in 1948.[19]

[18] E. A. Payne, *A 20th-Century Minister: John Oliver Barrett, 1901–78*, p.15

[19] K. W. Clements, *Twentieth Century Baptists*, BHS, 1983, pp.55–75 recount the subsequent Baptist involvement in 'Faith and Order'

However, there was a strong continuing reaction to the ecumenical issue after Shakespeare's period of office. The first Assembly for Aubrey was in 1926 when the Assembly theme was *The Faith of the Baptists.* The address of the President, J. H. Rushbrooke, typified the mood in the denomination. Rushbrooke, the founding minister of a united Baptist and Congregational Free Church, at Hampstead Garden Suburb, London, in 1910, was a pioneer of local ecumenism.[20] He was committed to Christian unity but he had many questions. Not surprisingly, he responded quickly to the 1920 Lambeth *Appeal to all Christian People* in an address to his Hampstead Garden Suburb Church.

He described the *Appeal* as 'tolerant and charitable', free, as it was, of the terminology of a pre-War generation that invidiously compared the 'Anglican Church' with 'Nonconformist Bodies'. Rushbrooke felt Christians, as members of a universal Church, should be willing to interchange ministries, pray with each other, and even join each other in communion at the Lord's Table, for which mutual recognition of ministries was vital. The weakness of the Lambeth *Appeal* was its excessive stress on external formalities, offering an organisational unity arranged by ecclesiastical statesmen. Rushbrooke chaired the committee of the Baptist Union that prepared for the Assembly an official response to the *Appeal*. After several drafts the Union's Council agreed a document for approval by the Assembly that 'was gracious in tone, firm in Baptist conviction, open to the continuing search for unity, but adamant that organic union upon the terms laid down by the Lambeth Conference was unacceptable.'[21]

His Presidential address to the 1926 Assembly was, as Dr Charles Brown described it, 'an undisguised blowing of the Baptist trumpet'. Why did he take such a denominational stance? His biographer, Bernard Green, suggests that he drew attention to distinctive Baptist principles to highlight the inescapable differences that had to be honestly faced if Christian unity was to be discovered. His address expounded the centrality of faith, under the sole Lordship of Christ, according to Scripture, which found expression in believer's baptism. He described Baptists as 'unashamedly children of the Reformation, irrevocably evangelical and evangelistic'.[22]

There was no official Baptist representative at the Lausanne Conference on Faith and Order in 1927. Two unofficial Baptist delegates who paid their own expenses were the Baptist historian, W. T. Whitley, and a former Baptist Union President, J. Roberts. When Roberts died in 1929, Aubrey himself took his place on the 'continuation committee' of Faith and Order and played an important part in its work. After 1930 eighteen representatives of the Federal Council of Evangelical Churches discussed church re-union and issued a report in 1938. Aubrey, Gilbert Laws and Hugh Martin were the three Baptist participants. However, the proposals were questioned as soon as they were issued, and nothing came of them.

At this time there were two national groups on the Free Church scene and these came together in 1940. The National Free Church Council and the Federal

[20] J. H. Y. Briggs, *English Baptists of the Nineteenth Century,* BHS, 1994, p239, fn.96
[21] B. Green, *To-morrow's Man*, BHS, 1997, pp.188, 194
[22] *Ibid.*, p.140

Council became the Free Church Federal Council, based in Tavistock Square. Two years later, in Baptist Church House, the inauguration of a new ecumenical group, the British Council of Churches, took place and continued until 1989, as an agency for the churches to discuss common issues and plan co-operation on public issues.

Although the World Council of Churches was not formed until 1948, funds were collected for Inter-Church Aid, the fore-runner of Christian Aid in Britain, to provide relief for the grave distress on the Continent that followed 1945. The leading Baptist MP at the time, Ernest Brown, who had been a member of Churchill's War Cabinet, and Aubrey, were both delegates at Amsterdam and they were appointed members of the Central Committee.

Movements In Mission

Just as ministry had dominated the opening decades of the century, in the thirties Baptists returned with an equal vigour to the challenge of mission in the inter-War period. Evident decline was an albatross around the denomination's neck, but as yet it was felt that the innate passion for mission that had characterised Baptists for centuries, would liberate them from the mission stalemate that followed 1918.

The Discipleship Campaign

In 1932 the Baptist Union again turned its mind to the need for 'aggressive evangelism', a phrase often used at that time. The first effort was the Discipleship Campaign that asked every church member to lead at least one person into the direct service of Christ and the Church. Although widely taken up by Associations and churches the results were generally less than impressive.

The Essex Five Phenomenon

The Discipleship Campaign worked out in the Associations in various ways, but what happened in Essex, chronicled in *An Adventure for God* published by the Baptist Union in April 1934, was significant. It tells the story of five ministers from Essex whom Hugh Redwood, of the *News Chronicle*, challenged to make a 'hundred-percent commitment to Christ'. The Essex Baptist Association had been planning to implement the work of the Discipleship Campaign and there was a 'tinge of disappointment at the seeming apathy' according to Ernest Wood, President of the Baptist Union, writing later. However 'here was a waiting team of men fired with enthusiasm ready to throw themselves unreservedly into the work of evangelisation.'

It began with a meeting at Dagenham Baptist Church chaired by its minister, the Revd Hugh McCullough, at which Hugh Redwood was the speaker. Stanley A. Baker, minister at Tabernacle Baptist Church, Grays, who was also present, had had a restless night before joining a prayer breakfast, to pray for the conversion of Essex. He had begun to experience a measure of renewal in his own congregation and felt constrained to call Hugh McCullough, to suggest that if a number of ministers shared the same vision, they could work together as an evangelistic team among the Essex churches. After months of prayerful waiting on God four young ministers met on 3 August 1933 to consider what God was saying to them about the level of their commitment to evangelism in

Essex. They were convinced they had to sacrifice everything for the sake of this call from God, even their leisure hours. Within days of agreeing to work this out, a fifth, but older minister, joined this diverse group of ministers who shared a common evangelistic vision, with McCullough as the leader.

McCullough, born in Ireland on 1 August 1898, was early orphaned and brought up in a Dr Barnardo's Home by a devoted foster mother in the East End of London. Converted at the age of twelve, he later gained a commission and served in the Royal Army Flying Corps during the First World War He felt called to serve God in China and went to Spurgeon's College to train. Rejected for China on health grounds, he entered the home ministry and was minister first at Rayleigh, Essex (1925–9), then at Dagenham, (1929–35). When he died in 1949 he was revered as 'a winner of souls, one who turned many to righteousness, he has left a memory that is as a star to guide and a proof of the Gospel he proclaimed.' For five remarkable years he led the 'Essex Five', already a tried and tested leader of work in the overspill estates of Dagenham, full of East Enders like himself. The *News Chronicle* had noted he was 'attacking with fierce understanding and stubborn insistence the problem of the soulless suburb.'

George Banks, the only unaccredited minister in the Five, was the Bible teacher in the team who also played the piano. Fred G. Missen, a native of Wiltshire, was born at Melksham on 9 June 1905. He left school early and was in business at Woking when, after training at Spurgeon's, he was called into the ministry. It was while he was at Burnham-on-Sea, Essex, his first pastorate, that he met Hugh McCullough and became involved with the Essex Five.

Tom Shepherd, the oldest member of the Five, was born in 1867. He trained at Spurgeon's College and his final pastorate was at Aldeburgh (1929–32), when he retired from active ministry and joined the Five.

Stanley Albert Baker was another product of the East End, always 'ready for anything ... six foot of London, and proud of it' as he would say. He was born at Stoke Newington, 17 November 1899, and experienced an early conversion at the age of 9. He married another East Ender, Jessie Hurdle, converted at 13, and they were indomitable partners in Christian ministry over the years, particularly among young people. He trained for the mission field, hoping to go to Africa, but the War had prevented that. He was listening to Douglas Brown in Westminster Chapel, after the War, when Brown pointed at him in the gallery: 'You, young man! What God wants from you is a little bit of movement!' It was this that brought him into Baptist ministry at home, first at New Barnet, (1924–8), then Upwell (1928–32), and next Tabernacle, Grays (1932–5) where he met Hugh McCullough and became the loquacious secretary of 'the Five'. He was a remarkable minister, and from 1935–7 he was released by the Baptist Union for evangelistic work with Hugh McCullough, after his time with the Essex Five.

Each of these ministers received permission from their churches to spend the last week of each month, from Monday to Saturday, working for the wider evangelistic goal of the Essex Baptist Association. During that team week each month there were mornings of prayer and Bible Study, where each had to face themselves and recognise by fearless self-examination how each must change if they were to work together effectively. Afternoons were given to house to house visitation or attending existing meetings in the local church that invited them. The evenings were evangelistic meetings that also encouraged believers to a deeper commitment for Christ. The 'follow up' was the local church's responsibility. Prayer partners were enlisted from all the churches.

Invitations came in quickly from town and village churches and within eighteen months the team had visited the large majority of the county's Baptist churches.

Inevitably other areas asked them to visit and the Five held a special day of prayer to reflect on their response. McCullough and Baker handled most of these invitations from beyond Essex. There was a joint venture that involved all the Free Churches in a north London borough that was successful. Another request from Wales meant McCullough and Baker were seconded for two months of work in some of the most deprived towns of the Rhondda, places like Mountain Ash, Nant-y-moel and Dowlais, where many were encouraged and challenged to give 'one hundred-percent for Christ'.

Changing social milieu

There was a growing culture of leisure in the twenties and thirties and many churches deliberately offered wholesome alternatives within their church programmes. The Waterbarn Baptist Church, Bacup, for example, owned a playing field for its own cricket teams that played in the Sunday School League, together with tennis courts and a crown green bowling club. All this was linked with the Sunday School and flourished alongside the Scout and Guide companies also run at, and by, the chapel. This approach was repeated widely across the denomination. Some ministers also promoted what John Clifford had called 'a social gospel'. It challenged Victorian individualism and laissez-faire attitudes and what was meant to be a strategy for mass evangelism, in the end allowed secularising forces to gain a foothold in many congregations.

In the inter-war years the Lord's Day Observance Society received a lot of Baptist support, particularly in its opposition to cinema opening on Sundays, the battle finally lost in 1939, as Sunday cinema opening was viewed a vital recreation for troops on leave.

The Twynholm Baptist Church, Fulham, London, formerly in membership with the Churches of Christ, joined the Baptist Union in 1931. Its leading personality, Robert Wilson Black, was a man of great wealth and energy, the father of a subsequent Baptist Member of Parliament, Sir Cyril Black. He provided money for the appointment of J. N. Britton in 1935 as Baptist Union Evangelist and Commissioner for Evangelism from 1935–8. He launched the Baptist Forward Movement on the back of the Discipleship Campaign in 1936. Between 1931 and 1936 nearly half a million pounds had been raised for new Baptist churches, and by 1941 a further half a million pounds had been successfully raised, but there was little real church growth.

Nominalism in the Churches

As Baptist churches at this time had a steadily growing desire to be effective in their outreach, it was only slowly recognised that nominalism was not only a problem for the established church, but also affected Baptist churches. The Council in 1933 believed one way to face the 'effects of industrial on religious work' was to plead 'that churches in districts where they can no longer secure congregations should seriously consider whether it is their duty to move to other districts where a better response can be secured.' This was in itself an amazing concession to 'class' and 'culture'.

The Assembly's President in 1933, Rowntree Clifford, of Barking Road Tabernacle in East London, analysed the dilemma facing the churches:

> Never was church life harder than it is today. An entirely new situation has arisen in changed conditions, in the wider interests and constant migrations of the people, in the breaking up of family life, in the growing secularism of Sunday, in the passion for pleasure, in the wonders of the wireless, in the daring and unregulated thinking, in the neglect of the Bible and the decadence of Public Worship. The passion for social welfare captures many who hold the ideals of the Church, but they spend themselves in all kinds of social enterprises and recognize no Church loyalty. The place, power and usefulness of the Church are being seriously challenged, and the situation demands the statesmanship and sacrifice of all who love our Lord and His Church ... The state of many churches in the poorest populations is a disgrace to common Christianity ... We need to do to death the wicked fallacy that anything in the way of ministry and buildings is good enough for the poor. The dilapidated, ill-kept, poverty-stricken edifice, with a ministry to match is a reproach to the name of Christ.[23]

Aubrey was convinced that Baptists needed to trust less in schemes and committees and 'more in prayer, dedication, obedience and self-sacrifice'. Others called for the 'surprise power of the pulpit' to be re-discovered and believed it possible if only the familiar stereotyped order of public worship, which most churchgoers could repeat in their sleep, could be changed. Faced with claims that Baptist worship was weak and boring, Aubrey called for Baptist ministers to 'preach a more adventurous Christianity as well as a more definite faith than has been the general custom for some time past.'[24]

'Forward Movement'

A 'Call to Advance' announced in March 1936 emerged as the 'Forward Movement': a fresh effort to bring churches into harmony with God's purposes for them and thereby 'kindle the fires of devotion in the hearts of the people.' It had a financial goal of raising a million pounds over the next decade for new church extension and had raised a quarter of the total by April 1936. The *Baptist Times* in January 1936 claimed decline was a consequence of the First World War, since those who would have been the churches' strength and support did not return from the Front. Michael Goodman believed that the national crises of the Thirties served to precipitate the realisation in the church that all was not well.

[23] Presidential address
[24] *Baptist Times,* 1938

> Sadly, it appears that all too often the very sense of decline and crisis that permeated church life caused introspection and intense reassertion of old values, and what were considered to be well-tried strategies. Neither proved adequate for the entirely new ethos now facing the churches and society at large ... A cycle of decline had become established, acute crisis had effectively evolved into long-term, pragmatic survivalism.[25]

Social And Political Issues

At the opening of the twentieth century 'a Baptist was, almost by definition, a Liberal' claims David Bebbington in a study of Baptists and Politics since 1914.[26] But the political agenda post 1918 was totally different as Adrian Hastings apt summary indicates:

> A self-governing southern Ireland, parliamentary democracy, female suffrage, a powerful Labour Party, a vastly stronger Trade Union movement, a British Communist Party (founded in 1920), important further steps in education and insurance towards the welfare state: such were the not inconsiderable characteristics of the new post-war political order.[27]

Not only at home, but also abroad. The October 1917 Bolshevik Revolution meant Russia was profoundly changed, after great suffering and violence, into the Union of Soviet Socialist Republics, and for the next seventy years, not just Russia, but the whole world was irrevocably altered.

Not surprisingly the party political solidarity among Baptists prior to 1918, united in support of Liberal politics, began to change after the War. This is clearly chronicled in the pages of the *Baptist Times.* As already noted, Shakespeare had controlled the editorial policy of the paper while General Secretary, and remained loyal to Lloyd George. This loyalty wavered after the election of the first Labour government, when the paper, now edited by J. C. Carlile, minister at Folkestone Baptist Church, thought a Conservative administration relying on Liberal support for a majority would be acceptable. Under Carlile's editorship from1925–1941 the paper endorsed no candidate from any political party and that, in some measure, was the end of the public identification of Baptists with Liberalism, symptomatic of a more general Baptist retreat from politics.

Although Lloyd George remained a hero to many rank and file Baptists, as many welcomed the contribution of Ernest Brown, Liberal MP and member of Bloomsbury; while others enthusiastically supported the organiser of the Christian Socialism Crusade, George Lansbury, a Labour MP.

After the 1931 election few Liberals still had the political will to win, having fought the election as prisoners of a Conservative-dominated coalition. The *Baptist Times* made less reference to political issues but its attacks on Lloyd George grew. Although denominational affairs dominated its pages for the next couple of years, the Baptist leadership steered the denomination away from

[25] Michael L. Goodman, unpublished Open University Ph.D, 1993, 'English and Welsh Baptists in the 1930s', p.332. See also: P. R. Clifford, *Venture of Faith: the West Ham Story*
[26] D. W. Bebbington, 'Baptists and Politics since 1914', pp. 76–95 in K. W. Clements, ed., *Baptists in the Twentieth Century*, BHS, 1983
[27] A. Hastings, *A History of English Christianity, 1920–85,* 1986, p.22

contentious political and social issues.

Aubrey and Carlisle increasingly supported the government of national unity. Prime Minister Ramsay MacDonald and Aubrey were members of the Athenaeum Club, met informally, and in 1934 MacDonald chaired meetings held to celebrate the 150th anniversary of Spurgeon's birth, at which he declared himself to be a Calvinist. The *Baptist Times* now supported the Conservative-dominated National government, not the Liberals, advocating the Conservative reduction in unemployment benefit in 1932 and called on Baptists to accept increased personal austerity. Lloyd George's marital unfaithfulness became an open secret during the thirties and was viewed as a betrayal by many Baptists. Apart from education, most of the issues that had once secured Baptist support for Liberalism no longer existed after the First World War. Greater geographical, and easier social, mobility, both played their part. After the War chapels were no longer the primary place for many community leisure activities. As family businesses gave way to more impersonal industrial corporations, employees were no longer to demonstrate support for employers, if they were chapel people. The Conservative and Labour parties now largely represented the interests of the two main social classes. In fact, communal politics was giving way to the politics of class.

The 'convoluted manoeuvres of that practising but insincere Baptist, Lloyd George', writes Bebbington, was the impetus for the self-destruction of the Liberal Party, and a united Baptist political front was now impossible. By the 1945 election, only half the political constituencies had a Liberal candidate, so compromise or change was inevitable.

Aubrey's political convictions were not as obvious as his predecessor's, and emerge only occasionally. In 1931 he commented on a Labour plan to nationalise banks, as playing with fire, and so 'wholly mischievous'. His firm opposition to 'politics' was seen when a last political intervention by Lloyd George in 1935, called for a 'Council of Action' and asked the Free Churches to agitate for peace and increased public spending. Aubrey thought it 'politicking' of the worst kind, a threat to the spirituality of the Church. Aubrey felt so strongly, he resigned from the Free Church Council executive over the issue. He protested vehemently against the Church 'being dragged through the mire of an electioneering campaign'.[28]

Peace and War: Baptist views

Baptist churches became more inward looking and after the Great War the link between Christian pacifism and Nonconformity was broken. Baptist support for a war in the defence of Christendom had grown as the First World War continued, and most Baptists recognised that Shakespeare's creation of a United Board of Free Church Chaplains for the armed services had been a necessary step. However, in the aftermath of War, a significant number of ministers and laity declared themselves openly pacifist, and many Baptist churches had become corporate members of the League of Nations.

[28] D. W. Bebbington, 'Baptist in Politics since 1914', in K. Clements, *Baptists in the Twentieth Century*, BHS 1983, p.83. S. Koss, *Nonconfomity in modern British Politics*, 1975, pp.187–215

The major change for ordinary people regarding war, as a result of the First World War, was the discovery of pacifism as a Christian life-style. Until then, war had been the domain of the professional serviceman, but once conscription was introduced then war was an issue for all citizens. Pacifism had arrived and would be part of the Christian response to war for the rest of the century, challenging any 'just war' position, however it was re-presented in the light of changing circumstances demanded by Fascism or Communism.

In 1929 the Revd W. H. Haden promoted the idea of a Baptist Ministers Peace Movement. He had over 300 responses and was given a place on the agenda at the Pastoral Session of the 1932 Assembly. Following this F. C. Bryan took responsibility to circulate peace literature and in 1934 a Baptist Ministers' Peace Fellowship was formed, with 580 members. In 1936 the Assembly passed a resolution that 'modern war means the organized killing of men, women and children on a wide scale, and is manifestly contrary to the will of God'. Churches also passed similar resolutions. Queen's Road, Coventry, called on the government to pursue a vigorous policy of disarmament and collective security and affirmed that 'reliance on Armed Force can neither be reconciled with our Master's Law of Love, nor give the world peace'.[29]

The absolutist position of the Christian pacifist between the wars, if only for a while, became popular in Britain through Dick Sheppard, a canon of St Paul's Cathedral, London. In 1934 he personally challenged the re-armament programme. In a famous letter to the press of 16 October he declared himself 'now convinced that war of every kind or for any cause, is not only a denial of Christianity, but a crime against humanity', and asked anyone who agreed with this to send him a postcard saying that he or she 'renounced war'. Fifty thousand did so, and the Peace Pledge Union was born on 14 July 1935. It was a short-lived popular movement, but many Baptists were seriously committed to it. On 3 September 1939 Britain declared war. The Peace, appeasement, Pacifism, the League of Nations, were all swept aside and the Church, Baptists included 'had very little to say. It had exhausted its wisdom.'[30]

The Baptist Union Council set up a group to consider *The Attitude of the Baptist Denomination to War*. In 1936 the group urged the surrender of a measure of national sovereignty to secure the formation of an appropriate world organization to keep the peace. The Council was hesitant about a view endorsed by a majority of the committee: '... that a peaceful world cannot be ensured apart from force organized in such form and on such a scale as to be equal to the task of restraining disloyal and aggressive states'.[31]

On the crucial issues of war and peace, many Baptists were determined pacifists, but the Japanese invasion of Manchuria brought home that sinister changes were coming in the world order. The pages of the *Baptist Times* spelt out the issues but scrupulously avoided the unacceptable cry for the country to be on a war footing. The arrest of Pastor Niemöller highlighted the issue of the German Church's struggle with Hitler.

[29] P. R. Dekar, '20th-century Baptist Conscientious Objectors', BQ, 1993, pp.35–44
[30] Hastings, op.cit., p.332, 352
[31] E. A. Payne, *The Baptist Union: A Short History*, 1958, p.207

However, while among English Baptists there was equal concern about the Italian fascist regime's actions in Abyssinia, there was little public action on behalf of fellow believers in Eastern Europe, with the exception of Romania, where J. H. Rushbrooke as European Secretary of the Baptist World Alliance worked tirelessly to overcome the active persecution by the Orthodox Church of Baptists.[32]

Wartime disruption

The effects of war on church life in Britain during 1939–45 were much more extensive than they had been during 1914–18. Men and women were conscripted into the armed services; the whole population was affected by evacuation programmes which emptied city churches over-night and filled small village chapels to overflowing; church buildings were requisitioned and evening services were cancelled because of inability to meet the 'black-out' requirements. There was also disruption to central denominational planning. The Baptist Missionary Society moved to High Wycombe for safety at the start of the hostilities, then moved back to Furnival Street, only to be bombed out, and moved to Kettering where the Society had begun in 1792! The Union remained in Church House and suffered considerable disruption, including the loss of its upper floor by enemy action.

Throughout the War ecumenical co-operation continued. In 1941 a delegation met the Secretary of State for Education, R. A. Butler, and agreed principles about religious education in schools, acceptable to all the churches, that were embodied in the 1944 Education Act.

Fred Townley Lord was minister at Bloomsbury in this period and was deeply aware of the change that the War brought to Bloomsbury.[33] Born in Burnley in 1893, his family moved to Accrington and joined the Cannon Street Church. He went to Manchester University and then to Rawdon for ministerial training. He became minister at Turret Green, Ipswich, in 1916. He spent time with the YMCA in France during the War, and in 1920 became minister at Acton, West London. While in Acton he gained a London DD researching on 'The Christian conception of soul and body in relation to modern psychology', at 25 the youngest recipient of the degree. From 1926 to 1929 Lord was minister at Queen's Road, Coventry. Approached by Bloomsbury, he first declined, but under denominational pressure to accept, he did so in 1930, remaining its pastor until 1958. Lord was a prolific writer and was one of the first successful religious broadcasters, and this medium occupied much of his time and talent. He was a powerful preacher whose commanding presence and brilliant mind made him popular with a wide range of people. His church secretary said of him: 'Scholar, writer, administrator, he could have reached the top of any profession he had adopted. He chose to be a minister of the Gospel ... he did not avoid modern problems, but he disdained sensationalism. The Christianity he preached was always a joyous religion; his message was the simple one of the all-embracing love of God through Jesus Christ.'[34]

[32] For Rushbrooke, see B. Green, *Tomorrow's Man*, BHS, 1997; and for the later development of the European Baptist Federation, B. Green, *Crossing the Boundaries*, BHS, 1999
[33] F. Bowers, *Called to the City*, 1989, pp.37–48
[34] F. Bowers, *A Bold Experiment*, 1999, p.330

When War was declared on 3 September 1939 the regular Bloomsbury morning and evening congregations of 500 and 800 respectively disappeared within weeks and about 40 people remained. Young men were called up, students dispersed, hospitals moved out of London, and Sunday School children were evacuated. Lord wrote regularly to those in the services, and in January 1940 he wrote to every child who had been evacuated, enclosing a gift. Services continued, sandbags surrounded the building, and until blackouts were provided for the chapel, evening services were held in the basement. One spire was damaged, windows were blown out in the bombing, and seven members were killed in the first wave of bombing. During one winter some one thousand people bombed out of their homes found temporary shelter in Bloomsbury.

In 1941 the London County Council requisitioned the basement as an emergency dormitory and put 250 bunks in it. Mrs Grant, the caretaker's wife, always called the refugees 'our guests' and would bring some up to the Sunday services. The LCC also took over the fourth floor and used it as rest rooms and offices for their staff. The lounge became a dining hall where 150 children were fed daily in 1942, and 300 in 1944.

The Treasurer was moved out of London by the Admiralty, for whom he worked, by 15 September, and the Secretary, Myrddin Evans, was busy in the War Cabinet Office and was loaned to the United States government in 1942. The minister and caretakers kept Bloomsbury open, and many service personnel were glad of its worship service during the duration of the War.

Ministry

What is a Baptist minister?

Although the War intervened on the routine affairs of Baptist churches, there was a widespread concern among Baptist ministers to secure a common definition of their role. Two books about the ministry, each with a very different view of what was involved, emerged in the mid-1940s. Were ministers like Ingli James and John Barrett simply to be understood in terms of the local church, or were they in some measure ministers of the world Church?

Arthur Dakin, the President of Bristol Baptist College, wrote:

> A Baptist minister is one who is actually doing to the full, the work of a minister in a Baptist Church … Baptists have no 'order' of ministry in the sense that there is in the Church a class of men made distinctive by some special endowment of divine grace regarded as being confirmed by an ordination ceremony, or the laying on of hands, or in any other way. In actual practice the minister is given a standing different from that of ordinary members of the church, but this is … not in any sense [because of] some special grace or "holiness" not available to others.

There was nothing to prevent any lay person fulfilling ministerial functions provided he or she had the gifts and was properly appointed by the church so to do. Dakin continued:

> [A] Baptist minister is one who is closely related to one Baptist Church which has given him an invitation and over which he presides. He is a

> Baptist Minister (with emphasis on the word 'Baptist') partly in virtue of that relationship, and if that relationship were entirely to cease, leaving him with no church over which to preside, he would for the time being cease to be a Baptist minister, just as a deacon ceases to be a Baptist deacon when he gives up the office.

Among Baptists, declared Dakin:

> ministry is defined in terms of the local community, and not in terms of a central authority or of an ideal whole. To give up this principle would be to alter profoundly the whole Baptist view both of church and ministry.

How did Dakin understand a Baptist minister's work in relationship to the universal Church?

> About this there is no difficulty. Baptists believe that every true Baptist Church is an expression and part of the Church of God. Therefore every minister of a Baptist Church is, *ipso facto,* a minister of the Church of God. Only, in Baptist theory, he is not first a minister of the Church of God in some general way and then a minister of the Church at Corinth. Rather the situation is exactly the reverse, first a minister of the local church and then by reason of that a minister of the Church of God.[35]

In the same year, 1944, Ernest Payne published *The Fellowship of Believers,* which looked at the themes of Church, ministry and sacraments in Baptist thought and practice over the previous three centuries. Payne's stated aim 'was to show that the mutual relations of Baptist churches are not a matter for voluntary decision.' In a revised and enlarged edition of his book, Payne declared: 'The local congregation is not truly a church if it lives an entirely separate life' and quoted R. C. Walton with satisfaction, who had maintained the Church is not a voluntary society, but one that is 'called into existence and its life maintained, not by the decision of men, but by the will of God ... The glory of the Church is a phrase without meaning unless we are thinking of the World Church.'[36]

The Baptist Union Council in 1948 had made a statement on the Church that supported Payne when he claimed that:

> Many among us hold that since the ministry is the gift of God to the Church, and the call to exercise the function of a minister comes from Him, a man who is called is not only a minister of a local Baptist church but also a minister of the whole Church of Jesus Christ.[37]

The statement confirmed that among Baptists the minister's authority to exercise his office comes from the call of God in his personal experience and after testing of the call and training, the minister is invited 'to exercise his gift' in a particular sphere. His authority is therefore, from Christ through the believing community.

[35] A. Dakin, *The Baptist View of the Church and Ministry,* 1944, pp.42, 44, 48
[36] E. A. Payne, *The Fellowship of Believers*, 1944 and 1952. R. C. Walton, *The Gathered Community,* 1946, p.179
[37] E. A. Payne, *The Baptist Union: A Short History,* 1958, p.287; text on pp.283–291

The Home Work Fund

During the War it had become clear that the Sustentation Fund would need total reorganization. Aubrey and Gordon Fairbairn had been working on a proposal for the Baptist Union to have a General Purposes and Finance Executive and a Home Work Fund, which would not only support ministerial stipends but also the general and departmental work of the Baptist Union.

After B. G. Griffith retired from the BMS, he gave himself to the Union with the same vigour he had served the Society. The shared Welsh origins created trust between him and Aubrey, and in the mid 1940s Aubrey and Griffith produced a major plan for the reorganisation of Baptist finances. They proposed a unified appeal by the Union within the churches and Associations to be called the Home Work Fund. The funds raised would meet all the central and local needs currently appealed for on an individual basis within the constituency. Apart from the gifts received from personal members of the Union and affiliation fees from churches, all monies received would be credited to one fund to meet the Union's administration costs and to make grants to ministers of churches in need of help. From the total raised by each Association a quarter would be returned every year to the Associations, to finance the local work of the churches. This radical plan changed the denominational pattern of work, giving flexibility and freedom to the Union's staff.

Griffith shaped much of the scheme's details and his authority and drive set it in motion for acceptance in the churches. Griffith was almost daily in Baptist Church House, Holborn. In February 1947, when preparations for the Copenhagen Congress of the Baptist World Alliance were at their height, Dr J. H. Rushbrooke died. Grey Griffith, a close friend of Rushbrooke, generously helped W. O. Lewis, the BWA General Secretary, to carry through the Congress. In 1955 at the Golden Jubilee Congress, Griffith was one of a small group present who had attended the Alliance's formation in London in 1905.

In 1951 Griffith was elected President of the London Baptist Association, and Dr Henry Cook, the London Superintendent, welcomed his business acumen in re-ordering the affairs of the London Baptist Property Board.

Since 1927 he had been a member of the Psalms and Hymns Trust and was appointed a member of the editorial committee for the new *Baptist Hymn Book*. The book's contents, its *Companion*, as well as the successful business arrangements for its publication, owed much to his wisdom and foresight. His eagerness and enthusiasm for the enterprise was all the greater because of the grants to widows and orphans that were made from profits on the sale of hymnbooks.

Before retiring, Aubrey 'determined to return to his "evangelistic pastoral mode". The Baptist Advance campaign was initiated in this context.' Morris West noted that, 'Throughout the Aubrey years, the denomination had to live with declining membership. In 1926 the membership was 416,000; by 1946 this was 355,000 and this against a rising total population. The loss in Sunday School scholars was even more striking: from 525,000 in 1926 to 302,000 in 1946 ... Retrospectively, one can perceive now how the leisure life of the local community at large detached itself from the life of the local church. There was now so much else to do, more attractive and less demanding than the church-organized leisure activities.'[38] From 1949 Aubrey travelled widely throughout the Baptist constituency, encouraging churches in programmes of renewal and evangelistic activity.

At the end of his Secretaryship the Assembly recorded its appreciation of his faith, courage and resolution, his fervent evangelistic zeal and deep concern for the spiritual health of the churches, and noted appreciatively his many-sided public and religious services.[39]

[38] W. M. S. West, *Baptists Together*, BHS, 2000, p.62
[39] D. C. Sparkes, *The Home Mission Story*, BU, 1995, tells the story of Baptist giving to mission at home

15

Understanding Faith, Enabling Ministry

THE Baptist Union moved into the 1950s under the careful leadership of Ernest A. Payne who had grown up in London at The Downs, Clapton. His commitment to a predecessor in office began when he was a boy and it marked him for the rest of his life. One of Payne's abiding memories was of when he first met J. H. Shakespeare, on a London tram. Years later he wrote:

> Even a boy could not fail to be impressed. One of my own earliest memories of him belongs to the time of the First World War, when his powers and influence were at their height. My mother had taken me to a meeting in North-east London at which Shakespeare was one of the speakers ... on the way home we found Shakespeare on the same electric tram ... As the tram rattled its way up the Lea Bridge Road I received an ineffaceable impression of a rare and almost majestic personality who seemed to dwarf his physical surroundings. On several occasions I saw him on the platform of the Baptist Union, usually looking grave, pale and worn, but always commanding. When his book, *The Churches at the Cross Roads,* appeared, I was swept off my feet by its eloquent plea for Christian unity and eagerly entered for an essay competition based upon it.[1]

Payne trained for the ministry first at Regent's Park College, then housed in London, and afterwards at Mansfield College, Oxford, fully intending to go overseas to India with the Baptist Missionary Society. This was not to be, however, and in 1928 he went to his first and only local pastorate at Bugbrooke, in Northamptonshire.

After a few years he was called to be the Young People's Secretary of the BMS. He served in that capacity and later as Editor of the Society's publications, until he was called back to Regent's Park College, by then in Oxford, to serve as tutor in Church History. He wrote a wide range of Baptist missionary books, including *The Growth of the World Church,* (1955), that set the missionary story in its widest possible church setting. He also reflected continuously on Baptist history and wrote the seminal study, already referred to, *The Fellowship of Believers.*[2]

[1] See A. S. Clement, ed., *Baptists Who Made History*, 1955, p.127

[2] A comparison of the two editions, 1944 and 1952, is very informative for understanding Payne's developing approach

Percy Evans, Principal of Spurgeon's College, led the search committee for Aubrey's successor. Payne came to the post of General Secretary with much hesitation but was widely recognised as the person most suited to the task which faced the denomination in mid-century. Morris West comments:

> Ernest Payne had no real expectation nor thought that the committee might look in his direction. Certainly he had little desire that they should. His part on the Baptist Union Council and his intervention in the debates had often been extremely critical of the official line. He had never had contact with nor been seriously under the influence of the Spurgeonic tradition which was very strong in certain parts of the country. He was known to be involved and becoming more deeply involved in ecumenical affairs ... It was an office to which the Baptist Union Council and then the Baptist Assembly called him with virtual unanimity. He accepted because of his loyalty to the denomination and because he believed that the call truly reflected the call of God.[3]

Baptist World Alliance 1955

One of his first tasks was to be involved with the Golden Jubilee Congress of the Baptist World Alliance which had first met in London in 1905. In 1954 Billy Graham had held his first Crusade at the Harringay Arena, and it was at BWA Golden Jubilee meetings in 1955 that many more Baptists from around the world became aware of the powers of Billy Graham who preached at the final BWA gathering held in the Arsenal football stadium.

In 1954 Payne had made a personal visit to the All Union Council of Evangelical Christians-Baptists in the Soviet Union and re-established contact with the Soviet Baptists. They now numbered over half a million members throughout the various states. Nine Soviet Baptists came to the London Baptist World Alliance Congress in 1955, the first to be present since the 1928 Congress. Payne gave much time to strengthening European Baptist contacts in both East and West, and between 1955 and 1958 he established contacts with Baptists in Hungary, Poland and Czechoslovakia, who came with other European representatives to a European Baptist Federation conference in Berlin in 1958.

The Baptist Union Ter-Jubilee

As the fifties moved into the sixties, Ernest Payne constructed a wide-ranging programme of celebrations to mark the 150th anniversary of the founding of the Baptist Union. To set the scene he published in 1959 *The Baptist Union: A Short History.* The four year celebrations produced a growing self-awareness among Baptists which resulted in discussions about the nature of the Church, its ministry, ordination, baptism and the place of children in the Church, as well as liturgical renewal. This last was summed up in a denominationally formative book, *Orders and Prayers for Worship* (1960), written by Payne and Stephen Winward, and the publication of *The Baptist Hymnbook* in 1962.

The Ter-Jubilee celebrations began with a renewing of the 1784 *Call to Prayer* that had been so important a factor in the formation of the Baptist Missionary

[3] W. M. S. West, *To be a Pilgrim: a memoir of Ernest A. Payne,* 1983, pp.73, 75, and chap.4

Ter-Jubilee Celebrations

Society in 1792. It was proposed to raise £300,000 during the four years 1959–63 that would be used to help strengthen the ministerial training programmes of the Union and augment the financial resources of the Home Work Fund.

Denominational Conference 1961

A conference was held in 1961 at Swanwick, Derbyshire, when representatives from across the Union's churches spent a few days considering denominational issues.[4] The Swanwick statement had a ripple effect in the Baptist Union over the next

[4] *Ibid.*, pp.122–125

decade, as many of the issues raised were addressed. Appropriate commissions were set in motion and there was a perception that this whole internal process must be set securely within the world scene and therefore the ecumenical dimension needed to be understood.

The statement from the conference reflected on a range of issues. On both biblical and pragmatic grounds it was agreed that the historic independency of Baptist churches must face the implications of, and necessity for, interdependency, both on theological and pragmatic grounds, an issue that Payne had argued in *The Fellowship of Believers* from the mid-forties onwards.

Since the seventeenth century the emergence of Baptist Associations had initially produced large geographical units. By the nineteenth century, industrialisation and overall population growth, meant they needed to be smaller. The Western Association, for example, during the nineteenth century was split on more than one occasion into the Devon and Cornwall, Bristol and District, Wiltshire and East Somerset, and Gloucestershire and Herefordshire Baptist Associations. A working group was set up to address rationalising Association boundaries but its report, when considered by Council, was left on the shelf.

The fifties and sixties were, for Baptists, a period of reflection upon Church and ministry, as once more the Richard Baxter maxim, that churches increase in direct proportion to the adequacy of ministry, was pursued in the interests of mission through local congregations. Swanwick urged changes in the settlement of ministers, questioned the status of deaconesses, and suggested that ministerial candidates over 40 years of age be accepted for training. In the light of the 'spiritual and numerical weakness evident in certain areas, pastors and churches should experiment with grouping neighbouring churches under one pastor'. The Union was asked to encourage Commissions to look at various issues. One of the first Commissions to report in 1964 was on the Associations. Swanwick had an impact on the denomination, it marked the beginning of a more complete acceptance of women in ministry, and the emergence of a generation of ministers who were not prepared to accept the drift into decline that had marked the denomination in recent years. Neville Clark later commented:

> The report from the denominational conference of 1961 reads ... like an advanced agenda for the actual Union business of the sixties. Independency must be supplemented by interdependency. Association structures and life must be renewed. Ministry matters must be thought through. The spiritual and numerical weakness of the churches must prompt examination and experiment, and teaching and training be better provided. The ecumenical dimension must be grasped and clarified.[5]

A Baptist view of the Church

The writers in *The Pattern of the Church* (1963), edited by Alec Gilmore, contended that the Baptist pattern of the Church is one of the most formative and most widespread in the world. But what was this understanding of the Church? What is the heart of its life and witness and how is this related to the whole church and its growing unity?

[5] In J. H. Y. Briggs, ed., *Faith, Heritage and Witness*, BHS, 1987, p.14

Morris West wrote about 'Baptist Church life Today'; Stephen Winward described the New Testament Church using Christ as the 'form' of the Church, whose ministry was mediated through Word and Sacraments, and who was Himself the Church's authority. Neville Clark contrasted the Old Israel and the New Israel under Christ, and Alec Gilmore wrote of Baptist churches today and tomorrow in terms of worship, ministry and unity.

> [Baptists] must be prepared to meet with other Christians and to worship with them ... to discuss matters of faith and practice with them and to see their point of view. In due course, the Baptist church, built on the self-surrendered rights and privileges of the local churches, will in turn be called upon to surrender its own independence and doubtless some of its principles before the wider church ... To achieve it is to enter into the fullness of the church and to give the Lord we love the full rights over those who are his.[6]

A final chapter, 'towards church union', urged the whole denomination to face the ecumenical challenge and the 'action now demanded.'

The authors identified inertia and complacency as obstacles since 're-union demands denominational crucifixion; and it is a hard demand.' Confessionalism on a world scale, which had developed side by side with ecumenism, was another obstacle. Re-union in Britain 'would menace global confessional relations, and to betray fraternity for the sake of unity is too high a price.' It is easier 'to sanctify the denominational will to live by extending it into the international field than to crucify it on the local hill outside our city wall.' Fundamentalism was judged the most positive and pervasive obstacle.

> Its intense concern with the Bible as sole and simple arbiter of faith, and with rightly formulated doctrine expressive of common belief and experience as the essential bond of unity, has rendered it on the one hand indifferent to churchly unity, and on the other profoundly distrustful of the familiar ecumenical approach and solution ... Fundamentalism may seem an insuperable barrier to re-union. But an attitude that takes scripture so seriously must surely yield to scripture at the last.[7]

Describing the nature of the unity to be manifested, the authors sought a 'unity of faith rather than formulation ... this is the irreversible order and connection ... Formulation is the necessary servant of faith—necessary, but servant.' Similarly, organization is the essential servant of order—essential, but servant. Again, they looked for 'unity in sacrament rather than liturgy ... Liturgy is the needful bearer of sacramental existence—needful, but bearer.' We must first act if we would fully understand what 'lies beyond the hills.'[8]

It was necessary now to educate Baptists into their true identity, the fullness of their denominational heritage and at the same time initiate conversations with other Christians. It required the denominational heritage be taught ecumenically. Just as scripture has been prized out of sectional interests, so Baptist identity must be understood afresh from the ecumenical context, which is

[6] A. Gilmore, ed., *The Pattern of the Church: A Baptist View*, 1963, p.156
[7] *Ibid.*, pp.159–60
[8] *Ibid.*, pp.161–2

a hard demand. 'The time for Free Church union has long since passed ... There is not even the will to secure a Free Church hymnal.' This particular chessboard 'is securely protected against the remotest possibility of checkmate.'

The four issues identified as important at that time were tradition, *episcope*, initiation, church and state. After discussing these, the chapter ended:

> Yet, at some point, if education be effective and conversations fruitful, a second stage in church relations must be inaugurated by means of a pledge to visible union ... [which] means that discussion is deliberately set within a new context and problems viewed from an altered standing ground.

This would have profound consequences for resolving denominational problems relating to new church building and training for ministry. The pledge to unite must be crowned by a deed of union, and it is at this point that intercommunion becomes relevant and necessary.

> For the deed of union is the act of surrender. It is the committal to the cross that opens the gates of resurrection.[9]

'Liberty in the Lord'

An immediate response to the Swanwick Conference came from the Commission on the Associations, set up in March 1962 and reporting to Council in November 1964. It provoked considerable discussion and in particular brought a significant reply from Conservative Evangelical ministers in the denomination, published as *Liberty in the Lord* by the Baptist Revival Fellowship (BRF) that had its origins in the 1930s.[10]

Council appointed a representative from each of the Baptist Union Areas to the Commission, and Dr Morris West to chair the whole. Its remit was to make a report with recommendations for consideration by Council on a number of issues: the relationship of the Associations to the Council, its committees and Departments, Association boundaries; and the representation to, and effectiveness of, those serving on Association committees. It also considered the increasing pressure for full-time Association appointments, and the right proportion of Home Mission money to be returned to the Associations. The 60 page report made 64 recommendations, 20 for Associations and the rest for Council. It argued that in the light of developments in the Baptist Union over 150 years that 'the concept of the Baptist Union as the Associations associating together could provide a starting point for such re-thinking.' It also suggested that if a 'strengthening of confidence' was needed and 'if a basis of doctrine is felt to be necessary for an Association', then the Declaration of Principle is commended for consideration.

On the matter of 'authority' the report argued for the servant model of Jesus (*ministerial*), rather than for that of domination by a Master (*magisterial*). 'Any authority which rests with the Association, rests with it, not that the churches

[9] *Ibid.*, p.168

[10] BRF arose from a group of London Baptist ministers who in the 1930s were burdened by their own spiritual weakness and need for renewal by the Lord and the need for a Revival in the Church. After 1945 a quarterly bulletin was issued, BRF numbers grew, and from 1954 annual conferences were held, mainly, though not exclusively for ministers

might become subservient but that through the Association local churches in their mission and all their activities may be served'. It further observed that 'the local church, Association and Union are not to be viewed as working one above the other, but as working *together*, each having its essential part in all matters which concern the wider fellowship beyond the local church'. There was a firm intention to take back responsibility from the Area Committees that Shakespeare had introduced when creating the Superintendency, and put all powers back in the Associations' control.[11] In the published Report it was noted that none of the recommendations were before either the Baptist Union Council or the Associations.

The peril of creeds

An editorial in the *Baptist Times* introducing the Report, headed 'The Peril of the Creeds', stated

> Confessions and creeds may be useful forms of making a witness. They become a peril when turned into rules of faith ... and that liberty of conscience and man's personal responsibility to God are matters with which no 'king, pope, priest, or theological committee can be allowed to interfere'.

The title of the leader caught readers' attention, and brought criticism from two different theological perspectives.

Alec Gilmore, a minister in Northampton, was not happy that yet another report was coming down to the churches. Judging by what had happened to the reports on Ordination and Ministry, he suggested that the report 'will make no difference at all' causing 'scarcely a ripple on the surface' of the churches because it was asking the wrong questions. Apart from one reference on p.26, he noted there was no attempt to set the discussion in the terms of Scripture or theology, but only in the light of Baptist principles, history and present practice.

Gilmore thought it was using a telescope to see the far distant scene of Reformation, when what was needed was good theology to re-interpret history and correct present practice—'alas, that is not what we are given'. What of the ecumenical challenge of the 1964 British Council of Churches Conference, in Nottingham, which asked churches to seek visible unity by Easter 1980? Gilmore concluded by giving his own questions. First, what is a church unit—local, regional, national or international? Second, what is the focal point of authority and power within that unit? Finally, what is the mind of Christ on these matters for our day, learned from Scripture as interpreted by the whole Church and not simply within our own tradition?

Leslie Larwood, from the perspective of the Baptist Revival Fellowship, and on the same page, described the report as 'realistic, but ...' He was glad the polity of both Methodism and Presbyterianism had been set aside; and that John Owen's distinction between 'magisterial' and 'ministerial' authority had been recognised, with 'ministerial' welcomed. He stressed that Baptists currently faced many important issues within their own sphere and ecumenically, yet regrettably it was true that Assembly deliberations were ineffective for this. Therefore he welcomed the concept of the Union as the 'association of Associations' because

[11] *The Report of the Commission on the Associations*, 1964, p.2, 54–5

it would give 'full opportunity for the voice of the churches to be heeded and their convictions expressed.' However, that would need an enlarged Council representation in *all* the Associations if this were to happen. He rejected giving the Council power to elect 35 members itself!

His deepest criticism was reserved for the failure of the commission to understand that historically, according to W. Lumpkin, 'the association of churches was based upon carefully defined confessions of faith which were subsequently elaborated in considerable detail.' It was not enough for the report to use confessions to establish *purpose* and ignore the doctrinal *basis* of associating. Unlike the commission, Larwood felt that a basis of doctrine was not only necessary, but essential. The weakness of the section *Towards a strengthening of confidence,* derived from the fact it did not go deep enough.

He concluded the Report's many recommendations 'will amount to mere organisation and machinery unless they arise from the foundations of the credal basis on which the associations came into being and which was the source of their fellowship and activities'.[12]

Six weeks later the *Baptist Times* carried a long article from David Kingdon, the Irish Baptist College Principal, which concluded

> The issues raised in this editorial need to be discussed and pondered throughout the denomination. It should be realised that those who advocate a more integrated denominational structure will increasingly encounter a demand from conservative evangelicals for a more adequate basis of faith upon which to associate than the present Declaration of Principle. Unless this demand is seen as the expression of deep conviction, and not written off as unfortunate obscurantism, it will be impossible to associate on the basis of 'mutual recognition and trust in one another as baptised believers in the Lord Jesus Christ'.[13]

Although Kingdon made no reference to the Baptist Revival Fellowship's publication, *Liberty in the Lord,* he reflected its views completely. The book attempted to state the views of 'Conservative Evangelicals' relevant to 'the present denominational debate on Church Polity'. It was a response to the Denominational Conference held in May 1961, which appeared to deal only with matters of organization, whereas 'true unity at the practical level can only be the outcome of unity at the level of fundamental belief'. It was also provoked by various county Association reports and more especially by *The Pattern of the Church: A Baptist View.* The book concerned itself with the exegesis of Scriptural teaching about the people of God; a re-examination of Baptist history; and with definite proposals by Conservative-Evangelicals 'for changing the present pattern of denominational life.'[14]

The contemporary discussions of 'the structure and nature of the Church were not giving the New Testament church the primacy that Baptists had traditionally given it'. The Church is 'visible' as well as 'invisible' and 'its life and nature is expressed in outward forms of organization'. Ministry, finance and

[12] Quotes from the *Baptist Times,* 14 January 1965
[13] *Baptist Times,* 25 February 1965
[14] *Liberty in the Lord,* 1964, p.5

evangelism were discussed as three focal points of inter-church relationships. Paul's apostleship is noted as only being exercised over churches he founded, and in such a way as to make the local church independent as soon as possible, with their own 'ruling elders'. Paul never became involved with inter-church organization. The chapter concludes:

> ... inter-church control is absent from the *practice* of the New Testament churches, though voluntary fellowship *between* them was strong. In dealing with the *principles* of churchmanship in the New Testament we have tried to indicate that each local church is a microcosm of the whole church, one body, as are all believers, with one Head ... If this is so, inter-church control of any kind would contradict the New Testament evaluation of the local assembly.[15]

The second chapter provided an historical survey of Baptist polity and began with a discussion of the meaning of 'independency', quoting W. S. Hudson, an American Baptist historian, with approval.

> The extent of their [Baptist] 'independence' was their assertion that a particular church, properly organized, has all the necessary means of grace appointed by Christ, and has no need to derive any further authority from outside its own life.[16]

In the thought of early Baptists, the author comments, 'a particular local church is the catholic church finding expression in a given localized and gathered church.' It is misleading to point to early local examples of co-operation between specific Baptist churches and 'to ignore the fact that such co-operation and consultation took place within a clearly defined context of agreed doctrine ... intercommunion of churches was sought on the basis of doctrine, not at the expense of it.' Any type of Association implies 'qualified independency' (Lumpkin), yet the author maintains the Association has no 'church power'. The recent report from the Northern Baptist Association, *The Way Ahead*, (1960) while 'advocating a considerable extension in the present powers of Association seems to emphasize the principle of "legislative" authority'.

National Synods, Messengers and pastors are each considered in turn and the particular influence of Payne noted and challenged. His use of both Particular and General Baptist writings to make a point, while not recognising their very different understandings, is contrasted with the care in this matter taken by the authors of the report, *The Doctrine of the Ministry*.

The final chapter surveyed present denominational trends, and began with general trends among Evangelicals and Liberals and the resulting confrontation. It then comments on theological trends, noting that agreement 'in the sentiments usually denominated evangelical', the basis of the re-organized Baptist Union in 1832, is often used without reference to its original meaning. It then notes the incarnational theology of *The Pattern of the Church*, centred in the fact of Christ's identification with the human race, and contrasts it with the Evangelicals' concern to centre their faith in Christ's cross and resurrection.

[15] *Ibid.*, pp.9–11, 15–16
[16] *Ibid.*, p.17, quoting W. S. Hudson, 'The Associational Principle Among Baptists', *Foundations*, 1, 1958, pp.10–23

The Council Chamber

A number of trends receive comment: the doctrine of Scripture, the 'gathered church' concept, and the status of the ministry, followed by ecumenical, administrative, and liturgical matters. Baptists needed to be alerted to the pace and direction of these modern trends, and all must be firmly based on doctrine, not on mere expediency. Ministers should give their congregations doctrinal teaching to cope with this. On the gathered church, 'we dare not give up or compromise this important New Testament doctrine and principle.' Inter-dependency construed in terms of connexional church polity, involving legislative and executive authority for Associations and National Assembly, would not remedy the spiritual malaise of our churches.

The Declaration of Principle must not be changed without the fullest consultation with local churches and full debate in Assembly. The paucity of leadership can be met 'only by the re-establishment of the Eldership' in local churches. Finally:

> We fully accept some recent words of Dr E. A. Payne: 'Faith and Order issues are inescapable and are becoming increasingly pressing *within* as well as *between* [churches] ... We repudiate isolationism as contrary to the spirit and practice of the New Testament and we affirm that all believers should have fellowship with one another on a wider scale than the local church, seeking always an adequate basis of doctrine and experience for such fellowship and provided always that its purpose is not legislative, but for mutual consultation and edification.[17]

[17] *Ibid.*, p.48

The Ministry

In the fifties and sixties, a number of reports dealt with the Baptist understanding of ministry, against a background of liturgical revival and ecumenism, and brought the concerns of Conservative Evangelicals, as evidenced by *Liberty in the Lord*, to the forefront of denominational life.

The meaning of Ordination

In the pragmatism of much twentieth-century Baptist life, the issue of ordination was considered before that of the ministry. The 1953 Baptist Union Council requested a report on *The Meaning and Practice of Ordination among Baptists together with an Order of Service.* The group was aware that after the excessive individualism of the nineteenth century, 'Baptists having made their protest against the excesses of the Oxford Movement, along with other Free Churchmen, are able to see these questions of church order in a new perspective'.

The report perceived the New Testament Church as a 'living organism' rather than an organisation people have decided to join. This corporate body is brought into being by God's gracious act and receives its life from him. It is a living organism sustained by the common life of Christ and it is a fellowship of free responsible persons. In the New Testament the Church and 'the churches' in a locality are the people of God. In worship the Church is turned towards God in adoration; and in witness it is turned towards human society in proclamation and service.

Just as God brought the Church into being so it is he who by the Holy Spirit appoints people in the name of Christ to various functions within the community. 'Ministry' is certainly for the service of the Church; but it is equally ministry in the name of Christ, and all these forms of ministry are ministries of the whole Church.

The Holy Spirit, who authenticates a call to ministry, works through people who are holy in their daily living and distributes to them the gifts necessary for ministry. In the New Testament 'there are three factors of outstanding importance in relation to the ministry: (1) its origin in the operation of the Spirit; (2) its sanction by the Christian community; and (3) its exercise for the edifying of the Body'.

The church possesses both adaptability and continuity as permanent features of its life. Therefore new patterns of ministry will emerge that call for valid experiments by the Church.

Ordination practice

Historically, a local Baptist congregation gave the call to pastoral office to a person already set apart as a preacher of the Word and in membership of the local church, before giving the invitation to become its pastor. The pastoral work often began some months before ordination that took place at special service, when questions regarding the pastor's faith and call would be asked and answered, together with prayer, sermons, and the laying of hands by other local pastors who were present. No unordained person took part in the service, and the appointment was to a specific charge, understood to be for life. If a pastor did move to another church, ordination was often repeated.

A more mobile population in the nineteenth century, and that included ministers, and the position of missionaries with the Baptist Missionary Society, both required further changes. Andrew Fuller suggested an 'ideal' pattern, drawing a distinction between missionaries overseas and local pastors. The missionary was sent to an area before a church had been formed—and is selected, trained, and commissioned for church planting work. However, this ideal was not followed either overseas or at home, and in 1805, Fuller noted 'the practice of dissenting ministers to receive ordination but once, is now becoming common'.

> The use of the word 'Reverend', which Baptists had used since the seventeenth century, was now challenged; the laying on of hands was omitted, and then the word ordination dropped out of use. By about 1885 Ordination and Commissioning Services had given place to Welcome Meetings.[18]

What is ordination?

The *Report* offered the following definition of ordination:

> Ordination is the act, wherein the Church, under the guidance of the Holy Spirit, publicly recognises and confirms that a Christian believer has been gifted, called and set apart by God for the work of the ministry and in the name of Christ commissions him for his work.[19]

The call of God is fundamental and is an act of the Church. 'The work of the ministry' was defined in the familiar phrase, 'the ministry of the Word and Sacraments' and is normally, but not exclusively, exercised in a local congregation. It is appropriate when the ministry involves 'leadership of the Church's worship, the administration of the ordinances of Baptism and the Lord's Supper, the proclamation of the Gospel and the teaching of the faith, the work of pastoral care and Christian service'. The report declined to make a list of such ministries beyond the local church, but did emphasise that 'only service which demands that a man shall exercise some of the ministerial functions mentioned ... may be regarded as within the scope of ordination.'[20] Ernest Payne correctly pointed out when the Report came to Council in 1953 that this issue would need further consideration.

Ministry in question

Five years later the Baptist Union Council had identified low stipends, the depressed state of the ministry, and the ease with which ministers could transfer to other professional occupations, particularly teaching and social work, as causes for decline among Baptists. A *Baptist Times* headline spoke of 'Grave decline in quality and numbers of those entering the ministry' (20 March 1958). When challenged, the Editor defended the heavy dependence upon untrained ministers as sufficient justification for his headline.

The *Doctrine of the Ministry*, 1961, was an independent Biblical and theological study that drew upon Baptist history and the wide knowledge and experience

[18] BU Report, *The Meaning and Practice of Ordination among Baptists*, 1953, p.19
[19] *Ibid.*, p.22
[20] *Ibid.*, p.24

of its three authors. Although the Baptist Union Council did not adopt the report, it suggested careful consideration by churches and ministers, because changes to current practice 'will only be salutary if they spring from theological insights.'

The Report chose three phrases to summarise New Testament teaching: 'the people of God', 'the body of Christ', and 'the community of the Spirit', and concluded 'the vital principle that the nature and functions of Christian ministry are determined by the ministry of the whole Church'. The whole Church is called to turn to God in worship, prayer, dependence; and the whole church is called to turn to man in love, service and sacrifice.

> This is the church's primary ministry ... and by the appointment and will of Christ some among his disciples have been authorised to exercise special functions of leadership.[21]

Baptist ministry was traced through the various confessions of faith, and its status and authority were seen to be 'from Christ through the believing community.'[22]

'The whole community' of Baptist Union Churches, echoing Shakespeare's phrase, 'the common church', had an obligation to train ministers, provide adequate material support and arrange means by which spiritual leaders could receive appropriate counsel.

The report then spelt out in clear terms the mutual responsibilities of church and minister. Local churches should 'accept as altogether adequate the spiritual leadership provided by the Union' and 'find its ministers from those thus accredited'. Local churches would act as members of the whole community and be willing 'to accept the counsel thus sought'. The local church was obligated to make proper provision for its minister's material needs, offer a discerning response to spiritual leadership, recognise the minister's status, and enable ministers to fulfil their proper function.

Ministers are obligated to live a personal life that embodies the calling, to build up the church in its faith under the Spirit's leading, to understand and interpret Scripture by regular reflection upon and reading about Scripture as the Spirit of truth directs. Ministerial status and authority would become clearer as 'the whole community' became 'aware of the real nature of church and ministry.'[23]

Local churches should continue to call out those with appropriate gifts for the work of the ministry and the whole Baptist community must test, train and recognise Christians so called and gifted.

The functions of a minister

The functions of ministry were defined as: preaching and teaching the Gospel, leading the worship of the Church, administering baptism and the Lord's Supper, caring for individuals and the fellowship. While not exclusively ministerial tasks, normally the church will appoint a minister for these functions and expect the minister to discharge them. All church members are responsible

[21] J. O. Barrett , L. G. Champion, W. M. S. West, *The Doctrine of the Ministry*, BU, 1961 p.12
[22] *Ibid.*, p.27
[23] *Ibid.*, p.41

for the total ministry of the church and where all accept their obligations, the church's ministry is greatly enriched.

The language of mutual obligation is a predominant feature of the report, and was important for contemporary ministry with increasing local 'sector' ministries, as well as denominational roles and world-wide associations like the Baptist World Alliance and the World Council of Churches. Yet, despite reference to Baxter's dictum in the introduction, and insistent calls for new Baptist evangelistic thrusts, mission, as a responsibility of ministers, nowhere appears in the report.

Ecumenism

'Baptism and the Baptists'

Anthony Cross's study of the Baptist theology and practice of baptism in the twentieth century, suggests Baptists went through three major phases in their thinking.[24]

Until 1940 the Baptist focus was predominantly on the mode and subjects of baptism, with H. Wheeler Robinson writing one of the most widely read books on baptism in the first half of the twentieth century, *Baptist Principles* (1925). It began with the assertion that believer's baptism was a Gospel principle, 'central and fundamental enough to justify the existence of the denomination.' Baptism emphasised 'the significance, the necessity and the individuality of conversion.' Baptism made central, unique and permanent the position of Scripture in the life of faith. Baptism carried with it an 'unmistakable definition of the Church, to which it is the door of entrance.'[25]

Two chapters follow on the historical abandonment of believer's baptism by the Western Church and various attempts to revive spiritual religion in the church prior to the Reformation. The final chapter looked at three contemporary issues: first, the catholicity of Christendom revealed in a conversion experience; second, the recovery of the New Testament emphasis on the Holy Spirit; and third, a deeper recognition of individual liberty of conscience. Believer's baptism, 'scripturally sound, psychologically true, and intellectually free,' was symbolically rich in meaning for Christians living in such times.

From 1940 to 1970 the Baptist focus was on the theology of baptism, initiated by Emil Brunner[26] but more particularly by Karl Barth's monograph, *The Teaching of the Church Regarding Baptism* (1943). It was translated by Ernest Payne for SCM and published in 1948, and went through five impressions over the next twelve years.

Only in 1959 was a Baptist response made to the theological challenge, through Alec Gilmore's *Christian Baptism* (1959) and two further books by two of Gilmore's collaborators, R. E. O. White and George Beasley-Murray.[27]

[24] Anthony R. Cross, *Baptism and the Baptists*, 2000
[25] H. W. Robinson, *Baptist Principles*, 1925, p.24
[26] E. Brunner, *The Divine-Human Encounter*, SCM, 1944
[27] R. E. O. White, *The Biblical Doctrine of Initiation*, 1960

Christian Baptism surveyed the Biblical and historical questions afresh, and urged Baptists to ground the doctrine of believers' baptism in the very nature of the Gospel, recognising that the Godward aspect of baptism needed to be re-stated, and that baptism has more to say about the doctrine of the Church, than personal witness.

George Beasley-Murray provided an exhaustive review of the New Testament teaching on baptism. He stated that baptism could not be viewed as purely a symbolic rite, since to do so was out of harmony with the New Testament.

> [Baptism] is the divinely appointed rendezvous of grace for faith ... Faith is needful before baptism, to receive what God bestows; and after baptism in order to abide in grace so freely given and to work out by that grace what God has wrought within.[28]

Baptism in the New Testament is of the Holy Spirit, and into the Church: a Church act made effective by the Spirit. Baptism is about hope, because in Christ the believer receives assurance that his future is safe in Christ. Beasley-Murray looked for a reform in the baptismal discipline of paedo-baptist communities, insisted there must be an end to regarding re-baptism as blasphemy; and urged the oneness of baptism, confirmation, and first communion. To fellow Baptists he commended the open-membership principle that allowed for tender consciences, asked for better pre- and post-baptismal training, and insisted that baptism and membership must go together.

In 1953 some paedo-Baptists felt the doctrine of baptism did not occupy a central place in the thinking of rank and file Baptists. They perceived most Baptists regarded baptism as a sign of effective evangelism, rather than an act of initiation into the Body of Christ. By this time baptism, in particular, and sacramental theology generally, had become an ecumenical concern; although, as David Thompson noted in 1987, 'this 'concern over baptism owed next to nothing to the discussion of the subject among the defenders of believer's baptism'.[29]

Among Baptist ministers, despite considerable attempts to co-ordinate training and practice through the colleges and the Ministry Department of the Baptist Union, a common understanding of the meaning and practice of baptism has remained elusive. The Baptist intuitive adherence to independency rather than interdependency means that Baptist ministers continue to exercise their 'liberty in the Lord' regarding the practice and teaching about this central rite, despite all Shakespeare's efforts, reinforced by his successors at the Union. For lay members of Baptist churches baptism remains an ordinance rather than a sacrament. Cross concluded:

> The emphasis placed on baptism continues to centre on the candidate, their decision to be baptized, and their personal testimony to what God has done in their lives ... This individualism has meant that Baptists have continued to find difficulty in expressing the prevenience of God's grace and the corporate dimension of the rite.[30]

[28] G. R. Beasley-Murray, *Baptism in the New Testament*, 1962, p.273f
[29] Quoted in Cross, *Baptism and the Baptists*, p.4
[30] A. R. Cross, *op.cit.*, p.457

Worship and Stephen Winward

In 1952 Ernest Payne could claim, 'The general pattern of church services has remained the same from the seventeenth century to the present day: scripture, prayer and sermon, interspersed with hymns.' He was an advocate of liturgical renewal among Baptists, and it was the pioneering work of Stephen Winward, who was minister at Higham's Park in London's East End from 1935–63, that challenged Payne and a whole generation of Baptist ministers. Winward put the emphasis on the Reformation pattern of word and sacrament, weekly communion became the norm and an integral part of the worship, not an 'add on' attended by a few on the first and third Sundays of the month, which it had been in many churches. Congregation members were encouraged to read the Scriptures in worship and offer intercessory prayers, while the whole congregation learnt responses to follow Scripture reading and prayers, and the *Sursum Corda* was used at communion. In 1958 *Responsive Prayers and Praises for Minister and Congregation* was published, but was not widely used in Baptist churches, although many ministers valued it as a tool for preparing public worship. In 1964 Winward in *The Reformation of our Worship*, his Whitley Lectures, given in Cardiff and Oxford in 1963, described this long experiment. He said in his Preface:

> For a quarter of a century I have worshipped with one particular congregation, and with their consent attempted *some* of the reforms suggested in this book. As such, I hope it may be of some help and encouragement to all those who are endeavouring to reform and enrich the worship of the church, under the guidance of the Word and the Spirit, to the greater glory of God.

The growth in sharing the worship of other traditions through the *Week of Prayer for Christian Unity*, encouraged by local Councils of Churches, to which many local Baptist congregations belonged, had helped to promote Winward's work. Michael Walker commented:

> Nonconformists found the catholic that lurked in their souls and catholics explored the freedom of extemporaneous prayer. Transcendence and immediacy were introduced to each other after a long period of illegal separation.[31]

However, Baptists who would discuss the conduct of the Lord's Supper seemingly had no relish for the deeper question of the Supper's meaning. There was a willingness in some places to unite baptism, the Supper, and reception into church membership, within a single service, but most Baptists continued to separate conversion, baptism, communion, church membership and, in the seventies and eighties, the gift of the Spirit, one from another. The ecumenical, liturgical and latterly the charismatic, movements have each had their influence on the way Baptists have worshipped in the second half of the twentieth century, as the pace of change and diversity have increased.

[31] K. W. Clements, ed., *Baptists in the Twentieth Century*, BHS, 1983, p.24

The Church

In 1948 the Archbishop of Canterbury, Geoffrey Fisher, in an address at Great St Mary's, Cambridge, had invited the Free Churches to take episcopacy into their system, to try it out for themselves. *Church Relations in England* (1951) was the resultant formal document. Baptists made it clear that they considered it fundamentally wrong to make inter-communion dependent on episcopacy, particularly in view of the unsubstantiated claims commonly made for the latter. Nonetheless, Baptists had been involved in the formation of the British Council of Churches in 1942, a useful forum for action in international and social matters. In 1948 British Baptists participated in the inauguration of the World Council of Churches, though the international Baptist community largely held back. It was in preparation for the Faith and Order Conference in Lund (1952) that the Baptist Union Council prepared a careful statement on *The Baptist Doctrine of the Church.* The opening paragraph stated:

> The origin of the Church is in the Gospel—in the mighty acts of God, the Incarnation, Ministry, Death, Resurrection and Ascension of our Lord and the Descent of the Holy Spirit. Thus it is the power of God in Christ which created the Church and which sustains it through the centuries. It is historically significant that Christ, at the outset of His ministry, 'chose twelve to be with Him' and gathered His people into a new community. In our judgement there is no evidence in the New Testament to show that He formally organised the Church, but He did create it. This 'New Israel', the expansion of which is recorded in the Acts of the Apostles and in the Epistles, is the heir to the 'Old Israel', yet it is marked by vital and significant differences. It is based upon the New Covenant; membership is not constituted by racial origins but by a personal allegiance; the ritual of temple and synagogue has given place to the ordinances of the Gospel and the national consciousness has widened to world horizons. The Messianic community was reborn by the events of the Gospel and is a 'new creation'. Therefore, whilst there is an historical continuity with the Old Israel, Old Testament analogies do not determine the character and structure of the New Testament Church.[32]

The 1964 Nottingham Conference

In 1964 the British Council of Churches called a special conference at Nottingham and challenged churches to covenant for unity by Easter Day 1980.

A small book from Leonard Champion, Principal of Bristol Baptist College, written against the background of the new ecumenical thinking among church leaders in Bristol, presented the 'hard facts of unity' that Baptists themselves and fellow Christians must consider if the ecumenical conversation was to be genuine.[33]

He set the Baptist testimony to Church, ministry, worship and sacraments within the theological and religious cause of separation that gave rise to the Baptist churches. Nonetheless, among Baptists there have always been men and

[32] E. A. Payne, *The Baptist Union: A Short History*, 1958, p.284
[33] L. G. Champion, *Baptists and Unity*, 1962

churches willing to reach out hands to fellow Christians. In spite of important convictions and practices, that Baptists have felt compelled to maintain and which have necessarily separated them from many Christians, 'a number of Baptists have always tried to overcome the separation and have cherished the vision of a church united in its witness to the Gospel, and its dependence upon the grace of God in Jesus Christ.'[34]

Champion gave five reasons why Baptist Christians should listen to each other. Baptists' historical stability, geographical expansion, and numerical growth, made such listening important. The absence of a large section of the 30 million strong worldwide Baptist communities from the World Council of Churches was another reason. Why were so many Baptist Christians outside the ecumenical conversation? Finally there are distinctive Baptist themes, shared by all Baptists, which are valid and valuable theological emphases, about baptism, the significance of the individual, the gathered church, and religious liberty.

When faced by other Christians, Baptists must consider the place of infant baptism and children in the church; orders of ministry, specifically episcopacy; and the nature of the Church and tradition. He continued:

> If Baptists are to venture along the way of Christian unity sharing with other Christians in this pilgrimage of faith, they will want the conversation to include four themes. They are the themes of evangelism, mission, freedom and fellowship. All Baptists accept these for they are the characteristic themes of Baptist witness. These four must be given proper place in any unity that Baptists could consider.[35]

Mission

The search continues

After the Second World War, the search for a relevant evangelism continued. Many Baptists were strongly influenced by the evangelist Tom Rees, from a Brethren background. Numerous young people went to his monthly rallies in the Royal Albert Hall, London, and attended regular Youth for Christ Rallies in their own locality. Youth for Christ, an American organisation, sent its youth organiser to England in the early fifties for a six month 'crusade' that was warmly welcomed in many Baptist churches. In 1954 Billy Graham returned to take a Crusade in his own right at Harringay, and this opened England to mass evangelism for thirty years, but 1986 was the final such venture. It produced many Baptist candidates for the ministry from among the converts.

Callum Brown, in *The Death of Christian Britain*, (2001), has made the unexpected claim that between 1948 and 1958 there were surges in British church membership, Sunday School enrolment, solemnisation of marriage, accompanied by the immense popularity of evangelical 'revivalist' crusades, particularly that of Graham. He also states the fifties were modern in terms of 'things', but the cultural climate was of 'the last Victorian decade'. Religion mattered and mattered deeply in British society as a whole in the fifties, but

[34] *Ibid.*, p.21
[35] *Ibid.*, p.93

in the 'swinging sixties' this all changed when 'new media, new gender roles, and the moral revolution dramatically ended people's conception that they lived Christian lives.'[36] Brown's controversial thesis re-brands the Britain of 1800–1963 as a highly religious nation and the period as 'the last Puritan age', a deeply Christian country of unprecedented churchgoing levels and the strictest religious rules of personal conduct. The book focuses on how piety was conceived as an overwhelmingly feminine trait that challenged masculinity and left men 'demonised' and constantly anxious.

> It was modern evangelicalism that raised the piety of woman, 'the angel of the house', to reign over the moral weakness and innate temptations of masculinity ... women rather than cities or social class emerge as the principal source of explanation for the patterns of religiosity that were observable in the nineteenth and twentieth centuries. More importantly ... women were the bulwark to popular support for organised Christianity between 1800 and 1963, and ... it was they who broke their relationship to Christian piety in the 1960s, and thereby caused secularisation.[37]

This original interpretation needs further consideration from a Baptist perspective, but is worthy of serious consideration in understanding the failure of Baptist mission initiatives.

Ecumenical Church-based Mission

An ecumenical approach to church planting under the impetus of the British Council of Churches led to increasing numbers of Local Ecumenical Projects (LEP). Baptists were involved in a significant number of them. At Corby New Town in 1965, for example, faced with several thousand people coming from Scotland to work in the new Stewart and Lloyd's steel works, Anglicans, Baptists, Church of Scotland, Methodists and Congregationalists planned this 'area of ecumenical experiment'. It was an attempt to 'ring-fence' an area, in denominational terms, that was free from the ancient 'parish system' and allow Christians to come together in a single congregation.[38]

Swindon in Wiltshire, a decade later, became a major redevelopment situation as the former railway industry drastically declined. Under the active leadership of the town's Anglican and Free Churches, and in co-operation with the town developers who wished to have only one Christian community in each of Swindon's new 'satellite' villages of about 10,000 people, the churches together took a policy decision to plant only ecumenical congregations. The Free Churches in the re-developed 'Old Town' set the pattern, each selling their church buildings and eventually opening a single new community called 'The Pilgrim Centre'. It had a café on the ground floor, a new chapel and offices on

[36] C. G. Brown, *The Death of Christian Britain*, 2001, pp.5–8. Brown challenges the general view that secularisation has been a long and gradual process, and claims it has been a catastrophic and abrupt cultural revolution starting in the 1960s. His book offers an unusual alternative to those usually offered to explain the decline of the Christian churches

[37] *Ibid.*, pp.9–10

[38] *Planning the Ecumenical Parish*, Northampton, 1966. As Milton Keynes emerged, it became another area of ecumenical experiment in which Baptists were involved from the start

the second floor, with rooms for a whole range of community organisations on the top floor. Within Swindon's Baptist community, the husband and wife ministerial team of John and Ruth Matthews played a leading role, and were fully supported by the Baptist Union's Area Superintendent at that time, Ronald Cowley. This pattern was repeated several times as the town grew to almost 200,000 by the year 2000, developers 'allowing' only one ecumenical church centre to be built in each new village centre. Swindon Baptists as a whole did not always favour this method of mission, but ecumenism in Swindon had a distinctly evangelical profile, and new churches were built at Toothill, Shaw, and Abbeymeads, while other congregations met in schools, or in one case, a seventeenth-century Anglican church which was eventually enveloped in the expansion of Swindon.

Social Issues

It was in 1961 that British Baptists returned to the political arena, and the purpose was to expose the atrocities of the Portuguese in Angola.[39] Information came to London from David Grenfell who reported the deteriorating situation as the Portuguese forces massacred 50,000 Africans to repress the Angolan revolt. It was Clifford Parsons, Associate Foreign Secretary of the BMS, himself an African missionary from 1939–59, who exposed the magnitude of this atrocity. Parsons went to Africa and reported back, emphasizing that the revolt was the result of African patience being exhausted after years of repression. The BMS General Committee sought time at the Baptist Assembly to present a public resolution.

> [on 2 May 1961] after a moving speech by Clifford Parsons, the Assembly passed unanimously a resolution which repeated the conviction that the revolt was 'largely due to lack of justice and charity in relationships between the races', registered 'grave disquiet at the reports of the large-scale terrorism by the armed European community', and appealed to the Portuguese authorities to exercise restraint.[40]

The Assembly was determined to follow through the resolution with action, and it fell to three Southend Baptist ministers to take up this challenge. Eric Blakeborough, Ferndale Road, Len Addicott, Earls Hall, and George Thompson Brake, of Avenue, drew up and signed a protest letter to the Portuguese ambassador. The letter of the Angolan Action Group was soon spread throughout the country. Other area groups were formed, most notably in Manchester where the leading organizers were Malcolm Purdy and John Nicholson, with active support from H. H. Rowley, the current chairman of BMS, who wrote a supporting introduction to Manchester copies of the statement. Through Rowley's influence the document and supporting evidence was taken up by the *Manchester Guardian*, and its leader on 19 June was, 'Angola Protest by Missionaries'.

Further articles, based on David Grenfell's evidence, followed and it was this that made it a national political issue. A petition organised by the Action Group raised 37,254 signatures on a single Sunday from members of various

[39] B. Stanley, *The History of the Baptist Missionary Society, 1792–1992*, 1992, pp.454–9. For a detailed account., L. E. Addicott, *Cry Angola*, 1962
[40] *Ibid.*, p.454

churches countrywide, and a debate initiated by George Thomas, MP, came on 5 July. The Labour opposition leader, Hugh Gaitskell, used the testimony of BMS missionaries to challenge the Conservatives under Macmillan to confront Portugal with the evidence of atrocities. Portugal's propaganda machine denied the situation, Blakeborough and George Thomas went on a fact-finding tour to the Angolan-Congo border at the end of July. They found no evidence for the revolt being caused by Communist agitators, as Portugal claimed, and attributed it rather to forced labour, the denial of the Africans' political rights and other grievances, and the 'exploitation and massacre of Africans in Angola' by the Salazar regime. Stanley comments:

> In the history of British nonconformity, the campaign marks the most recent (and arguably the last) example of the power of the 'nonconformist conscience' to affect political events … [however] on arrival in Britain in August, David Grenfell was 'very distressed to find that the Angolan tragedy had become a Party issue instead of a humanitarian concern'.[41]

'Empire Windrush'

When the 'Empire Windrush' sailed from Jamaica with its Caribbean passengers seeking work in Britain, it brought a profound challenge to the country as a whole, but in particular to Baptists, not least because of the historic links through the Baptist Missionary Society whose missionaries had worked hard to secure the end of slavery, in the early nineteenth century.[42] Those who came settled in the industrial centres like London, Birmingham, Bristol, Manchester, Nottingham, Leeds and Sheffield. There was a parallel migration that brought Asian workers into the cotton towns of Lancashire, the wool and steel mills of Yorkshire, the clothing factories of the Midlands, and the London transport system. A third wave of African migrants came from Angola and Congo, Ghana, Nigeria, and from East Africa, particularly when Idi Amin evicted former Indian migrants with British passports. Initially both the Baptist Union and the Baptist Missionary Society were remarkably slow to take any action regarding the increasing numbers who came to England. Local ministers and churches were largely left to their own devices, either in dealing with the problems arising or with seizing the opportunities clearly presented, and many did remarkably well.

A few Baptist churches in England, during the years of Empire, had had a cultural mix of members from a range of countries, particularly so in ports like Liverpool, Bristol and London, as well as industrial centres in the Midlands and Manchester.

The Baptist Colleges had been involved in training overseas students for Baptist ministry over the years, a steady trickle of candidates training in England for overseas Baptist ministry. At Oxford W. G. Wrickramsinghe had studied with Ernest Payne, and became Principal of Carey College, Colombo, Sri Lanka.[43] Horace Russell, later Principal of Calabar College, Jamaica and then Eastern Baptist Seminary, Philadelphia, had also trained at Regent's Park.

[41] *Ibid.*, p.457

[42] B. Stanley, *The History of the Baptist Missionary Society, 1792–1992,* 1992, chap.3. For the earlier period: D. Killingray, 'Black Baptists in Britain, 1640–1950', BQ, 40, pp.69–89

[43] See, W. Wrickramasinghe, 'Church Union: A Call to obedience', BQ, 22, 1967, pp.166–175

Perhaps the most significant Regent's person was Sam Reid, sent by BMS staff member David Jelleyman, Principal at Calabar, for further training. On the initiative of Norman B. Jones, the North-West Superintendent, Reid was encouraged to spend some years in an English Baptist Church before returning to minister in Jamaica. He accepted the pastorate at Moss Side, Manchester, when the church was near to closure. There were seventeen in the congregation when Reid began, six white and eleven West Indians. Within five years the church was teeming with West Indians from all over Manchester. In one year Reid was estimated to have taken almost 200 weddings! Reid was put into a 'team ministry' with J. F. V. Nicholson at Fallowfield, and Jack Swanson at Chorlton-cum-Hardy. In Fallowfield, Manchester, a significant Black member was Joe Linton, a deacon of the church. When he died, aged 50, the church decided to name its new student hostel, Linton House, in memory of him. At his funeral, the church was filled with people from across the whole social spectrum of Manchester, who wished to acknowledge his contribution to the city.

The Moss Side church was given a completely new lease of life by the time Sam Reid returned to be pastor of Montego Bay, Jamaica, where he has continued to minister. Brian Tucker, whose father had been a missionary in Jamaica, became the minister in 1965, by which time the church was better equipped to face the re-building of Moss Side, as that part of Manchester was pulled down, prior to redevelopment.[44]

In Yorkshire, the Cemetery Road church in Sheffield had a former BMS Jamaican missionary couple, the Browns, in the fellowship at the end of the fifties. Sydney Clark, then the minister, put them on the leadership team and this enabled the church to integrate the West Indian migrant workers effectively. The church continues to have a strong mixture of nationalities to the present, a number of whom share the leadership.

Spurgeon's trained some Sri Lankan pastors who stayed in England for their ministry, among them V. Fred George, who settled at East Barnet in 1969 and became President of the Baptist Union in 1997. Delvin Knower, came to England from Sri Lanka, after time spent in training for the ministry in America and Bermuda. His desire was to train at the College that his mentor Spurgeon had founded. It was from a link in Bermuda that the Parkstone Church called him to their pastorate from 1964–1970. It was another personal contact through the Association that brought him to be minister at Eastleigh for the next thirty-two years, during which time he offered significant leadership within the Baptist Missionary Society, being its chairman and one of its trustees.

From the 1950s the migration of workers from the former British Empire to Britain challenged English society about how these disparate communities could live together. Initially the key word in this emerging phenomenon was 'integration', but it proved difficult, and in many ways unacceptable to all concerned, as a way forward. The migrant communities did not find it easy to integrate into Baptist churches, despite their shared Christian commitment, and there is little doubt that many felt rejected. Part of that rejection was

[44] The author is grateful to J. F. V. Nicholson for his personal help with these paragraphs

an inability of English Christians to understand the migrant culture. In one church, for example, a few Jamaican Baptists still retained their betting slips for use at the Kingston racecourse. The earlier 'slave culture', that had clearly left its mark on the understanding of loyalty in marriage relationships, was difficult for English Baptist congregations to understand. There was also the intense rivalry between the different island communities of the countries that comprised the West Indies that could manifest itself in English Baptist church life. Caribbean Christians in Southall, Middlesex, where there was a significant Asian community side by side with them, would sometimes express the perception that they were 'white', because in religious terms they were Christian, not Muslim; and in terms of language, English was their mother tongue, not one of the Indian languages.[45]

Those from the Caribbean sometimes brought an idealised picture of English Christianity as a vital force in society, but this was nowhere to be found in the Baptist churches they visited. The culture in Jamaica had been of predominantly all black churches, some using the English *Baptist Hymn Book*, but many preferred Sankey's *Sacred Songs and Solos*. In a number of leading Caribbean churches Canadian and European ministers led wholly black congregations.

Most of the Baptist migrants were not Pentecostal in style or churchmanship. However, some who felt unwelcome turned in the direction of forming Black and Black-led churches, entirely outside the Baptist Union structures. The political pressure to 'integrate' migrants was perceived by some as an unwelcome intrusion that often ended in a tokenism that was unacceptable to all.

Among the first generation of Caribbean migrant workers much was tolerated in this unhelpful situation because they did not see themselves as in Britain permanently, but working towards a time when they would return to the Caribbean. The second generation, born and brought up in Britain found themselves in tension with both their own culture and the English norm, which was changing rapidly through the increasingly permissive sixties and seventies. It was the second generation of Caribbean Christians who also encouraged the formation of Caribbean Black and Black-led Baptist churches

Some Baptist churches within the Baptist Union soon became predominantly Black as the society around the church reflected the ethnic change. The Small Heath Baptist church, Birmingham, was just one such example. Norman Moon, pastor from 1944–53, was very much aware of the impact of the 'Empire Windrush' changes, as was Bernard Mason after him. By the time Bill Dixon began his ministry that stretched from 1971 to 1999, the change to a Black Church with an English, white pastor, was complete. However, it was not until David Ellis, a British-born West Indian, became the Small Heath minister, that the church had its first Black pastor in 2000. Ellis had grown up in Enoch Powell's Wolverhampton constituency in the West Midlands, trained for ministry at Spurgeon's in the late eighties, and had his first ministry at Totterdown, Bristol.

[45] P. Thompson and others: *Here to Stay*, Lion, 1991, tells something of this experience from a female Caribbean view point

English pastors of 'Black' churches

Among English Baptists, it has been some of their own white Baptist ministers who have been effective in ministry to multi-racial, multi-cultural congregations. Stuart Cook, Bristol born and trained at Spurgeon's, for example, was one who spent a decade at Brixton Baptist church as the whole area went through a serious time of racial tension, culminating in the Brixton riots.

At Western Road, Southall, the church was strong when Donald Cranefield became minister in 1956, and it was a year later that he became aware of the first Caribbean and Asian migrants in Southall. The first Asians were usually Sikhs, who had been encouraged to work at the Firestone Rubber Company, initially by a retired Army Colonel. At this time some Black Pentecostal Christians bought a disused chapel from the Methodists on the Western Road, Southall.

It was through the Southall Council of Churches, led by Cranefield that these various merging groups were 'welcomed' in to the Christian community. Cranefield attempted some 'evangelistic' work among the growing Asian community. A Baptist Asian teacher and an Asian Christian woman, who had joined the Southall Baptist Church, made it clear to Cranefield that Asians would be the best people to win Asian converts. The Church therefore decided to sponsor and encourage an Asian Christian Fellowship as the way forward. Cranefield believed that 'integration' would not help migrants to develop their own Christian lifestyle. Through the Council of Churches a variety of work was undertaken. At the close of the century, Boyd Williams, Cranefield's eventual successor, and a former BMS missionary in Brazil, underlines the appropriateness of these beginnings:

> The Church is now multicultural with over 30 nations represented. We have also been involved in church planting in other parts of London and are at present helping three Brazilian groups. We have a large African Church associated with us and are seeking to help them find a home in Bedfont, near Heathrow. They will remain associated with Southall and continue to be a multi-cultural church.[46]

In the Yorkshire Baptist Association, faced with Asian communities, help came for the Bradford Fellowship of Baptist churches in the person of Donald F. Hudson, trained at Regent's Park, before working with the BMS in India from 1940–1969. On return to Britain he took an educational appointment in the area. He was Associate Minister at the West Bradford Fellowship of Baptist Churches from 1971–4, and from 1975 to 2003 ministered at Central Bradford Fellowship. The knowledge of Asian language, culture and religion was an essential factor in Christian witness in the area. However, Hudson writes:

> An Asian project was in operation for 10 years from 1969, which made contact, mostly with women from the Asian community, but it never got the interest of the majority of Church members, and did not bring in any Asians … As far as Baptist churches are concerned there are no black-led Baptist churches in Bradford. They are all Pentecostal …

[46] Letter to author, March 2003

> The Westgate Church has a good proportion of members of a Caribbean origin, two of whom are on the diaconate. As far as Asians are concerned there is one Sikh convert, and there are occasional visitors, either students or doctors from the hospital who come for a short time and then return home.[47]

Among second generation Black Christians, who have heeded the call to ministry, trained for it, and then ministered in the Union's churches, would be Glenford Gordon, from Birmingham, who trained at Bristol College, before becoming the full-time Black pastor at Acocks Green, Birmingham, in 1988. Desmond Gordon, another second generation Black minister who trained at Bristol, returned to Caribbean in 1974 and served with the BMS in Trinidad for five years, returning to Britain in 1979 to be minister at Church End, Finchley, London.

From this 'second generation' have come some Baptist ministers who felt able to challenge what they perceived as the incipient racism within Baptist churches. The previous generation knew about this, but always felt themselves to be against a brick wall in their struggle to secure an adequate hearing within the Baptist Union and its churches. It was only in the 1990s that this issue was addressed better, but for many, not yet satisfactorily.

Payne's retirement

Ernest Payne retired as General Secretary of the Baptist Union in 1967. Payne's long time friend, American Franklin Fry, was invited to speak at the Assembly and told people that at the meetings of the WCC Central Committee, for a number of years, the final session had been led by Ernest Payne.

> He has never slouched or sidled into the presence of God. He has been God's respectful son and has been able to lead many of us along paths of worship. We honour a man tonight with profound gratitude to God, a man whom I love and whom you love.[48]

In his reply Payne commented on a number of features in his Secretaryship that had given him pleasure. Much had been done to improve ministers' pay and job security through the Home Work Fund. He was thrilled to have shared in re-establishing meaningful contact with Baptists in Eastern Europe. He was pleased to have been involved in the new 1962 hymnbook and co-authoring with Stephen Winward a new service book. Finally he was glad to have represented Baptists to other Christians and vice-versa.

He was disappointed that revival and renewal of the churches had still not happened; and that BU and BMS had not become an integrated organisation under one roof. He concluded by quoting from Phillips Brooks: 'To seek for the reproduction of Christ's mind in the mind of the community, is the greatest aim that we can cherish.' R. L. Child said of Payne:

> He has kept the future open for Baptists. Ecumenism is not the only issue that perplexes British Baptists today. We also differ among ourselves about the meaning and message of the Bible in the light of modern knowledge.

[47] Letter to author, March 2003

[48] W. M. S. West, *To be a Pilgrim: A memoir of Ernest A. Payne*, 1983, p.152

And we differ as to what the Baptist Union is and what we think it ought to become. Payne has never disguised his distrust of all attempts to resolve them prematurely, and has consistently maintained, in effect, that since no one knows what the church of the future will be like, we must be patient with one another and with God until he is pleased to reveal his will to us.[49]

[49] L. G. Champion, *Outlook for Christianity*, 1957, pp.7–8

16

Baptist Identity and the Future for our Past

WHEN David S. Russell began his work as General Secretary of the Baptist Union, in May 1967, the Council elected by the Assembly, and the staff, were ripe for significant change in both structure and daily working. Russell, born in Glasgow in 1916, was ready for the challenge, having gained a wide experience of the English scene. After early years in the Cambuslang Baptist Church, he entered Glasgow University and took a general Arts degree before entering Trinity College, Glasgow, to take a BD, the only Baptist among a hundred Presbyterian theological students.

From 1939-41, while continuing his studies, he served Berwick-on-Tweed Baptist Church, and then moved to Oxford for Old Testament Studies with Wheeler Robinson at Regent's Park College. This was the beginning of a life-long fascination with the period between the Old and New Testaments, summed up in the word 'apocalyptic'. While researching in Oxford he was minister at Woodstock Road Baptist Church, and when his studies were completed in 1945, he accepted an invitation to Church Road, Acton, in London.

In 1953 an invitation to teach at Rawdon Baptist College, near Leeds, was accepted, although the future viability of the college was in doubt. However, even Russell's imagination, effort and sacrificial commitment, together with considerable and growing support from Yorkshire Baptists, were not enough to secure the College's independent future. In 1962 Russell took soundings with K. C. Dykes, then Principal of the Manchester Baptist College, about a merger. Russell dealt with Rawdon's closure prior to becoming joint Principal with Dykes of the new Northern Baptist College, on the Manchester site, in 1964. Russell's considerable administrative gifts, energy and warm personality did fit him to follow Payne as the Union's new General Secretary.[1]

Re-structuring the Union

Two changes were made as Russell came to office: one respecting the running of Baptist Church House and Baptist Union Committees; the other regarding the representation of the Baptist constituency on Council.

Russell began by re-structuring the Council's Main Committees, with Morris West chairing a Structure Group. It proposed all the Union's committees be brought

[1] Peter Shepherd, *The Making of a Northern Baptist College*, BHS, 2004, pp.204–16

within three new departments, Ministry, Mission and Administration, each with a departmental Head answerable to the General Secretary as chief executive. When these appointments were agreed, Ernest Clipsham, who had looked after ministry matters for Payne, and R. W. Thomson, who had been responsible to Payne for the daily administration of the house, left the employ of the Union, the former returning to pastorate, and the latter retiring because of ill-health. A layman, J. B. Morris, was brought in to head Administration; Geoffrey Rusling, former Vice-Principal of Spurgeon's was made responsible for Ministry, and eventually Norman B. Jones, the former North-West Superintendent, led Mission.

A resolution of the Berkshire Association resulted in an Assembly decision in 1969 whereby the annual Assembly divested itself of the power to nominate and elect fifty Council members, and increased the direct representation of the Associations by a similar number. This was a seemingly small step, but in fact it was a turning point in the Union being more obviously 'the Associations, associating'.

Russell fulfilled the routine tasks of his office, preaching in the constituency, broadcasting on radio and television, and began a monthly letter to all Baptist ministers containing news and information, 'a personal, pastoral epistle in which he shared with ... ministers some of his own hopes and fears ... and strengthened the bonds of understanding.'[2]

Negatives ...

In re-structuring programmes there were negative as well as positive outcomes. On the negative side, Russell had to wind up the Baptist publishing house, Carey Kingsgate Press. The Haven, which since 1945 had undertaken the care of unmarried mothers and their babies, had to be closed in 1970, a result of changing social conditions. The capital monies were put in to the 'New Venture Fund' and the first appointment, in 1973, was of Miss E. Bichard, the Union's former Adoption Officer, to serve as a social worker in the South West Durham Group of Baptist churches.

In 1975 the Deaconess Order was wound up as the call for their specialised services declined, as did the number of applicants. Those still active were transferred, some after further re-training, to the list of accredited ministers.[3]

The Baptist Women's League established under Shakespeare had celebrated its 60 years with the building of Newington Court, a North London hostel with accommodation for business girls and students, a project made possible by a large gift from Sir Herbert Janes. In the seventies it became clear that an increasing number of women's groups in the churches did not see themselves as aligning with BWL and were reluctant to join it. Russell facilitated many hours of consultation and committee work until it was agreed, in 1979, to disband the BWL and replace it with a new programme sponsored by the Union for all women's work across the denomination.

[2] J. H. Y. Briggs, ed., *Bible, Church and World*, BHS, 1989, pp.13–14, for a series of essays in appreciation of D. S. Russell

[3] Nicola Morris, *Sisters of the People: the Order of Baptist Deaconesses, 1890–1975*, Bristol University, 2002, for a full account of the Deaconesses

... and positives

On the positive side of change Russell worked hard for the uniting of the offices of the Union and the Baptist Missionary Society, but like Payne before him, was unsuccessful. Russell changed the lay-out of offices in Baptist Church House to reflect the new committee re-structuring. He launched the Strategy Building Scheme in 1980 to release needed finance for capital building schemes by the churches, and in its first year it realised £75,000 for such purposes. As Joint Chairman of the United Navy, Army and Air Force Board he supported service chaplains, 'happiest when ferreting out the views of all ranks', and so, not surprisingly, in particular was responsible for securing better career prospects for those serving.

Ecumenism

Baptists and Unity Report

The Baptist Union responded quickly to the 1964 Nottingham Conference 'call' for unity by Easter 1980, publishing its report, *Baptists and Unity*, in 1967. It concluded that Church unity was an urgent yet complex issue.

> It seems clear, that Christian unity is of great importance, urgency, and complexity; whilst there is an undeniable spiritual unity binding together all believers to our Lord Jesus Christ and to one another, this needs to be given visible expression in a clearer and more unmistakable manner than at present.[4]

The unity of British Baptists was a major area of concern, and the report called on the United Kingdom Baptist Unions, with the Missionary Society, to consider these issues and include the Strict Baptist Associations and the Baptist Union of Ireland within the discussions. The latter hope was proper, but proved impossible, as both the Strict Baptists in England and the Irish Baptist Union, were totally unwilling to enter meaningful conversations.

It suggested Baptists remain within both the British and World Councils of Churches, a position later affirmed by 1125 to 361 at the 1969 Assembly. There was a need for Baptists to remain in future discussions as official 'observers', but it would be wrong for the Baptist Union to move towards organic Church union by Easter 1980.

The Church Relations Advisory Committee received and evaluated responses from 655 Baptist churches, 17 Associations, numerous ministers meetings, as well as individuals. It presented its conclusions to the 1969 Assembly in *Baptists and Unity Reviewed*. Neville Clark believed this provided 'something like an agreed platform' so far as the Baptist understanding of, and attitude towards, the visible unity of the Church, was concerned.[5]

These ecumenical discussions were difficult and needed clear-minded, patient, yet committed leadership from the Church Relations Advisory Committee to secure agreement. In this, the commitment of an evangelical ecumenist like George Beasley-Murray was important. He had already made his position clear in *Reflections on the Ecumenical Movement*, Baptist Union, 1965.

[4] *Baptists and Unity*, Baptist Union, 1967, p.49
[5] J. H. Y. Briggs, ed., *Faith Heritage and Witness*, BHS, 1987 p.17

In January 1967 he was invited to speak in Ipswich at a meeting at which Roman Catholics would also speak. The Protestant Truth Society claimed the meeting was organised to 'unite the Protestant churches under the Church of Rome'. Beasley-Murray was incensed and in the meeting gave his own testimony before turning to Father Angellus of the BBC, and asked him to declare his own faith by answering three questions. Angellus did so in the affirmative and Beasley-Murray then held out his hand to Angellus and said publicly:

> Then I humbly own you as a brother in Christ. There are many elements in the creed of your Church I cannot accept, for I believe them to be wrong. But you and I have been made one with God in Christ, and we cannot be one in Christ with the Father, and not be one with each other.

In a subsequent article Beasley-Murray wrote:

> I am not ashamed of the Gospel. But I confess to being ashamed of some of its defenders … There appears to be a competition among some Evangelicals to see who can vilify most effectively the people of Christ who believe it is the will of God to end hostilities within the Church.

In the 1960s there was deep suspicion of the World Council of Churches by many evangelical Baptists. Among these was Theo Bamber, chair of the Baptist Revival Fellowship, who asked Beasley-Murray to stem 'the ecumenical tide' in which, he feared, 'evangelicals will be drowned'.[6]

Other ecumenical pressures

Among other churches, the Anglican-Methodist Scheme of Union failed, but Congregationalists and Presbyterians successfully formed the United Reformed Church in 1972. In 1966 the Congregational Union had moved from a 'gathered church' understanding of its life, to become the Congregational Church in England. The formation of the URC was particularly sensitive for Baptists, who for the past three hundred years had been part of the historic 'three denominations' of classical Dissent, but this was about to change. Russell was concerned to safeguard the Baptist position as the necessary Act of Parliament went through. Arthur Macarthur of the URC said of Russell,

> while he welcomed the ecumenical agencies he remained and remains a Baptist. Thus in efforts in the late seventies to establish a covenant between the Churches he always made it clear that Baptists would stand in a different position.[7]

All these pressures in 1972 were focussed, as often happens, in a particular case, the establishment in Skelmersdale, Lancashire, of an ecumenical congregation. All the participating denominations, including the Baptists, each applied to join all the constituting bodies, providing *Baptists and Unity* with a critical test.

During the 1970s, when *The Ten Propositions* were issued for discussion, Baptists agreed to consider what 'covenanting together' with the mainstream denominations, excluding the Roman Catholics, might mean. The proposals provided for the mutual acceptance of various forms of baptism, intercommunion, the mutual acceptance of ordination and a proposal for episcopal re-ordination

[6] P. Beasley-Murray, *Fearless for Truth*, Paternoster, 2002, pp.132–142
[7] J. H. Y. Briggs, *Bible, Church and World*, BHS, 1989, pp.16, 35–55

of existing ministers. Morris West produced an Occasional Paper for the Union, *Church, Ministry and Episcopacy*. Nonetheless, the Baptist Union Council felt unable to recommend the *Ten Propositions* as a way forward for Baptists. The reply concluded:

> It is our clear judgment that at present no unqualified recommendation to accept the Ten Propositions can be made.

The sticking point for most Baptists was an unwillingness to contemplate the re-ordination of its ministers by Anglican bishops. Organic union by 1980 would be a mistake, as it could seriously endanger denominational unity.

Since the Second World War all the churches had had to face the growing ecumenical tension of mission as together they faced the pressures of national, cultural and religious diversity in an increasingly pluralist society. Local Baptist churches were involved with other Christians more than ever before, and although there was a national reluctance to covenant together with other Christians, at the grass roots there was steadily increasing participation by local Baptist congregations in 'areas of local ecumenical experiment'.

The response of the Baptist Revival Fellowship to the 1969 Assembly decision was to explore different possibilities for Conservative Evangelical Baptists who felt unable to work within a denomination that had active links with the WCC. In the wider Christian world the sixties was the decade of the Second Vatican Council giving birth to a total shift in relationships between the Roman Catholic Church and other Christians. There was at last the chance for a genuine rapport between Protestant and Catholic. However,

> The heady freedom of the sixties, refreshing as it was for many Christians, did nothing to halt decline. Astonishingly, [in the seventies] the pendulum swung in a conservative and more authoritarian direction. Many Baptists turned their backs on any pilgrimage towards greater catholicity, choosing instead sectarianism.[8]

Ministry

Recruiting ministry tomorrow

Norman B. Jones introduced *Ministry Tomorrow* (1968) and stated the basic concern of the *Commission on the Ministry Report* was to 'suggest a scheme of ministry that will maintain and make more effective the life and witness of the local church.' and to this end considered the 'use, deployment and maintenance of the ministry'.

> There is an underlying principle within the report for which we plead acceptance. It is that the local church should be responsible for its own ministry and as far as possible the money raised nationally should be used for the larger purposes of mission and evangelism ... Our examination has convinced us that the denomination cannot support as many full-time ministers as in the past; hence the need for 'supplementary' ministry ... In the light of our present declining membership, we cannot see how the denomination can support more than 400 full-time ministers. We believe

[8] Michael Walker, in K. W. Clements, ed., *Baptists in the Twentieth Century*, BHS, 1983, p.27

> the statistical evidence we have gathered supports this contention, but shall be delighted to be proved wrong and to discover that more ministers can, in fact, be adequately supported.[9]

The dissatisfaction with existing patterns of church and ministry had arisen in part from the perception that church and ministry are not 'entirely faithful to the abiding reality of God's purposes' in so far as they serve yesterday rather than to-day, and were marked by rigidity rather than flexibility. 'To foster a relevant and contemporary ministry is to assist materially in the growth of a relevant and contemporary Church'. The problem was that the inherited pattern of church 'expression' is ill equipped to face the fast changing world around the Church. The denomination is comprised of a majority of small, isolated churches that struggle to maintain all the paraphernalia appropriate to relatively large and economically viable communities. Churches are too busy with survival to give themselves to their primary task, and the ministry is the sensitive barometer that registers these shifting pressures.[10]

One deep root of ministerial unease was believed to be the financial impoverishment that financially struggling churches imposed on ministers and families. An increasing number of ministers were taking part-time work to supplement their income, and alongside this having an increasing dependence on income from working spouses. The ministry had sub-consciously become a depressed class, and the cost to the churches was incalculable, for 'a depressed class is rarely renowned for vision and imaginative leadership.'

The 'smallness' of most churches was a significant factor in ministerial unease and ineffectiveness.

> Frustration arises where men are denied the diverse kind of community that would stretch them, call forth their best, give scope for their God-given talents; where they are expected to be ecclesiastical mechanics with the expertise to maintain the machinery and produce bigger churches and rising budgets; where they are physically over-worked and spiritually under-employed.[11]

The pattern for the future still required the local church and crucial to the health of those churches would be a

> ministry which builds up the Body and equips the saints for their work of ministry in and to the world. The central requirement for a 'general-practitioner ministry' remains and this consists in bringing the Word and sacraments to the People of God, the giving of pastoral oversight and service, and the representing of the whole Church in and to the local manifestation of it.[12]

The *Report* proposed two strands of ministry: a 'full-time, properly paid, professional ministry of smaller numbers and generally speaking higher qualifications, and more rigorous training', interwoven with 'a properly trained, supplementary ministry, equally esteemed and recognised, normally drawn from

[9] *Ministry Tomorrow*, 1968, pp.2–3
[10] *Ibid.*, pp.5–6
[11] *Ibid.*, p.7
[12] *Ibid.*

those earning their living in trades, professions and skills of society.' The total ministry would need to work in teams serving large and smaller congregations, some of the latter being grouped geographically for ministry purposes.

The view that a 'call to ministry' was inherently for life was seriously challenged. The proposals meant the Dakin view, propounded as already noted in 1944, was re-considered, because the ministry needed to have a more temporary aspect than many ministers understood, which arose in part from the changing nature of the society in which the Church now worked.

The person of Christ questioned

A theological controversy, connected with Michael Taylor's address to the Assembly in 1971, put David Russell at the centre of a storm and he found himself absorbing the indignation which came from many quarters, not least in the 800 letters to which he responded over the next two years. That the Union came through as positively as it did owed much to Russell's abilities.

The issue originated when Dr Gwynne Henton Davies, the Principal of Regent's Park College, Oxford, was elected President of the Baptist Union for 1971. Henton Davies set the Assembly theme for his Presidential address, *The Incarnate Presence,* with the text, 'Seek the Kingdom of God'. In his address he claimed the contemporary Church spent too much time addressing it own ills. He then asked whether Baptists in particular were not suffering from a 'a devalued Christology' and went on to assert that even the New Testament summary, 'Jesus is Lord', was in fact 'insufficient doctrine' as far as the fullness of Christian faith was concerned. He said:

> The Christology of rank is a devalued Christology and reflects lower levels of thinking, confession, and proclamation—it becomes a Unitarianism of God the Son ... Why do conservative churches send us ministerial students who are prone to these Unitarian tendencies?[13]

He affirmed that the 'Jesus is Lord' formula, in isolation, would eventually tend to dispense with the incarnation, and if there were no incarnation, where was the resurrection, and where indeed Christianity itself?

Having taken this initiative, as was normal practice for the Union Presidents at that time, he invited three other platform speakers to address his theme. The three addresses were: 'The Royal Presence: How dead is God?', to be given by John Huxtable, Secretary of the newly founded Congregational Church; second, 'The Incarnate presence: How much of a man was Jesus Christ?', that Michael Taylor, Russell's successor at Northern Baptist College; was to give, and the third, 'The Presence of the Holy Spirit: Is the Holy Spirit a Ghost?', to be given by Dr Barrie White, also of Oxford. The proposed subjects, however treated, given in the context of an inspirational address of twenty minutes at an Assembly, would always be extremely difficult, if not impossible to handle, for any of the speakers.

It was Michael Taylor's address, robust in style and having intellectual integrity that caused a problem for many present, but by no means all. He saw

[13] As reported in *Baptist Times,* 29 April 1971. See also, G. Henton Davies, *Seek First His Kingdom,* BU, 1971, p.13

his assignment as writing about the doctrine of the incarnation in a 'modern paragraph' that would deal with 'the mysteries of the Nicene Creed'. He said 'I personally have no great enthusiasm' for this, but nonetheless attempted it and shared his draft paragraph with the Assembly.

> The story of Jesus makes such an overwhelming impression that I am not content to say he was an extraordinary man ... I believe that in the man Jesus we encounter God. I believe that God was active in Jesus: but it will not quite do, to say categorically: Jesus is God. The difference between him and ourselves is not in the manner of God's presence in Jesus. The difference is in what God did in and through this man, and the degree to which this man responded and co-operated with God.[14]

As he explained his 'highly compressed statement' he made further comments. 'Jesus is the same as me, because like me he is a man' ... How can he be the clue to what it means to be human if he is not a man himself?' Taylor felt that however remarkable the life of Jesus, 'I must stop short of saying categorically; Jesus is God, and I understand the New Testament probably stops short of it. Jesus is a man. I do not say that Jesus is God, but I do say with the New Testament, that God was in Christ or that I encounter God in Jesus.' Taylor then moved on to make it clear that he had no enthusiasm for 'Christian faith based on doctrinal agreement'. He continued:

> I am not committed to a confession of faith. I am committed to a Person, and the truth about that person is not carried for me by a number of intellectual propositions. The truth about Him is carried by a story ... I would rather sign my name on a dotted line under the Gospel story and declare that here for me is the bearer of truth about God and man, than give my assent to a statement of faith and suggest that here is the truth about Jesus.'

Taylor's address precipitated a major denominational Christological debate. The letters pages of the *Baptist Times* were inundated with letters for several weeks, the editor drawing correspondence to a close as he announced a series of articles to be written in July and August by a wide variety of contributors who would address the Christological issue.[15]

Taylor suggested there were a number of possible reactions to an unbelievable incarnation. Taylor himself concluded that who Jesus was in the Gospel story, was more important for the mission of the Church , as it sought to relate to the world, than arguments about the incarnation.[16]

Principal Beasley-Murray of Spurgeon's College, Union President in 1968–9, was one who found the content of Taylor's address difficult. He resigned as Chairman of Council in order to address the issue.[17] He felt the 'argument' that followed for weeks in the *Baptist Times* could not just be ended, as the editor

[14] All quotations from text of Michael Taylor's address in possession of author
[15] See *Baptist Times* from 29 April to end of August, 1971, for correspondence and articles
[16] An expanded form of the themes in the address can be read in M. Taylor, *A Plain Man's Guide to the Incarnation*, 1977
[17] G. R. Beasley-Murray, *The Christological Controversy in the Baptist Union*, privately printed

wished. The job facing the churches was to preach the Gospel, but, as George Beasley-Murray recognised, the address had seriously challenged that Gospel.

> An interpretation of Christ has been set forth among us which maintains that the belief that Jesus is truly God and truly man is a contradiction. Jesus, it is said, was a man in whom God was present just as He is in the rest of us. The uniqueness of Jesus lay in his response to God and in the way God worked through him.[18]

For Beasley-Murray the problem was that Taylor appeared to set aside the New Testament teaching that God *was* in fact uniquely present in Jesus, and was differentiated from all other men by virtue of being the Son of God. More fundamentally Taylor was advocating that the incarnation of Christ was no longer to be received as the faith of the Church. Any idea that Christ is the pre-existent Son of God is no longer to be accepted. Taylor's view, pressed to its logical conclusion, would call the doctrine of the Trinity into question as well as that of salvation itself. What is the point of praying 'through Christ' and to God on this basis? All worship and prayer is called into question, and the idea of believers being united by the Holy Spirit to the glorified Christ is rationally excluded.

While the 1971 Assembly was still in progress a regular meeting of its Council was invited, but declined, to repudiate Taylor's address. Nor was it prepared to call him to account for being in breach of the Union's *Declaration of Principle*. The issue came to the November 1971 Council, when a resolution was put affirming the *Declaration of Principle* and asserting the Council's belief in the deity of Christ.[19]

Ernest Payne and Leonard Champion, noting doctrinal statements to which the Baptist Union had in the past given its assent, and reminding Council of the historic Baptist concern for religious freedom and tolerance, sought to amend the resolution but failed. A lengthy resolution came to the next Assembly, proposed by Sir Cyril Black, MP, which reasserted the *Declaration of Principle* and required all those who appear on the Union's accredited list to affirm it.

David Russell wrote of the issue in the 1972 Annual Report, the

> note of reconciliation was struck by a motion in the name of Sir Cyril Black, MP … Its purpose was, by God's help, to seek for the removal of divisions and misunderstanding which had grown up within the Union since the previous Assembly. It gladly and explicitly reaffirmed the wholehearted acceptance of and belief in the Declaration of Principle as set out in the Constitution and acknowledged Jesus Christ as both 'Lord and Saviour' and 'God manifest in the flesh' understanding these words as expressing unqualified faith in His full deity and real humanity. It recognised the Declaration as representing the basic requirement for fellowship in the Baptist denomination and asserted the unacceptability of an interpretation of the person and work of Christ which would obscure or deny this fundamental tenet of the Christian faith that Jesus Christ is Lord and Saviour, truly God and truly Man.

[18] *Ibid.*, p.1
[19] Baptist Annual Report, 1971, Appendix 9, a–b, pp.64–5

The Assembly voted overwhelmingly in favour of the resolution, with only 45 against, and 72 abstaining.

Over forty churches, including several large and influential congregations, left the Baptist Union and sixteen leaders of the Baptist Revival Fellowship resigned their place on the accredited list of the Baptist Union.

Mission

'Signs of Hope'

When Donald Cranefield became the London Baptist Association President in 1976, his theme was simply and starkly, 'Survival'. A life-long London Baptist, reared at Drummond Road, he had trained at Spurgeon's, ministered first at South Lee, and then spent 17 years at Western Road, Southall, till he moved to Bromley in 1973. He began by commenting, 'churches of all denominations in Britain today, are passing through a time of crisis that I can only describe as a survival situation, in that our survival as churches is in jeopardy, and our extinction is a real possibility'. He noted that the statistics for 1975 show that 'the familiar pattern of losses has not varied'.[20]

> The deterioration of the majority of our London Baptist Churches in the past forty years has been no less than heart-break for all those old enough to remember their former glories. In my own group [of the LBA] in one place a 600 membership has dwindled to under 30; 400 members have declined to around 80; 300 members have become less than 60. Today 25% of our London Baptist Churches have fifty members at the most, 10% have 25 or less ... I am not playing with figures. I am talking about a clear, consistent numerical decline for half a century. The graph line falls as relentlessly as the tide ... Neither a world war nor Billy Graham have produced more than a kink in that remorseless line. It has held its course for fifty years ... Our current figures put us right on the line which runs to zero around the year 2000.

Cranefield commented on community changes, social tension, economic stringency, militant and increasing humanism and atheism in schools, collapsing standards of behaviour, and amid these, he asserted, the churches stand 'like sea-walls, already leaking and crumbling, facing the threat of a rising Spring-tide'. The 'city of God' may stand as Augustine averred, but the churches are another question. He brought his analysis to the following conclusion:

> So I come like Solzhenitsyn with his latter day warnings to the West, opening our eyes to what he calls the abyss beneath our feet; so I come to deliver you from any fantasy world into which ecclesiastical enthusiasts, in their blinkered confidence would lead us, and to try and come to terms with the reality as it is for the churches today existing in their survival situations.[21]

Cranefield went on to examine from Scripture the way in which churches could act positively in a survival situation, issued a personal 'Teach Yourself

[20] D. Cranefield, *Survival*, President's address, privately printed, 1976, p.1
[21] *Ibid.*, p.2

Survival' Bible Study Guide, commended group Bible studies on Revelation 1–3, prepared by Arthur Thompson, for use in the churches, and himself advocated a deepening of prayer for revival and renewal.

It was not surprising that at the following year's Baptist Union Assembly, when Ernest Payne, a decade after his retirement, was President of the Baptist Union, a resolution proposed by Douglas McBain and Paul Beasley-Murray, called for a commission to look at the spiritual and numerical decline within the denomination, and to consider whether there was a link between the two.

Payne was resistant to the motion but the Assembly carried it. A leading Baptist historian at Keele University, John H. Y. Briggs, chaired the commission that published its report, *Signs of Hope,* in 1979.

The report began by summarising the approach to mission work since 1945. There was a 'dispirited air' within the churches of the Baptist Union and a perception that 'decline' was inevitable and 'retrenchment' the only proper response. It noted, however, various initiatives within local churches, specific schemes in the Yorkshire, Kent and Sussex Associations; individual programmes like 'One Step Forward', the Baptist Men's Movement call to discipleship, and the large number of churches that supported 'crusade evangelism' particularly that of Billy Graham. The Union had made its own response through 'Baptist Advance', led by Aubrey in the 1950s; a denominational statistical and geographical survey made by Sir Herbert Janes in 1956–7, the Ter-Jubilee campaign in 1959–63, and George Beasley-Murray's 'Renewed for Mission' in 1969. David Russell's recent evangelistic theme, 'The Wholeness of the Gospel', which he enlarged as 'the whole Gospel for the whole man in the whole world', was also noted.

The setting up of a Mission Department, with its twin aims of mission and social responsibility was a positive move, as was the Stewardship Department which the Baptist Union supported for over a decade from 1963, were both mentioned. More significant was the expanding work of Home Mission, judged to be an 'incalculable' contribution to Baptist life and witness for the over 200 churches that had been enabled to have full-time ministry through it. By the churches' support between 1952 and 1963, 73 new causes had been opened, and by 1973 fourteen had a membership of over 100, one 200, and another 300.

A 'crude' comparison of the figures given in the Baptist Union Handbook in 1952 and 1977 made the situation clear. In 1952 there were 205,000 members in 2109 churches; in 1977 there were 147,200 members in 1745 churches; a decline of 28 per cent. The report noted changes in the way statistics had been gathered over these years, but it still amounted to a decline of 22 per cent.

The report suggested the factors that impinged on the size and health of Baptist churches are: the level of personal commitment to Christ, to mission in the local church, the changing society where the mission takes place, and the wider denominational structures and ecumenical realities of the day.

> The attack on the institutional church in our own day, coupled with certain emphases in parts of the charismatic movement, would seek a spiritual religion divorced from any institutional or structural framework but the precedents in history for such movements are not promising. As the Spirit

> brings new life into our churches old structures may well be challenged and overthrown, but it is equally certain that the ongoing work of the Spirit may demand new institutions and structures.[22]

A critical examination of the Church Growth Movement concluded that while not without its weaknesses,

> it is important that such thinking does not become a focal point for more talk, but a challenge to new faith and love that overflows into obedience and into joyful, intelligent and effective evangelism.[23]

The conclusion of the report considered matters of quantity and quality, drawing upon a Kenyan and British assessment of the position. A Kenyan, T. Tuna, in a paper preparing for the 1978 Lambeth Conference, had claimed:

> The main reason for the loss of members in the older churches is the failure of those churches to respond effectively to a situation in which secularisation is predominant and secularism is rapidly gaining ground.

This was set side by side with Birmingham Professor J. G. Davies' assertion, a decade earlier:

> To seek success in terms of numbers gathered in or of churches planted, is to deny Christ's way of service and suffering. As long as we hold before ourselves the objective of church extension, we are deliberately planning not to die; we are devoting our energies to ensuring our own survival. We thus replace self-giving by self-aggrandizement, acceptance of the cross by self-sufficiency.[24]

On the key issue of linkage between spiritual and numerical issues, it was all too easy for the living experience of one generation to become a hollow and second-hand form in the next. The danger for the denomination was holding to outdated structures and practices, where some churches were open to the criticism that they had become closed in outlook, backward looking, concerned to maintain a legacy from the past in terms of church plant and former glories, uncertain how to throw off the shackles of yesterday in order to give themselves in totality to the mission of the day. Social and economic changes had increased the irrelevance of the church generally as more efficient social or government agencies had been generated. As the eighties opened, Britain was not only becoming less Christian, it was increasingly anti-Christian. It was evident that Baptist problems were centred in three major tensions: theological polarization, the charismatic movement and tensions over ecumenism.

Theological polarization

The situation in the twenties and thirties over *The Fundamentals,* while only peripheral at the time, still lingered within the Baptist family. A small number had moved to the Fellowship of Independent Evangelical Churches. The Baptist Revival Fellowship had, since the 1930s, brought together a significant minority of ministers within the Baptist Union who looked for a return to a more

[22] *Signs of Hope, an examination of the numerical and spiritual state of the churches in membership with the Baptist Union of Great Britain and Ireland, March 1979,* Baptist Union Council, p.36
[23] *Signs of Hope,* p.42
[24] *Signs of Hope,* p.43. Quoting J. G. Davies, *Dialogue with the World,* 1967

conservative theological position. Following the 1961 Swanwick denominational conference there was a growing pressure from this quarter for a denominational statement of faith to the extent that at a repeat Swanwick Conference in 1981 one section, led by Bernard Green, the General Secretary of the Union from 1982, considered the value of a new confession of faith. However, by then it was already too late, as the attempt to discuss Christology at the 1971 Baptist Assembly had effectively closed off the possibility of an open debate.

Evangelical and 'Mainstream'

From 1971 evangelicalism was resurgent among Baptist ministers and churches and became increasingly dominant, challenging the broader theological basis of earlier in the century. This was focused in *Mainstream*, a Baptist group that sought to bridge the gap between traditional and charismatic Baptists. *Mainstream*'s introductory leaflet stated its constituency would be

> people who see themselves standing in the mainstream of Christian life in general and Baptist life in particular. Believing that our denomination is on the verge of one of the most exciting periods of its life, the aim of Mainstream is to encourage, co-ordinate, publicise and support every venture that will lead to further life and growth within the Baptist Union of Great Britain and Ireland, and to give wholehearted commitment to the Gospel as expressed in the Union's Declaration of Principle and also the life and work of the denomination.[25]

A variety of causes were at work, but there is no doubt that the 1967 Keele Conference of Evangelical Anglicans had provided a model that some evangelical Baptists found attractive. Principal Raymond Brown met with Douglas McBain and Paul Beasley-Murray after the 1977 Assembly to consider a way forward. Mainstream had its first 'fringe meeting' at the 1979 Baptist Assembly and its first Swanwick Conference in January 1980.

At that Conference Dr Barrie White, Principal of Regent's Park College, gave a significant paper, *Opening our Doors To God*, that noted the movement of the Holy Spirit in both liturgical and charismatic renewal, and urged that the Lord's Supper be re-discovered as the place where worshippers would be able to affirm the priority of Christ and receive him afresh in their lives.

McBain's own perceptions were published by Mainstream in *No Gentle Breeze*, 1981. He proposed reform of denominational finances, in the level of ministry support to which Baptists aspire, the identification of new evangelistic activity in areas of special need, revitalising national leadership especially the Union's Presidency, and a fresh approach through Associations to local ecumenism and mission. He concluded:

> I am conscious of the incredible resilience of any religious establishment, however weak and sickly it may appear. It is all too easy for the negative forces of ecclesiastical inertia to kill off enthusiasm among the people of God. I understand why it is that some Christians despair of the very institutions in which they were nurtured ... I do not share their pessimism.

[25] McBain, *Fire over the Waters: Renewal among Baptists and others from 1960s to 1990s*, 1997, p.208

> I actively oppose the view of those who would propose that Christianity must start again with every new generation ... [however] if we do not move reformingly while we may, there will come a time when ... patience with us will be exhausted ... What I am advocating is not a contracting out of our present responsibilities but the most determined contracting into them by all of us.[26]

However, by 1982 the impact of charismatic renewal was such that the coalition of concerned evangelicals was soon divided over the way forward. McBain, in particular, was not satisfied that the Baptist Union leadership were really prepared to change national structures. He left the pastoral ministry and set up an independent 'apostolic' ministry through a new para-church group, *Manna Ministries*. This produced a conflict of interest between McBain and the Union's Superintendents, particularly those in the North-West, South-West and Metropolitan areas, where McBain directly challenged the Union's level of pastoral care for ministers and churches.

Mainstream continued to develop evangelical concerns within the denomination and by 1990 many of its key members, including McBain, Derek Tidball and David Coffey, were in positions of leadership in the Baptist Union, spearheading a radical agenda for Baptists presented particularly in the writings of Nigel Wright, and specifically in *Challenge to Change*.[27]

A Call to Commitment

There were others who accepted the challenge of change and believed that the foundations of renewal were more likely to be found in a re-statement of historic Baptist theology and ecclesiology. L. G. Champion stated that new denominational structures of church life needed to be fashioned that would be effective means of

> communicating the gospel and sustaining both faith and fellowship amid the radical changes occurring in contemporary society, we need a clearer, more coherent and more widely accepted theology than prevails among us at present.[28]

David Russell made his own response to *Signs of Hope* at the 1980 Assembly, producing a discussion document, *Call to Commitment*. The Council of the Union asked Russell to examine and collate the responses to the *Call*. From this emerged a strategic pattern for action that presented a challenge to the churches to work out what it meant to be a 'Baptist Christian to-day'. It was a 'strategy of faith' by which Baptists together would respond to God's call to witness and service. Sections of the report challenged churches to a new commitment to worship and prayer, evangelism, learning, caring, and service, and the releasing

[26] D. McBain, *No Gentle Breeze*, Mainstream, 1981, pp.25, 32

[27] See Nigel Wright, *The Radical Kingdom*, 1986; *Challenge to Change*, 1991; *The Radical Evangelical*, 1996; *New Baptist, New Agenda*, 2002. Also D. W. Bebbington, *Evangelicalism in Modern Britain, from the 1730s to the 1980s*, 1989, especially chap. 8, 'Evangelical Resurgence in the Later Twentieth Century'. pp.248–70

[28] L. G. Champion, 'Evangelical Calvinism and the Structures of Baptist Church Life', BQ, 28, 1980, p.206

of leadership potential within the churches. It was a continuation and expansion of what was already being done, but 'none the worse for that'. It was hoped that every church in the denomination would set aside one Sunday in the year to express its commitment.

Mainstream was unhappy the Union challenged churches to change, but was unwilling to accept radical change itself. However, a group of Baptist ministers accepted the challenge of Champion's earlier lecture. They were Keith Clements, Tutor at Bristol; Richard Kidd, of Botley, Oxford; Paul Fiddes of Regent's Park College; Roger Hayden of Haven Green, Ealing, London, and Brian Haymes of Mansfield Road, Nottingham. Working together over a couple of years, they published *Call to Mind* in 1981, outlining a 'theology of commitment' for Baptists as they faced the secularism of the day, accepted the challenge of what it means *to be* the people of God, and looked for a deeper definition of *Signs of Hope* than the report's title offered. They attempted to set Christian faith within the wider context of other faith communities, and offered an understanding of being the Church.

In 1985 the same group produced a second volume of essays, *Bound to Love*, that offered a covenantal basis for Baptist life and mission, and it was this covenant theme that eventually emerged in the major changes proposed in 2000.[29]

Charismatic Renewal

Baptists in the fifties and sixties had looked for revival, as evidenced not only in *Liberty in the Lord*, but also in others, including E. A. Payne, who had written warmly of the 1784 Prayer Call in 1942 and again in 1959. By 1970 a renewal movement was well under way, affecting large numbers of Baptist churches, deeply influencing many Baptist ministers who were conscious of the 'depressed air' in the denomination. In 1980 the Union published *Charismatic Renewal: A Baptist View*, a report received by the Union's Council with a commentary on the text by Paul Fiddes, of Regent's Park College.

The renewal, concerned with 'the gifts of the Spirit', was first called 'charismatic renewal' in America in 1962. Its initial impact was on individuals who sought to 'speak in tongues', then it became a corporate concern of weekly congregation meetings that sought to develop these 'spiritual gifts' in the whole fellowship. The initial impact was in existing mainstream Protestant churches that had a distinctly evangelical outlook, but Roman Catholic congregations were involved from 1967 onwards. The first principal promoter of charismatic renewal was Michael Harper, a curate at All Souls', Langham Place, London. Harper and his colleagues early recognised the movement's potential for fracturing churches, but instead of creating para-church organisations, they adopted a strategy of permeating existing denominational churches, and that is how most Baptist churches first encountered the movement.[30]

The Fountain Trust, established in 1964, with *Renewal* as its magazine and Harper as its leader, had no membership as such, did not organize regular London-based meetings, and encouraged people 'baptized in the Spirit' to return

[29] For a full account of this group, see P. S. Fiddes, *Doing theology in a Baptist Way*, Whitley Publications, Oxford, 2000
[30] D. McBain, *Fire over the Waters*, p.6

to their own congregations. By 1980 the Fountain Trust had concluded its work as vigorous renewal movements had been planted in all the main Protestant denominations, as well as the Roman Catholic Church. It was over the conduct of worship that tensions developed within denominations, as 'traditionalists' and 'charismatics' confronted each other.

At the same time, outside mainstream denominational groups, there emerged what were originally known as 'House Churches'. Andrew Walker, in *Restoring the Kingdom,* (1985), has charted the course of 'the radical Christianity of the House Church movement', and subsequently described these churches as 'restorationist'. They set aside the old denominations and set out to 'restore' their understanding of the original biblical concept of 'God's kingdom people.' Restoration's origins were largely among independent Evangelical groups with a (Plymouth) Brethren background and their ablest leader was Arthur Wallis. He wanted to restore the pattern of church life allegedly found in the New Testament, and set out his programme in *The Radical Christian* (1981).

By the mid-1980s there were several categories of Restorationists, some based in Bradford, Yorkshire, led by Bryn Jones who published the magazine *Restoration,* and ran Bible Weeks from 1976, attracting thousands of people, many from Baptist churches. Gerald Coates and John Noble led a more loosely organized group that was strongest in the South-east, and organized Christian festivals from 1983.

In the 1960s 'renewal created a Christian version of the counter-culture' where 'tradition', the institution of the church and its bureaucracy, were replaced by self-expression and the search for a new ideal of the Christian community. McBain wrote:

> In a very real sense it can be claimed that British restorationism of the 1970s was the reinvention in the twentieth century of the Baptist wheel of the seventeenth century ... like our Baptist forefathers, they have a hearty dislike for all forms of establishment religion and a strong commitment to biblical authority. They are warmly evangelical in their general outlook and hold to the necessity of demonstrating their enthusiasm in their worship. Unlike our forefathers they model their worship not so much on the passages in the New Testament that usually apply but on their own understanding of Davidic worship in the Old Testament.[31]

These churches also looked for major change in the structures of church government. The control of the body of Christ through members in Church Meeting submitting to Christ revealed in Scripture through the Holy Spirit, must give way to the leadership of an eldership team in whom authority resides. This idea appealed to a growing number of Baptist ministers at the close of the twentieth century, although those BRF ministers who had advocated 'elders' in the sixties were probably surprised at the way this concept developed.

To Michael Walker, the charismatic movement was a 'Trojan Horse', housing those who

> were a new breed of authoritarians come to lead us to a style of fideism long unfamiliar to Baptists and a far remove from the Free Church

[31] D. McBain, *Fire Over the Waters*, 1997, p.77

tradition in these islands. It has itself been a sign of the times which are marked by a new fundamentalism in many areas.[32]

The charismatic movement produced its own ecumenism and some Baptists found themselves asking why the Lord's Supper was so vital for charismatic Catholics. New freedom in charismatic worship reached across the Catholic-Protestant divide as 'Alleluias heard regularly in many of our Baptist churches could be heard rising from the vast crowds of young people that waited for the Pope on his visit to Murrayfield Stadium, Edinburgh, during the summer of 1982'.[33]

Walker noted the negative side of charismatic renewal, as loosely knit congregations experienced secession and divisions. The slender Baptist theological resources were inadequate, he felt, in the face of a rising tide of renewal, particularly in the blows it dealt to serious worship in churches.

> The Reformation pattern of word and sacrament is only dimly discerned in the self-indulgent chaos that aspires to be worship of the holy, living God. It is likely that little attention will be paid to the underlying theological issues for one characteristic of many charismatic churches is their numerical growth and their success where others have failed. After years of decline success is seductive. Yet the merest glimpse at similar movements in the past, of which the Welsh revival is but one example, show that renewal that does not address itself to theology and undergird experience with a strong concept of the church, ministry and sacraments, will not only fail to survive but will leave the church weaker than it found it.[34]

Church Growth Movement

For the whole of the twentieth century numerical decline had been staring Baptists in the face. By the seventies, when Donald McGavran, of Fuller Theological Seminary, had expounded his theory of Church Growth, published in *The Bridges of God* (1958), and *How Churches Grow* (1959) it seemed to many Baptists that he had discovered the way out of the maze of constantly downward spiralling statistics. This movement had began when two missionaries in India asked why some churches grow and others do not, though both within a similar context. McGavran's research gave birth to the Institute of Church Growth at Fuller Theological Seminary, Pasadena, California. A simple summary of the research was given by Peter Wagner in *Your Church Can Grow* (1976). In the United Kingdom the Bible Society took up church growth as a major part of its programme, and an English Baptist minister, Roy Pointer, became a leading exponent of it for the Bible Society for almost twenty years.

Pointer had served as a British Merchant Navy Officer from 1956 until 1967, then trained for Baptist ministry at the London Bible College. He studied cross-cultural issues and was awarded a doctorate in Missiology from Fuller Theological Seminary. He joined the staff of the Bible Society in 1976, first as their Church Growth Consultant, then as Director of Church Training from 1986. His Baptist roots meant he was a significant denominational person who

[32] K. W. Clements, ed., *Baptists in the Twentieth Century*, BHS, 1983, p.27f
[33] *Ibid.*, p.28
[34] *Ibid.*, p.29

brought mission and ecumenism together powerfully by promoting Church Growth principles through all the churches that supported the Bible Society. Many Baptist ministers went on the courses he organised and delivered, along with significant numbers of Baptist lay people. The movement was not without its critics, but it caught the Baptist imagination in a way that many previous 'campaigns' had not .

The Mennonite W. R. Shenk, in *The Challenge of Church Growth,* offered a sympathetic critique of the ideas, but in 1982 Michael Walker wrote of this movement, 'it organises the church for growth. Using the insights of sociology and market research, it plots the course of action that will lead to expansion. Goals are set and success is looked for.'[35] The temptation for congregations wanting to escape the depressive atmosphere of constant decline was to shape worship to meet consumer needs. This often proved successful but in the process set aside worship as owed to God and for his glory, for worship that cultivated a sense of well-being that the secular world of the eighties claimed almost as a basic human right. The movement also struck at preaching, believing it to be an ineffective means of proclaiming the Gospel.

At the Pastoral Session of the 1980 Baptist Union Assembly, Michael Walker noted that ministers were advised to pay less attention to preaching and more to congregational management, on the basis that 'anyone can get up and spout', an astonishing description of preaching to which no dissentient voice was offered. Michael Walker, however, was clear that what seemed simply a matter of method would increasingly affect deep theological issues. He wrote:

> Not for the first time in the history of the church liturgy is the focal point of deeper theological issues. Earlier reference was made to numerical decline as the joker in the pack. That card has now appeared on the table, throwing into doubt and confusion the value of everything else we hold in our hands. If truth is to be equated with success and error with failure, then a criterion has been introduced of which truth itself will be the first and greatest victim. We are no longer faced with questions of liturgical renewal. What is at issue is nothing less than our view of the Bible, the sacraments, our reformation tradition and the catholicity of the people of God. If preaching continues to be devalued, if the Lord's Supper is made marginal to the church, if catholicity is rejected in favour of charismatic hedonism and ... fundamentalist authoritarianism then, whatever success may be ours numerically, it will have been purchased at the price of bankruptcy.[36]

John Wimber

A later American with this concern for growth was John Wimber, author of *Power Evangelism* (1985), who attempted to draw Evangelicals, denominational charismatics, and Restorationists together on a common platform.[37] He believed that an essential New Testament element in evangelism were the 'signs and wonders', typical of the *Acts of the Apostles,* and these could still be expected

[35] *Ibid.,* p.27
[36] *Ibid.,* p.30
[37] D. McBain, *Fire over the Waters,* 1997, chap.7

when churches grew. The emphasis was on 'power' and it dominated Wimber's work to such an extent that it led to serious misgivings, best summarised by Tom Smail, ordained a Church of Scotland minister in 1953, who became Harper's successor as Director of the Fountain Trust, and subsequently Vice-Principal of St John's College, Nottingham until 1985.

> My own experience of charismatic renewal strongly suggests that if some of its leaders were as concerned with being men of love as they are with being men of power, because they saw that the only power the Spirit has is the power of love, it would be a more wholesome thing than it has sometimes been.[38]

Theological polarisation, charismatic renewal and the Church Growth movement were a heady cocktail for Baptist churches facing numerical and spiritual decline. The linking of numerical with spiritual decline was once more accepted, unchallenged. In the seventies and eighties the denomination largely lost its 'reformed' roots, and experienced a reformation in worship and liturgy that moved it towards a much more narrowly conceived evangelical formation, in every aspect of its work.

The leadership in the churches and the national Baptist institutions, became involved with 'personality' in contemporary culture, acceptability in a media dominated age, and all matched with an insistent call for relevant management skills among all congregation leaders. All of which prepared the way for the radical institutional changes made at the Baptist Union and Baptist Missionary Society in the closing decade of the century

Bernard Green as Secretary

David Russell concluded his work at the 1982 Assembly. The *Baptist Times* leader on Russell's retirement noted that in 'a period of decline in all British churches he has given positive and constructive leadership in re-organisation of the Baptist Union and by his *Call to Commitment*.[39] He had made 'a notable contribution to ecumenism', locally, nationally and internationally, and as one critical observer said, 'not least by restoring the balance of the evangelical view'. Russell himself saw his years in office as 'an honest attempt to examine our weaknesses as well as our strengths, to confess our shortcomings and to hold ourselves ready to respond as a denomination to the leading of God's Spirit.' They had been 'years of consolidation and strengthening of the ties which bind us together.' In particular Russell welcomed a deeper Baptist commitment to Europe after the successful 1979 European Baptist Federation Congress held in Brighton, which had introduced many English Baptists to their European sisters and brothers of East and West Europe.

Bernard Green was Secretary until 1991, with his Deputy Secretary, Douglas Sparkes the former London Area Superintendent. From Rushden, Northamptonshire, Green had been conscripted in to coal-mining, like many others, who were dubbed 'Bevin boys' during the Second World War, before he proceeded for ministry training first at Bristol, then Oxford. The thirty years prior to his appointment were spent in ministry at Birmingham, Nottingham and

[38] *Ibid.*, p.107
[39] *Baptist Times*, 22 April 1982, p.2

Bristol, which meant that when he took on his new responsibilities he came to the task from thirty years in pastorate, as well as with many years of experience on the Council. Green had been a member of the Baptist Union Council since the early 1960s, served on a number of committees, particularly Christian Education and International Relations, and was a member of two commissions, one looking at 'The Child and the Church', the other concerned with the future of the Baptist Colleges. He had also done considerable local radio broadcasting in Nottingham and Bristol, and been a student chaplain while in Nottingham. However, many thought that what he brought to the task in particular, was a wide experience of ministry in the local churches.[40]

Signposts for the Eighties

As Green began at the Union there were some who felt that a certain balance needed redressing after Russell's period in office. Douglas McBain comments:

> He had considerably more experience in local church ministry than either of his immediate predecessors ... While in Bristol he encountered some expressions of the charismatic interest in healing ministry in which he had been involved from his Nottingham days ... He had developed his own prayer ministry for healing, though without any presumption that he possessed a gift for healing.[41]

McBain considered Green to be sympathetic to evangelicals and willing to listen when they expressed their convictions. For a generation Evangelicals had felt 'they had not received even-handed treatment within the denomination.' However, when Green began his first Council after becoming Secretary, he did so, not as 'a closet charismatic', as Mc Bain suggests, but as someone who recognised that the denomination had, at that time, a broad range of theological conviction and worship styles, which it was vital to hold together. It was not for the Union to take one side or the other, but neither should the Union allow any group to take over entirely. He often said that historically the Union was at its strongest when truly united in its diversity.

To make his position clear, he asserted in his opening speech to Council in November 1982, some signposts for the future of the Union. He openly acknowledged the charismatic emphasis abroad in the churches, but equally deplored the extremes of authoritarianism that had done so much damage in local church congregations. He believed Baptists needed to direct their energies to securing a new generation of young people by the close of the century. He asked for the development of special ministries that would address the widely divergent areas of city centre and countryside, and called for ministers who would pilot such experimentation. He hoped for a renewing of the 'nonconformist conscience' in matters of public concern, for further ecumenical commitment alongside the renewal of local churches and Associations. It would be important to have better and more personal links between the national Baptist Union and local churches. He saw the Union's objectives as 'to grow churches, to spread the Gospel, and to be agents for the Kingdom.'

[40] H. L. McBeth, *The Baptist Heritage*, 1987, Broadman Press, Nashville, USA, p.504
[41] D. McBain, *Fire Over the Waters*, 1997, p.142

One of the first reports he commended to the constituency was *Half the Denomination* (1983). It was concerned with the better use of lay preachers and pastors, and appropriate styles of church life that get away from the traditional concept of a small church as a scaled-down version of a large church. He hoped the report would be used in forward-looking mission rather than survival techniques, and enable churches, large and small, to 'abandon false independence or resistance to change so that this important half of the denomination can become a true missionary spearhead'. The report was considered in Associations, and in Bristol, for example, it led to a thorough investigation of all the small churches in the Association, both urban and rural. This led to the appointment of a 'consultant' to the smaller churches, Tom Elsby, who ministered in one of them, but was available to all the small churches to help them plan their life together and their mission strategy. However, it proved extremely difficult to secure long-term national resources for such opportunities countrywide.

Bugbrooke, Northamptonshire

Unfortunately, Green's energies were all too soon absorbed in a time-consuming dispute with one Northamptonshire Baptist church, Bugbrooke. It had become a very large community-based church calling itself the Jesus Fellowship, with an authoritarian leadership style, under the guidance of its one time lay-pastor, now Elder, Noel Stanton, and his eldership team. There were many claims and counter-claims; but the church clearly no longer operated a form of church government that placed the ultimate authority in a members' meeting gathered under Christ as Lord, and had therefore ceased to be a Baptist church.

Early in the dispute a *Baptist Times* article likened the community to a Franciscan Order, in its revolutionary concern for the radicalism of the Gospel and its care for society dropouts, particularly drug addicts.

After Bugbrooke was asked to withdraw from the Evangelical Alliance, and following prolonged further debate within the Baptist Union, Green felt there was no alternative but to expel it from the Union. Bugbrooke's actions and reputation brought considerable correspondence from those whose family members had come under its spell. This in turn brought considerable pressure from the media with widely broadcast television documentaries calling much in question. The local Association as well as churches further afield were conscious of the competitive nature of the 'New Creation Community', later to be called 'the Jesus people'. As they were no longer operating as a Baptist Church, and the Union meant nothing to the community, it was decided to discontinue their membership of the Baptist Union. Bernard Green had a meeting with Stanton and some of the leadership at Church House, and Green made a personal visit to Bugbrooke in the company of the Area Superintendent, and Peter Clark, the Area Committee Chairman. This was before making a report to the General Purposes and Finance Committee that came to Council with the recommendation that Bugbrooke's membership of the Baptist Union be terminated.[42]

[42] See P. S. Fiddes, *A leading question: the structure and authority of leadership in the local church*, 1983, for a theological discussion of the issues involved

Women in Ministry

A report to the Baptist Union Council in 1965 had indicated that although more women were applying for ministry, 'Superintendents were finding that churches are reluctant to appoint women ministers', and this was reflected by the fact that there were still only two accredited ministers and three probationer women ministers on the ministry list. *Women in the service of the denomination* addressed this issue a year later re-affirming the place of women in Baptist ministry but noting the continuing prejudice in the churches against calling them in to pastoral service. It was only in 1972 that the BMS Secretary, J. B. Middlebrook, proposed to Council that the names of women be included with men in the printed list of Baptist Union ministers as a clear sign of equality.

Margaret Jarman

The flow of women ministers had been hindered in some measure by the fact that the Deaconess movement already provided an avenue of service for women.[43] Deaconess work had begun under the inspiration of F. B. Meyer, then minister at Regent's Park chapel in London, who brought together a group of women to provide medical help for London's needy women. The alleviation of distress among the poor was a significant part of the mission of local churches, with the Baptist Women's League raising support for the Deaconess work countrywide. Throughout the first 60 years of the century Deaconesses were increasingly involved with church pastoral work and were often indistinguishable from accredited ministers in their responsibilities. Financial difference in stipend levels between ministers and Deaconesses resulted in women being called to pastor churches that otherwise had little hope of full-time accredited ministry. As the number offering for Deaconess work declined in the sixties the Baptist Union took a decision to close the Order and by 1975 twenty serving Deaconesses were transferred to the accredited ministers list.

Margaret Jarman had trained first as a deaconess at Struan and Carey Hall, and then served the Pontesbury Group of Baptist churches in Shropshire. She became the organising secretary of the Deaconess Department of the Baptist Union, and after further training at Spurgeon's College, became an accredited

[43] See earlier, chap.12, pp.161ff

minister of the denomination, serving in London, Coventry and Kings Stanley, Gloucestershire. In 1987 Margaret Jarman became the first woman minister to be elected President of the Baptist Union. However, the first woman to serve as Baptist Union President, had been Mrs Nell Alexander, of Zion, Cambridge, elected a decade earlier in 1978. Nell Alexander was a gifted dramatist, deeply committed to women's work in the European Baptist Federation, as well as within the Baptist Union, and a lively advocate of women's issues within and beyond the denomination.[44] The changing situation for women in Baptist ministry is recognised when the figures for 1980 and 1990 are compared. In 1980 there were 51 women ministers listed, and just under 100 in 1990.

Baptist Identity

As Baptists moved into the eighties and nineties a number of key questions were being asked within and beyond the Baptist denomination that meant the whole understanding of who Baptists are, as well as the very important question of who they once were, gave birth to the debate on Baptist identity that continues into the twenty-first century.

It was the Yorkshire Baptist Association pamphlet, *A Question of Baptist Identity* (1986), by Brian Haymes, then Principal of Northern Baptist College, that initiated a wide-ranging debate that is still proceeding. Given to the Yorkshire Baptist Ministers' Annual Retreat in February 1986, the material was left largely in the form in which it was given.

Writing from the 'liberal-evangelical' tradition of the denomination, Haymes felt that there were important features of Christian identity to which Baptists have born witness as a way of being Christ's Church, that were worth developing and guarding. It is 'for more than our own good that Baptists be true to their inheritance', and 'we are presently in danger of neglecting these features and in some instances actually betraying them'. He was concerned about the increasing 'polarity in all British churches around such matters as theological perceptions, the liturgical movement, the theology of mission and Charismatic renewal'. His next concern was about the rise in the

> last fifteen years of what I call 'non-rational conservatism' … an attitude to the Christian life [that reveals] an impatience with demanding questions of belief and practice. These are dismissed as 'theology'. 'Real Christians' just get on with praising God.[45]

His third concern was the rise of 'personality cults within the church' that was 'not unrelated to the modern longing for the authoritative leader and the charismatic personality'. Having established the importance of such a debate, Haymes discussed the nature of the 'true' Church, the question of authority, the tradition of Dissent, and the necessity of right belief. He concluded what was in many ways a combative argument with words from Oliver Cromwell to Parliament.

> There is a phrase Cromwell used in Parliament that I often say to myself, as I recognise my own temperature rising as theological debates get hotter. Cromwell said to those who were so absolutely sure of their assertion:

[44] For a detailed discussion of women in Baptist ministry, BQ, 1986, July and October
[45] B. Haymes, *A Question of Identity*, YBA, 1986, p.4

> 'I beseech thee, in the bowels of Christ, consider that thou mightest be mistaken'.[46]

Haymes's contribution focussed attention on what was becoming a key issue for the denomination and it produced an immediate response from Baptist 'conservative evangelicals'. In 1987 Mainstream published addresses that originated at a consultation to consider Haymes's arguments. The organisers expressed 'delight' that Bernard Green, the Union's Secretary, had shared in the consultation process, although he himself regarded it as simply an opportunity to hear what Evangelicals were saying. However, the Baptist identity debate was also an important aspect in the wider ecumenical context. It had implications as the British Council of Churches was being re-formed as Churches Together in England, and it impinged upon the challenge of Restorationism and its excessive authoritarian structures that were appearing in many erstwhile Baptist churches.[47] Although *A Mainstream Perspective* was not widely circulated, the book's ideas and aspirations were shared by many Baptists, and set an agenda for evangelical Baptists in the nineties.

The Union's new leaders, in 1991, were David Coffey and Keith Jones. Coffey had been pastor at Upton Vale, Torquay, Devon, and a leading member of Mainstream. He took office as the Head of Mission at the Baptist Union, before being appointed General Secretary. His Deputy was Keith Jones, the former Secretary of the Yorkshire Baptist Association that had published Haymes challenge. Together they created a ten-year plan that would take Baptists towards 2000 with a common national mission strategy for all the churches. Mainstream members found themselves increasingly in office within the Union, its Council and Departments, and were able to put these issues at the centre of their concerns.

An agenda for the Nineties

A Perspective on Baptist Identity (1987) was put together, wrote its editor, David Slater, minister at Kingsbridge, Devon, and Secretary of Mainstream, so that 'our denomination take a lead in the advance of God's Kingdom' for which a clear grasp of Biblical theology, the wider sweep of Church history, as well as 'Baptist history and traditions', were required. There was much to learn from other Christians, and yet again a call was made for a modern 'Confessional Statement', and for 'practical structures' to be put in place within the denomination 'which will advance our mission more effectively'. Baptists needed to

> co-operate more fully and more widely with others, but remain in *the Baptist way*. There is a call to recognise the variety and diversity of expressions, but not at the expense of orthodoxy.[48]

Analysis of the present

Derek Tidball, then the Senior Pastor of Mutley Baptist Church, Plymouth, formerly a lecturer at the London Bible College and a well-known conference

[46] Ibid., p.29

[47] For 'restorationism', see Andrew Walker, *Restoring the Kingdom: The Radical Christianity of the House Church Movement*, 1985; and for a Baptist evaluation, see N. Wright, *The Radical Kingdom*, 1986

[48] David Slater, ed., *A Perspective on Baptist Identity*, Mainstream, 1987, p.5

speaker, and soon to be Head of Mission at the Baptist Union, responded to Haymes booklet by noting that,

> in the past 25 years the Church has undergone a ferment of change. The cultural and moral revolution of the 60s was the seed bed in which another revolution grew—that of the charismatic movement. In the 70s that movement widely affected the mainline churches and became known as the Renewal movement. That in turn gave way in the 80s to the Restoration movement. In such a lively and changeable context it is essential that we be clear-sighted about the traditions and principles that are distinctive to our churches, especially those we regard as fundamental and enduring—even if the expression of them will rightly change.[49]

Tidball's perceptive analysis ended with a concern that Haymes had not given sufficient attention to the cultural context. Not liking Restorationism, or aspects of evangelicalism, or Church trends is one thing—but he had failed to ask what gave rise to these developments. Answering his own concern, Tidball wrote:

> the growth of conservative evangelical churches as well as the rise of more fundamentalist groups is saying something of importance both about the society in which we live and about the Christianity which our churches have been offering ... scientific humanism has reigned ... It is time we faced the fact that such a reasonable, tolerant, undemanding and anti-supernatural perspective breeds a personal and spiritual barrenness in people. The boredom of a world without gods (to paraphrase Peter Berger) was bound to provoke a reaction sooner or later. Secularisation, so confidently expected among many to go on its way unchallenged until a transcendent perspective no longer existed, has produced a reaction. The reaction may not always be balanced and wise—but it is a real cry to fill an aching void ... In a world where we have been in decline and where our spirituality has often degenerated into being the ethics of respectable bourgeoisie, I am not surprised that many are looking for something different within our churches. Our tradition has not always been successful at meeting the needs of the people in the context of their times. There have been times when it has done so gloriously—but not today. The challenge is to mould our tradition and to do it again.[50]

Associating Again

Barrie White, Principal at Regent's Park College, Oxford, addressed the nature of Baptist associating and began:

> I am very uneasy and have been uneasy for a long time with the Baptist Union's Declaration of Principle which says: 'Each church has liberty, under the guidance of the Holy Spirit, to interpret and administer God's laws'. That statement about liberty sounds to me all too much like an assertion of unbridled independence. It is a virtually absolute

[49] *Ibid.*, p.7
[50] *Ibid.*, pp.15–16

> independence which has led to many of our troubles over the years ... many are happy with it as a statement of principle. Others, like myself, will see it as a statement of unfortunate fact ... The heart of the matter lies in that clause which refers to the 'guidance of the Holy Spirit ... especially in days when the ministry of the Holy Spirit is being newly recognised, valued and experienced.[51]

White's critique of Baptist identity came from a critical review of the 1964 *Commission on the Associations*, and he concluded that 'fellowship' is the life style of the gospel.

> *Inter*dependence is the mark of the converted—the search for independence was Adam's sin ... I am reminded of that famous passage from Martin Luther about the way the Reformation was launched from Wittenberg: 'I simply taught, preached and wrote God's word; otherwise I did nothing. And while I slept or drank Wittenberg beer with my friends ... the Word so greatly weakened the Papacy that no prince or Emperor ever inflicted such losses upon it. I did nothing, the Word did everything ... let the Word do its work.' We need not drink the beer, but should we not allow the Word to do its work for our Reformation?[52]

Truth, love and creed

Alastair Campbell, a member of the Mainstream Executive, trained at Regent's Park College, had ministered at Broadmead, Northampton from 1973, leading the church in a programme of radical renewal, and since July 1987 had been involved in research studies at Spurgeon's College, London.

He argued that the grounds of Christians associating were truth and love. Quoting Haymes, 'the true ground of fellowship is something more than doctrinal agreement, or common experience, or preferences in worship, or understanding of mission', Campbell retorted,

> But it was exactly on such grounds that Baptists came into separate existence at all! ... Many of us joined a Baptist church in the first place, forsaking the Church in which we had been brought up, for those very reasons.

Campbell looked critically at ministers' gatherings, Association meetings and particularly church meetings, and submitted that

> in a union of independent Churches, the passing forms of church government assumed in various places and times by different local churches should not be made grounds of association.

He welcomed Haymes plea for 'serious open discussion about the faith' and commented,

> Certainly it is fear, not wisdom, that has turned us away from creeds. With many Baptists it has become a mark of their Baptist identity that they do not express their faith in creeds and confessions. There is clearly no historical legitimacy in such a claim. Creeds and confessions are the proper outcome of theological debate; their absence points to a loss of nerve among us.[53]

[51] *Ibid.*, p.19
[52] *Ibid.*, p.29
[53] *Ibid.*, pp.36–7.

Baptist way of being Church

Nigel Wright, lecturer in Biblical and Historical Theology at Spurgeon's College, was previously the Senior Minister at Ansdell Baptist Church, Lytham St Annes for 13 years, during which time three new congregations were planted. He had published *The Radical Kingdom: Restoration in theory and practice* (1986). He addressed the Baptist way of being the Church and noted

> The similarities and contrasts of Restoration and Baptist churches make this movement simultaneously attractive and threatening to us … [Those who are] sympathetic to the Renewal and Restoration movements of our time … have asked whether they can remain within the Baptist fold with integrity … are reassessing their Baptist heritage and are finding it biblical, wise, liberating and exciting … [and requires us] to recover our Baptist roots … among the Continental Anabaptists in the 16th century…[54]

Wright looked at Scripture, the 'believers' church', believer's baptism and freedom of conscience, and described Anabaptist thought as nothing less than a new way of 'being the Church'. Restorationism, far from threatening Baptists, is an attempt to pursue the same vision of the New Testament church in a different generation.

Similarly, 'Baptists are by definition evangelical. A departure from evangelical theology entails a fatal loss of Baptist identity'.[55] By 'evangelical' Wight meant loyalty to the Reformation centralities of Scripture, faith, and grace alone, and in this what is distinctively evangelical is the *intention* to live under the authority of God's Word, wherever that may lead. In respect of the ecumenical movement, Wright said:

> The New Testament presents us with a picture of variety in unity. The unifying factor was not how the church was organised in this or that particular culture but the New Testament theology of the Church and its ministry … this theology is the norm for the Church and to which the Church is called to submit itself … Baptist identity therefore is something that we need to surrender to the greater and wider movement of God as he reaches out to all men to gather them into his Kingdom.[56]

Patterns of ministry

Mike Nicholls, the Vice-Principal of Spurgeon's College, London, had been pastor of Alder Road Baptist Church, Parkstone, for five years before returning to teach at the College. He contrasted Baptist understanding with those of Episcopalians and Restorationists and noted that worldwide, 90% of Baptist churches adhered to a two-fold ministry of pastors and deacons. After a wide-ranging discussion he asserted that

> every believer has a ministry and true ministry is the work of the whole church. Ministry is recognised locally, but is also worked out regionally. Baptists hold to two vital principles: variety and unity in ministry. It is in this striving for patterns of ministry that are locally, nationally and universally expressed that Baptists make a major contribution to the ecumenical debate about ministry.[57]

[54] *Ibid.*, p.41
[55] *Ibid.*, p.44
[56] *Ibid.*, p.45
[57] *Ibid.*, pp.47–59

Worship: meaning and style

Stephen Ibbotson, trained at Spurgeon's, had been minister at Harris Street, Peterborough, since 1976, was a member of the Mainstream Council, with a particular interest in church planting. He examined Baptist distinctives that have a bearing on worship. There were three fundamental truths about the Church, which influence worship, these are 'that the Church consists of God's people who are a community that is evangelical, catholic and charismatic'.[58] He stressed that the Word proclaimed through Scripture and in preaching must shape God's people, but it was in danger of being relegated to a lesser place in the pursuit of more time for praise. Baptism and the Lord's Supper expressed Baptist identity as a community of people gathered by God's grace to be 'a priesthood of all believers'. The Church is a family of God that needs to bring humility and openness to its worship, and in a family setting allow for interaction between worshippers. In the family it is important to give due place to family history and origins. Charismatically, worship needs to recognise the way God gifts all his people, and as they open themselves to the Spirit, it is important that there is opportunity for their gifts to be used to build up the Body of Christ.

Ibbotson picked up a criticism of contemporary charismatic worship made by Keith Clements, who was responsible for promoting the planned new Baptist hymn Book, *Baptist Praise and Worship*, and by Haymes, who suggested charismatic worship was shallow and lacked content. He offered a defence of the charismatic material and suggested that worship should be culturally related and relevant. At this level hymns were culturally distant from modern people and are no longer known nor sung by the community at large, and the denomination needed a new hymnbook that was culturally relevant. The new hymnbook appeared in 1991 but never achieved the place in the denomination that earlier Baptist hymnbooks had done.[59]

A new Confession

The final chapter by George Beasley-Murray noted the great variety of identity within the worldwide Baptist community. He suggested that what made Baptists distinctive was the coalescence of their principles within one community. Baptist convictions can be likened to genes in a body: others may have one or other of them, but this set makes Baptists what they are to-day.[60] He pleaded that Haymes be heard and

> Baptists pluck up courage and do for our day what our Baptist forefathers did for theirs: namely produce a contemporary Baptist Confession of Faith. Such an undertaking is desirable for God's sake, for our sakes, for the sake of other Churches and for the sake of the world.

Beasley-Murray elaborated each of these themes, offered an example from the American Baptist Churches as an encouragement, and concluded by pleading such a Confession be seen not negatively, but as a charter with a vision for action.

[58] *Ibid.*, pp.66–73
[59] C. J. Ellis, *Baptist Worship To-day,* Baptist Union, 1999, for a detailed analysis
[60] D. Slater, ed., *A Perspective on Baptist Identity,* 1987, pp.75–85

Ecumenism

'Baptism, Eucharist and Ministry'

In 1982 a first draft of the so-called Lima text, *Baptism, Eucharist and Ministry*, (BEM) appeared and soon became 'the most widely publicized and discussed ecumenical document of the twentieth century' with Morris West 'at the heart of the process.'[61] As editor of the *Baptist Quarterly* in the 1950s he had revived its place in the denomination as a journal of significant research and knowledge that was vital if there was to be a new understanding of Baptist identity at the heart of the denomination. In 1959 he wrote a small booklet for the Ter-Jubilee series, *Baptist Principles*, which was constantly reprinted and studied by four generations of new Baptist church members. Involved in the Union's Council, key committees and commissions for forty years, West regarded the Baptist tradition as something which was not fixed and final, but always in process, and therefore capable of continual development.[62] West was one of the most gifted servants of the Union and Neville's Clark's assessment was that West had 'been a Union and Association man from the beginning'.[63]

However, West was totally committed to the ecumenical renewing of the whole Church. For over thirty years he served on the Faith and Order Commission of the WCC and played a key role in producing *Baptism, Eucharist and Ministry*. In 1964, when Ernest Payne resigned from the Plenary Commission of Faith and Order, West took his place. This Commission of a hundred delegates met every four years and a much smaller Standing Committee met yearly to do detailed work. West was appointed to this inner group in 1971 and remained on it until 1983. It was in 1971 that a momentous ecumenical decision was taken to develop a 'consensus' document on baptism, eucharist and ministry that set in train the process leading to the 1982 Lima document. It proved difficult to get consensus. Nonetheless a report was sent to the churches for their reaction to be voiced at the World Council of Churches Assembly at Nairobi in 1975, which West attended as a Baptist delegate. The Standing Commission was reduced in size after Nairobi and West was now the only Baptist on it, making his role crucial.

A critical stage in the baptism discussions was reached in 1978 when Faith and Order organized a conference with Baptists at Louisville, Kentucky, at which West, George Beasley-Murray and J. H. V. Nicholson were the British Baptists present.[64] Throughout this consultation, West, according to Nicholson,

> resolutely played the role of one who wished to set the foremost item of discussion in the wider context: to let justice be done to real differences while seeing that *both* traditions were recognizing initiation as a process, always within a believing *community* in which children had a real place,

[61] K. Clements, 'The Larger Context: Morris West, Servant of World Ecumenism', Briggs and Bowers, eds., *Baptists Together*, BHS 2000, pp.19–29

[62] West, *The Bristol Tradition—Now and Then*, Bristol, 1986

[63] J. H. Y. Briggs, ed., *Faith, Heritage and Witness*, BHS, 1987, pp.13–20

[64] W. M. S. West, 'Towards a Consensus on Baptism? Louisville 1979', BQ, 28, 1980, pp.232–9, and this is followed by the consultation's report

> and always within a particular historical and societal context. This perspective was to be liberating for the ecumenical debate on baptism, and to confirm the shape which the section on baptism would take in the eventual Lima text.[65]

So it was in 1982 at Lima that Morris West was present when it was unanimously agreed that the text had reached a mature enough stage to be sent to the churches of the WCC. The text was published in more than 30 languages and sold nearly a million copies worldwide. He saw BEM as an opportunity and reception of it would be a very long process. Nonetheless, in his clear enthusiasm for the text, as his critical review for the Roman Catholic *One in Christ* makes clear, to say with Lima that 'Any practice which might be interpreted as "re-baptism" must be avoided' would in its absolute form be totally unacceptable to Baptists, a statement that demonstrates West's creative attachment and critical loyalty to BEM.

Churches Together in England

In the English ecumenical scene concern had been expressed for some years about the operations of the British Council of Churches that acted on behalf of the denominations, yet sometimes consulted them very little, if at all. Bernard Green was one who was keen to have new ecumenical instruments for the future, one that would involve Baptists, and also Roman Catholics, as more than 'observers'.

When the 'Covenant Talks' between the English churches failed in 1982 the denominations had to face the question how the churches went forward. At a meeting of the church leaders it was decided to initiate a process of reflection and prayer, waiting upon God for his guidance, rather than planning yet another church unity scheme. This produced a series of united meetings for prayer among the church leaders, including a week-end in Canterbury waiting upon God, and was followed by a series of study booklets, and another Swanwick Conference at which the seminal report, *Not Strangers, but Pilgrims* appeared. Baptists and Roman Catholics both participated in this new process. After active discussion in each denomination the new 'ecumenical instruments' were agreed. Baptists in every local church, the Associations, Council and Assembly discussed these ideas. Cardinal Basil Hume had described the new ecumenical instruments as concerned with 'unity with legitimate diversity'. Green corresponded endlessly with churches, ministers, Superintendents, and Colleges, until a final decision was taken in favour of the new proposals at the Leicester Assembly in 1989. After the decision was taken, Baptists agreed that fellow Baptists who did not wish to participate in Churches Together in England could register that fact with the Baptist Union, which a very small number did. This was not sufficient for some Baptist evangelicals and a few churches and ministers resigned from the Baptist Union.

[65] W. M. S. West, *Baptists Together*, BHS, 2000, p.24

Baptist House, Didcot

A new Baptist House—Didcot

The possibility of a united Baptist Headquarters for the Union and the Missionary Society, which had eluded Baptists for fifty years, became a reality at the end of the 1980s under Bernard Green.

At the Baptist Missionary Society, Reg Harvey had become the Home Secretary, and for the first time in many years, the two denominational leaders were not only personal friends of long standing, with a strong bond of partnership between them, but were also both keen to pick up David Russell's theme of the 'wholeness of the Gospel' to convince the widest possible Baptist constituency that there was only one mission.

It was this firm theological conviction that was the foundation of the possibility of joint Headquarters, as was the development of the Joint Baptist Assembly pattern they evolved. A joint meeting of the Baptist Union Council and the Baptist Missionary Society at Bloomsbury made an overwhelming vote in favour of the project. The votes were taken in the two bodies separately and simultaneously, and finally laid to rest the obstacles that had prevented the action fifty years earlier.

By no means all Baptists welcomed it, and without doubt the move from central London had some drawbacks. Many thought contact with other denominations, and even direct links through to the centres of political power, would suffer, but this was addressed carefully in the initial stages and many of the early fears allayed. Modern buildings improved staff conditions at a stroke, easy communications to London, together with national and international communication through increasing use of the burgeoning information technology available strengthened the effectiveness of both the Union and the Society. The move released substantial sums of new money that enabled significant changes to follow, not least the strengthening of the Pension Fund for ministers, finance to support students training in the Colleges, and a substantial increase in Baptist Loan Fund facilities to provide more realistic help with the rising costs of new church buildings. Money once held in bricks and mortar was released for mission.

Baptists since 1945

Professor John Briggs, writing in 1987, concluded that for much of the previous forty years of the twentieth century Baptist leadership had been 'largely concerned with managing the contraction of well-ordered churches, attempting to halt the retreat'.

The invigorating wind of charismatic renewal revitalized moribund churches and brought new patterns of life to churches that had largely forsaken the traditional style of earlier Baptist churches. Other churches have found the experience divisive, with an unhealthy seeking for signs, and the emergence of naïve theology. However, both are signs not of death and decline but of life and growth. Briggs quotes approvingly Adrian Hastings' judgement that Baptists are best perceived as sitting between ecumenical Christendom and evangelical sectarianism.

> It is not in fact a bad strategic position to occupy though involving very considerable pressures on denominational leadership to ensure that a proper balance of positive affirmation is secured: in polity, an order both congregational and associative; in ministry, both the vocation of the whole people of God and the separated ministry of word and sacrament; in worship, a liturgy at once structured but free; in mission, a commitment to both evangelism and prophetic action.[66]

Organizationally, the Union was stronger in 1990 than it had been in the past. One sign of this, Briggs believed, was the increased number of applicants to train for ministry in these years. Following a ground-breaking initiative taken by Northern College, under Michael Taylor's leadership, all the colleges have experimented with various congregation-based patterns of training that put the emphasis on practical aspects of learning through theological reflection on specific issues. A separated ministry, adequately trained in biblical and theological awareness is important for Baptists who have all too often been prone to pragmatism in the search for outward success.

In the conduct of worship Baptists have shown their vulnerability to the claims of the 'immediate', in 'the development of patterns of worship that omit major elements of the reformed liturgy in favour of unstructured immediacy'. This is evident not least in the rejection of a 'Book of Common Hymnody' in favour of 'popular, praise-orientated' material, all too often sentimental, introspective and emotional, that is unlikely to meet Wesley's definition of his collection of hymns as 'a little body of experimental and practical divinity.'[67]

[66] J. H. Y. Briggs, ed., *Faith, Heritage and Witness*, BHS, 1987, p.60

[67] For assessment of contemporary hymnody and worship, C. J. Ellis, *Baptist Worship Today*, Baptist Union, 1999, which summarises two worship surveys by the BU Doctrine and Worship Committee

Baptists in Britain still feel the double pull of social responsibility issues and mission.

> The late twentieth century has not lacked large issues of social responsibility: the stock-piling of nuclear weapons, South Africa and Central America, sexual permissiveness and the instability of so many marriages, the polarisation of wealth and poverty, to name but a few … When, however, in 1978 E. R. Norman used his Reith Lectures to attack the World Council of Churches for 'politicizing' the church, a number of Baptist voices were raised in support of his position. It is probably symbolic that whereas in 1906 there were seventeen Baptist MPs (fifteen Liberal and two Labour), since 1983 there have been only two, both Conservatives. Certainly Baptist political affections have become more volatile than the almost total alliance with the Liberals at the beginning of the century. At the same time evangelicalism has become less pietistic … in 1974 the Lausanne Conference underwrote a both/and approach to evangelism and social responsibility, whilst TEAR Fund allowed the Evangelical constituency, including many Baptists, no excuse for opting out of relief and development in the Third World … Baptists, particularly in Britain, feel the double pull of ecumenical and evangelical demands, in many respects providing a bridge between those allegiances.[68]

The seventies and eighties

Dr Paul Beasley-Murray gave a different assessment of Baptist thought as the twentieth century closed. 'The tide of defeatism and decline began to turn [in the 1970s] and in the 1980s a new spirit of optimism and commitment to church growth and church planting emerged. There were four reasons for this. 'First, a growing evangelical identity among Baptists that made Baptists 'the chief beneficiaries of the general evangelical renaissance in England' at the end of the twentieth century. This idea receives considerable support from Baptist historians like David Bebbington, Ian Randall and Nigel Wright. Second, Baptist 'openness to charismatic renewal,' despite its occasional excesses, has meant a renewal of Baptist churches through a changed worship perception, the new understanding of 'the body life' of the church especially through small groups, and the valuing and use of spiritual gifts within local congregations. Third, Baptists 'played a key role in the 1980s when the insights of the American church-growth school were introduced to Britain.' Baptist churches, facing a survival situation, accepted the clear-cut conviction that God intends his church to grow, and this proved revolutionary for them. Finally, 'Baptists have always been a missionary people. Where a church is committed evangelically, influenced charismatically, and convinced that Jesus is building his church, there evangelism is likely to become increasingly effective.' Beasley-Murray concluded with a quotation from the 1977 *Signs of Hope* report:

> There does seem to be a new move towards more openness and less hypocrisy, a greater sense of flexibility and an unwillingness to be bound by precedent, a new concern to proclaim the eternal gospel in terms relevant to the contemporary scene, and a greater willingness to serve the needs of the community in the name of Christ.[69]

[68] J. H. Y. Briggs, ed., *Faith, Heritage and Witness*, BHS, 1987, pp.63–4
[69] Paul Beasley-Murray, *Radical Believers*, p.118

Bibliography

T. M. Bassett
The Welsh Baptists, Ilston House, Swansea, 1977

George Beasley-Murray
Baptism in the New Testament, Macmillan, 1962
Baptism Today and Tomorrow, Macmillan, 1966

Paul Beasley-Murray
Radical Believers: The Baptist Way of Being the Church, Baptist Union, 1992, 2005
Fearless for Truth: A Personal Portrait of the Life of George Beasley-Murray, Paternoster, 2002

D. W. Bebbington
Editor, *The Baptists of Scotland: A History*, Glasgow, 1989
The Nonconformist Conscience: Chapel and Politics, 1870–1914, Allen & Unwin, 1982
Evangelicalism in Modern Britain: A history from the 1730s to the 1980s, Unwin Hyman, 1989
Editor, *The Gospel in the World: International Baptist Studies*, Paternoster, 2002

C. Binfield
Pastors and People, 1984, published by Queen's Road Baptist Church, Coventry

Malcolm Bonnington
Chard Baptists, 1992, Forum Books, Silver Street, Chard, Somerset

Faith Bowers
A Bold Experiment: The Story of Bloomsbury Central Baptist Church, 1999, Bloomsbury Central Baptist Church

W. H. Brackney, P. S. Fiddes, J. H. Y. Briggs
Editors, *Pilgrim Pathways, Essays in honour of B. R. White*, Mercer University Press, 1999

G. Breed
Particular Baptists in Victorian England, BHS, 2003

J. H. Y. Briggs
The English Baptists of the Nineteenth Century, BHS, 1994

Raymond Brown
The English Baptists of the Eighteenth Century, BHS, 1986

Keith W. Clements,
Editor, *Baptists in the Twentieth Century: papers at BHS Summer School, July 1982*, BHS, 1983
Lovers of Discord, SPCK, 1988

Rosie Chadwick,
Editor, *A Protestant Catholic Church of Christ: Essays on the History and Life of New Road Baptist Church, Oxford*, New Road Baptist Church, Oxford, 2003

Anthony C. Cross
Baptism and the Baptists: Theology and Practice in Twentieth Century Britain, Paternoster, 2000

A. C. Dakin
The Baptist View of the Ministry, Kingsgate Press, 1944

Kenneth Dix
Strict and Particular: English Strict and Particular Baptists in the Nineteenth Century, BHS, 2001

Christopher J. Ellis
Baptist Worship Today, Baptist Union, 1999
Gathering: A Theology and Spirituality of Worship in the Free Church Tradition, SCM, 2004

Paul S. Fiddes
Tracks and Traces: Baptist Identity in Church and Theology, Paternoster, 2003

A. Gilmore
Editor, *Christian Baptism*, Lutterworth, 1959
The Pattern of the Church: A Baptist View, Lutterworth, 1963

Bernard Green
Tomorrow's Man: A Biography of James Henry Rushbrooke, BHS, 1997
Crossing the Boundaries: a History of the European Baptist Federation, BHS, 1999

Stanley C. Griffin
A Forgotten Revival, Day One Publications, Bromley, 1992

Adrian Hastings
A History of English Christianity, 1920–1985, HarperCollins, 1986

Michael Hambleton
A Sweet Hopeful People: Abingdon Baptist Church, 1694–2000, Abingdon, 2000

Mike Nichols
C. H. Spurgeon: The Pastor Evangelist, BHS, 1992

Roger Hayden
Editor, *The Records of a Church of Christ in Bristol, 1640–87*, Bristol Record Society, 1974
Editor, *The Baptist Union Documents, 1948–1977*, BHS, 1980
Editor, *English Baptist Records*:
1 *Chesham, Bucks*. Transcribed by L. G. Champion, Introduction by Arnold H. J. Baines. BHS, 1985
2 *Church Book St Andrew's Street Baptist Church, Cambridge, 1720–1832.* Transcribed by L. G. Champion, Introduction by L. E. Addicott, Notes by K. A. C. Parsons, BHS, 1991
3 *Association Life of the Particular Baptists of Northern England, 1699–1732.* Transcription and Introduction by Stephen L. Copson, BHS, 1991

B. Haymes
A Question of Identity, Yorkshire Baptist Association, 1986

D. M. Himbury
British Baptists: A Short History, Carey Kingsgate Press, 1962

D. W. Lovegrove
Established Church, Sectarian People: Itinerancy and the Transformation of English Dissent, 1780–1830, Cambridge, 1988

W. L. Lumpkin
Editor, *Baptist Confessions of Faith*, Judson Press, USA, 1959

D. McBain
No Gentle Breeze, Mainstream, 1981
Fire over the Waters: Renewal among Baptists and Others, 1960s to1990s, DLT, 1997

H. Leon McBeth
The Baptist Heritage: Four Centuries of Baptist Witness, Broadman Press, USA, 1987
A Sourcebook for Baptist Heritage, Broadman Press, USA, 1990

G. F. Nuttall
Visible Saints: The Congregational Way, 1640–1660, Quinta Press, 2nd Edition, 2001

E. A. Payne
The Free Church Tradition in the Life of England, SCM, 1944
Henry Wheeler Robinson, Nisbet, 1946
The Fellowship of Believers, 1944, second enlarged edition, Kingsgate Press, 1952
The Growth of the World Church, Edinburgh House Press and Macmillan, London, 1955
The Baptist Union. A Short History, Carey Kingsgate Press, 1959

Ian Randall
The English Baptists of the Twentieth Century, BHS, 2005

Ian Sellers
Editor, *Our Heritage: Baptists of Yorkshire and Lancashire, 1647–1987*, Yorkshire Baptist Association, 1987

Peter Shepherd
The Making of a Modern Denomination: John Howard Shakespeare and the English Baptists, 1889–1924. Paternoster, 2001

D. C. Sparkes
The Home Mission Story, BHS, 1995
The Constitutions of the Baptist Union, BHS, 1996
An Accredited Ministry, BHS, 1996

David Slater
Editor, *A Perspective on Baptist Identity*, Mainstream, 1987

Edward C. Starr
Editor, *A Baptist Bibliography: being a Register of Printed Materials by and about Baptists*, Judson Press, USA. 26 volumes of information on who wrote what, when, and where it can now be found; supercedes W. T. Whitley's two-volume bibliography, 1916–1922

Don A. Sanford
The History of the Seventh Day Baptists, Broadman Press, USA, 1992

B. Stanley
The History of the Baptist Missionary Society, 1792–1992, T & T Clark, 1992

Joshua Thompson
Century of Grace: The Baptist Union of Ireland, A Short History, 1895–1995, Baptist Union of Ireland, Belfast, 1995

Murray Tolmie
The Triumph of the Saints: The Separate Churches of London,1616–49, Cambridge, 1977

A. C. Underwood
The History of the English Baptists, Carey Kingsgate Press, 1947

Michael Walker
Baptists at the Table: Theology of the Lord's Supper amongst English Baptists in the Nineteenth Century, BHS, 1992

R. C. Walton
The Gathered Community, Carey Kinggate Press, 1946

Michael Watts
The Dissenters: from the Reformation to the French Revolution, Oxford, 1978
The Dissenters: the Expansion of Evangelical Nonconformity, Oxford, 1995

W. M. S. West
To be a Pilgrim: a memoir of Ernest A. Payne, Lutterworth Press, 1983
Baptists Together, BHS, 2000

B. R. White
The English Baptists of the Seventeenth Century, BHS, 1983
The English Separatist Tradition, Oxford, 1971
The English Baptists of the Seventeenth Century, BHS, 2nd Edition, 1996. Pages 164–70 provide a helpful review of historians of the English Baptists from Crosby to McBeth
Association Records of the Particular Baptists of England, Wales and Ireland to 1660, three parts, BHS, 1971–4

R. E. O. White
The Biblical Doctrine of Initiation, Hodder & Stoughton, 1960

S. F. Winward
The Reformation of our Worship, Carey Kingsgate Press, 1964

Nigel G. Wright
The Radical Kingdom: Restoration in Theory and Practice, Kingsway, 1986
Challenge to Change: A Radical Agenda for Baptists, Kingsway, 1991
New Baptists, New Agenda, Paternoster, 2002

Index